GALATIANS—DIALOGICAL RESPONSE TO OPPONENTS

SOCIETY
OF BIBLICAL
LITERATURE

DISSERTATION SERIES

William Baird, Editor

Number 65
GALATIANS—DIALOGICAL RESPONSE TO OPPONENTS
by
Bernard Hungerford Brinsmead

GALATIANS—
DIALOGICAL RESPONSE
TO OPPONENTS

Bernard Hungerford Brinsmead

Scholars Press

Published by
Scholars Press
101 Salem Street
P.O. Box 2268
Chico, CA 95927

GALATIANS—DIALOGICAL RESPONSE TO OPPONENTS

Bernard Hungerford Brinsmead

Th.D., 1979
Andrews University

Advisor:
James J.C. Cox

© 1982
Society of Biblical Literature

Library of Congress Cataloging in Publication Data

Brinsmead, Bernard Hungerford.
    Galatians, dialogical response to opponents.

    Dissertation series / Society of Biblical Literature ;
no. 65)
        ISSN 0145–2770)
    Originally presented as the author's thesis (Th.D.)—
Andrews University, 1979.
        Bibliography: p.
        1. Bible. N.T. Galatians—Criticism, interpretation,
etc. I. Title. II. Series: Dissertation series (Society of
Biblical Literature) ; no. 65.
BS2685.2.B74 1982   227'.406   81–18535
ISNB 0–89130–549–1   AACR2

Manufactured in the U.S.A.

ACKNOWLEDGMENTS

I would like to thank firstly the chairman of my dissertation committee, Professor James Cox, for the patience, wisdom, and thoroughness with which he guided the writing of this dissertation, and the generosity with which he gave so much of his time. The other two members of my committee, Professors William Johnsson and Gerhard Hasel, also made invaluable contributions, and were a great encouragement. Dr. Robert Johnston took part in the defense of the dissertation with much thoughtfulness and helpful generosity. The work could not have been done without the helpfulness, resources, and financial assistance of the Theological Seminary of Andrews University, and its library.

Particular thanks must be extended to Professor Dieter Georgi, of Harvard, not only for his great kindness in interrupting his busy schedule, to make the long trip to Berrien Springs for the defense of the dissertation, but also for the scholastic inspiration and friendship that have extended far beyond the brief time the writer spent under his professorship.

One of the most indispensable people behind a dissertation is the one who is asked to perform the miracle of typing it. Carmen Holland must be thanked not only for the carefulness and calmness with which she did so, but also for the fact that it was all a real gesture of friendship.

It is impossible to thank my father and mother adequately, for supporting us all financially, and for foregoing the pleasure of their grandchildren, for so many years.

The people who suffer through a dissertation most are those who are roped to the wild-eyed recluse by marriage and birth. Prue has been more understanding, patient, and *interested* than any wife could be expected to be. Regina, Faye, Gabrielle, and even Simon, have tiptoed, whispered, stayed home at weekends, and accepted meekly that "Daddy's busy" for *so long*, that he will be a *long time* making it up to them.   It can only be hoped that they will all share fairly in the satisfaction of the dissertation's completion.

CONTENTS

ix

ABBREVIATIONS

Collections, Periodicals, Reference Works

ANF
    Alexander Roberts and James Donaldson, eds. *The Ante-Nicene Fathers*. 10 vols. New York: Christian Literature Company, 1885-1897.

AUSS
    Andrews University Seminary Studies

BAG
    Walter Bauer, *A Greek-English Lexicon of the New Testament and Other Early Christian Literature*. English trans. from the 4th German edition by W. F. Arndt and F. W. Gingrich. Chicago: University of Chicago Press, 1954.

BJRL
    Bulletin of the John Rylands University Library of Manchester

CBQ
    Catholic Biblical Quarterly

CH
    Corpus Hermeticum

HE
    Eusebius, *Historia Ecclesiastica*.

HNT
    Handbuch zum Neuen Testament. Tübingen: J. C. B. Mohr.

HTR
    Harvard Theological Review

ICC
    The International Critical Commentary. Edinburgh: T. and T. Clark.

IDBS
    The Interpreters' Dictionary of the Bible: Supplementary Volume. Nashville: Abingdon Press.

JBL
    Journal of Biblical Literature

JTS
    Journal of Theological Studies

LCL
    The Loeb Classical Library. Cambridge, Mass: Harvard University Press.

LS
    H. G. Liddell and R. Scott, *An Intermediate Greek-Englixh Lexicon*. Oxford: Clarendon Press, 1975.

NHL	James M. Robinson, ed. *The Nag Hammadi Library in English.* New York: Harper and Row, 1957.
NovT	*Novum Testamentum*
NTA	Edgar Hennecke and Wilhelm Schneemelcher, *New Testament Apocrypha,* trans. R. McL. Wilson. 2 vols. Philadelphia: Westminster Press, 1963–65.
NTD	Das Neue Testament Deutsch. Göttingen: Vandenhoeck und Ruprecht.
NTS	*New Testament Studies*
PG	Migne, *Patrologia Graeca.*
RGG	*Die Religion in Geschichte und Gegenwart.* 3rd ed. Tübingen: J. C. B. Mohr.
RQ	*Revue de Qumran*
ST	*Studia Theologica*
StrB	H. L. Strack and P. Billerbeck, *Kommentar zum Neuen Testament aus Talmud und Midrasch.* 4 vols. Munich: C. H. Beck, 1922–26.
TDNT	G. Kittel and G. Friedrich, eds. *Theological Dictionary of the New Testament,* trans. and ed. Geoffrey W. Bromiley. 9 vols. Grand Rapids: Eerdmans, 1964–72.
ZNW	*Zeitschrift für die neutestamentlicher Wissenschaft*
ZTK	*Zeitschrift für Theologie und Kirche*

Works of Philo and Josephus

Philo	
Abr	*De Abrahamo*
Aet	*De Aeternitate Mundi*
Cher	*De Cherubim*
Conf	*De Confusione Linguarum*
Cong	*De Congressu quaerendae Eruditionis gratia*
Decal	*De Decalogo*

xii

Det	Quod Deterius Potiori insidiari solet
Ebr	De Ebrietate
Flacc	In Flaccum
Fuga	De Fuga et Inventione
Gig	De Gigantibus
Heres	Quis Rerum Divinarum Heres
Immut	Quod Deus immutabilis sit
Jos	De Iosepho
Leg All	Legum Allegoriae
Leg ad Gaium	De Legatione ad Gaium
Migr	De Migratione Abrahami
Mut	De Mutatione Nominum
Opif	De Opificio Mundi
Plant	De Plantatione
Post C	De Posteritate Caini
Praem	De Praemiis et Poenis
Prob	Quod Omnis Probus Liber sit
Prov	De Providentia
Qu Ex	Quaestiones et Solutiones in Exodum
Qu Gen	Quaestiones et Solutiones in Genesin
Sacr	De Sacrificiis Abelis et Caini
Sobr	De Sobrietate
Som	De Somniis
Spec Leg	De Specialibus Legibus
Virt	De Virtutibus
Vit Con	De Vita Contemplativa
Vit Mos	De Vita Mosis

Josephus

Ant	*Antiquitates Judaicae*
Apion	*Contra Apionem*
Bell	*Bellum Judaicum*
Vit	*Vita*

LIST OF TABLES

Table   Page

INTRODUCTION

This thesis seeks to discover the center of Galatians
--its unique theological statement--by approaching the question from the perspective of the dialogical nature of the
letter as a piece of literature and of the theology of the
opponents with which it is dialogical.

The significance of this study lies not only in the
possibility of a more precise comprehension of a foundational
document of the Christian church. It also offers deeper
insight into earliest Christianity, some of the circles of
thought from which these Christians came, the theological
"baggage" they brought with them, and the influence this
"baggage" had on early understandings of Jesus.

Certain recurring issues suggest that some new attempt
to grasp the essentials of Galatians is timely. There is much
less than unanimity on the place of the letter in Paul's theology. For some, "Paul" is found more clearly here than any-
where else.[1] But if this is the case, then he is the protag-
onist par excellence in conflict even with the other apostles
and the Palestinian wing of Christianity.[2] For others, "Paul"
is not really found here at all.[3] Galatians is a letter of
excesses, perhaps due to the heat of the moment in which it
was written, and Paul himself strays dangerously close to
Gnosticism.[4] In the extreme form in which the doctrine of
righteousness by faith here appears, it is said, he lays the
basis for later problems in Corinth. However, in his other
letters he has learned his lesson; he never again proclaims
Christian freedom so boldly.[5] Others even conclude that this
"extreme" letter is the result of a later addition to and
alteration of "Paul."[6]

Closely allied to this issue is the question of the
"Judaism" of the Galatian opponents. Hans Joachim Schoeps is
rather typical in his assumption that it is an "orthodox" or
Pharisaic Judaism; but he concludes that, if this is so, Paul

1

basically misunderstands Judaism.[7] Others see behind Galatians
an error closely related to the one behind Colossians[8]--and
therefore not of Rabbinic type, but associated more with sectarian and apocalyptic Judaism.[9] Precision in this respect
becomes even more difficult in the face of the apparent breakdown of traditional categories of intertestamental literature.[10]

      A third and vital issue is the place and meaning of
the doctrine of "righteousness by faith" in Galatians. As it
has a central place in only two of Paul's books, is it really
a "Pauline" doctrine? Is it that an opponent has led him to
use an "un-Pauline" argument?[11] Or, if it is Pauline, is it a
doctrine which speaks only to Pharisaic Judaism, therefore
being totally irrelevant in the Galatian situation? Is Paul
using an argument against opponents who could not possibly be
answered in this way?[12]

      In the face of such issues, this thesis suggests that
it is in Paul's opponents that explanations will be found for
the form of the theology in this letter, and the particular
way in which the argument holds together.[13] And yet, as the
review of literature will demonstrate, there is anything but
consensus concerning the identity of these opponents. Is the
letter written against Jewish intruders? Then why does it
refer to them only in terms of their methods, and not of their
theology? Why is the theology directed to the Galatians themselves? And why is it that some practices in Galatia seem
very "un-Jewish" in traditional terms (4:8-9, 5:19-21, 6:13)?
Is it written, then, to Gentile Galatians? Then why does the
argument suggest a direct assault from a form of Judaism? Are
there two groups of addressees (legalist intruders, libertine
Galatians; or legalist intruders and Galatians, and a party of
libertine Galatians)? Then why are there strong suggestions
of the same concerns in all sections of the epistle (3:1-5,
5:13-24, 6:1, 2, 7-8)? Why are the Galatians always referred
to as a homogeneous group (1:6-10, 3:1-5, 5:13-15)? If it is
the Galatians who are the libertines, how are they in danger
of accepting a legalist heresy?

      In all the attempts at approaching Galatians from the
perspective of the opponents, the most crucial and recurring
question is that of the unity of the letter. Which parts

address the Galatians? From which parts is the intruding
theology to be assessed? No clear answer is possible without
a careful examination of the structure of the letter, its
literary nature, and the unity of its argument.

      This thesis therefore seeks to approach the question
of the opponents from a particular direction, an analysis first
of the dialogical nature of Galatians as a piece of literature.
As will be noted below in the review of methodology, this
approach has not yet been fully explored. Moreover, it may
provide some form of control over the way the parts of the
epistle are related to each other, suggesting to what extent,
and with whom, the letter is dialogical.

      Once the structure of the argument in Galatians has
been clarified, the key traditions at work in the letter are
analyzed in terms of external literature. This is not only to
safeguard against any "vague combinations and hypotheses" but
is also to fill out the picture of the opponents and their
theology as suggested by the literary analysis. This last is
not here left behind but is used to provide a framework in
which the "structural function" of the traditions in Galatians
itself can first be determined.[14]

      The steps in the thesis will now briefly be described.
It begins with a review of literature, divided into two chapters, the first of which examines various theories regarding
the identity and theology of the opponents. The second crit-
ically considers methodologies for locating and characterizing
the opponents, concluding with a statement of the method to be
used in this thesis.

      The following part is devoted to an analysis of Gala-
tians as a piece of literature, and a determination of the
literary genre to which the letter belongs.[15] The first chapter examines the genre of letter, or epistle, indicators within
Galatians of appropriate genre, and the "apologetic letter"
genre, with suggestions of the structure to which it gives
rise. The second chapter looks for indications of smaller
scale of the structure and unity of the letter, continuing and
confirming the genre analysis. Using the conclusions for the
pattern of argument, it ends with a sketch of the intruding
theology.

The final part of the thesis seeks to confirm and fill
out this sketch or hypothesis in terms of Jewish and Christian
literature of the period. Beginning from within the movement
of the debate in Galatians, it examines five prominent traditions involved in the controversy: the tradition of apostle,
the tradition of Abraham, traditions of Moses and the law,
sacramental traditions, and ethical traditions.

The conclusion, of course, seeks to draw the whole work
together. It sets forth the theology of the opponents, and the
essentials of Paul's theological statement in the letter, now
that it is understood as a dialogical response to these opponents.

There are naturally some self-imposed limitations to
the study, although at times their restrictions are keenly
felt. Such matters as the precise destination (North or South
Galatia) and date of the letter (especially relative to Acts
15, 1 and 2 Corinthians, and Romans) must be largely left to
one side. Five traditions are considered; of course there are
more, but space excludes them. For Jewish literature, attention is concentrated on so-called "apocalyptic" texts, the
writings of the sectarians (Qumran), Philo, Josephus, and some
"apologetic" literature, with briefer attention to other
sources. And it has not been possible to trace exhaustively
the anti-Pauline or "Judaising" traditions through the rest
of the New Testament and early Christianity.

This is an appropriate place for some definitions of
terms. By "nomism" will be meant not only a concern for law
but a conviction that compliance with law is essential for the
initiation of access to God, or for full acceptance with God.
"Enthusiasm" is used to refer to an attention to the inward
and personal experience of religious powers, especially the
experience of the Spirit, which lifts above the ordinary and
confers an advanced standing in that religion. A "literary
genre" is a literary type with respect to larger units such as
"gospel" or "epistle."[16] "Genre analysis" is used to refer to
the identification of literary genres, and determination of
the suitability of any one for an evaluation of a particular
piece of literature.[17] The "apologetic letter genre" is a sub-
category within the larger category or literary type of

"letters" which is at the same time rhetorical or apologetic
speech in a literary mode.[18] "Rhetoric" refers to the long-
developed and studied methods and devices for public speech or
oratory.[19] The term "apocalyptic" is used in two typical
senses. Firstly, it is used as a commonly-accepted designation for certain Jewish pseudepigraphical literature ("apocalyptic literature"), in particular 1 Enoch, 2 Baruch, 4 Ezra,
the Assumption of Moses, and Jubilees.[20] Secondly, it is used
to refer to a realm of ideas, or a form of eschatological
thinking, which has its own way of viewing the world, the
cosmos, and history--that is, ideas contained in "apocalyptic
literature."[21] "Eschatology" refers to an orientation to the
movement of history towards its conclusion or perfection, an
orientation to last things.[22] "Realised eschatology" means a
participation in some sense in the benefits of the last days.[23]

PART ONE

REVIEW OF LITERATURE

CHAPTER ONE

THE IDENTITY AND THEOLOGY OF THE OPPONENTS

From Paul to Irenaeus

Because of the work of Ferdinand C. Baur, Joseph B.
Lightfoot, etc., the postapostolic age, with its controversies,
has become part of the Pauline debate itself. In the second
century, the Galatian opponents were identified by both orthodoxy and the Marcionites as radical Jewish-Christians from
Jerusalem.[1] But there is more to the picture than this. The
early Fathers evidently lost the heart of the argument in
Galatians. Judaism was wrong, not because it nullified the
cross, but because it was ἀφροσύνη;[2] the law was said to lead
to belief in Christ;[3] Christ was in fact a "new law."[4] Walter
Bauer, after examining the tenor of such literature, concluded
that it left no room for Paul as an authority.[5] On the other
hand, the gnostic opponents of the Fathers seemed to make much
use of Galatians;[6] and later, Paul became almost the "Gnostic
apostle."[7] To further complicate the picture, Jewish-Christian
literature painted Paul as the bogus apostle, the Gnostic, and
caricatured him in the person of Simon Magus.[8] The Gnostics
saw Galatians as written against Peter and the ψυχικοί Christians of the Great Church.[9] The Church did not understand it
as being written specifically against contemporary Gnostics,
Jewish-Christians, or Jews; and certain Jewish-Christians
closely identified Paul and Gnosticism. One conclusion is
that Galatians does not counter Gnosticism: if the opponents
are Gnostics, Paul has misunderstood them, and given them much
ammunition.

From Luther to Baur

John Calvin made some distinction between those who preached a "different gospel" in 2 Cor 11 and those who did so in Galatia; and between both these and the heretics encountered in the Pastorals.[10] However, along with Martin Luther most Protestant writers have identified Paul's opponents as Jewish-Christian fanatics from Jerusalem.[11]

About a century after Luther and Calvin, Henry H. Hammond of Oxford anticipated some later scholarship in identifying virtually all Paul's opponents as Gnostics, including those in Galatia.[12] Another century later, Johannes L. von Mosheim joined Hammond and the Reformation tradition. There were two heretical tendencies within the New Testament, one, Gnosticism, the other (as in Galatians), Jewish Christianity which later became Ebionism.[13] In 1829 Edward G. Burton again proposed that Paul's opponents were, in the main, Gnostics. In Galatia they were either Jewish teachers or Gnostics who espoused Jewish ordinances for reasons political. Burton worked partly from Tertullian's apparent use of Gal 4:3, 10 and Col 2:12, 20 against Gnostics, who, he said, were clearly present in Colossae, though the predominant emphasis in Galatians is the scrupulous enforcement of the Jewish religion.[14]

The Modern Period

Jerusalem Theories

The majority of modern commentators see the Galatian opponents as being connected in some way with the Christian church in Jerusalem.

Two-Party Theories

Baur was perhaps the first to make Paul's opponents a decisive key to the whole of the apostle's writings. The course of early Christianity, and of Christian history as a whole, was said to have been determined by a dialectic between Pauline (Hellenistic) and Petrine (Jewish) Christianity.

Gnosticism was restricted to the second century. Paul's opponents were the Jerusalem apostles themselves, preaching circumcision as the first step in the Christian faith.[15] They
first appeared in Galatia, then later in Corinth, where the
conflict entered another stage. Sources for this conflict
were the four "authentic" letters of Paul, and especially the
Clementine romance.[16]

Later followers took Baur's historical-critical theories to some of their logical conclusions, tending in the
process to refute his own positions. The controversy between
Peter and Paul became the controversy in the second century
between Gnosis and Jewish legalism, now the orthodoxy of the
Great Church. The New Testament documents were made reflections of this second-century struggle. Because that struggle
was clearest in Galatians, Bruno Bauer made this the last
"Pauline" letter.[17] W. V. van Manen pressed this logic even
further. Because the struggle between law and gnosis climaxed
in Galatians, its author was a Gnostic, endeavoring, with the
aid of other Pauline literature, to defend liberal Gentile
Christianity against the Church itself, the "anti-Pauline
opponent."[18] In demanding such an unlikely dating of the whole
New Testament, this theory has tended to disqualify its own
assertions about the antagonists in Galatia.[19] However, one
position has remained: Galatians rejects legalism in terms of
theological principles.

Despite reservations with Baur's theory at many places,
Albert Schweitzer agreed in identifying Paul's Galatian oppo-
nents with the Jerusalem "Pillars." The apostles themselves
had insisted that the Gentiles accept circumcision and the law.
However, the tension between Petrine and Pauline Christianity
is in terms of different eschatologies.[20] The occasion of
Galatians was said to have arisen from a particular aspect of
Pauline eshcatology. Because of the unique form in which the
Messianic kingdom had arrived in Christ, Paul developed a
theory of spheres within Christianity, one Jewish and one
Gentile--two separate churches. The Galatians had somehow
learned that these two churches were two levels of privilege
and salvation, and hence wanted to live as the Jewish church.

Paul's answer is an eschatological one. For Gentiles to live
as Jews is to deny all belief in Jesus as the Messiah (Gal
3:10-25, 4:4-5). Schweitzer has prompted the question of the
place of eschatology in the opponents' argument, and in Paul's
answer.

Hans Lietzmann modified Baur's position by postulating
three parties in early Christianity. It is barely a modification. The third party is a "behind-the-scenes" party, secretly
supported by James and Barnabas.[21] However, the principle of
a third party has become perhaps the most popular modern solution.

Three-Party Theories

A series of commentators have chosen this position
for at least one outstanding reason: there is no direct
attack in Galatians on the Jerusalem pillars, and certain
portions of the letter (1:18-24, 2:1-10, 15-16) reveal a basic
agreement between the latter and Paul.

Joseph B. Lightfoot, like Baur, placed the Pauline
controversies within the whole of Christian history of the
first two centuries. He too felt the need to account for the
second-century antagonism of Ebionites and Marcionites, and
believed that "the epistle to the Galatians is the true key to
the position."[22] However, he suggested that Paul was not confronting a "party" but a "movement." It was distinct from the
Jerusalem apostles, but was a Judaising movement that took two
forms--Gnosticising and Pharisaic--which only became distinct
and separate in the second century (libertine Gnosticism and
ascetic Jewish Christianity). In Galatians Paul encountered
the Pharisaic form, though there may also have been an anti-
Judaistic, antinomian party, as in Corinth (shades of the
"Two-Front" theories).

William Ramsay began by positing the trustworthiness
of Acts, and the syncretistic background of the "South Galatians."[23] It is a party of over-zealous followers from James
(though not officially connected with James) who create the
occasion for Galatians. They assert that there are two stages
in Christianity: those who keep the Apostolic Decree (Acts 15)

achieve the lower stage, and those who keep the whole law
reach the higher stage. The anti-syncretistic and ethical
passages of Galatians were directed against ways in which the
Galatians themselves had modified this "new gospel."

H. J. Schoeps, though in some ways returning to the
positions of Baur, opposes the latter's school with a three-
party theory.[24] Besides Paul's party and the "Pillars" (a
moderate Jewish-Christian group), there are τινες τῶν ἀπὸ τῆς
αἱρέσεως τῶν Φαρισαίων (Acts 15:5), who espouse the stricter
views of Shammai. The great gulf is not between Paul and the
"Pillars,"[25] but between Paul and this stricter group, the
ancestors of the Ebionites. This group is directly countered
in Galatians.[26] They did not demand the keeping of the whole
law for Gentiles (Gal 5:3); but Paul opposed the Jerusalem
Decree as well as these Judaisers when he rejected the entire
Mosaic law in principle (Gal 3).[27] To Schoeps, the different
opponents behind Paul's letters are all related to the one
basic conflict running through Christianity, and all stem from
the strict Pharisaic party (even in 1 and 2 Corinthians).
These opponents, in their Jewishness, are closer to true
Judaism than Paul himself, who, in his attacks on works of
law, has totally misunderstood the law in Judaism.[28]

Most conservative writers see the opponents as a
third, stricter Jewish party.[29] To all of them, the witness
of Acts, especially Acts 15 and its views of the conflict
within the early church, is crucial.[30] Francis F. Bruce goes
so far as to say that Galatians refutes Baur, since it shows
basic agreement between Paul and the "Pillars," against a third,
Pharisaic group.[31] For him, the main issue of the letter is
not theology but principles of mission. The central term in
Galatians is not "gospel" but "gospel to the uncircumcised"
(2:7). Paul is an independent authority in his sphere, as the
"Pillars" are in theirs--and in this there is agreement.[32]
Certainly apostleship is central in Galatians. But if Paul
and the pillars have one and the same "gospel" (as Bruce
affirms), then where does the "other gospel" come from? Is
it not this "other gospel" that is the main issue?

Several other commentators also prefer a "third-party"
theory that has the opponents come from Jerusalem.[33]

There is general agreement among these writers on one
fundamental point: a "legalist" cannot be an "antinomian" or
"libertine."[34] The issue in Galatians 1-4 is clearly one of
law--a point of the Tübingen school that has been constantly
reaffirmed--so Galatians 5-6 cannot be dealing with the same
issue. This is, in fact, an implicit two-front theory: therefore several of these writers must be considered again under
that heading.

Gentile Theories

Ernst G. Hirsch and Wilhelm Michaelis have suggested
that the Galatian opponents were pre-Pauline Gentile Christians,
circumcised before their baptism, now advocating the same to
Paul's converts.[35] Johannes Munck has more recently advocated
this position as part of his attack on Baur and the Tübingen
school, and on the historical assumptions behind their literary
conjectures--that everywhere Paul was fighting with Jewish
Christianity.[36] If the literary conjectures are untenable,
he claims, the historical ones are too, and we should not look
for Jewish-Christian opponents.[37] Munck makes much of the
present participle in Gal 6:13;[38] and the suggestion that the
Judaisers themselves do not keep the whole law or teach their
converts to (3:10; 6:13). Elsewhere in the New Testament the
central issue between Jerusalem and Gentile Christians is proposed to be table fellowship, of which there is no mention in
Galatians. And he stresses the unlikelihood of a Judaising
countermission from Jerusalem in Pauline missionary territory.
Rather, he says, the situation has been created because Paul's
own converts, taking seriously the apostle's sympathetic portrayal of Judaism (as in Rom 9-11),[39] gathering material from
the Greek Old Testament which he himself had given them,[40] and
hearing that the Jerusalem Christians were themselves circumcised, decided that they would conform to Judaism.[41] The
erroneous theology is Jerusalem seen from a distance, a Gentile
version of Jerusalem religion.

There has been plenty of criticism. The participle
in 6:13 could be a middle of personal advantage;[42] the questions of keeping the law, and of a countermission, are

answered better in other ways;[43] the Judaisers seem clearly to
be intruders;[44] and the questions raised by the Jerusalem
theories are still unanswered.[45] Munck's overall thesis, of
which this material on Galatians is a part, has been strongly
criticised.[46] However, for Galatians, it is a theory that
bears further examination.[47] He is correct in asking the
traditional interpretation how it can adequately account for
a Judaising mission from Jerusalem--in Galatia!

Two-Front Theories

Wilhelm Lütgert posited that Paul had to wage war on
two fronts simultaneously--against legalists (Gal 5:1) and
libertines (5:13).[48] Like Lightfoot, he saw in Galatians a
group of "free spirits" similar to those in Corinth, who charge
that Paul teaches circumcision, re-establishes the law, has his
gospel from men, and gives up Christian freedom in face of
pressures from Jerusalem.[49] The argument of the letter meets
the two groups in a complex way. The charge concerning
apostleship is one of dependence on Jerusalem, not independence
(1:11-12, 16-17), and it is libertines, not legalists, who make
this charge. The attack on legalism is restricted to 2:11-
4:31; and in chaps. 5-6 the attack on libertinism is resumed.
Both positions are distortions of Christian freedom.

James H. Ropes produced his own "singular" version of
this theory.[50] Paul is said here to face the same two opponents, but Gal 3:6-29 is assumed to be against libertines,
errant Gentile Christians who fail to understand their obligations as sons of Abraham. This turns the traditional understanding of the passage on its head and reduces the legalist
thrust to a few specific items (circumcision, feasts). He can
therefore say that the "Judaisers" are Gentiles, not from
Jerusalem at all: they seek to impose circumcision to escape
persecution from local Jews. This historical argument has not
found much support.[51]

For all their weaknesses, these theories have highlighted three things: the force of the apparent contradiction
between anti-legalist and anti-libertine sections of the
epistle; the complex attitude of the opponents to Jerusalem

and Judaism (the opponents have their own version of liberty);
and the complexity of Paul's own answers, in which theology is
intertwined with ethics.

Other writers who see something less than a unity in
the thrust of Galatians should be considered here. Theirs is
an "implicit" two-front theory. Bruce disconnects Paul's section on "works of the flesh" from the theological portion of
the letter. It is directed to an uninfluential minority of
libertines.[52] Hans Dieter Betz proposes that, initially, an
over-enthusiastic interpretation of Paul's gospel among the
Galatians led to a problem of "sarx."[53] Anti-Pauline Jewish-
Christian legalists siezed the opportunity and proposed adher-
ence to the Torah as a solution. The key to both false positions is "pneuma."[54] Others see here an answer to a hypothetical situation charged by the legalists--that Paul's gospel of
"antinomianism" leads to licence.[55] Another alternative is
that of Jost Eckert.[56] The opponents are Judaisers who, if
not identical with the "false brethren" of Gal 2:14 and the
"James-party" of 2:12, are at least one in spirit with them,
belonging to the same Jewish-Christian front.[57] The place of
circumcision and the law in the dispute is to be determined
principally from the teachings of the Old Testament.[58] The
paraenetic section of the letter is traditional rather than
occasional,[59] and is therefore "unpolemical,"[60] elucidating
neither the nomism of the opponents nor the actual behavior of
the Galatians. Its function is to stress the new basis of the
life of the believer, the basis of the Spirit.[61] Robert Jewett
sees a real nomistic threat, a real moral problem, and an inti-
mate relationship between the two. The background is zealot
terrorism in Judea, which leads Judean Jewish-Christians to
undertake a circumcising mission among the Gentiles to escape
persecution.[62] They find the Galatians with a background of
cosmological syncretism, a Hellenistic desire for perfection,
with enthusiastic traits; and they cunningly integrate their
pragmatic demand for circumcision into this context.[63] Nomism is
an imported danger; enthusiasm is native. Each is dealt with
in separate parts of the epistles. This comes under the criticisms that have been levelled against other writers;[64] and

Jewett does not seem to have been successful in avoiding a
two-front theory.[65]

In a recent dissertation on the Galatian opponents,
John G. Hawkins has reached a conclusion similar to Jewett's.
The opponents are only "Judaisers"; the Galatians themselves
are self-styled πνευματικοί and devotees of the στοιχεῖα. The
sections of the letter dealing with these issues are attacks
on "popular religious attitudes and ideas," not on the intruding opponents. And the most enthusiastic and pneumatic of all
is Paul himself, who uses language that puts him on the road
to Gnosticism.

Gnostic Theories

Rudolf Bultmann, having assumed Gnosticism to be a pre-
Christian phenomenon, asserted that Paul's theology made use
of the framework of the Gnostic redeemer myth.[66] In keeping
with this, Galatians is said to share in Paul's use of Gnostic
language.[67] And yet there are also crucial differences between
the two religions:[68] and in the ethical portion of Galatians,
with its call to love grounded in faith (5:6), Paul finds a
positive solution to the problem so fatal to Gnosticism, that
is, the unworldliness of the self.[69]

Walter Schmithals, going even further, has made all
Paul's major opponents Gnostics, including those in Galatia.[70]
His theory for this letter has six basic supports:

(1) The unlikelihood of Judean missionaries, more
radical even than James, in Galatia.

(2) The specific nature of the question of apostleship
in Galatians. It does not accord with a Jerusalemite view of
the relative validity of message and apostolate. Paul is
charged with denial of a Jerusalem tradition and with dependence on other apostles. In the context, an apostle is validated by ἀποκάλυψις.

(3) The concern for circumcision not being a nomistic-
Jewish one (the opponents do not keep the whole law, 5:3,
6:13), but a Gnostic one of liberation of the pneuma-self from
the prison of the body. When Paul puts circumcision

in the context of Judaising (3:1-5:12), he has misunderstood
the situation.

(4) The concern for cultic festivals fitting better
with Gnostic angel-worship (στοιχεῖα) than with Judaism.[71]

(5) The unity of the letter, and the "enthusiasmus"
of the opponents, as revealed in the use of "pneuma" and
"pneumatikos." The lists of virtues are integral to the argument against circumcision (5:1, 13, 23)--in fact, a quarter of
the letter is against "sarkic" conduct--and exactly fits a
Gnostic context (the main concerns are dissensions, divisions,
et cetera, and their opposites).

(6) The similarity of the opponents here to those
behind 1 and 2 Corinthians, Philippians, and Colossians, who,
it is asserted, are also Gnostics.

Others have agreed that there are "Gnostic colorings"
to the Galatian opponents.[72] But they are also much more
Jewish in character than Schmithals has admitted[73] and would
better be labelled "syncretistic." He appears to be correct
in linking this heresy to those behind Colossians, 2 Corinthians, and Philippians (though not 1 Corinthians), but incorrect
in labelling them all "Gnostic."[74]

Willi Marxsen has followed Schmithals rather closely
in identifying the opponents as "Christian-Jewish-Gnostic"
syncretists, though he disagrees at certain points.[75] Elements
in the letter point so clearly to Gnostic libertines that the
only conclusion can be that, in discussing the heresy in relation to law, as if the opponents were Pharisaic Judaists, Paul
has completely misunderstood the situation. In fact, the historic Galatian formulation of justification by faith was
developed in the face of a situation that was misconceived.

Specific points of Schmithals' system have come under
attack.[76] However, some of his positions carry weight--the
question of apostleship, the unity of the letter (theological
and ethical portions addressing the same problem), and the
significance of other anti-Pauline missionary movements.

Enthusiastic Theories

In these theories, as for several other writers mentioned above, the Judaism in question in Galatians is assumed
to be of a sectarian, mystical type. But a step is taken that
enables the problem of the unity of Galatians to be overcome:
a legalist could be an antinomian or libertine, in a certain
sense--or at least, both parts of the letter could be called
forth by the same speculative source. These writers continue
the work of Bultmann, though with significant differences.[77]

Frederick G. Crownfield offered a version of this
alternative.[78] Galatians is against Judaisers; and Paul only
addresses one group throughout the letter. Thus, Judaisers
and "pneumatikoi" are the same people--syncretistic Christians
who had been adherents of Jewish mystery cults, now combining
Jewish rites with a quest for a Christian form of illumination
and deification. They are from Jerusalem, pretending to belong
to the Petrine "legalist" party, but are "false brethren."
Their purposes are unacceptable to both Peter and Paul. Galatians was written after Acts 15, but Paul does not invoke the
decision of the council, as it is here irrelevant. It was an
agreement reached with "normative" Judaism, not syncretists.

Helmut Koester claims that the opponents' observance
of law cannot be explained by Rabbinic sources, as they stress
the law's spiritual and cosmic dimensions.[79] However, they
have a real interest in law and its redemptive value.[80] Especially important is the role assigned to Jesus--the revealer
of the cosmic rule of God. All the major elements of the
letter must be considered collectively as relating dialogically
to the opponents' system, that is:

(1) The central place of the discussion of law

(2) The cosmos-language and mythology-language (3:19-
20, 4:3-11)

(3) The language of promise and covenant (3:6-25)

(4) Paul's eschatological-historicising argument (1:4;
3:17-18; 4:4)

(5) Christological statements (3:13, 4:4)

(6) Ethical statements that stress "agape"--human
responsibility to an existing, visible community[81]

(7) The "mystery-language," which is the counterpart
of the Christological statements (2:20; 6:14, 15). The heresy
must be related to the ones behind Philippians, 2 Corinthians,
and especially Colossians.

Dieter Georgi has set forth a portrayal of the Galatian heretics and their theology which has had great influence
on recent scholarship.[82] The heretics are pneumatics,[83] and
in some senses they anticipate Gnosticism.[84] They are gospel-
preachers who stress the necessity of combining the law and
the gospel.[85] But they are nomistic Jewish pneumatics, with
roots in wisdom movements.[86] Their legalist interest includes
the "elements of the world" (4:3-11) interpreted in terms of
the speculative and liturgical interests of intertestamental
Judaism in angels. These στοιχεῖα or angels are mediators of
the law (3:19), mediators between heaven and the world. Moses,
and even Jesus, may be seen by the opponents as angels as well.
Christ is the last landmark in a long development of revelation of law.[87] This law reveals the structure of things,
brings the Spirit (3:1-3), and makes believers participate in
the innermost of the cosmos and God (4:21-31). The opponents
simultaneously practice baptism[88] and circumcision,[89] which
are understood in a mystical-sacramental sense. This legalism
leads to individualistic nomistic-enthusiastic problems, which
are confronted in the ethical portion of the letter.[90] The
attack on Paul and his mission, and especially on his doctrine
of righteousness by faith, that here comes into the open,
stems from a widespread church intrigue set in motion by
Jewish-Christians, perhaps beginning in Jerusalem itself. The
agitators were equals with the Jerusalem apostles and argued
for the priority of all Jerusalem apostles.[91] Jerusalem to
them was the holy center of Christian mysteries, and the
apostles were its mystagogues.[92] Paul was charged particularly
with contempt for the traditions and institutions of Jerusalem.[93]

Others have seen validity in such an assessment of
Galatians. In a recent review of literature on the Pauline
opponents, E. Earle Ellis would venture to say little more
than that Galatians was "problematic": but that "it is quite
conceivable that one group might have been both ritually strict

(regarding circumcision) and at the same time theologically
syncretistic and morally lax."[94]

Conclusions

Each of these theories has something essential to
contribute to the question of the Galatian opponents.

What is Paul's relation to Jerusalem and the apostles?
What are their relative positions on law and gospel? Baur
heightened these questions, but the persistence of "three-
party" theories suggests that his answers were not adequate.
Lütgert, Bruce, and especially Schmithals have each shown the
complexity of the question of apostleship in Galatians.

The place of Judaism in the whole context is significant. The difficulty of reconciling Galatians on this point,
not only with Acts but with Paul's own letters, has been
pointed out by Munck and Drane. Lütgert shows that the opponents' relation to Judaism, too, is complex (as it is to the
Jerusalem apostles). Luther, and later, Bultmann and others,
quickly assumed that Paul was attacking "normative" Judaism.
Schoeps has retorted that Paul has completely misunderstood
it, if that is the case. Is it a question, then, of some
other form of Judaism?

How are anti-Pauline missionaries in Galatia to be
explained? Is it really unlikely that they are from Jerusalem (Munck)? It must be borne in mind that they bear important resemblances to the "Hebrew" opponents behind other Pauline letters, especially 2 Corinthians and Philippians
(Schmithals, Gunther, etc.).

It has been frequently affirmed (the Tübingen extrem-
ists, Schweitzer, et cetera) that Galatians deals with law as
a theological principle. But did the opponents keep the
"whole law" (Munck, Jewett)? If not, then in what sense does
Paul deal with law in principle? How is it that the one
letter deals with the apparently opposite questions of legalism and ethical laxity? The strength of the "two-front" solution since Lightfoot, Lütgert, and Ropes forbids a minimising
of the real tension in the letter in these terms (Schmithals).
And yet these very two-front theories overlook the essential

unity of the letter (Jewett, Koester, Georgi), and, within the
framework of these theories, the epistle inevitably flies
apart (Jewett, Betz).

The question of the place of eschatology in Paul's
theology, and, therefore, in Galatians, was raised by
Schweitzer. It is probably directly associated with the significant use in Galatians of mythical and speculative language,
wrestled with by many since Ramsay. Both may be subheadings
within the larger category of Christology (Koester).

Later movements and literature of the second century
are also part of the question. How could Galatians be against
Gnostics (Schmithals, Marxsen) if it became so popular with
Gnostics (Pagels)? How could it be against the ancestors of
the Ebionites (critics of Schoeps)? Can the two second-century
movements of Pharisaism and Libertinism be so clearly separated
in the first century (Lightfoot)?

The Galatian opponents and their theology appear to
remain "problematic" (to use Ellis' term). These seem to be
some of the conclusions reached so far--which are at the same
time questions that remain. Hence they will be used as somewhat fixed points from which the following chapters will take
their bearing.

CHAPTER TWO

OPPONENTS AND METHODOLOGY

This chapter will attempt to examine the most significant contributions to methodology for locating and character-
ising opponents, not only in Galatians but in other contexts
as well.

Interpretation out of the Context

Several attempt to interpret the Galatian conflict out
of a preestablished context. Helmut Koester suggests that the
teachings of opponents can be found by subtracting Paul's
interpretation of certain terms, concepts, and forms of speech
from those terms and concepts themselves, and replacing it with
an opposite interpretation, in the historical context most
appropriate to the terms and motifs in question.[1] Behind this
method there would seem to be two concerns in particular.
Firstly, in Paul's letters the apostle's thought is to be
found not so much in the terms, concepts, and myths that may
be used. These may belong to his readers, or opponents.
Paul's own thought is to be seen in the direction of the
interpretation.[2] Secondly, and arising out of this, the syncretistic character of the theology of Paul and his environ-
ment forbids a facile preoccupation with history-of-religions
parallels. There must be some overall frame of reference and
ordering of the history-of-religions context for the parallels
to be useful.[3] The frame that Koester has chosen is a historical one, and thus the foremost task becomes that of defining
most precisely the historical background of Paul's theological
vocabulary and interpreting the movement of arguments out of
this context.[4]

These criteria are unquestionably essential in themselves. Paul must be seen as an interpreter of tradition; and

23

there can be no faithful exegesis without attention to context.
But the question of priority must be asked. What is to be the
beginning point, the primary frame of reference? Koester himself comments that many forms of syncretistic-Jewish development may have disappeared altogether, "often leaving no more
traces than the Qumran community before the year 1945."[5] In
this case, we may crush a fragile piece of evidence for earliest Christianity if we too quickly interpret Galatians out of
systems reconstructed from external materials. As far as possible, the essential frame of reference within which movements
of interpretation are traced should come from Galatians itself.

Interpretation out of the Text

Johannes Munck has set forth several principles for
beginning exegesis with the text of the New Testament itself,
two of which are relevant here:[6]
(1) Paul's letters are to be interpreted as such.
Statements from other sources must not determine the exposition of the letters.
(2) Paul's individual letters, and the situation that
forms the background of each individual letter, must be viewed
on their own merits in each case. Material in the letters may
be unified only if this does not violate the individual nature
of the particular letter and of the situation that lies behind
it.
Others concur that, when studying any of Paul's writings, the letter in question must be the primary source,[7] and
that the uniqueness of each New Testament document must be
allowed to stand.[8] However, it must be asked whether Munck
has been able to achieve this openness to the text of Galatians.
He himself earlier states that Paul must first be understood on
the basis of the "uncontroversial" texts, and then the "controversial" texts must be interpreted in this light.[9] His "uncontroversial" texts are 2 Thess 2:6, Rom 9-11, and Rom 15:14-33.
So Munck *does* have a "context" in which he places Galatians,
admitting that the letter is controversial and difficult to
exegete in itself.[10] Here is the rub: it is to be desired
that Galatians be understood on its own basis; but the very

controversial nature of the letter makes this exceedingly
difficult.

Joseph B. Tyson has also postulated principles for
understanding the letter on its own terms:[11]

(1) We must limit ourselves to the internal evidence
provided by the letter itself.

(2) We must analyze Paul's defense in Galatians,
attempting to identify specific charges or objections to certain contrary teachings. Galatians is a defensive letter. We
must find statements in the letter which seem to be direct
answers, those which seem to be countercharges, and those
which reflect charges made by the opponents.

(3) On the basis of Paul's defense, we must decide
what specific charges were made by Paul's opponents and what
positions they held. Mostly, the charge can be seen by taking
the negative of the defense.

(4) We must attempt to discover the source or sources
of these charges.
The difficulty is that the charges Tyson postulates, using
this method,[12] would not call forth some of the most distinctive passages in Galatians,[13] suggesting that this quest for
the mirror-image of defensive statements must be inadequate,
on its own, for reconstructing the Galatian opposition.
Tyson is incorrect in concluding that Galatians is only
defensive. It is also offensive,[14] but even further, it is
dialogical. It is significant, too, that Tyson's defensive
statements come mostly from the "historical" portions of the
letter, portions which, on the basis of literary analysis,
would not be expected to yield the essence of the opposing
theology.[15]

Further, defensive statements are, to an extent,
blanks to be filled in on other grounds. They could be denials
of misconstructions of facts, denials of untruths, or denials
of inferences.[16] John J. Gunther has seen further complica-
tions within the argument of Galatians.[17] Paul does not react
to the opponents by direct denial alone. He uses insult and
caricature, asks rhetorical questions, reduces the opponents'
views to absurdity, accepts one part of an argument and denies
another, repeats the opponents' charges only to refute them,[18]

uses mere affirmation to counter what he has attacked elsewhere,[19] and steals the enemies' thunder by using terms in a
different sense[20] or by repeating their teachings with approval
while putting them in an entirely new frame.[21]

  With one who, like Paul, can use so many subtle methods of argument, the "mirror-image" approach to the discovery
of opponents will be very unsatisfactory. But how can these
criteria be used, and the exact nature of each pericope and
argument be determined, while still making Galatians rather
than some external priority the reference-point for exegesis?
Munck's starting-point seems desirable, but, given the complex
nature of the epistle, how is it to be done?

  Franz Mussner suggests that the opponents' theology
should be reconstructed by locating "Stichworten" and determining how Paul is using them. The majority of his catchwords
come from chapters 1 and 2.[22] But considerations of genre and
structure may suggest that these are the very chapters where
the essential issues in dispute may not be found. Moreover,
Mussner's own summary of the opponents' teachings reveals that
the catchwords cannot fully yield the theological complex
necessary to account for essential portions of the letter.[23]
And how is an opponent's catchword to be isolated? Claus
Bussmann summarized the various arguments used to justify the
presence of non-Pauline material, but notes that they are all
inconclusive without a larger frame of reference.[24] In fact,
catchwords may more appropriately be used for tracing a theme
or determining a pattern of argument.[25]

  Schmithals and Wilckens have relied heavily on the
significance of "Gnostic terminology" from within Galatians,
in order to assess the context and the source of opposition.
A synchronic investigation of the milieu of various terms,
phrases, et cetera, will be essential, and to this extent
Schmithals' method is not wrong. However, he may read a whole
theological system into certain terms, failing to realise
fully the syncretistic nature of Gnosticism,[26] which "pirated
elements of earlier myth" and grew in a situation in which
there was "a free-floating availability of traditions that are
no longer binding, but pregnant with redefinable meaning."[27]
Vocabulary was useful to Gnosticism only because it was

important in other theological systems; and Paul's use of
certain terms may only indicate that he drew from a literary
and intellectual context common to other systems and writers.
The linguistic method reaches extremes when, in the case of
Schmithals and Marxsen, the system out of which the text is
being understood is retained at the expense of the text--that
is, it is deduced that Paul has misunderstood his opponents,
and that they can be sketched only from certain portions of
Galatians.[28]

*Interpretation out of a Portion
of the Text*

Further problems are raised by the suggestion that
Galatians in part attacks the opponents and in part rebukes
the Galatians themselves.[29] Then what signals would we look
for to decide that Paul had shifted audiences? Here Galatians
is more problematic than Paul's other letters. In 2 Corinthians, problems of unity aside, most agree that it is possible
to see where Paul addresses the church and where he debates the
opponents.[30] Again, in Philippians, such a distinction is
fairly clear.[31] But in Galatians, the whole letter is polemical, and yet only brief verses refer to the opponents themselves.[32] Paul does distinguish sharply between the congregations themselves and the opponents;[33] but the distinctions are
not between the opponents' theology and the theology of the
congregation. Mussner notes that the direct personal references to the opponents reveal their method of propaganda, but
not their teachings.[34] These must be reconstructed from other
parts of the letter.[35] Just as the direct defensive statements
do not yield the opponents' theology,[36] neither do the direct
personal references. It becomes apparent that Paul's handling
of the opponents' theology is bound up with the structure of
the letter as a whole.

How, then, would it be known that there were two opponents, or that the letter was directed to two groups? Lütgert
and Ropes began working from the paraenetic section of the
letter. Without discussing the literary relationship between
theology and paraenesis in the Pauline letters, or the literary

characteristics of paraenetic material,[37] they assumed that
the vocabulary of the ethical passage must directly reflect the
situation in Galatia, which must be libertinistic. This group
and its teachings can therefore not possibly be in view in the
portion of the letter which confronts a nomistic heresy. There
must be two fronts involved, a legalistic and a libertinistic
one. However, Lütgert and Ropes managed to arrive at contradictory conclusions about the central passage of the book,[38]
and the overall result of their work is to show the complexity
of the argument of Galatians and the difficulty of making such
a distinction.[39] The letter resists subdivision that starts
from within its final section. The same concerns appear in
the so-called anti-legalist and anti-libertine sections,[40] and
to suggest two audiences may be to misunderstand Paul's
polemic against the law,[41] as well as to misunderstand the
relation between theology and paraenesis in his letters.[42]
Jewett has noted that all two-front theories fail to explain
why Galatians deals with the congregation as a homogeneous
group.[43] The literary signals that Paul has two audiences
are lacking, and the entire congregation seems as much in
danger of the one extreme as of the other (if they are
extremes).[44]

        Regarding distinctions within Galatians, three con-
siderations stand out:

        (1) There is a clear distinction between the Galatians
and the opponents, which is not a theological distinction.
Direct references to opponents fail to adequately supply their
theology.

        (2) Defensive statements (referring back to Tyson) are
also inadequate for constructing the opponents' theology.
There is an important way in which the letter as a whole confronts the opponents.

        (3) The Galatians themselves are treated homogeneously,
and there are no literary signals that there are two groups
within the congregations.

        It would appear, then, that there is no clear method,
using the internal evidence of Galatians, for distinguishing
two groups that hold different theologies, have different

problems, et cetera. Two-front theories have not supplied a
methodology for distinguishing the theology of the opponents.

     Two other writers, though partially discussed above,
must be considered again here--Jewett and Hawkins.[45] Jewett
finds a distinction within the letter between the Judaism of
the opponents and the speculative-syncretistic Hellenism of
the Galatians themselves. Any suggestions of Hellenistic
religion are native, not imported.[46] Such a distinction
encounters several problems. The vocabulary of the vice-list
does not imply, as he assumes, that the Galatians themselves
are ethical libertines.[47] Account must be taken of the degree
of both tradition and contextuality in the Pauline ethical
passages. Further, if it is said that the calendrical observances are non-Jewish, then it should probably also be said
that circumcision in this context is non-Jewish,[48] as has
Schmithals. But as the latter is very unlikely,[49] the former
would appear unlikely too, especially in the light of abundant
parallels to Gal 4:10 in Jewish sources.[50] Finally, it seems
improbable that 4:8-11 is to be taken out of the sequence of
Paul's attack on the intruders' program. 4:3 brings the
experience of Judaism under the same head as the matters dealt
with in 4:8-11,[51] and 4:8-11 seems very much to refer to a
turning back that is directly occasioned by the intruders.[52]
There seems therefore to be an intrinsic connection between
this turning back and what the opponents teach, and 4:10
appears to be a part of the treatment of law begun in chapter
3 (to Jewett, an anti-Jewish argument).

     It would appear that Jewett encounters the same prob-
lems of structure that he raises against the more "classical"
two-front theories,[53] because he really works from the same
basis as they did--the assumed picture of the Galatian church
derived from a mirror-reading of the paraenetic section. He
concludes that the libertinism of the Galatians is irreconcilable with an interest in nomism, and there must therefore be
two problems, one native, one imported. He cannot explain why
the Galatians should fall prey to nomism--and the letter was
obviously written because they did.[54] Jewett has put such a
distance between the theology of the Judaisers and that of
the Galatians that he cannot hold the letter together. Whereas

Marxsen says that the classical expression, justification by
faith and not by works of law, was formulated in the face of
a situation that was not understood, it must be concluded from
Jewett's reconstruction that it does not address the Galatians'
real concerns at all. This is the predicament. If the language of the ethical section is assumed to demand a party of
libertines, then if it is a separate group among the Galatians
there is no accounting for the way Paul addresses the congregation as a homogeneous unit. But if it is the Galatians in
distinction from the intruders, there is no accounting for the
way Paul writes the first part of the letter--to the Galatians!

        Hawkins makes a distinction similar to Jewett. Terms
such as στοιχεῖα, πνευματικοί, et cetera, are suggestions of
speculative Hellenism, "popular religious ideas and attitudes"
that belong to the Galatians themselves, not to the opponents.[55]
The above objections therefore apply to his thesis too. He
claims to base his study only on an exegesis of Galatians,[56]
but ignores the complicated nature of the book, and begins by
examining various verses in isolation.[57] His work is based on
an important a priori assumption--that the "traditional understanding of the situation in Galatia is generally correct."[58]
By "traditional understanding" he means the assessment of the
Galatian situation by the Fathers, and the equation of the
opponents with Jewish-Christians as pictured by Justin Martyr
and the later heresiologists.[59] It is not for internally
derived literary reasons that he makes his distinctions between
Galatians and intruders.

        These two most recent attempts to characterize the
opponents by making distinctions within Galatians seem to lack
an adequate literary basis. When there is such abundant evidence of a Judaism capable of being responsible for such a
"syncretistic" theology as is suggested by 3:19, 4:8-11, et
cetera,[60] there must be sound methodological reasons for saying
that these verses cannot be attributed to a Jewish opposition.
The need for an overall, holistic appreciation of Galatians,
and a larger frame of reference derived from the epistle itself,
is still apparent.

Interpretation out of the
Literary Genre

It is evident from the above analysis that one of the
most recurring and as yet unresolved problems for the identification of the opponents is the relationship of the parts of
the letter to each other.[61] There are obvious weaknesses in
methods that begin from a reconstructed history-of-religions
context, rather than the text.[62] But there are also glaring
weaknesses in those methods claiming to begin with the text.[63]
Obviously, there must be some holistic control over the way
the parts of the letter are related in order to handle adequately its complicated, dialogical nature, and over the way
it is motivated by an offending theology coming from offending
individuals, referring to those individuals in terms of theology only scantily, and addressing the theology almost exclusively to the congregations who have been "bewitched."[64]

It is suggested therefore that an important step in
the identification of the intruding theology must be a search
for some indication of the structure of the letter of the
largest possible scale. Galatians should be examined as a
piece of literature and should be classified in terms of literary genre.[65] This may help to uncover possible suggestions
of structure and to provide some sort of control over subjective or predetermined dissection of this very difficult text.[66]
Such a method has not yet been applied to the question of the
opponents, their theology, and Paul's response. And it seems
a logical step. Galatians was not written in a vacuum, and,
if the writings of Paul himself should prove too small a sample
for analysis of the letter,[67] some other analogous literature
should be expected to exist.

This approach should not contradict the beginning pre-
supposition that it is preferable to start with the text rather
than the context.[68] Genre analysis must be determined in conjunction with a simultaneous analysis of internal indicators
in the piece of literature itself which confirm that a particular literary genre is appropriate.[69] It is important to notice
that this internal analysis has begun already. There is a distinction between intruders (1:8-10, 5:12, 6:12-13) and the

congregation (3:1-5, 4:8-16, 5:7-8),[70] but the theology of
the intruders is the theology of the congregation,[71] and the
whole letter deals with the heresy in a particular way.
Further, there are evidently the same concerns in the so-called
"anti-legalist" and "anti-libertine" sections (3:1-5, 5:13-24,
6:1, 2, 7-8).[72] And the congregation is treated as a homogeneous group in which all have equally accepted the opponents'
propaganda (1:6, 3:1-5, 5:7).[73] In this letter, Paul pursues
one particular object, an intruding theology, with unique
singleness and vigor. It appears, then, that this is an appropriate stage to raise the question of literary genre.

        Again, this is not to leave the text behind. It is
never simply a question of dealing with the text, and then
external literature, or of dealing with the external literature, and then the text. One can never be lost sight of in
absorption with the other,[74] especially when dealing with
such a complex piece as Galatians. Hence the following chapters will move constantly from Galatians to possible genres
and back in an attempted process of suggestion, confirmation,
and elaboration.[75] Genre analysis will be used with an awareness that it is not a method to be used on its own,[76] and that
the very genres themselves demand a sense of flexibility.[77]
The section will include "a comparative literary analysis of
the arrangement and construction of the entire composition,"[78]
that is, an analysis of the form and function of smaller seg-
ments of the letter such as transitional statements, vocabulary,
catchwords, and pieces of pre-Pauline tradition.[79]

        Using the evidence of structure of argument and rela-
tion of the parts to each other that these chapters will provide, an hypothesis will be constructed regarding the probable
theological positions of the opponents. The remaining section
of the thesis will then test this hypothesis against "contextual" or external evidence such as the Jewish literature of
the period, other Pauline letters, and some of the later "trajectories" of Christian theology into the next century.

        Perhaps this is following the lead of Günther Bornkamm.
After looking for the major polemical thrusts in Colossians,
the pattern of the argument of the book, and the most likely

theology that would have called it forth, he confirms his
work from "contextual" sources:

> If we succeed in assigning the details of the whole (of
> the reconstruction of the Colossian heresy) to a place
> in the history of religions, then we shall have attained
> the desired degree of certainty and avoided the suspicion
> of vague combinations and hypotheses.[80]

PART TWO

GENRE ANALYSIS

CHAPTER THREE

GALATIANS AND LITERARY GENRE

This chapter will seek to relate Galatians to a known
literary genre--assuming that a literary genre gives expression
to a corresponding thought pattern.[1] It seems to be customary
to pay no attention to genre at all in analyzing the structure
of Galatians;[2] or to assign the book to a genre of letters
(Pauline or Papyri[3]) which allows us to say little more than
that we should expect an opening, a middle, and a conclusion.[4]
This seems inconsistent with the growing awareness that Paul's
letters (Galatians included) evidence careful arrangement and
structure.[5] It will be the thesis of this chapter that the
epistolary nature of Galatians has little consequence for the
structure of its contents, and that the body of the letter may
be closer to something other than simply epistolary genre.

The Genre of the Pauline Letter?

It should first be decided whether one can speak of
a "typical Pauline letter" and whether an examination of the
various structures of Paul's letters can suggest anything
about the relation of the parts of Galatians to each other.

It does seem possible to differentiate between Pauline
and non-Pauline New Testament letters.[6] Because, in the
latter, epistolary features tend to become convention, they
are best classified as literary tracts.[7] James is paraenetic
throughout, stringing together general moral maxims.[8] 1 and 2
Peter and Jude have no sequence of interrelated and mutually
supportive units but are theological reflections around Christian traditions.[9] 1 John has lost all epistolary characteristics.[10] 2 and 3 John appear to be a move in another direction,
approximating even more closely than Paul's epistles the Greek
common letter traditions.[11]

37

          In comparison, Paul's letters reveal a much more
lively use of epistolary features.[12] The customary salutation
and closing are a strikingly Christianized form of both Jewish
and Hellenistic letter conventions.[13] An opening prayer or
thanksgiving is also a regular feature,[14] which often serves
the function of a prooemium,[15] tending to "telegraph" the content of the letter to follow.[16] There are quite regular formulae that open the main segment of the letter (i.e., the
letter body), such as παρακαλῶ ὑμᾶς, ἀδελφοί,[17] γνωρίζω . . .
ὑμῖν,[18] et cetera. Paul also seems to incorporate regular
features into his letters, such as autobiography,[19] travel
narrative,[20] and paraenesis, so-called.[21] Such consistency of
structure and style in Paul's letter-writing has led to an
"hypothesis concerning the structure of the Pauline letter
form,"[22] of salutation (sender, addressee, greeting); thanksgiving; body (opening formulae, connective and transitional
formulae, concluding eschatological climax, and travelogue);
paraenesis; and closing elements (greetings, doxology, bene-
diction).

          However, it must be asked whether this "letter form"
is fixed enough to be the basis of an analysis of structure
in any one of Paul's letters and to explain the presence of
various parts and their relation to each other. There is no
lack of awareness of diversity of form among Paul's letters.[23]
1 Corinthians breaks all the rules of Pauline structure: there
are evidences that it is "genuine correspondence,"[24] and the
unique arrangement of the development of Christ as wisdom
(chaps. 1-4) followed by extended paraenesis (chaps. 5-15)[25]
is best explained by a relationship between form and content
where wisdom speculations are being related to existence and
faith.[26] 2 Corinthians is widely held to be composite and so
cannot be used as a basis for the structure of the Pauline
letter.[27] If Philippians is not composite[28] then at least it
must be said that 3:1-4:1 gives the appearance of an independent letter and is not the expected paraenetic section.
1 Thessalonians is also unique in the way the body of the
letter flows out of the thanksgiving (which occurs at 1:2-10,
2:13-16, and 3:9-13).[29] If Colossians is Pauline, then still
it is difficult to separate body from paraenesis, as the two

are inseparable (i.e., 2:16-20), and "paraenesis" takes up
more than half the letter.[30]   Philemon is different again,
most closely approximating the Greek private letter.[31]   Only
Galatians and Romans are constructed according to the homiletic
schema of dogmatic teaching and paraenesis.[32]   Even Galatians,
in many respects the only real approximation to Funk's "hypothesis," has such significant departures from it that Funk himself calls for an examination of the structure of Galatians on
its own grounds.[33]   Thus, on the one hand, if one speaks of
the "Pauline letters," it must be said that identification of
both overall structure[34] and parts within the structure is
still tentative;[35] and on the other hand, for any individual
letter, some factor other than its being a letter best explains
its construction.[36]   Doty has concluded that "There is more
differentiation between any of several of his (Paul's) letters
than between hundreds of hellenistic letters."[37]

Other Letter-Genres?

Will other contemporary letter-traditions be more
productive in providing a genre on which to base a structure-
analysis of Galatians?
There seems to be wide and well-established agreement
that Adolf Deissmann[38] was wrong in equating the Pauline letter
too closely with the private Greek letters among the nonliterary papyri.[39]   These objections are based on such things as:
(1) The awareness that Deissmann's distinction between
"literary" and "nonliterary" breaks down, both for pagan Greco-
Roman letters[40] and for later Christian letters.[41]
(2) The fact that Paul's letters are not private
letters, except for Philemon.[42]
(3) The presence of paraenesis in Paul's letters suggests that they stand nearer to literary than epistolary conventions.[43]
(4) The papyri give no help in understanding the overall structure of Paul's letters.[44]
(5) The awareness that factors other than epistolary
ones are crucial in determining the structure of individual

Pauline letters,[45] passages within those letters,[46] and the
style and language of the letters.[47]

(6) The growing awareness, based on style, form, and
sequence analysis, that there is a careful structure in Paul's
letters, and that they were not dashed off hastily in the
midst of a busy apostolic career.[48]

It seems rather strange, therefore, that new attempts
should be made to analyze the structure of the Pauline letter-
body on the assumption that "the common letter-tradition . . .
is the primary literary *Gattung* to which the Pauline letter
belongs."[49] These investigations of the nonliterary letters
have fulfilled Weiss' prediction--we are told little more than
that a letter has an opening, a middle, and a closing.[50]

Are other categories of letter-writing more appropriate for understanding the structure and content of Galatians?
It has been noted by Wendland that the essential themes of
Galatians come firstly from the missionary and theological
thinker and only secondarily from the letter-writer.[51] In
fact, one wonders what the typical letter-writer was like, as
letters in the ancient world performed such a variety of literary and communicative functions. Plato used the letter-form
for apology and self-justification;[52] Isocrates' letters are
general in subject-matter, best classified as political writings;[53] and the letters of Appolonius of Tyana are religio-
philosophical tracts.[54] The essential criterion among Cicero's
letters is whether they are public or private.[55] Seneca's
letters are mostly brief, artistic discourses in which form
is dominated by Stoic diatribe style,[56] although he could also
write "discursive letters."[57] Even such Jewish examples as
those in 2 Maccabees and the Letter of Aristeas are better
classed as "letter-essays."[58] It becomes apparent that one of
the least significant things about letters is that they are
letters.[59] The letter as a written form was "almost as flex-
ible as oral speech itself,"[60] and the letter was in fact
often regarded merely as another medium of oral speech.[61] The
fact that material should come in the form of a letter, then,
will not be essentially relevant for understanding the structure of that material.[62] The typical lament, in letter-
handbooks, over the mistreatment of letter-form only indicates

further the wide variety of functions the "letter" was made
to perform[63] and the small influence the handbooks had on
letter-writing.[64]

The research of Bultmann[65] and Thyen[66] into Cynic-
Stoic and Hellenistic-Jewish letters (as well as other forms
of literature)[67] has led to important conclusions about style,
but not about overall structure. The main techniques of diatribe are the disputative question, the imaginary opponent who
holds an opposing philosophy, taking up part of an opponent's
point to win one's own point, plays on words, et cetera. Particular phrases are characteristic,[68] and forms such as virtue
and vice lists are frequent. Writings are often hortatory or
imperative in tone. There is no clear pattern of overall con-
struction--structure is dominated by subject-matter, and
rhetorical influence is confined to phrases, expressions, and
literary devices (antithesis, analogy, etc.).[69] There are
clear parallels to Paul's letters, though the diatribe style
is most apparent in those that are farthest removed from the
personal letter, that is, Romans and 1 and 2 Corinthians,[70]
where Paul shows least personal acquaintance with his readers
and deals mostly with conjectured opponents.[71] And Paul's
diatribe style is softened in comparison with the Cynic-Stoic
authors,[72] while there is at the same time a move towards the
Jewish-Hellenistic homily.[73] Concerning Galatians, it is significant that, though the diatribe style of answers to questions posed does occur, there are here comparatively few
examples of diatribe, and little use of a conjectured opponent.[74] This further suggests that Galatians was written to
perform a particular function.

Three conclusions can be drawn from the material
examined so far. Firstly, the letters most closely approximating conventional epistolary form, the nonliterary epistles,
are too distanced from Paul's letters to help in understanding
their structure. Secondly, the literary epistles, though true
epistles, are not dominated by epistolary form. If they add
anything to the investigation, it is that the essential structure and nature of their material is to be explained in some
other way than by calling them letters. And thirdly, if the
genre of the letter or epistle is not adequate to analyze

Paul's writings, then some other appropriate genre should be
sought. Though the letter does not explain the structure of
Galatians, neither does the diatribe, suggesting that there is
some meaningful structure involved.

Apologetic Speech and Rhetorical Canons

        In the light of some of the suggestions by letter
theorists and rhetoricians regarding the relationship between
letter and speech referred to above--that is, the tendency for
rhetoricians to dominate letter-writing and for letters to
serve the purposes of oral speech[75]--Hans Dieter Betz appears
justified in carrying out[76] what others have suggested before
him,[77] an examination of Galatians in terms of rhetorical
structure. He refers to an "apologetic letter" genre, evidenced particularly by Plato's *Letter 7*.[78] This genre itself
stands close to autobiography and apologetic speech,[79] which
in turn stands in the one stream of development of the autobiographical letter.[80] It is here, then, that a speech form
and a letter form come together.[81] The "apologetic letter"
can be classified as a subheading under the genre of "apologetic speech" which, as with other categories of rhetoric,
could be conveyed in either oral or written form.[82] The
"apologetic speech" appears in literary form in such examples
as Plato's *Apology* of Socrates,[83] perhaps the first example
of the conversion of a speech of defense into a literary form
and confession of faith;[84] Demosthenes' *De Corona*;[85] Isocrates'
Antidosis,[86] "a blend of forensic oratory, self-defense, and
autobiography,"[87] itself influenced by Plato's *Apology*;[88] and
Cicero's *Brutus*, in turn influenced by Isocrates' autobiographical apology.[89]

        Besides these speeches in literature, there are pur-
ported records of speeches, particularly in Greek and Latin
historiography.[90] Although rhetoric had a strong and unfor-
tunate influence on history-writing in the Hellenistic period,[91]
the rhetoricians themselves distinguish between historiography
and oratory,[92] and an examination of these historiographic
speeches itself reveals that, on the whole, they were recorded
in the briefest manner.[93] It is justifiable then to limit

this investigation to literature that is concerned to present
speeches themselves, or literary imitations of speeches,
rather than to include the reports of speeches in literature
that has some other purpose.

When Betz examines the structure of rhetorical apology,
he turns firstly to the rhetorical textbooks.[94] This procedure
seems in fact to be correct. Although rhetoric was primarily
intended for the forensic situation of the law-court,[95] its
scope was much wider than this, and it was seen as providing
a vehicle for persuasion in any sphere.[96] On the other hand,
rhetorical canons were typically formulated in terms of forensic speech, and it is clear from the examples above that
apology was fond of the forensic setting, even if artificial,
to present its case.[97] Thus the rhetorical textbooks reveal
the accepted way of structuring any apology.

Further, William Beardslee makes a distinction between
two classes of larger form or genre.[98] Beginning perhaps with
Aristotle's *Poetics*, there is a line of tradition in which the
literary form is an essential part of the work. The form
itself is part of the message and content, revealing something
of the life-situation of the writer and audience. But beginning with Aristotle's *Rhetoric* is a line of tradition which
treats the form as a vehicle for a content which can stand
in its own right. Form is simply a means of communicating
content, a way of making a point of view persuasive. Ancient
rhetoric belongs to this tradition. In this case there must
be a clear distinction between content and form; the form cannot be analyzed in terms of the content conveyed by the form.
Because of this particular characteristic of a rhetorical
genre or larger form, rather than defining the structure of
the genre by attempting to analyze instances of it in terms of
each other (which may give an untrue picture of wide variation
within the genre[99]), it would seem preferable to place each
instance of the genre alongside accepted models of speech structure, that is, canons of rhetoric.

When this is done, it becomes evident that there is a
significant correlation between canons of rhetoric and the
structure of the various instances of "apologetic speech."[100]
The textbooks themselves, then, are important literary evidence

for the structure and dynamics of apologetic speech, as well
as representing the theory of rhetoric as it was in Paul's own
time.[101]

Rhetorical theory was based on a discourse of six
related parts, although some parts were often combined into
larger categories:[102]

(1) Introduction, also called *prooemium* or *exordium*.[103]
This was used to prepare the hearers' minds and gain attention,[104] and also to state the case or *causa*, that without
which there would be no dispute.[105]

(2) The narrative or statement of facts. Here the
events that have occurred are set forth, the historical background to the case itself.[106] This is not material that is in
dispute. The function of the part is not merely historical,
but also persuasive.[107]

(3) The *divisio*,[108] also called *partitio*[109] or *propositio*.[110] Its purpose is to make clear that which the speaker
and his opponents agree on, and what remains contested.[111] In
this sense it sums up the legal content of the *narratio* and
provides a transition to the *probatio*.[112]

(4) The proof or *probatio*,[113] also called the *confir-
matio*.[114] This is the essential part of the speech, the presentation of the argument. It is here that the case will
stand or fall, and much attention is given to methods of
argument, best order of presentation, et cetera.[115] It is
essential that it be directly related to the *narratio*: the
latter is a connected exposition of that which is to be proved,
and the former is the verification of that which has been
stated.[116]

(5) The refutation, called *refutatio* or *confutatio*.[117]
It is negative in tone, being a destruction of the adversaries'
argument.

(6) The *peroratio* or *conclusio*.[118] It is the last
chance to remind the judge or audience of the case and is to
make a strong emotional impression. It could be subdivided
in various ways,[119] but has to be related to the individual
parts of the speech.[120]

Looking ahead to Galatians, it is interesting to note
that the body of a forensic speech, excluding *prooemium* and

conclusio, and including *divisio* with *narratio* as does
Cicero,[121] would have three major parts, a *narratio*, a *probatio*
and a *refutatio*.

Apologetic Speech in Paul's Context

But could the use of rhetorical forms be expected in
Paul's context? Firstly, the canons of rhetoric had an integral place in Greco-Roman life and literature. Rhetoric was
fundamental to Hellenistic education, comprising the curriculum
for intermediate schooling, and having an important place in
advanced education.[122] The Roman schools took over this tradition with little or no modification.[123] Education tended to
reinforce basic patterns,[124] and rhetorical imitation was fundamental to the system.[125] These canons, and probably also
several of the above apologetic speeches, could be expected
to be fundamental to the education of anyone who received a
careful schooling in the Roman empire in the first century
A.D.

Secondly, Judaism came under the influence of this
system of education, directly or indirectly, both within and
outside Palestine. For the Diaspora, the Greek school and
gymnasium had been planted in almost every Asian city.[126]
Jewish names are common in lists of ephebes in Greek cities.[127]
Josephus implies that Jews attended the gymnasium in Antioch,[128]
and the letter of Aristeas, with its stress on καλοκαγαθία,
shows that the Jewish upper class in Alexandria had accepted
Hellenistic educational ideals.[129] There was evidently a
close association between admittance to the gymnasium and
acceptance into Alexandrian and Roman citizenship.[130] Philo
took it for granted that upper-class Jews would be at the
gymnasium[131] and speaks of the necessity of a knowledge of
rhetoric.[132] Palestine did not escape this influence. The
Greek literature of Palestine and even the synagogue and
temple schools bear its mark,[133] and the region produced its
writers and rhetors, though they were Pagans.[134]

Thirdly, Paul's "own city," Tarsus, was famous for
its university. Strabo writes that not only in philosophy but
in education in general the city even surpassed Athens and

Alexandria, and he particularly mentions schools of rhetoric.[135] Even if Paul did not attend these schools, he would
have been influenced by them.[136] But his letters give evidence that he had received a Greek education[137] and that he
knew Roman law.[138] Many have noted rhetorical characteristics
in his letters,[139] both on a larger[140] and smaller scale.[141]
Not only did rhetoric surround him on all sides; it has also
directly influenced him.

      One other piece of evidence for rhetoric in Paul's
context, though a very sensitive one, is the speeches of Acts.
The three defense speeches of Paul before Pagans in Acts 24
and 26 show clear rhetorical structure, especially the more
complete one in Acts 26.[142] Acts 17 is the centre of much
debate, but there is good evidence that it is to be understood
as a trial speech,[143] and it shows a definite rhetorical structure.[144] In these two respects, then, it proximates the genre
of apologetic speech and the literary models referred to above,
perhaps standing in the Socratic tradition of Plato's *Apology*
and Isocrates' *Antidosis*. Even further, the speech ends with
a missionary exhortation[145] which may still be considered to
be the rhetorical *conclusio*.[146] This is of even further significance for the analysis of Galatians.[147]

      All this material at least indicates that, by suggest-
ing that Galatians should be examined in terms of rhetorical
canons, Paul as a writer has not been placed in an unlikely
context. Those who see in him the "Platonic precedent" and
the influence of larger rhetorical structure may not be far
wrong.[148]

Galatians and Apologetic Speech

      In accord with the principle that a genre should
function as both an external and an internal control, there
should be here a consideration of indications from within
Galatians that it is to be understood in terms of apologetic
speech.

      The previous chapter has already suggested that the
nature of the direct references to the opponents, the defensive statements, and references to the Galatians themselves,

indicates that the letter as a whole confronts the opponents'
theology, though the letter as a whole is also written to the
Galatians.[149] In terms of epistolary form, too, Galatians is
polemical in the sense that the "whole letter is body" in a
unique way, with an unusually sustained interest in one problem.[150] Further, there is here a departure from typical
Pauline style in the smaller use of diatribe and the contrived
opponent.[151] This suggests that Galatians is written to perform a unique function--and so probably uses a unique larger
form.[152]

          There are phrases in Galatians that suggest that Paul
is presenting a case and demanding a decision in his favor.
Gal 1:8, 9 uses a double curse (ἀνάθεμα ἔστω) in a unique
way,[153] which is, however, a known rhetorical feature in
"apologetic speech."[154] In 1:20 Paul professes an oath of
truthfulness (ἃ δὲ γράφω ὑμῖν, ἰδοὺ ἐνώπιον τοῦ θεοῦ ὅτι οὐ
ψεύδομαι), also used in Roman law in the presentation of a
legal case.[155] And in 5:10 Paul makes an appeal for a decision in his favor, ἐγὼ πέποιθα εἰς ὑμᾶς ἐν κυρίῳ ὅτι οὐδὲν
ἄλλο φρονήσετε, having a decidedly forensic flavor.[156] There
are at least ten interpretations for 6:17, τοῦ λοιποῦ κόπους
μοι μηδεὶς παρεχέτω, ἐγὼ γὰρ τὰ στίγματα τοῦ Ἰησοῦ ἐν τῷ
σώματί μου βαστάζω.[157] It seems most plausible that Paul by
στίγματα is referring to marks or bodily scars that have
resulted from his apostolic office,[158] powerful to persuade
because the trials of the apostle are part of his share in
the crucified Jesus.[159] He is speaking in the context of the
"scars" (ἡ περιτομή, 6:12-15) in which the opponents boast.
They have only flesh-wounds, the στίγματα of slavery under the
law; Paul's wounds are στίγματα of freedom in the service of
the crucified Christ.[160] What, then, is the significance and
function of such a remark at this point? Rhetorical texts and
literary examples reveal that one of the most effective final
appeals, in a forensic case, was to present one's wounds
received in action, at the same time belittling the claims of
the opposition.[161] Paul here evidently makes a last appeal
for a favorable decision.

          The modifications of the typical Pauline letter-
opening and letter-closing are significant. There is an

epistolary framework that easily separates from the body of
the letter, almost like an external bracket,[162] and, when
separated, the body is left with few epistolary features. The
letter-opening itself is striking for its "apologetic" tone,
showing Galatians to be no private letter but an official
apostolic missive directed to particular concerns.[163] The
postscript departs even further from Pauline custom. Apart
from 6:11, 18, which are epistolary, the section is analyzed
more satisfactorily in terms of a rhetorical *conclusio*. It is
striking in the way it recapitulates the main themes of the
epistle (personal attacks of the troublemakers, circumcision,
the cross, the new people of God, and Paul's personal struggle),
and in its strongly personal references to both Paul and to an
opponent. This is unusual for a postscript, but typical of a
conclusio.[164] It can be divided into a *refutatio* (6:12-13, a
negative final appeal and denunciation of opponents); *recapitu-
latio* (6:14-16, a recapitulation in the form of a final exhortation); and *conquestio* (6:17, Paul's personal worth as grounds
for a favorable decision).[165] These modifications in the
letter-opening and the letter-closing suggest that the body of
the letter, too, is to be understood in terms of a particular
form and function.

     There is also a striking modification of the typically
Pauline *prooemium* or thanksgiving--that is, there is no thanksgiving at all,[166] which is such a departure from the Pauline
practice that it calls for explanation.[167] In terms of the
rhetorical model, the explanation is simple: Paul is using
a particular kind of *prooemium* or *exordium* in conformity with
the nature of a certain type of situation.[168] The use of
θαυμάζειν, which Paul nowhere else uses in a letter-opening,[169]
was a familiar rhetorical expression in connection with the
exordium.[170] Paul is here setting forth the *causa*, that without which there would be no dispute.

     Another fact noted by most commentators, though not in
the light of rhetorical structure, is that, apart from the
"epistolary envelope," the body of the letter divides into
three clear sections, which Lightfoot has labelled "narrative"
(chaps. 1 and 2), "argumentative" (chaps. 3 and 4), and "hortatory" (chaps. 5 and 6).[171] This is in fact what would be

expected of a forensic speech constructed in terms of rhetorical canons.[172]

The larger structure of Galatians will now be examined
in terms of these rhetorical canons, as an external criterion
(introduced into the discussion for internal reasons) for distinguishing the parts of the letter-body and ascertaining how
they hold together.

The *Prooemium*, 1:6-10

As already noted, this section sets forth the *causa*,
that without which there would be no dispute. In this case,
the central issue to which the argument of the whole letter is
directed is not only the "different gospel," serious though
this is,[173] but it is also that the Galatians are turning to
it (θαυμάζω ὅτι οὕτως ταχέως μετατίθεσθε ἀπὸ τοῦ καλέσαντος
ὑμᾶς . . . εἰς ἕτερον εὐαγγέλιον).[174] Certainly the issue has
been raised by intruders, as Paul appeals for a decision
against them (5:10, 6:17). The Galatians are both judge and
jury.[175] But the Galatians have identified themselves with the
offending party. If they had not deserted (μετατιθέναι), the
letter would not have been written.[176] The letter is not
written against two or more problems (a false gospel, deviant
Galatian praxis, etc.),[177] but against one central problem
(with several implications)--the Galatian acceptance of the
false gospel.[178] This explains why Galatians as a whole disputes a theology that has been introduced by intruders; and
yet the book is directed specifically at the Galatians themselves. Being understood as a *prooemium*, 1:6-10 stands at the
head of the whole letter as the *causa*.

The *Narratio*, 1:12-2:14

The "apologetic letter" genre explains why this historical passage is here. The *narratio* gave the background to
the dispute, the events that elaborated the situation. It is
significant that 1:13 begins with ἠκούσατε. Paul is giving
no new information, and it is an interpretation of history,

not history itself, that is in dispute, as is expected in a
forensic *causa*.[179] In the light of Paul's autobiographical
statements elsewhere, he here gives not "an historical but
rather an historic, that is, significant" or even apologetic
account of his early life as a Christian.[180] This is to be
expected in a rhetorical *narratio*, which must be "adapted to
persuade."[181]

In the light of rhetoric, three things can be said
about this difficult passage. Firstly, Paul has not here taken
up a different subject to the one raised in the *causa*; he is
still primarily concerned with the defense of his gospel, not
of his apostleship alone.[182] Throughout the letter, arguments
about gospel are bound up with arguments about apostleship,
and the two cannot be separated.[183] As well as a defense of
his apostleship, the passage is an alibi for his gospel:[184]
it is not κατὰ ἄνθρωπον.

Secondly, because these two issues are so closely
bound together, the charge of dependence on Jerusalem evidently
discredits both apostleship and gospel. If, to the opponents,
the Pillar apostles' gospel was the authentic one, the charge
of dependence would discredit Paul as an apostle, but it would
be a commendation of his gospel.[185] This becomes even clearer
in 2:15-21, where Paul claims that his gospel is the one
originally taught at Jerusalem (it is not Paul who is the
innovator, but somebody else)--and yet it is clearly a gospel
that the opponents cannot accept.[186] This suggests that the
thrust against Paul is two-pronged: that both Paul's apostolic
authority and his gospel derive from human sources and he is
dependent on other apostles; and that he is denying the authentic Jerusalem tradition while preaching this gospel κατὰ
ἄνθρωπον.[187] He is apparently dealing with a movement that is
hostile to the Jerusalem church as well as to himself.[188]

Thirdly, the *narratio* deals with the historical events
without which the case cannot be understood, not necessarily
the historical events of the case itself.[189] The issue in
Galatians is not to be understood to be exactly the same as
that in Jerusalem (2:1-10 and circumcision of Gentiles from
the point of view of Pharisees) or Antioch (2:11-14 and table
fellowship between Jews and Gentiles), just as the issue in

Antioch was different to the issue in Jerusalem, but the principle was the same.[190] Nor do the opponents in the *narratio*
have to be the opponents behind the *causa*. The account in the
narratio is only intended to illustrate Paul's struggle to save
the freedom of the gospel. The rhetoricians taught that the
narratio should end where the issue to be determined begins.[191]
The issue with which Paul confronts Cephas in 2:14 is therefore
in principle the issue that confronts the Galatians themselves:
πῶς τὰ ἔθνη ἀναγκάζεις 'Ιουδαΐζειν. And this is, in principle,
the issue that Paul has always struggled against. But the
exact form this issue takes in Galatia must be decided from the
rest of the letter, not from the *narratio*.[192]

The *Propositio*, 2:15-21

The *propositio* or *partitio*[193] could be considered part
of the *narratio* or a section in its own right.[194] Either way,
it was intimately related to what had preceded, summing it up
in terms of the precise issue to be discussed in the *probatio*.
It made more precise that which was agreed upon and that which
remained to be disputed.[195] Most commentators have noted the
change of tone after 2:14 that indicates that Paul has begun a
new section in his argument.[196] This is precisely what is to
be expected if Galatians is constructed according to rhetorical
canons. Then 2:15-16 is probably that which is agreed upon
(including the doctrine of justification as stated here).[197]
The Judaisers are, by their teaching and behavior, denying
something which Jewish and Gentile Christians have always
agreed upon, and that the Judaisers in principle must accept
--that a man is not justified by works of the law but through
faith in Christ. The exact point in dispute appears to be
2:17-18, where the tone changes from agreement to disagreement:[198] εἰ γὰρ ἃ κατέλυσα ταῦτα πάλιν οἰκοδομῶ, παραβάτην
ἐμαυτὸν συνιστάνω. The *propositio* was to provide a transition
to the *probatio*, and look forward to it.[199] The striking
change in language in 2:19-20 (from forensic terms to ἀποθνήσκειν, ζῆν, etc.) must sharpen the issue under debate in
those terms that are most relevant to the Galatians situation.[200] In this way 2:15-21 makes more precise that which

is agreed upon, that which is in dispute, and the language in
terms of which it is to be disputed.

The *Probatio*, 3:1-4:31

The *probatio* was the central argument against the
accusers, on which the case stood or fell. It is to be
expected, then, that the central assertions of the opponents
are to be debated here, and that the essentials of their theology are to be found here, rather than in the *narratio*.[201]
Several pericopae within these chapters can be
expected to be serving particular functions. 3:1-5 appears
to be an *interrogatio*,[202] or examination of witnesses, which
was assigned to the *probatio*, though relating directly to the
partitio.[203] Its language was to be most relevant to the issue
and most understandable to those involved.[204] Here the Galatians become witnesses to the debate: their own experience,
past and present, is essential to the case, and the language
in which the *interrogatio* is framed is understood by all
involved to be carrying on the main point at issue, sharpened
in 2:15-21, justification.[205]
The piece of evidence produced by the witnesses under
interrogation will be constantly referred to throughout the
proof, which itself will be a carefully reasoned piece.
Because of their place at the centre of the *probatio*, it is
not to be expected that 4:1-11, or even 4:8-11, are a turning
to a new issue; rather, they are probably a reactivation of
the original argument against the new theology which the Galatians have adopted.
The material in 4:12-20, probably to be designated by
the title περὶ φιλίας, could also be included in a *probatio*
and was understood to have inherent persuasive value.[206] This
places the passage and the events it refers to directly in the
debate itself. Again, the behavior of the Galatians is part of
the *causa* of the letter. The passage also shows the repudia-
tion of Paul by the Galatian churches, revealing that the opponents have taken his place as the community apostles.[207]

The *Refutatio*, 5:1-6:10[208]

This section was negative in tone, and destructive of
the adversaries' argument. 5:1-12 seems to be a *refutatio* in
the classical sense. Paul's tone clearly changes from chapters 3 and 4, and his attention turns, perhaps more than elsewhere in the letter, to the intruders themselves (5:7, 10, 12).
Their influence is only bad (5:9), and the section ends with
a curse that is unusual in its bitterness even for Paul (5:12).

It is in this pericope that Paul appeals for a decision (5:10). The most suitable place for such an appeal was
after the strongest argument.[209] In this case it is significant that the sharpened issue of the *divisio*, justification by
faith without the works of the law, has been brought to a
climax in this unsparing denunciation of circumcision.

For the rest, it must be admitted that it is difficult
to get from rhetoric to paraenesis, as 5:13-6:10 is usually
considered to be, although there may be another instance in
Acts 17.[210] However, this passage is not paraenesis in the
sense of disconnected topoi[211] but is still carrying through
the debate. The language of the *interrogatio* (σάρξ, πνεῦμα,
νόμος, πίστις) is central to this passage (5:13, 14, 16-25,
6:1-2, 7-8).[212] And chapters 5 and 6 divide into three parts
(5:1-12, 5:13-24, and 5:25-6:10), each beginning with an indicative statement that assumes that Paul's argument of 3:1-5 has
been won:

> 5:1   τῇ ἐλευθερίᾳ ἡμᾶς Χριστὸς ἠλευθέρωσεν . . .
>
> 5:13 ὑμεῖς γὰρ ἐπ' ἐλευθερίᾳ ἐκλήθητε . . .
>
> 5:25 εἰ ζῶμεν πνεύματι, . . .

Each of these passages pushes the argument to its conclusions
in practical terms. So it could be said that Paul is not
abandoning a rhetorical model but is following sound rhetorical procedure in adapting his material to the specific speech
situation[213] and putting his forensic refutation in terms of
ethical exhortation.[214]

The refutation was the destruction of the opponents'
argument. Since the *causa* (1:6-10) states that the letter is
written because the Galatians have adopted an alien theology,
5:1-6:10 must be related directly to the acceptance of that

theology. But even more than this, the *refutatio* was typically
the destruction of the opponents' argument in the opponents'
own terms, by an appeal to norms to which even the opposition
had to agree.[215] So in terms of rhetoric, there will be a
subtlety to the passage. The standards of the opposition will
be used for an attack on an ethos that is owned by the opposition. This is in keeping with the dialogical nature of the
whole of Galatians.

This becomes particularly applicable when the *refutatio*
takes on a paraenetic function, because this subtlety is a
characteristic of paraenesis too: it is both traditional and
contextual. An examination of the forms used in Pauline
paraenesis[216] makes it clear that there is a heavy drawing on
traditions.[217] To this extent the problems enumerated may not
be the problems of the community.[218] Yet on the other hand,
Paul argues by adapting traditional material in a particular
way.[219] There is always a contextuality and concreteness in
his ethic growing out of his apostolic concern.[220] Thus the
paraenesis is dialogical; and the task becomes that of determining both tradition and contextuality[221]--the place where
Paul is echoing his readers' sentiment, and the place where
he has turned that sentiment firmly against them. In these
terms, too, the *refutatio* is the destruction of the opponents'
case, denying an ethos attributable to their theology in terms
of norms to which the opponents must agree. Here Paul will be
claiming that the debate has been won, demanding compensation
--on the opponents' own grounds.

Galatians as a Dialogical Response
to Opponents

The genre of apologetic speech tells something about
the overall structure of the letter to the Galatians. It suggests the sense in which it is a dialogical response to opponents. Every speech or letter is in a sense a dialogue,[222]
but genre-analysis here gives some external criteria (which
are at the same time internal criteria) for deciding what form
the dialogue takes, dialogical to what extent, and dialogical
with whom. The "apologetic speech" genre suggests that

Galatians is dialogical throughout; it is a dialogue with
opponents who are intruders; but it is a dialogue especially
with the Galatians who have accepted the theology of the
intruders.

In indicating something of overall structure, the
genre also indicates something about the intruders' theology.
At this preliminary stage, it is suggested that this theology
has an interest in both δικαιοσύνη and νόμος. It expresses
itself in certain language, such as σάρξ, πνεῦμα, δύναμις, ζωή,
ἐλευθερία, et cetera. It must have some interest in the στοιχεῖα τοῦ κόσμου and in calendrical observance, while the climax
of the works-program of which these are a part is circumcision.
And it leads to a particular practice, which Paul claims his
gospel refutes.

Because of the form-tradition or genre-tradition to
which rhetoric belongs, it will not tell something of the
Sitz im Leben of the opponents or their theology. Rhetoric
is simply a vehicle for a content which can stand in its own
right.[223] It is not incongruous to a Diaspora opponent, but
neither is it incongruous to a Palestinian opponent. Rhetoric,
and even the "Socratic tradition," was deeply imbedded in Palestinian literature.[224] But the genre suggests that Galatians
is a carefully-written piece in which all the strands of the
argument are in some way being woven together. It provides
an overall frame for an analysis of the structure of the argument.

CHAPTER FOUR

INTERNAL INDICATIONS OF STRUCTURE

This chapter will examine various indicators of
smaller scale (transitional devices, sayings formulae, inclu-
sions, word-patterns, mots crochets, etc.), partly to illumine
more fully the parts of the letter and their relationship to
each other and partly to confirm the above structural suggestions based on genre-analysis.[1] The various themes and antitheses that run through the letter will also be examined in
terms of their contribution to the structure of the argument.[2]

Others have elaborated on the methods to be used here.
Epistolary practice is of help in 1:1-4 and 6:11-18.[3] The
studies of John L. White and J. T. Sanders on Pauline transitional phrases are useful.[4] James A. Fischer and others have
shown the importance of "mots crochets," words used a significant number of times and in significant places.[5] Bultmann
points to Paul's use of catchwords as part of his diatribe
style,[6] and to the way he organizes passages around antitheses.[7]

There will be a detailed exegesis only where it is
essential to the present purposes; and it will not be possible
to assess fully the dialogical nature of Paul's argument until
possible sources have been examined in detail. The attempt
will be made here to work from the outside to the center of
the letter.[8] The examination of genre has suggested that the
central argument is in the central chapters, but these are
integrally related to what precedes and follows. It may be
that the precise form in which the central argument is to be
understood will become more apparent if it is approached
through the ways Paul is developing and concluding it.

The Prescript

There is a close relationship, in Paul's letters,
between particular modifications in the prescript and the following subjects dealt with in the letter.[9] Thus the contents
of Gal 1:1-5, and the particular ways Paul has shaped this
material,[10] will indicate in a significant way the central
theological issues of the letter.

Apostleship

A comparison with 1 Cor 15:4 suggests that Paul has
opened Galatians with a piece of Christian tradition,[11] which
makes his own modification of this tradition in Gal 1:1 more
striking: ἀπόστολος, οὐκ ἀπ' ἀνθρώπων οὐδὲ δι' ἀνθρώπου. . . .
Paul typically opens his letters with a reference to his
apostleship,[12] but never with such polemical force. Apostleship is an issue in Galatians because the authority of the
office is seen to guarantee the truth of the gospel.[13] In
1:6-8 the Galatians have turned to another gospel; in 4:12-20,
5:2-12 they have turned to other apostles. Throughout the
epistle Paul's mention of himself is inseparably bound up with
the purpose of the letter, the defense of the gospel.[14]

The central place of ἀποκάλυψις in these verses should
be commented on. It has already been noticed that, to a
degree, the attack on Paul's gospel is also an attack on the
Jerusalem apostles.[15] It is clear from Galatians 1 and 2 that
Paul defends his relationship to the circle of the Jerusalem
apostles.[16] The obvious importance of ἀποκάλυψις in the opponents' scheme may well be part of their rejection of the
Jerusalem church: if apostleship comes by ἀποκάλυψις, there
is a basis for criticism of the Jerusalem apostles too.[17]
Thus there seems to be a complexity in the charge of the opponents: not only that Paul was taught his gospel from men
(1:11, 12), but that he is denying authentic Jerusalem tradition as he teaches this gospel. However, for Paul there is
one central Jerusalem tradition that holds together these
questions of apostle, gospel, revelation, and authority, and

it is a tradition that he uses with great polemical force:
the tradition of the death of the historical Jesus.[18]

The importance of ἀποκάλυψις for the opponents need
not therefore lessen their interest in παράδοσις, but may even
enhance it.[19] Any connection between the intruders and later
Gnostics would also suggest an enthusiasm for tradition.[20]
The connections between apostleship and gospel that the opponents have promoted is to enhance their own traditions, not to
eliminate tradition from the argument.[21] No doubt they have
their own version of Paul's apostolic curse (1:8, 9), as not
only Paul's gospel but Paul himself has been repudiated by
the Galatian community.[22] This indicates that they have a
strong sense of missionary calling and teaching office--and
have rejected Paul in both senses.

These suggestions about the opponents' missionary
calling and teaching office have consequences for the unity
of the letter. Given the authoritative nature of the intruders,
their pride in authentic tradition, and their rejection of any
other gospel than their own, it is extremely unlikely that the
Galatians, under their administration as community apostles,[23]
have spontaneously taken up some religious practices of their
own.[24] If the opponents label Paul a heretic, they would be
very quick to condemn any other forms of syncretism (as they
regard Paul's gospel),[25] especially if they are as Pharisaic
as the Judaisers of Acts 15. Gal 4:8-9 is a thoroughly Jewish
criticism of Pagan religion.[26] If the practices here belong
to Pagan religion and not to the Judaisers' propaganda,[27] the
opponents become very poor propagandists and community
apostles. They would probably be as critical of this behavior
as Paul. The very stress here on the relationship between
apostolicity and doctrine, and the importance of the issue of
apostleship, suggest strongly that the whole letter is directed
against problems that can all be related to the one intruding
theology.

Deliverance from the Present Evil Age

In Gal 1:4 there is a further significant modification
of Christian tradition:[28] ὅπως ἐξέληται ἡμᾶς ἐκ τοῦ αἰῶνος τοῦ

ἐνεστῶτος πονηροῦ. The Christ-event is interpreted in such a
way that Jesus is made the eschatological freer of mankind.[29]
Paul refers to this Christ-event in the same way at the end of
the letter: δι' οὗ ἐμοὶ κόσμος ἐσταύρωται κἀγὼ κόσμῳ (6:14).
In Paul's letters, κόσμος and αἰών are common equivalents,[30]
as they are in Jewish apocalyptic.[31] Just as the present aion
can be represented as a powerful dominion of sin and evil that
grasps men and rules over them,[32] the present kosmos is the
domain of superhuman powers, including angels, which rule in
connection with the sin of men.[33] Paul apparently asserts,
in Gal 1:4, that through Christ's death on the cross he is
free from the authority of these powers.[34] Whereas he goes on
to speak of the Christ-event in terms of justification, the
opening and closing of the letter place the debate in an
apocalyptic-cosmological frame.[35] This must be the basis for
Paul's Christological answer to the opponents; and the apocalyptic language in which he couches it must be significant to
them.

     The Christological language of Gal 1:4 is eschatologi-
cal language as well, and the phrase τοῦ αἰῶνος τοῦ ἐνεστῶτος
πονηροῦ strongly suggests the eschatological scheme of the two
ages as it appears in the New Testament and Jewish apocalyptic
literature.[36] Thus Paul's modification of tradition here
stresses the *presence* of eschatological deliverance in Christ.
Eschatology apparently plays an essential part in Paul's argument. The central issue of the letter, δικαιοσύνη, is to be
understood as deliverance from the enslaving powers of the
cosmos. In these verses it is placed on a Christological and
eshcatological basis; it conforms to the "shape" of the eschatological Christ-event.[37] When Paul rebukes the Galatians for
returning to subjection to these eschatological powers (4:8-11),
this must be the same polemic against the intruding theology.

     The polemical thrust of 1:4, and of eschatological
restatement throughout the book (4:4-5, 5:24,[38] 6:13-14), suggests clearly that the opponents hold something much less than
a realized eschatology. For them, the deliverance from the
present age has not yet come, and cannot come without obedience
to the covenant and the Torah.[39] It is Paul who would appear
to border on eschatological enthusiasm. From a comparison of

parallel passages in the New Testament[40] and similar traditions
in later Christian literature, both orthodox and heterodox,[41]
Gal 3:27-29 is a bold interpretation of baptism which would be
far too explosive in an eschatologically enthusiastic setting
and can only mean that the opponents (and the Galatians, for
that matter) have a far less than realized eschatology.[42]
They have a great interest in angels,[43] but are still concerned, through the cosmic significance of the law, to reach
the angelic state at some future time.[44]   It is Paul who is the
enthusiast.

The Will of God

        Here in the prescript, Paul emphatically states that
the deliverance effected in Christ was according to the will
of God. This, too, is an important premise for his following
argument. He says that there can be no other gospel than his
gospel (1:8-9), that his calling to apostleship was according
to the will of God (1:15-16), and that his gospel does not
deny the grace of God--implying that it is actually those who
try to maintain the possibility of both faith in Christ and
righteousness by works of law who resist the will of God. He
maintains that the law cannot annul the will of God as revealed
in His promise to Abraham (3:15-17). He seems to be constantly
attempting to refute the charge that he has introduced an inconsistency into saving history. Apparently the opponents
stress the consistency of any new revelation or saving act of
God with all past revelations and saving acts.[45]
        Schoeps builds much on the tradition that "the law
ceases when the Messianic kingdom begins."[46] However, W. D.
Davies and others have rightly questioned whether this tradition, or this interpretation of it, ever existed in pre-
Christian times.[47] The tradition to which Schoeps refers was
perhaps related to discussions about the applicability of Torah
to the Messianic age,[48] and may even be relevant to the debate
in Galatians, because of Paul's unique scheme in Galatians 3
of Abraham-Moses-Christ[49] and the unique expression "the law
of Christ."[50] But it does not seem to have been understood as
meaning that law would cease to exist in the Messianic age.[51]

Apocalyptic was as interested in the fulfillment of the Torah
as the rabbis,[52] the Damascus Document looks for a Messianic
Teacher of Righteousness who will lead Israel to keep the law
more perfectly than ever before,[53] and Hellenistic Judaism
also expected that, in the coming time of salvation, the
heathen would finally submit to the law of God.[54]

The opponents apparently have similar notions. They
have accepted Jesus and have given Him some saving significance.[55] But for them, Abraham, the law, and Christ must be
harmonized: Jesus has come especially to renew the Mosaic
covenant.[56] This explains why Paul must fight so hard (in
3:15-17) to draw the line of God's salvific will directly from
Abraham to Christ.[57]

In this apocalyptic stream that is looking for a new
authentication of the covenant will of God by a Messianic
figure (such as in the Damascus Document), there was much
criticism of Jerusalem Pharisaism--just as the opponents evidently stand in criticism of "orthodox" Jerusalem Christianity,[58] and Paul can criticise the opponents from a Pharisaic
point of view.[59] In this debate, Paul never caves in nor
denies his Pharisaic heritage. His gospel at no point annuls
the will of God, and he alone is the one who is true to the
real heroes of Israel's past, maintaining the consistency of
saving history.[60]

Slavery and Freedom

As antithesis is an important key to Paul's meaning,[61]
the announcement of deliverance in 1:4, becoming the "keynote
of the epistle," is particularly significant.[62]

This antithesis runs through the whole epistle. There
is ἐλευθερία in Christ, while the goal of the opponents is
bondage (καταδουλοῦν, 2:4). The ἐλευθερία that Paul preserves
is the ἀλήθεια τοῦ εὐαγγελίου (2:5). Under the dispensation
of law, ὑπὸ νόμον ἐφρουρούμεθα (3:23). The law is a παιδαγωγός (3:24), and the end of its jailorship is not just freedom
but justification (ἵνα ἐκ πίστεως δικαιωθῶμεν, 3:24). He calls
the period under the ἐπίτροποι καὶ οἰκονόμοι (4:2), that is,
the period ὑπὸ νόμον (4:5), a period of slavery to the στοιχεῖα

τοῦ κόσμου, from which Christ, at the exact time, brought
freedom (ἵνα τοὺς ὑπὸ νόμον ἐξαγοράσῃ, 4:5). But now the
Galatians are turning again to bondage under the same powers
(οἷς πάλιν ἄνωθεν δουλεύειν θέλετε, 4:9). The final pericope
of the *probatio* contrasts the children of παιδίσκη and ἐλευθερία (4:21-31). Paul begins the next section by reminding
the Galatians of their call from δουλεία to ἐλευθερία (5:1),
reiterated in 5:13. Here it is the basis of the imperative.[63]
Thus the antithesis again brings together cosmology and eschatology, and law, faith, and justification.

In Romans, freedom is always in relation to some particular object;[64] but in Galatians the object is freedom
itself, τῇ ἐλευθερίᾳ ἡμᾶς Χριστὸς ἠλευθέρωσεν (5:1).[65] Typically for Paul, the powers which grasp man in this age are
law, sin, and death.[66] But in Galatians man's problem as
ἁμαρτία quickly becomes man's problem as bondage,[67] and ἁμαρτία is used surprisingly infrequently.[68] Even less is man's
problem death. The only death referred to is Christ's death,
and man's death with Christ. Whereas, in Romans 5 and 7, law
produces sin and death, in Gal 3:23-4:11 law comes bringing
bondage. Whereas, elsewhere, the gospel is the way to life,
in Galatians it is especially the way to freedom.

"Justification" in this letter must be interpreted in
this context of freedom, which is also a cosmological/escha-
tological context. Justification is evidently being defined
as freedom from the enslaving powers of the present evil aeon.
The opposing assertion must be that Christ has *not* brought
such freedom from the enslaving powers; that is left for the
believer yet to work out, with the aid of the law.

The Postscript

The postscript is both epistolary, written in Paul's
hand, his own personal summary and apostolic pronouncement,
and rhetorical, functioning as a *conclusio*, summarising the
letter and pointing to the main themes.[69] In both senses it
will have much significance for the argument of the letter.

The *Refutatio*, 6:12-13[70]

Paul immediately takes up the question of circumcision,
οὗτοι ἀναγκάζουσιν ὑμᾶς περιτέμνεσθαι (6:12). It is hard to
avoid the conclusion that the opponents teach the necessity of
circumcision for salvation.[71] It is clearly a vital issue, as
can be seen from its place in the *narratio* (2:3), the *refutatio*
(5:3-6),[72] and the *conclusio*. This speaks against other explanations of its place in the debate which make it something less
than a salvific necessity.[73] These last are not able to explain
the absoluteness of 5:3-4,[74] Paul's utter despair over the
Galatians, and his fierce and uncompromising assertion of the
inviolability of the gospel.[75]

But this raises another problem: how to explain the
Galatians' sudden enthusiasm for the rite, when history and
archaeology provide so few examples of acceptance of circumcision by Gentiles.[76]

Then Paul asserts not only that the opponents have
failed to explain to the Galatians the full implications of
Jewish law (5:3), but that they do not keep the law themselves.
It is unlikely that, in perverting the gospel, they "were in
Paul's view rejecting God's will as revealed in Torah."[77]
This equates law and gospel, whereas in Galatians Paul makes
them antithetical.[78] It does not take account of the concrete
sense in which law keeping is an issue (2:14-15, and especially
the term 'Ιουδαΐζειν, make it clear that it is a question of
national and cultic laws, those laws which separate Jew from
Gentile);[79] and it brings in arguments that have not yet
appeared already in the body of the discussion. This contradicts the function of a *conclusio*. The expression in 6:13
therefore is to be understood much more logically in terms of
the way only certain aspects of legal observance are brought
in to elaborate what Paul means by "works of law" (that is,
circumcision, and ἡμέρας . . . καὶ μῆνας καὶ καιροὺς καὶ ἐνιαυτούς, 4:10).[80] The opponents are only partial observers of
the national and cultic inheritance of Judaism, and it is Paul
who appears to be the Pharisee in 5:2-5 and 6:13.[81] He and
the Judaisers of Acts 15 appear to be quite orthodox,[82] whereas

the opponents of Galatians do not, if it is left to Paul to
state the connection between circumcision and the "whole law."

This is further evidence that the opponents at the
same time see themselves as the true heirs of the covenant and
keepers of the law; and yet they stand over against Pharisaic
Judaism, having dispensed with some aspects of Jewish law.

The *Recapitulatio*, 6:14-16

Over against the opponents' teaching of circumcision,
Paul stands the cross in both its cosmic (δι' οὗ ἐμοὶ κόσμος
ἐσταύρωται) and personal (κἀγὼ κόσμῳ) significance.

As noted already, there is a parallel here to 1:4. In
6:14 the cross has brought an end to the dominion of κόσμος or
αἰών. But this language now draws to a conclusion the central
argument of the epistle, and echoes 2:19 in the distributio:
ἐγὼ . . . διὰ νόμου . . . ἀπέθανον.[83] Here Paul stresses that the
Christ-event has for him brought about a complete end of the
earlier relationship between himself and the powers of the
cosmos. Again he stresses the "realised eschatology" in his
gospel. The result is καινὴ κτίσις, life in a totally new
dimension. This proclamation of a saving work of God in a
radically new dimension is the summary answer, not to libertinism, but to the circumcision program (6:15). This not only
points to the unity of the epistle and its argument: it shows
the central place in the debate of Christology and eschatology
--expressed in cosmological terms.[84]

Paul here speaks of deliverance from the cosmos in
terms of the cross. The eschatological newness of Christianity is usually expressed in terms of the resurrection of
Christ:[85] but in Galatians there is only one brief mention of
the resurrection, probably in traditional language (1:1), and
attention rather is on Christ crucified.[86] The postscript is
here drawing together a central issue in the Galatian controversy, the cross, which becomes a polemical doctrine against
cross-less apostles who pay more attention to both κόσμος and
νόμος. The cross expresses the full humanity of Jesus, the
paradox of the saving act of God in the context of human weakness and suffering (4:4).

It is significant, too, how Paul links theology and
experience in terms of this theme. The cross brings to an end
the dominion of αἰών, νόμος, and κόσμος, but only for those
who themselves experience the cross (2:19, 6:14). The σκάνδαλον τοῦ σταυροῦ (Gal 5:11) evidently refers to both theology
and experience. Paul characterizes the opponents only in terms
of καύχησις (6:13), but his life is characterized in terms of
the cross (2:19-20). The human weakness and suffering of
Christ comes to epitomize Christ's apostle--but not the opponents.

It is in this context that the place of 4:12-20, the
passage περὶ φιλίας, in the whole argument concerning justification, can be seen. Paul pleads with the Galatians, γίνεσθε
ὡς ἐγώ (4:12)! Because they have turned to works of law, he
cries, τέκνα μου, οὓς πάλιν ὠδίνω μέχρις οὗ μορφωθῇ Χριστὸς ἐν
ὑμῖν (4:19), referring no doubt to the crucified Christ. These
two verses form a bracket to the passage. Here the apostle of
the cross inserts in his rhetorical case for justification by
faith a call for a personal return to the message and experience of the cross, as well as to the apostle of the cross.
The Galatians have been deceived and drawn away by cross-less
apostles (4:17). Paul notes that, previously, in his bodily
weakness, he was received as an angel of God, as Christ Himself (4:13-14). But the new apostles, with their rejection
of the cross, and their religion of νόμος and attention to the
κόσμος, have brought a profound change to the attitude to "weak
apostles." Evidently, in the new program, angels can have
nothing to do with one who is physically weak and poor. A
genuine apostle, who knows all the secrets of the cosmic powers,
must be a perfect priestly specimen, the epitomy of Christ
glorified, not Christ crucified.

*   *   *

The prescript and postscript together reveal the central concerns of Galatians, and the terms in which the central
argument concerning law and grace is to be fully understood.
In these sections of the letter several important strands are
initiated and drawn together. The concern of apostleship

stands at both the beginning and the end; and the apostle
becomes the epitomy of the gospel he preaches, so that apostleship and gospel are inseparably bound up together. Cosmology
is also crucial and reveals the way in which law, justification, slavery and freedom, et cetera, are to be understood.
Eschatology, typically bound up with cosmology, is a central
issue, and the "realized" eschatology of Paul's gospel, the
present end of the old *aiōn* and the present participation in
God's new creation, is an important part of the answer to the
circumcising program. And the roots of the two opposing positions, the two assessments of cosmology, eschatology, apostleship, gospel, and experience, are in two opposing Christologies
and two different assessments of the significance of the cross.

The Prooemium or Causa, 1:6-10

        This passage states the issue without which there
would be no debate--not only the intrusion of the opponents
and their theology but also the Galatians' desertion (μετατιθέναι) to the opponents. It is characteristic of rhetorical
procedure to restate the *causa* in various places throughout
the defense.[87] The concern here will be to determine whether
this happens in Galatians; and, if it does, to determine from
these restatements the precise nature of the *causa*.
        In 2:14 Paul brings the *narratio* to a climax by return-
ing to the central issue of the debate: εἰ σὺ 'Ιουδαῖος ὑπάρ-
χων ἐθνικῶς καὶ οὐχὶ 'Ιουδαϊκῶς ζῇς, πῶς τὰ ἔθνη ἀναγκάζεις
'Ιουδαΐζειν;[88] The abandonment of 1:6-10 is here given particular form.[89] The *distributio* restates the disagreement in
other terms again: εἰ γὰρ ἃ κατέλυσα ταῦτα πάλιν οἰκοδομῶ, παραβάτην ἐμαυτὸν συνιστάνω (2:18). The ultimate transgression is
a turning back,[90] a Christian heresy. As the *distributio* puts
the debate into new language in 2:19-20, δικαιοσύνη becomes
equated with ζωή, confirming the suggestion in 1:6-10 that the
Galatians' own experience is an essential part of the debate.
Again, 3:1 takes up the *causa* of 1:6, ὦ ανόητοι Γαλάται, τίς
ὑμᾶς ἐβάσκανεν, ... Here again, the Galatians' own past
experience is essential to the discussion of δικαιοσύνη,[91] but
instead of "How were you justified?" the question becomes

τοῦτο μόνον θέλω μαθεῖν ἀφ' ὑμῶν, ἐξ ἔργων νόμου τὸ πνεῦμα
ἐλάβετε ἢ ἐξ ἀκοῆς πίστεως; (3:2). This is probably a reference to the Galatians' baptism and its eschatological significance.[92] But the shift from δικαιοσύνη in 2:21 to reception
of the πνεῦμα in 3:2-3 to δικαιοσύνη in 3:6 shows that the two
are in essence the same question.[93] The debate in Galatians
concerns the *life* of justification, how the beginning point of
Christianity radically determines the rest of space-time exis-
tence--the *life* of sharing in the new creation of God.[94]

The restatements of the *causa* so far make more precise
the abandonment, the beginning one way and ending another way,
of 1:6-10. This essential pattern appears again in 3:15 (ὅμως
ἀνθρώπου κεκυρωμένην διαθήκην οὐδεὶς ἀθετεῖ ἢ ἐπιδιατάσσεται;
there is no adding or subtracting after a covenant is ratified),
and again in 4:9 (νῦν, . . . γνόντες θεόν, μᾶλλον δὲ γνωσθέντες
ὑπὸ θεοῦ, πῶς ἐπιστρέφετε πάλιν ἐπὶ τὰ ἀσθενῆ καὶ πτωχὰ στοιχεῖα). Following the line of the development of the argument,
this is only a restatement of 1:6-10 and the turning from
Paul's gospel to the false gospel.

The *refutatio* begins with a thrust at the same scheme
of abandonment (5:2). The specific term of abandonment here
is circumcision. So Paul continues, ἐτρέχετε καλῶς. τίς ὑμᾶς
ἐνέκοψεν [τῇ] ἀληθείᾳ μὴ πείθεσθαι; (5:7). And he makes
another reference to the reason for the letter in 5:12, ὄφελον
καὶ ἀποκόψονται οἱ ἀναστατοῦντες ὑμᾶς. Finally, 5:24 puts the
double catalog of 5:19-23 into terms of beginning with the
crucifixion of the flesh (οἱ . . . τοῦ Χριστοῦ . . . τὴν σάρκα
ἐσταύρωσαν) and ending by living in terms of the flesh (ἐπιθυμίαν σαρκὸς οὐ μὴ τελέσητε).

Words such as abandonment (μετατιθέναι, 1:6) and
expressions such as beginning and ending (ἐνάρχεσθαι and ἐπιτελεῖν, 3:3), turning back (ἐπιστρέφειν, 4:9), building up
what was torn down (καταλύειν and οἰκοδομεῖν, 2:18), ceasing
to obey (μὴ πείθειν, 5:7), and crucifying the flesh and then
fulfilling the desires of the flesh (ἡ σάρξ σταυροῦν and ἐπι-
θυμία σαρκὸς τελεῖν, 5:24, 16), on the part of the Galatians,
and words such as to trouble (ταράσσειν, 1:17), bewitch (βασκαίνειν, 3:1), persuade (ἡ πεισμονή, 5:8) and unsettle (οἱ
ἀναστατοῦντες ὑμᾶς, 5:12) on the part of the opponents, appear

Internal Indications of Structure   69

in every section of the letter, tying together the various
items that these words and expressions refer to (εὐαγγέλιον,
δικαιοσύνη, 'Ιουδαΐζειν, σάρξ and πνεῦμα, νόμος, διαθήκη, στοιχεῖα τοῦ κόσμου, περιτέμνειν) into the one *causa* that lies
behind the letter, the treacherous embracing by the Galatians
of the opponents' theology. This tends to confirm the suggestion that 1:6-10 is a rhetorical *causa*. The Galatians are in
an important sense the offending party, and the whole letter
is written because of their espousal of an offending theology.
It also confirms the suggested unity of the letter. There is
no division into heresies of the intruders and heresies of the
Galatians. The *causa* and its restatements are typically in the
second person plural,[95] and there is never any suggestion that
they refer to only part of the Galatian congregation. The
whole community is addressed in both chapters 1-4 and the
ethical portion of the letter (5:1, 13, 16).[96]

The Propositio, 2:15-21

There is here a substantiation of the claim that
2:15-21 sets forth the precise terms of agreement and disagreement in the whole debate; though it is the movement of the
whole argument, from prescript to postscript, which indicates
more precisely how these terms are to be understood.[97]

The *narratio* is brought to a climax in 2:14. The issue
in Galatia is apparently that some who are Jews by race are
forcing Gentiles to live like Jews.[98] The beginning of the
propositio[99] continues the debate in the same terms: ἡμεῖς
φύσει 'Ιουδαῖοι καὶ οὐκ ἐξ ἐθνῶν ἁμαρτωλοί (2:15). The meaning of ἁμαρτωλός here is evidently national and cultic, not
ethical. It refers to one who by race stands outside the Jewish covenant and all its provisions.[100] The term φύσει
'Ιουδαῖοι is probably applicable to the Galatian opponents
themselves.[101]

Chapter 2:16 introduces the issue of justification by
faith in Christ without the works of the law, here a particularly polemical doctrine.[102] Only the verb form δικαιοῦν is
used in this verse, where it has "declaratory force," referring
to acceptance or acquittal that is undeserved.[103]

It has been suggested that this verse states a point
of agreement between Paul and the opponents.[104] But can the
intruders really accept a justification ἐξ ἔργων νόμου?

Several have noted the existence of a common formula
in 2:16, which, from the way it is used here, is widely
accepted among Jewish Christians.[105] The verse begins with
εἰδότες . . . ὅτι, a "Glaubenswissen" in Paul's letters, introducing a "dogmatic proposition as something commonly known."[106]
Paul substantiates the first part of the verse with a quotation
from the Old Testament[107] with his own significantly apocalyptic modification[108]--as elsewhere he substantiates his doctrine
of justification by faith, without works of law, from the Old
Testament.[109] So far, then, there are indications in the text
of agreement between the intruders and Paul.

Further, the language of the verse is not strange to
Judaism and pre-Pauline Christianity. The Qumran literature
taught that righteousness comes from God, who justifies the
sinner out of pure grace: "It is by Thy goodness alone that
a man is justified and by the immensity of Thy mercy" (1 QH
13:16); "If I stumble because of the sin of my flesh, my justification is in the righteousness of God . . . by His immense
goodness He will pardon all my iniquities" (1 QS 11:13-15).
The Qumran sectaries knew of a "justification without the
works of the law."[110]

As for early Christianity, many Pauline texts speaking
of justification also reflect Christian tradition (i.e., Rom
3:24-26, 4:25, 1 Cor 6:11),[111] and some at the same time have
close parallels in the Qumran scrolls.[112]

In this light, the force of οἴδαμεν . . . ὅτι should
be allowed to stand as introducing a point of common agreement.[113] In fact, for a Jew to become a Christian[114] he would
have to profess a belief that there was a justification without the works of the law.[115] Various circles believed in the
justifying grace of God. The Christian kerygma demanded that
one see that grace eschatologically displayed in Christ. So
throughout the passage the reference is not merely to justification by faith without the works of the law, but to justification by faith *in Christ* without works of law. The last is a
controversy-statement, with meaning only because of what it is

against.[116] The whole verse is looking forward to the future
debate, as is suggested further by the change in 2:16 from
διὰ πίστεως to ἐκ πίστεως, due probably to the anticipatory
force of Hab 2:4.[117]

Then the opponents accept a justification by faith
without the works of the law. But it is also clear that they
believe in a justification by works of law (2:21, 5:4, etc.).
The argument in 2:15-21 evidently moves from an antithesis
between faith and works which is acceptable to the Judaisers
(2:16) to one which is unacceptable (2:21).[118] It is in this
development between 2:16 and 2:21 that the points at issue
become sharply defined.

The debate is intensified in 2:17. It is perhaps
easiest to exegete this difficult text backwards. μὴ γένοιτο
is used by Paul as a strong negation, usually after a rhetorical question.[119] It functions "where a hypothetical opponent
takes a principle of Pauline Christianity and develops it to
a completely unacceptable conclusion."[120] ἄρα is probably the
preferred reading here, expressing bewilderment at the conclusion now being rejected.[121] If Paul is using the terms of the
passage consistently, he means by ἁμαρτωλός in this verse what
he means in 2:15--one who nationally and sociologically stands
outside Israel.[122] The beginning of 2:17 then follows from
what has been agreed on in 2:16. When a Jew becomes a Christian, he acknowledges that the Jew is a sinner--as is a
heathen--so that, in terms of δικαιοσύνη before God or before
the law, there is in fact no distinction between them.[123] The
structure of the verse does not conform to a contrary-to-fact
condition,[124] which would imply that 2:17a was in fact not the
case. Rather, "Paul and those with him must have actually been
found sinners in someone's eyes,"[125] and, in terms of the
definition of ἁμαρτωλός here, Paul accepts that estimation.[126]

Paul has shifted from the aorist ἐπιστεύσαμεν of 2:16,
the moment of coming to belief in Christ, to the present participle ζητοῦντες (with a continuous sense)--referring to the
life of faith--and to εὑρέθημεν, with the sense of the sustained experience in time of being a Christian. The discussion has now moved to justification by faith as a *process*.[127]
This also changes the meaning of the verb δικαιοῦν, so that in

2:17 it comes to signify the relational/moral as well as the forensic.[128]

Then Paul and the opponents agree that there is a justification by faith in Christ. But the disagreement is over whether or not this justification removes the historic distinctions between Jew and Gentile; and, if it does, whether this constitutes Christ an "agent of sin." For Paul, 2:17b is an illogical conclusion from a correct premise.[129] It is not true to say, using a play on the word ἁμαρτωλός, that, in extending the principle of justification (or righteousness) in Christ through time in the same direction, Christ is made an agent of sin and His followers become nothing but enemies of God. So the debate is sharpened by extending the question of δικαιοσύνη through time.

2:18 apparently continues Paul's μὴ γένοιτο[130] and takes up the opponents' play on ἁμαρτωλός by suddenly introducing the word παραβάτης. " . . . conduct such as he now describes is a more direct and more serious violation of God's law than that which the Judaisers call 'sin.'"[131] By continuing to live in time on the basis of justification by faith in Christ without the deeds of the law, one could perhaps be called ἁμαρτωλός; but if one revoked this principle and returned to a nomistic basis for living, one could only be called παραβάτης.[132] This understanding of the verse grows directly out of the climax of the narratio in 2:14 and the definitions of 2:14-15. It also shows the precise issue: "The guilt is not in abandoning the law, but in seeking it again when abandoned."[133] In 2:17-18 the principle of δικαιοσύνη ἐξ ἔργων νόμου is only a Christian heresy, a way of seeking justification (or righteousness) through time which sets aside the eschatological finality of Christ and the eschatological significance of being ἐν Χριστῷ.[134]

The propositio, as it develops, is in perfect accord with the causa and its restatements, where the issue is beginning and ending. The debate has shifted from an antithesis between faith and works which the opponents could accept, to an antithesis which they can now not accept. As attention shifts from a point in time (2:16) to a process through time (2:17-18), the debate centers as much on the meaning of

πίστις[135] as on the meaning of δικαιοσύνη. Paul here defines
πίστις in such a way that it is impossible to speak of justification through faith in Christ and justification by works of
law at the same time.

Verses 19 and 20 should be examined together. Both
use a new vocabulary (ἀποθνήσκειν and ζῆν) which shifts the
debate from forensic to existential and relational terms. And
both share a particular pattern of construction:

Dying	Living
ἐγὼ γὰρ διὰ νόμου νόμῳ ἀπέθανον	ἵνα θεῷ ζήσω
Χριστῷ συνεσταύρωμαι	ζῶ δὲ οὐκέτι ἐγώ, ζῇ δὲ ἐν ἐμοὶ Χριστός. ὃ δὲ νῦν ζῶ ἐν σαρκί, ἐν πίστει ζῶ τῇ τοῦ υἱοῦ τοῦ θεοῦ τοῦ ἀγαπήσαντός με etc.

The first dying/living construction makes anthropological
assertions, whereas the second centers in Christological assertions.

This language and construction appear to reaffirm the
heart of the argument and the sharpened issue established in
2:17-18. There is much to suggest that Paul is sharpening the
issue further by introducing the subject of baptism.[136]

Firstly, both the verbs used in these verses, and
their construction, suggest baptism. Paul characteristically
refers to the death and life of the baptized in different
tenses.[137] Here he uses the aorist (ἀπέθανον) and perfect
(συνεσταύρωμαι) for the Christian's dying, just as he used the
aorist (ἐπιστεύσαμεν) to refer to the beginning of the Christian life; and the life that follows the dying is in different
tenses.[138] The pattern of anthropological and Christological
assertion has a close parallel in the baptism-passage in Rom
6:5-10.[139] It is through the medium of baptism that Paul draws
on the experience of Christ to speak of the present experience
of the Christian;[140] and it is because of incorporation into
Christ's death that Paul is able to say "I died."[141]

Secondly, there is in the New Testament a typical
association of baptism with justification, especially in the
pre-Pauline material.[142] It is baptism which is sacramentally
effective in bringing about a union between the believer and

Christh;[143] and it is "in Christ" or in the "body of Christ"
that justification becomes a reality.[144] In this passage, too,
Paul is arguing out of the implications of being "in Christ"
(ζητοῦντες δικαιωθῆναι ἐν Χριστῷ . . . , 2:17), as he is in
one of his final arguments against circumcision.[145]

Thirdly, there are recurring baptismal statements
throughout Galatians which are closely linked to the sharpening of the argument here in the *propositio*. The discussion of
the Spirit in 3:1-5 presupposes baptism.[146] The function of
the passage as an *interrogatio* links it directly with the
issue elaborated in 2:15-21.[147] Paul brings forth the evidence of the Galatians' own experience to establish his proposition about justification.[148] 3:27-29 is of course a baptism-
passage. The question is whether or not it belongs in the
stream of Paul's argument. The way Paul uses it suggests that
it does.[149] The very rhetorical nature of Galatians, and its
unity as a carefully structured argument, suggests that it
does; and the way it naturally brings a sequence of argument
to a conclusion (if 2:15-21 revolves around baptism) suggests
that it does.[150] This suggests that, in these last verses,
Paul has not suddenly shifted his argument. Baptism has been
in his thinking all along.[151] Others have seen 4:5-6, referring to the reception of sonship and the cry "Abba" at the
coming of the Spirit, as a baptism-passage.[152] If so, it
would be a return to the *interrogatio* and the evidence of the
Galatians' own reception of the Spirit and so would logically
belong in the argument. There may be a reference to baptism
in 5:6.[153] And 5:24 also appears to be a reference to baptism,[154] itself having important links with the earlier
baptism-passages.[155]

In rhetorical terms, then, 2:19-20, as a baptismal
statement,[156] clarifies the point of the debate, which is to
be elaborated in the following sections of the argument. In
this case, the recurrence of baptism throughout the letter is
no coincidence. The later statements grow naturally out of
the place of baptism here at the head of the argument in the
divisio.

Paul expounds the meaning of baptism in 2:19-20 to
counter the opponents' teaching of justification by works. He

usually uses baptism to clarify the meaning of the new life
in Christ.[157] Here he uses it to clarify justification. The
two must then, in Galatians, come to mean the same thing. We
must speak of the *life* of justification, the *course* of the
justified life--and this is the center of the debate.[158]

Further, Paul introduces the subject of Christ's
death to settle the question of the believer's relation to the
law. The phrase "died to the law" should be understood in
accordance with the context. Because in the death of Christ
law and life are revealed as opposites,[159] then the one who
has died with Christ has closed the door to law as a life
principle.[160] By bringing baptism into the debate, Paul gives
a sacramental answer to the opponents, a sacramental answer
that lays a Christological foundation for his rejection of law
as a life principle,[161] and of the Judaisers' suggestion that
the Christ-event confirms the covenant of law by implementing
a δικαιοσύνη ἐξ ἔργων νόμου that places us where we must maintain this relationship by ἔργων νόμου.[162] He now poses the
antithesis of faith and works in Christological and existential terms: νόμῳ ἀπέθανον ἵνα θεῷ ζήσω.

Chapter 2:20 follows the same trajectory. That which
is signified in baptism, at the beginning of the Christian
life, is constitutive for the whole of life thereafter--that
is, for justification. Baptism is not one step among many,[163]
and neither, therefore, is justification by faith *in Christ*.
Justification is here expressed in terms of the eschatological
finality of the Christ-event and of the believer's incorporation into Christ. It conforms to the present lordship of
Christ, and is as comprehensive as that lordship. Because
nothing can be added to the lordship of Christ, nothing can
be added to the believer's justification. Here the eschatological and cosmological motifs of the letter begin to be taken
up into the central debate of justification[164] in a way that
effectively refutes the false gospel with its pattern of
beginning and ending, made clear in the *causa* and its restatements. Justification is a *life* which, because of its Christological basis, can only be understood as the life of the
new age.

In 2:21, Paul returns to the possibility of justification by law. This is evidently what he has been wrestling against in 2:19-20. Seeking righteousness by law is the opposite of dying to the law and living to Christ. Justification by law is that which denies the grace of God: it is a reversion to one way of life after commencing with another. Christ died in vain, not only if the declaration of justification comes in some way other than the cross (2:16), but also if justification (or righteousness) as a process through time, the *life* that naturally follows that declaration (2:17, then 2:19-20), is founded on anything other than God's deed in Christ and the eschatological newness of the age to come. Justification by law is only a Christian heresy.

The way in which 2:16-21 makes precise the terms of agreement and disagreement and elaborates the *causa* of beginning one way and ending in another can be analyzed in two ways. The first analysis is in terms of the linguistic and verbal breaks in the pericope:

16   Agreed: the antithesis of being justified by faith and being justified by works (declarative) acceptable to both parties

17-18   The point of dispute: the *life* of being justified (moral/relational) which follows the declaration of acceptance in Christ. The true παραβάτης as the one who builds up what was torn down

19-20   The point of dispute put into the language of baptism: anthropological statements out of a Christological base. Justification accords to the lordship of Christ

21   Precise statements of the antithesis unacceptable to the opponents (summarizing 17-20): justification by faith excludes justification by works

The second analysis is in terms of the major antithesis in the pericope and its repetitions:

16   Agreed: Being justified by faith as a point in time

17   Being justified in Christ extended through time   (A)

18	Justification by law as beginning and ending, a system which contradicts A	(B)
19-20	Being justified in Christ as *life*, that is, extended through time	(A)
21	Justification by law rejected as a system which contradicts A	(B)

Thus the structure of the pericope, as it unfolds,
conforms to the rhetorical pattern expected of a *propositio*--a
making more precise of that which is agreed upon and that which
is disputed. It is also seen to be functioning as a *propositio*
in that it forms a transition from the *narratio* to the main
argument, the *probatio*, by putting the dispute into the most
appropriate terms--terms which are consistent with the Christology and eschatology of the prescript and postscript.
Thirdly, it functions in this expected way when it is seen
that it sharpens the debate by introducing the language of
baptism: for after this pericope, baptismal statements run
like a thread throughout the epistle, appearing at crucial
places in the argument (3:1-5, 3:27-29, 4:6, 5:6, 5:24). The
rest of the letter then develops these terms of dispute as set
out in 2:19-20. Baptism also links the two major sections of
the letter, the dogmatic (3:1-5, 3:27-29, 4:6) and the paraenetic (5:6, 5:24). The whole letter grows out of the polemical statement of justification in baptismal terms. In both
sections, Paul expounds the significance of the new creation
as an answer to a nomistic system.

This detailed analysis has been necessary for a further
reason. It has been consistently difficult to relate the doctrine of "justification by faith in Christ" to the whole of
the letter. Those who stress its place in the dogmatic argument usually link the intruders with "normative" nomistic
Judaism and, thereby unable to maintain the unity of the
letter, resort to some sort of two-front theory.[165] It is
believed that the nomistic opponents are countered only in
parts of the letter. Suggestions of speculative cosmology,
ethical deviations, et cetera, are not part of the argument
concerning justification by faith. On the other hand, those
who see a unity in the letter, or stress the polemical nature
of the last two chapters, see the opponents as something other

than nomistic; and then the argument of justification by faith
could not possibly answer them.[166]

However, as 2:15-21 is analyzed in terms of a rhetorical *propositio*, the central place of justification in the argument is retained (because of the function of a *propositio*),
and the doctrine itself is seen to develop in a way in which
it stands at the head of the whole book. The opponents themselves must have a real concern for justification and its
meaning. The stress of this passage, as it sharpens the difference between the two meanings of justification, comes to
fall on the life of faith, so that justification is consistent
with the contexts of Christology, cosmology, and eschatology
provided by the rest of the book. The question becomes, Under
what law-requirements is the believer placed when he is justified? What is left yet to accomplish for his deliverance?
This is really a Christological question, and the concerns of
the rest of the letter--freedom, the cosmic powers, the two
ages, et cetera--now become relevant. And as justification is
developed in baptismal terms, as the *life* of faith, the pericope comes to stand at the head of both the dogmatic and ethical
portions of the letter. Each is exploring the consequences of
the eschatological deliverance brought about ἐν Χριστῷ (2:17;
compare 3:28 [ἐν Χριστῷ ᾽Ιησοῦ]; 5:6 [ἐν Χριστῷ ᾽Ιησοῦ]; and
5:24 [οἱ . . . τοῦ Χριστοῦ]).

The Interrogatio, 3:1-5

This passage begins the *probatio*, or main argument
against the intruders; and rhetorically, is to be directly
related to the *partitio*. Here the witnesses to the case, the
Galatians themselves, are brought to the stand, and the evidence of their own experience is presented in language most
relevant to the argument against the system of justification
by works of law.[167] Paul here uses direct address, which he
has not used since 1:11, indicating a return to the same subject as 1:6-10, the Galatians' apostasy,[168] though now with
the added force of the intervening *partitio*. The object here
will be, firstly, to examine the language in which this experience is referred to, as a clue to determining the nature of

the experience the opponents themselves are offering, and the
form of the apostasy of beginning and ending; and, secondly,
to note the way the evidence of this experience, and the language in which it is referred to, is used throughout the rest
of the argument.

Paul begins, τίς ὑμᾶς ἐβάσκανεν: The word βασκαίνειν
means to bewitch by words, to exercise a harmful magic independent of the subject.[169] The Galatians have yielded to magicians without realizing the nature of the powers to whom they
have surrendered. This word indicates strongly the complete
mastery of the opponents over the Galatians. It may also indicate a mystical, even magical, form of mastery.

In 3:3 Paul uses together the verbs ἐνάρχεσθαι and ἐπιτελεῖν (ἐναρξάμενοι πνεύματι νῦν σαρκὶ ἐπιτελεῖσθε). ἐνάρχεσθαι often has the meaning of an act of initiation;[170] ἐπιτελεῖν commonly means a performance of ritual or ceremony
which brings to completion or perfection.[171] The two verbs
also appear in the same sequence in 2 Cor 8:6 and Phil 1:6[172]
and may comprise a technical formula for progress in a religious mystery from a lower to higher stage.[173] They may even
belong to the opponents' propaganda. They have told the Galatians that their earlier experience was only the primary stage
of religion, but they are now, in the program of works of law,
offered the stage of perfection.[174] These terms suit perfectly
the elaboration of the heresy as a program of beginning one way
and ending another way;[175] and their mystical connotations must
be taken into account in the theological assessment of the program.

But the opponents' propaganda is turned on its head
with the introduction of the antithesis σάρξ and πνεῦμα. The
Spirit, received at baptism (3:2),[176] is a gift and sign of
the new age, bringing the *order* of the new age, the eschatological age (3:3). πνεῦμα comes to stand for an order of existence, the life of the new age.[177] Similarly, σάρξ has moved
here from the neutral sense it had at the beginning of the
letter to the sense of the world of the flesh, the sphere of
this age,[178] invested even with demonic qualities.[179] Used
together in this way, σάρξ and πνεῦμα stand for the two apocalyptic ages,[180] two antithetical spheres or powers, and two

ways of existence as conceived from the angle of the world to
which one belongs.[181] They are absolutely exclusive of each
other; man must live in one order or the other, the old age or
the new, last age (1:4).

These antithetical terms are reinterpreting the two
opposing programs elaborated in the *propositio*. The experience of σάρξ is the equivalent of justification by works of
law, and the experience of πνεῦμα is the equivalent of justification by faith in Christ. The Galatians were justified by
faith in Christ at their baptism. They cannot deny that this
was an experience of the Spirit.[182] Therefore the gospel
which brought them justification in Christ brought them the
Spirit (3:2) and brought them into the age of the Spirit (3:3).
Then that which the opponents refer to by the verb ἐνάρχεσθαι,
their own past experience of the Pauline gospel, was in fact
the highest level of religious experience possible. There can
be no talk of perfecting it further. If the intruders are
offering a program of ἐπιτελῆσις, it cannot be a part with the
religion they entered at baptism--which was the religion of
the new age. It must be a perfection in a *different* religion
--which can therefore only be a religion of the old age, the
σάρξ. Their undeniable experience of the Spirit shows that,
in this program of initiation and perfection offered by the
opponents, they are only making progress--backwards.[183]

This adds poignancy to Paul's question, τοσαῦτα ἐπάθετε
εἰκῆ; εἴ γε καὶ εἰκῆ; (3:4). If the Spirit should come, bringing the ultimate religious experience, and find the recipients
so "unreligious" that they should fail entirely to appreciate
its significance, even turning afterwards to continue their
religious quest in new directions, could anything at all be
done for such people? The question rings of eternal doom. As
Paul twice laments that the coming of the last age may have
been for the Galatians εἰκῆ, so he twice calls them ἀνόητος
(3:1, 3). In a religious context the word can mean one who is
blind to religious realities, "deficient in an understanding
of salvation."[184] By calling their first experience a beginning initiation and seeking now to perfect it, they are so
perverting the sense of that first experience as to render it

void. They are ἀνόητος in the sense of *uninitiated*.[185] Their
attempt at perfection is "fleshy" (3:3).

Two conclusions about this language stand out. Firstly,
the mystical and even magical vocabulary (βασκαίνειν, ἐνάρχεσθαι, ἐπιτελεῖν, σάρξ, πνεῦμα, ἀνόητος) strongly indicates that
these are the terms in which the opponents themselves present
their program. Secondly, the strong antithesis of σάρξ and
πνεῦμα in this pericope, and the way it is used to reinterpret
the Galatians' apostasy of beginning and ending, must be kept
in view throughout the book. νόμος and σάρξ are powers of the
present age and the present state of bondage; πίστις and
πνεῦμα are signs of the new age and of freedom. These two
ways of existence come to epitomize the whole debate.[186]

The antithesis, in terms of which 3:1-5 redefines the
debate, recurs throughout the book. Though the terms σάρξ and
πνεῦμα are not used in 4:8-11, the pericope turns around the
same ironic contrast: the Galatians, knowing God, yet turn to
the powers of the old age (νῦν δὲ γνόντες θεόν, μᾶλλον δὲ
γνωσθέντες ὑπὸ θεοῦ, πῶς ἐπιστρέφετε πάλιν ἐπὶ τὰ ἀσθενῆ καὶ
πτωχὰ στοιχεῖα, 4:9). This suggests again that the pericope
is a restatement of the *causa*.

The same antithesis is used in 4:21-31. The present
Jerusalem has come into existence κατὰ σάρκα (4:29) in contrast to the one κατὰ πνεῦμα (4:29).[187] So the *probatio* begins
and ends with the antithesis of σάρξ and πνεῦμα.

There is good evidence that, in chapters 5 and 6, Paul
takes up further aspects of the problems dealt with in chapters 3 and 4, because of the continued use of this same antithesis. Law, Spirit, and flesh function in the same way in
5:13-24 and 6:1, 2, 7-8 as they do in 3:1-5.[188] In 5:16-24
σάρξ and πνεῦμα are again personified powers; σάρξ does works
(5:19), and πνεῦμα plays the role of leader or teacher (5:18).
They are cosmic spheres which do not merely exclude one
another, but struggle against each other. Man must live under
one power or the other.[189] In 5:18 the life ὑπὸ νόμος stands
over against the life κατὰ πνεῦμα, as it does in 3:1-5. One
of the fruits of the Spirit is πίστις. Thus σάρξ and πνεῦμα
still stand in the same relationship to νόμος and πίστις.

It appears, then, that the same two apocalyptic
spheres, and the same two life possibilities, as in 3:1-5, are
in view here. In 3:1-5, behavior characterized by works of
law was *sarkic*; here, behavior characterized by departure from
the commandment to love is *sarkic*. "Paul moves intentionally
from the contrast of Spirit and law to the contrast of Spirit
and flesh. In each instance, he is dealing with the one human
predicament."[190] This is the more apparent in that 5:24
reveals that, in the ethical portion as in the dogmatic portion, Paul is filling out the significance of baptism for the
believer.[191]

The Probatio, Chapters 3 and 4

This central argument of the epistle, to which every
section and facet of the letter is related, will be examined
more closely below. The particular concern here is to explore
the relationship of 4:8-11 to the rest of the argument.[192]

Analysis reveals that Paul uses the literary device
of the "mot crochet" to hold the argument together between
3:1 and 4:11. The passage is broken up into smaller pericopes,
each of which does not use a particular word, or uses it
infrequently, until the last phrase. This suddenly appearing
"mot crochet" will then occur in the first phrase of the next
pericope, where it will become a key word used several times.
In the last phrase a new word will appear again, which becomes
the key word in the next pericope, et cetera. Thus, 3:1-5
only uses πίστις once apart from 3:5 (ἡ ἐξ ἀκοῆς πίστεως).
However, the word is picked up in 3:6 ('Αβραὰμ ἐπίστευσεν τῷ
θεῷ); and πίστις or πιστεύειν is used eight times in 3:6-14.
Then in 3:14, at the end of the pericope, ἐπαγγελία suddenly
appears. This word is picked up in 3:16, and 3:15-22 uses it
seven times, whereas πίστις is not used at all--until 3:22 (ἵνα
ἡ ἐπαγγελία ἐκ πίστεως . . . δοθῇ). Chapter 3:23 again picks
up πίστις, and 3:23-29 uses it five times, whereas ἐπαγγελία
is not used at all, except at the very end of the pericope.
Then 3:29 introduces a new word, κληρονόμος (although used
before in 3:18). This word is picked up in 4:1, and appears
again in 4:7, evidently functioning here as a bracket.[193] In

4:7, κληρονόμος is associated with θεός,[194] and 4:8 begins
with the question of the believer's relation to θεός, so that
this word becomes the "mot crochet" tying 4:8-11 into the argument. Moreover, the whole sequence is bound together with the
word εἰκῆ (τοσαῦτα ἐπάθετε εἰκῆ; εἰ γε καὶ εἰκῆ [3:4]; φοβοῦμαι
ὑμᾶς μή πως εἰκῆ κεκοπίακα εἰς ὑμᾶς [4:11]). The poignant
meaning of εἰκῆ in 3:4 has been elaborated above;[195] and it
comes to have the same meaning here in 4:11, as 4:8-11 is
based on the same pathetic contrast as the earlier pericope.[196]
It has been noted, too, that both 3:1-5 and 4:8-11 are reaffirmations of the *causa* (1:6-10).[197] Now it is evident that they
have been carefully placed at the beginning and end of a
sequence of argument. Both immediately after the first statement of the *causa* and immediately before the second, the issue
is that of sonship (οἱ ἐκ πίστεως, οὗτοι υἱοί εἰσιν ᾽Αβραάμ
[3:7]; ὅτι δέ ἐστε υἱοί [4:6]; ὥστε οὐκέτι εἶ δοῦλος ἀλλὰ υἱός
[4:7]).

    Thus the structure of the argument looks something
like this:

3:1-5	εἰκῆ	restatement of *causa*
3:6-14	sonship	
3:15-22		
3:23-29		
4:1-7	sonship	
4:8-11	εἰκῆ	restatement of *causa*

It seems clear that 4:8-11 has not fallen out of the argument
but is intimately bound up with the attack on the offending
theology.

    It has already been noticed how 4:12-20 has a function
in the overall structure of chapters 3 and 4[198] and how Paul
ties the two chapters together by a particular use of σάρξ and
πνεῦμα.[199] It also becomes evident that Abraham has an essential function in the argument. He does not appear before
chapter 3 or after chapter 4, but holds the whole section
together from 3:6, and the issue of sons of Abraham, to 4:21-
32, and the two τέκνα (or sons) of Abraham, as paradigms of
the two spheres of σάρξ and πνεῦμα. Abraham, and the assurance of being sons of Abraham, has a central place in the
opponents' propaganda.

The way Paul has heightened Abraham's role is only
evident from a comparison with the way he has negated almost
all other elements in Jewish salvation-history. The preeminence is given to Abraham and promise[200] and to Abraham's salvation in terms of "faith alone" rather than faith and
obedience.[201] Moses and Israel have dropped out completely.[202]
Moses has become a symbol of slavery (3:19, 4:24), and thereby
stands alongside a whole series of enslaving powers (νόμος
[3:24]; ἐπίτροποι καὶ οἰκονόμοι [4:2]; στοιχεῖα τοῦ κόσμου
[4:3]; οἱ φύσει μὴ ὄντες θεοί [4:8]; and οἱ ἄγγελοι through
whom the law is given [3:19]).[203] This identification by
Paul of Moses with a series of enslaving powers is made credible by certain Jewish literature which asserted that the law
of Moses was the law of nature and the cosmos[204] and that Moses
himself was a divinized revealer of the secrets of cosmic law
and order.[205] But because, in Paul's eschatological scheme,
the cosmos is identified with the present evil age, such cosmic laws could only bring bondage. It would seem that this
rather un-Pauline belittling of Moses and Israel is in response
to the particular way the opponents have of attaching them to
the cosmos and the present age.

Because these terms and motifs are held so closely
together by the careful structure of the argument, the sense
in which Paul uses any one of them is lost when it is treated
in isolation from the others. The question becomes, How can
he hold *all* these terms *together* in a particular way? It is
the holistic picture that Paul here creates that must be
accounted for.

There are suggestions that the argument in this chapter fits well into the context suggested for it in the pages
above. The parallel of 3:1-5 and 4:8-11, their particular
meaning, and their place in the argument against justification
by law, reveals the importance of cosmology.[206] Law is seen
only in terms of enslavement; and justification is in terms of
deliverance from law and all the enslaving powers associated
with it. Eschatology is central to the whole argument. Chapter 3 is built around a particular time-sequence, and the
argument climaxes in the eschatological statement of 4:4. This
last text grounds eschatology in Christology--particularly a

Christology which stresses the humanness and humiliation of
the Christ-event. The law is evaluated particularly in terms
of its role in the death of Christ (3:10-14). Concern for the
will of God is evident in the way Paul asserts that the line
of God's will as promise runs directly from Abraham to Christ.
And Paul's careful but unusual treatment of Abraham, Moses,
law, covenant, Israel, Jerusalem, et cetera, agrees with the
picture of the intruders as efficient missionaries who at the
same time claim an immediate, revelatory source for their gospel and the absolute authority for their traditions.

Above all, the central antithesis of slavery and freedom, the tyrannical powers associated with the law and the
deliverance of the gospel, and the experience of the Spirit
as the equivalent of justification, indicate that justification (or righteousness) is being discussed in terms of *life*,
a continued existence through time.

Conclusions

In conclusion, it is suggested that this chapter has
accomplished two things in particular. Firstly, it has
elaborated the essential unity of the whole argument of Galatians in a way that tends to confirm the rhetorical analysis
of the book. Indications of this essential unity are:

(1) The nature and significance of apostleship and
the stress on the relationship between apostleship and doctrine
which appears at the beginning and the end of the book. The
opponents are now community-apostles in Galatia, thorough propagandists who have *bewitched* the communities.

(2) The continued restatement throughout the book of
the reason for the debate--not only the intruders' theology
but the Galatians' acceptance of it. This experience of the
Galatians of beginning (πνεῦμα) and ending (σάρξ) is evidence
essential to the debate concerning justification.

(3) The eschatology at both the beginning and the end
of the book, which is also directly related to the question
of justification.

(4) The stress throughout the book on Christology, which is the basis of the eschatology and cosmology, and which appears at the climax of the central argument.

(5) The polemical interpretation of justification as *life* through space and time, so that both justification and ethics are different sides of identification with Christ and the cross. Justification takes the "shape" of Christology and the eshcatology which derives from it; and it is against the circumcision program that Paul proclaims the life of the "new creation" (6:14).

(6) The evident importance throughout the letter of baptism and the Spirit, revealed in the way the two sections of the letter (dogmatic and ethical) grow from the baptism-language of 2:19-20.

(7) The function of "mots crochets" and other unifying devices in chapters 3 and 4, and the unifying theme of Abraham (along with the negative unifying theme of Moses) in these chapters.

(8) The various antitheses that run throughout the book, functioning in the typical diatribe pattern of express-ing the central nature of an argument. These antitheses are slavery and freedom, law and faith, law and promise, and flesh and spirit as two ways of existence.

Secondly, as these unifying strands were developed, and as a limited exegesis of certain passages was necessary in order to understand these strands, the theology of the opponents was further elaborated.

(1) The intruders are Christians, and their heresy is essentially a Christian heresy. They are evidently also of Jewish origin.

(2) They have a strong sense of their missionary call, their teaching office, and the importance of their own tradi-tions, especially law, Moses, circumcision, calendrical obser-vances, revelations from angels, Jerusalem, et cetera.

(3) Cosmology is important for them, and law has a particular place in their understanding of cosmology. What must be explained is the holistic picture that results from the terms and expressions of chapters 3 and 4.

(4) The intruders have a particular Christology which minimises the significance of the cross and its eschatological consequences.

(5) The opponents are concerned about consistency in the revelation of the will of God, especially the consistency of Abraham, Moses, and Jesus. Their propaganda leads Paul to reinterpret the traditional Jewish understanding of Abraham and righteousness and to belittle Moses, probably in response to the way the opponents have related the two.

(6) They have a real interest in justification (or righteousness), the meanings of the term, and the relationship between those meanings. The debate comes to center on righteousness as life, that is, the covenant relationship of righteousness into which one is brought when one is "rightwised" without works of law.

(7) The language of σάρξ and πνεῦμα, so important in the *interrogatio*, probably has a significant place in the propaganda of the opponents. These and other mystical/religious words such as ἐνάρχεσθαι and ἐπιτελεῖν may reveal the way in which the opponents themselves present their program.

(8) They do not keep all the law. The sense in which this is true becomes evident as the debate about law as a principle moves to the particular terms of circumcision, days and months, et cetera. In rebutting them, Paul appears more Pharisaic than they, and they apparently stand in a stream which is critical of "orthodox" Jerusalem traditions, Jewish and Christian.

PART THREE

THE TRADITIONS OF THE OPPONENTS

CHAPTER FIVE

INTRODUCTION

This part of the thesis is an attempt to avoid the
suggestion of "vague combinations and hypotheses"[1] by testing
the above conclusions regarding the opponents, their theology,
and their traditions against the "contextual evidence" of the
wider literature of the Pauline period.[2] The method to be
used in the following chapters will in each case involve two
principal steps. To begin with, the evidence internal to
Galatians itself will be considered, using as much as possible
the results of genre analysis and the analysis of the structure of the argument. These results will then be applied to
specific theologoumena in an attempt to determine, in a preliminary way, how they are functioning in the argument. As
a part of this step, and in order more fully to elucidate the
"historical singularity" of the function of the theologoumena
in Galatians, there will be a comparison with the way the
same theologoumena are used in Paul's other letters, or
letters belonging to the Pauline tradition.

Secondly, relevant external evidence will be assembled,
and the ways in which this evidence relates to the theologoumena in Galatians and their function will be proposed and
tested. It is important not only that a parallel theologou-
menon be found but that it be found to be working as it is in
Galatians.[3]

As the external evidence is assembled, it may appear
that the stones of the opponents' theological building are
coming from a variety of quarries, or circles of literature.[4]
Is this reasonable or likely?

Scholarship is becoming more and more aware that the
traditional categories for the literature of the New Testament
world more often impede research than assist it.[5] One is able
to speak less and less of "normative" Judaism or to identify

Judaism of the New Testament era with the Judaism of the
Mishnah.[6] Not only is the distinction between "Palestinian"
and "Hellenistic" Judaism now unacceptable or, to say the
least, blurred:[7] but so also are the distinctions between
"Rabbinic" and "apocalyptic" Judaism,[8] "Hellenistic" and
"apocalyptic" literature,[9] and even between Philonic, apocalyptic, and Rabbinic Judaism[10] and "apocalyptic" and "gnostic"
literature.[11] Even though one is able to speak of Jewish
"apologetic" literature,[12] who was this apologetic for, and
should it be thought of merely as "Hellenistic"?[13] The motifs,
and treatment of such motifs, commonly labelled "apologetic,"
have appeared even in Qumran literature,[14] just as Essenes
feature so prominently in so-called "apologetic" literature.[15]

One further source should be stressed. Though the
opponents are Jewish, and their dependence on various Jewish
traditions is apparent, they are also Christians. In fact,
their heresy is a peculiarly Christian one, that of seeking
the law again when it has been abandoned.[16] Paul's polemical
doctrine of righteousness by faith, without the deeds of the
law, stands here not against any form of Judaism in itself,
but against a merging of Christ and Judaism. Therefore some
of the intruders' traditions will be Christian ones, to be
illuminated from other Christian sources--though they have
been found to be congruous with Judaism for an evident reason.

It does not therefore seem to be methodologically
unsound to cross the traditional literary "frontiers" in pur-
suing the use and meaning of various theologoumena; and an
opponent who should turn out to be "syncretistic" in these
traditional terms is perhaps exactly what is to be expected.

CHAPTER SIX

THE TRADITION OF APOSTLE

There is a particular reason for starting with the
opponents' tradition of apostleship. This tradition, perhaps
more than any other, will reveal the opponents' self-
understanding: and self-understanding is an important clue to
one's theology and the nature of the traditions used to authenticate that theology.[1]

The Function of the Tradition in Galatians

From Gal 1:1-2 " . . . the accusation is clear: Paul
is said to have received his apostolate, not immediately from
God, as befits an apostle, but from men."[2] He is charged with
having received his gospel as an academic tradition from the
"pillar apostles,"[3] making his apostolicity suspect. In the
face, no doubt, of the intruders' own self-claims, he must
assert his independence by pointing to his commission by ἀποκάλυψις (1:11, 12).[4] It is clear that his defense of his
pneumatic apostolate is intricately bound up with his defense
of the gospel.[5] In the apostolic tradition against which Paul
struggles, an authentic proclamation must be received in a
particular way, unmediated on the human level. "Purity of
the gospel and the nonmediated character of the apostolate
are inseparable."[6]

Further, the opponents must, in their absolute rejection of Paul and the gospel (1:6-9, 4:16, 6:12), make apostolic
claims for themselves.[7] Where such a view of the relation
between apostle and gospel is operating, the "other gospel"
could only be a real competitor to Paul's gospel if there were
other apostles preaching it.[8] These apostles must lay claim
to the unmediated type of apostolate which they deny to Paul.

The very charge of Paul's dependence on the Jerusalem
apostles implies a criticism of the Jerusalem apostles, too.[9]
There is a subtlety in the opposing apostolic tradition. It
sets great store by Jerusalem[10] and a particular estimate of
the Jerusalem church and leadership.[11] However, the charge of
dependence would not discredit Paul's gospel if the Pillars'
gospel were above question.[12] Further, the very circumcising
activity of the opponents, despite the decision reported in
2:6-9, suggests that they hold a gospel that is in contempt of
the Jerusalem Pillars.[13]

Above all, the notion of apostleship by ἀποκάλυψις
harbors a base for the most radical of attacks on the authority
of the Pillars. Whereas the Jerusalem view of authority sees
the Pillars as the repositories of unique traditions about
Jesus which must be passed on horizontally[14] (because of the
nature of the post-resurrection appearances and their cessation),[15] therefore giving the Jerusalem apostles a unique place
in the church,[16] this stress on ἀποκάλυψις bypasses the Jerusalem apostles completely, and places authority in immediate
encounters with heavenly wisdom, and perhaps with the risen
Christ Himself. The way the opponents use this notion both as
propaganda for their own traditions and as a means of fragmenting opposition to them is revealed by three things. Paul
must say that a "vain" mission is one in which there is some
discrepancy between the preaching of the missionary and that
of the Pillars (2:1-2). He must use an eschatological-
historicising argument in the main section of the letter (1:4,
3:6-4:11) that focuses on the earthly Jesus of history and his
cross (3:13, 4:4, 6:14, etc.).[17] And he must appeal to the
oneness of the community brought about by the Christ-event
(3:27-29) and point to the way the intruders have brought a
breakdown in responsibility to the visible community (5:1-
6:11).[18] Each of these issues involves a vigorous attack on
the Pillars themselves.

The opposing tradition is further highlighted by
examining Schoeps' claim that it is "utilized and preserved"
in the Kerygmata Petrou.[19] It is claimed that the document
is Ebionite in theology and a witness for a direct succession
from the Pharisaic ζηλωταί τοῦ νόμου of Acts 15:5 and 21:20,

the τίνες ἀπὸ 'Ιακώβου of Gal 2:12, the παρεισάκτοι ψευδαδέλ-
φοι of Gal 2:4, and the opponents Paul encounters in 1 and
2 Corinthians, to the later Ebionites.[20] The document's three
major objections to Paul's apostleship are therefore the same
as the attack in Galatia: firstly, that the apostolic office
is limited to the twelve;[21] secondly, that a true apostle is
authenticated by his teaching and that "Paul,"[22] by his attack
on Peter (referring to Gal 2:11) has shown himself untrue;[23]
and thirdly, that a charismatic apostolate, based on a vision
of the risen Lord, is quite unacceptable.[24] In fact, the
document plays down charismatic gifts among believers.[25]

        Great doubts remain as to whether the document is
simply of Pharisaic descent.[26] But laying this question aside,
its objections to Paul's apostolate are not those of the Galatian opponents. For the latter, the twelve are not an authoritative group, for Paul only claims the blessing of the Pillars.[27] If they were, the opponents could make no claim to
apostolic authority, and would cut the ground from under their
own feet.[28] Further, Schmithals appears to be correct in saying that, for the opponents, the authenticity of the message
is measured by the apostolate of the messenger: hence the
demand for authentication by ἀποκαλύψεις (Gal 1:7-8, 11-12).
This is exactly the opposite of the apostolic tradition held
in Jerusalem--and in the Kerygmata Petrou.[29] Thirdly, the
latter document flatly rejects an apostolate based on a vision,
whereas the very demand made of Paul in Galatians is that he
give proof of his ἀποκαλύψεις.[30]

        Schoeps' association of the Galatian opponents with
both the Pharisaic Christians of Acts 15 and the later Ebionites, by way of the pseudo-Clementines, must be questioned.
But further, three characteristics of the opponents' tradition
of apostle now stand out more clearly. The authentic apostolate is not the circle of the twelve, but interest centers
instead in the στῦλοι.[31] Further, the opponents make a programmatic demand for ἀποκαλύψεις and an apostolate received
immediately from heaven, which guarantees the truth of the
gospel. This is not merely the בת קול of later Rabbinism.[32]

        Though Schmithals has in some respects assessed the
opponents' apostolic tradition more correctly than Schoeps,

he, too, must be questioned when he says

> The Gnostic apostle is not identified by means of a chain
> of tradition, by the apostolic succession, but by direct
> pneumatic vocation. When Paul says, "Am I not an apostle?
> Have I not seen our Lord?" (1 Cor 9:1), this combination,
> which represents an equation, is in origin typically
> Gnostic.[33]

Schmithals' case rests partly on a distinction between
"chain of tradition" and "direct pneumatic vocation." But, in
the first place, Paul seems aware of no incompatibility between
these two.[34] In 1 Corinthians, with its stress on παράδοσις,
Schmithals finds his "gnostic" formula (1 Cor 9:1; see also
1 Cor 11:23: ἐγὼ γὰρ παρέλαβον ἀπὸ τοῦ κυρίου . . .); and
even in 1 Corinthians 15, it is the risen Lord who deems Paul
an apostle (ἔσχατον δὲ πάντων ὡσπερεὶ τῷ ἐκτρώματι ὤφθη κἀμοί
[1 Cor 15:8]).[35] In both Galatians and 1 Corinthians, chain
of tradition and pneumatic vocation are functioning dynamically
together, as they did in many Jewish circles.[36]

Secondly, Gnosticism, while undeniably exalting "direct
pneumatic vocation," was also concerned with "chain of tradition."[37] The term ἀποστολικός may have come into being to
counter Gnostics,[38] but it soon became the common property of
Gnostics too.[39] Schmithals' distinction breaks down within
the Gnostic texts themselves. On the other side, the Great
Church showed a remarkable interest in immediate, pneumatic
authority.[40] Schmithals' distinction is worse than "anachronistic."[41] The ancient world saw no contradiction between
vertical revelations and horizontal transmission of tradition,[42] and it is quite invalid to isolate one from the other
and call it "Gnostic."[43] In Galatians there is a programmatic
demand for ἀποκαλύψεις and a cherishing of traditions; in fact,
it appears that vertical revelations make tradition a live
issue.

Further characteristics of this demand for ἀποκαλύψεις
in Galatians should now be examined. Schmithals appears correct in positing that the same widely held criteria of apostleship which are functioning in Corinth (the demonstration of
religious power and authority by gaining a large following
[1 Cor 9:1-2]; the σημεῖα καὶ τέρατα which signify an apostle
[2 Cor 12:11-12]; and the experience of ὀπτασίαι καὶ

ἀποκαλύψεις which divulge hidden, heavenly secrets [2 Cor
12:1-11])[44] are also at issue in Galatians.[45] This is evident
from 6:12-13 (the opponents' boast of the winning of the Galatians),[46] 3:5 (the criteria of the presence of the Spirit and
the working of miracles),[47] and 1:8 (the opponents' apparent
boast of angelic revelations). This would explain why it is
that the revelatory source of Paul's apostolate, which must
have been widely known and of which even the opponents must
have been aware,[48] has not been accepted in Galatia. 2 Corinthians 12 makes it clear that this same tradition of apostle
demanded that the recipient of the authenticating vision should
preach himself as a pneuma-self and recount his visionary
experiences.[49] The simple claim to have seen the Lord (Gal
1:11-12, 15-16; 1 Cor 9:1-2) is not enough.[50] In the face of
the opposing apostolic tradition Paul has not authenticated
himself as a true apostle until he has divulged the contents
of the ἀποκάλυψις (2 Cor 12:1-2).[51] The person is to be identified with his revelation, and divulging of heavenly secrets
is a way of speaking about oneself as an apostle. No doubt an
appropriate Christ of heavenly wisdom is also involved (1 Cor
1:17, 2:4, 12:3). But for Paul, here in Galatians as elsewhere, apostolic authority is bound up with faithfulness to
the significance of the earthly Jesus and His death on the
cross.[52] There is no heavenly secret or revelation that can
compare to the revelation of the son of God dying in extreme
human wretchedness on his cross.[53]

    It seems significant that Paul should claim authentica-
tion of his apostleship, in Galatians, in terms of a prophetic
call.[54] The suggestion is that, for the Galatian opponents,
authentication is to be in terms of a prophetic tradition.
There is some evidence that, in early Christianity, the office
of ἀπόστολος was connected with that of προφήτης. Rengsdorf
has noted some relation between שלח and ἀποστελλειν.[55] The
early church connected the two titles,[56] as does Eph 2:20, in
a context where there are other significant theological tendencies.[57] In the above tradition of apostle there is the suggestion that visionary-revelatory experiences were connected
with prophecy.[58] So Paul may have had to deal with a tradition
in which an apostle was to be validated by traits connected
with prophecy.[59]

The apostolic tradition is further revealed in the
opponents' relationship with the Galatian communities. They
have completely displaced Paul as the community apostle (ὥστε
ἐχθρὸς ὑμῶν γέγονα ἀληθεύων ὑμῖν, 4:16).[60] The language of
4:14 (οὐκ ἐξουθενήσατε οὐδὲ ἐξεπτύσατε) suggests that they
have made him scorned and despised (spat out!). No doubt they
have their own counterpart of Paul's apostolic curse (1:8-9)
under which Paul now stands. Their propaganda has resulted
in a complete reversal of the estimation of him; he is a "weak"
apostle, an imperfect physical specimen, and therefore is no
longer fit company for those who fellowship with angels (4:14),
as the opponents evidently claim to do (1:7, 3:19).

The opposing tradition is revealed further in 4:17,
ζηλοῦσιν ὑμᾶς οὐ καλῶς, ἀλλὰ ἐκκλεῖσαι ὑμᾶς θέλουσιν. . . .
Several meanings have been suggested for the phrase,[61] which
may not be exclusive of each other. Paul sees a vital relationship between Christ, the church, and the apostles of the
church,[62] and exclusion from one would imply exclusion from
all. The greatest demand for loyalty is to what God has now
done in Christ (2:21); there is also a real sense of identity
with the apostles' preaching of the Christ (2:1-2) and with
the reality of the new community that now adheres in Christ
(3:27-29). In that the intruders are apologists for certain
Jerusalem traditions,[63] at the same time rejecting the Jerusalem leadership in important senses, the verb ἐκκλεῖειν
probably refers to their separatist, exclusivist program and
self-understanding in which they stand over against Paul's
gospel, the apostles, and the church in a programmatic sense.
Further, they seem to be hierarchical separatists, demanding
positions of honor and separation from the common members
among their followers (ἐκκλεῖσαι ὑμᾶς θέλουσιν, ἵνα αὐτοὺς
ζηλοῦτε [4:17]; θέλουσιν ὑμᾶς περιτέμνεσθαι ἵνα ἐν τῇ ὑμετέρᾳ
σαρκὶ καυχήσωνται [6:13]). Their "extravagandising" of the
office of the Pillars (2:6) is probably accompanied by an
"extravagandising" of themselves.[64]

This self-understanding lends weight to the suggestion
that in 4:26 (ἡ δὲ ἄνω ᾿Ιερουσαλὴμ ἐλευθέρα ἐστίν, ἥτις ἐστὶν
μήτηρ ἡμῶν) Paul has picked up a slogan of the intruders and
twisted it against them.[65] Such a slogan would be appropriate

for those who extravagandize themselves as superlative apostles
of Jerusalem traditions, to such an exalted state that they are
above human weakness and suffering, and accords well with the
other aspects of the tradition that are at work: the concern
for proofs of an apostle that demonstrate an impressive presence of God, such as visions, converts, and magical or miraculous powers. There seems to be a consistency between self-
understanding and theology.

In looking for possible sources of such a tradition,
it will be essential to hold these and other facets together,
such as concern for the στύλοι and interest in prophetic authentication. Further, the most likely sources will be those in
which the tradition is being used in the same way as in Galatians.

Possible Sources of the Tradition
of Apostle

The opponents' demand for the heavenly vision should
have first attention. Interest in both the experience and the
content of ἀποκαλύψεις, in Hellenistic times, appears even in
non-Jewish literature.[66] But the later examples in the apocalyptic New Testament apocrypha,[67] the Fathers,[68] and even in
Gnosticism[69] all have features suggesting that they are drawing on common origins in Jewish apocalyptic literature.[70]
Apocalyptic insisted that an authentic message must come by
revelation, for written revelation had hardened, and any new
word had to come by divine self-impartation.[71] The new
"prophetic self-awareness" was at work now in "inspired"
interpretations of prophetic writings.[72] The one difference
to the Galatian tradition is the characteristic of pseudonymity.[73] This rule was broken in favor of contemporaneity of
the visionary experience--as it was in Galatians--in Qumran
and the early church.[74]

The content of validation required by the opposing
tradition also appears close to apocalyptic Judaism. 2 Cor
12:1-4 refers to only three heavens, typical for apocalyptic
Judaism.[75] The later Christian apocrypha commonly speaks of
seven heavens,[76] the early Fathers speak mostly of eight,[77]
and Gnosticism multiplies the process even further.[78]

As well as in apocalyptic literature, the phenomenon
of visions and journeys appeared in other quarters in Judaism.[79] But the community in which these experiences were both
programmatic and contemporaneous was that of the Qumran sectaries.[80] This is evidenced firstly in the "Pesher," the community's particular way of "knowing" Scripture.[81] The "Pesher"
is a way of predicting what is "presaged" in Scripture so as
to corroborate that the "latter days" have set in. Its affinities are not with Rabbinic literature but with apocalyptic.[82]
In the Qumran community, scripture is "known" particularly in
an apocalyptic sense. Secondly, "knowledge" was of central
importance to the sectaries.[83] Here it was entirely a gift of
God to the elect, a result of divine revelation.[84] It was
only the Spirit who brought the knowledge of these mysteries
and insights,[85] which included insights into the cosmos, its
order and organization, and the powers which rule over it.[86]
This revelatory "knowledge" was so divinely effectual that it
actually lifted its participants above earthly existence and
made them co-dwellers with the angels in the supernatural
realms.[87]

It appears that the intruding Galatian tradition
demanded authentication of an apostle in terms associated with
prophecy.[88] Therefore circles showing an interest in prophecy
in some form will now be examined.

Prophecy was not as absent from inter-testamental
Judaism as is sometimes suggested,[89] although Rabbinism as it
is now known does not seem to be representative in this
respect.[90] For Philo, all the great religious figures of
Israel's past were prophets,[91] and he believed himself to
have had prophetic/ecstatic experiences.[92] Josephus too, by
his reporting of prophetic activity in Palestine, indicates
the great interest of Hellenistic Judaism in prophecy. Besides
the reference to the prophetic office of Hyrcanus,[93] and even
to Pharisaic prophets,[94] it is among the Essenes that he
reports the greatest prophetic activity. As well as Manoemus[95]
and Simon,[96] there was Judas, evidently head of a whole prophetic school.[97] These prophets have predictive prowess
because of their "virtue,"[98] their purificatory rites,[99] and
their ceaseless study of the "prophets," the "holy books," and

the "ancients."[100] Their gift of prediction was probably a
sign of the possession of the "prophetic spirit."[101] Josephus
himself had his own prophetic vision, fulfilled miraculously
in the career of Vespasian.[102]

An even wider form of "prophetic" activity was the
literature produced by the "Hasidic apocalyptic wisdom tradition," especially the Jewish apocalyptic literature.[103] This
"new prophecy" now took the form of inspired interpretations
of prophetic writings.[104] There is often a clear imitation of
Old Testament prophetic models and authentication in Old Testament prophetic terms.[105] Here wisdom and prophetic consciousness are intertwined: wise men acquire prophetic features,
prophets become wise men, and the scribe and the prophet are
no longer distinct.[106] What is even more interesting about
this prophetic tradition is its authentication of itself in
terms of a succession of heroic personalities of the past.[107]

In the light of Josephus' portrayal of the Essenes,
and of the "prophetic" characteristics of the apocalyptic wisdom tradition (in which the Qumran community shared)[108] it is
interesting to examine the role of prophecy in Qumran.[109] The
community had a messianic expectation, probably at least
partly in terms of a messianic prophet, though the question
is complicated.[110] The Teacher of Righteousness also had the
prophetic task of explaining the words of the prophets.[111] In
this sense, the prophet has again become a contemporary figure.[112] Further, 1 QM 11:7-8 speaks of "Thine anointed, the
men who had vision of things foreordained," a group evidently
designated as prophets, reminiscent of Josephus' Essene
prophets.[113] CD 2:12 also refers to "the annointed" in the
plural, men to whom God has "revealed His Holy Spirit" and
"disclosed the truth," that is, men with a prophetic function.[114]

The community has a prophetic self-consciousness
further in that it shares in the apocalyptic wisdom tradition,
in which knowledge and insight come by direct revelation and
inspiration.[115] There is great interest in contemplation and
exposition of scripture,[116] reminiscent of Josephus' Essene
prophets.[117] But it must be remembered that exposition of
scripture is a mystical/apocalyptic task.[118] The exegete is

the "wise man,"[119] the "wise man" is the "prophet,"[120] and
vision and ecstasy are the confirmation of the "prophetic wise
man."[121] In this sense, in particular, the prophet has become
a contemporary figure in Qumran.[122]

Thus there were circles in first-century Judaism which
showed great interest in a contemporary prophetic manifestation
that has affinities to the demands the opponents apparently
make on Paul's apostleship. The Qumran sectaries, in particular, maintained the apocalyptic traditions of Judaism, insisted
on a "knowledge" that could only be attained through immediate
access to God and that authenticated one as being in contact
with God, saw themselves as the ultimate expositors of scripture, and had a self-understanding in terms of which they were
on the one hand separated from the rest of mankind and even
Israel and, on the other, lifted into the company of the divine
and other-worldly powers and made one community with angelic
beings.

Possible parallels to the self-understanding of the
Galatian opponents will now be sought in two respects: in
terms of a self-designation such as "heavenly Jerusalem" and
of an understanding of the community that could lead to interest in the στῦλοι.

The Rabbis spoke of a heavenly city called Jerusalem,[123] as did Philo, though he used the expression in his
own particular way.[124] But apocalyptic literature seems to
provide the most relevant parallels. It spoke of a heavenly,
eschatological city, a counterpart of the earthly Jerusalem,[125]
though having a strong continuity with earthly and historical
Jerusalem.[126] The traditional, national hopes of Judaism still
win out.[127]

Because of the way apocalyptic sees a dynamic relationship between things on earth and things in heaven,[128] and
because of its doctrines of predestination and the remnant,[129]
the apocalyptic visionary, or wise man, in effect participates
already in the future redemption.[130] The remnant can be called
the "children of heaven,"[131] who understand themselves in the
present better by contemplating future certainties than by contemplating common human mortality.[132] They are already, in a
vital sense, "children of Jerusalem above."

This is no "realized eschatology" in the sense of
removal of the tension between this age and the age to come;[133]
rather, it intensifies the tension between the ages and assures
the righteous that they are on the verge of the regeneration of
all things.

The Qumran literature seems to make no mention of a
heavenly city called Jerusalem.[134] Jerusalem at present is
the abode of the wicked,[135] is to be the center of the final
eschatological war, and is to be afterwards restored to para-
disal conditions.[136] But in the present the community sees
itself as a supramundane dwelling place of the holy angels and
God, having real though invisible communion with the heavenly
world.[137] And the community sees itself as, in a sense, "Jerusalem."[138] This again does not seem far from the self-
designation, "Heavenly Jerusalem."[139] And again, this consciousness of a realization already of heavenly citizenship
does not reduce the intensity of future hope.[140]

This self-understanding of the Qumran community may
have a further parallel with the self-understanding of the
Galatian intruders. Gal 4:12-20 suggests that they have introduced a profound change in attitude to Paul in his weakness
and infirmity. Now one with a physical defect cannot be
accepted as a genuine apostle.[141] The Qumran community, too,
excluded any with bodily defects--because of the presence of
angels in the congregation.[142] Perhaps the opponents' preoccupation with angels has given them another reason for rejecting
(spitting out!) Paul.

Sources such as the literature of apocalyptic Judaism
and Qumran do reveal a self-awareness that could coincide with
the opponents' claim to be "heavenly Jerusalem;" and these are
the same sources that have a great interest in apocalyptic-
mystical revelations and present manifestations of prophecy.
In both these sources, the awareness of being the companions
of the celestial beings is accompanied by a strong sense of
being a "remnant."[143] At the same time, there is a strong
sense of continuity between earthly and heavenly Jerusalem,
Jerusalem of the past and Jerusalem of the future. The opponents, too, see Jerusalem still as the center of holy mysteries and zealously maintain certain religious traditions of

the past associated with Jerusalem (Abraham, Moses, the law,
circumcision, etc.). In these circles, as among the intruders,
Jerusalem of the past and Jerusalem of the future, the world
above and the world below, are being held together; and it is
the community of the elect that holds them together.

But for Paul, in Gal 4:21-31, the new aeon has come,
and is manifested "in Christ,"[144] and in such a way that there
is only discontinuity between the earthly and the heavenly,
Jerusalem past and Jerusalem present (i.e. future).[145] And
yet the new aeon comes in such a way that the Jerusalem apostles have a real place of authority (Gal 2:1-2 and Paul's constant reference to Jerusalem in his "alibi").[146] For the
opponents, there is authority in Jerusalem's past traditions
and freedom with respect to the Pillars and the traditions
they embody (particularly traditions of the earthly Jesus and
His cross).[147] For Paul, Christ and His cross have brought a
freedom from past Jerusalem traditions and a collegiality with
the Pillars.

If Paul's opponents were Gnostics, then he has badly
misunderstood them, for they present their own system of the
two Jerusalems just as he does.[148] Paul is here almost a
"Gnostic apostle."[149] But over against the self-designations
of apocalyptic circles, the dialogical force of his language
makes perfect sense. He has taken up the very designation of
the opponents in order to break the continuity between the
traditions associated with earthly or present Jerusalem and
heavenly Jerusalem.

Finally, possibilities arising from the use of στύλος
in Galatians should be considered. Only three more times is
the word used in the New Testament, none of them in Paul's
major epistles.[150] Barrett and Wilckens have suggested that
the concept of the apostle as Pillar comes from an apocalyptic
context in which the church or community is seen as the Temple
of God.[151] Early Christianity saw the community in this light,
as did the Qumran community,[152] with its strong sense of sharing in the גברה of God.[153] Moreover, the Qumran community was
ruled over by an inner group of twelve laymen and three priests,
reminiscent of three Pillars of Galatians.[154] Thus the terminology and its function suggest that Paul is authenticating

himself in the terms of a group that is close to apocalyptic
circles.

Self-Understanding and Tradition

From the above analysis, the probable demands made of
an apostle by the Galatian intruders can be filled out. He
must meet a programmatic demand for revelations and for the
esoteric preaching of the content of those revelations. He
must be one who can give evidence that he has communed directly
with God, since "knowledge," that is, understanding of scripture, comes only in this way. He must manifest certain characteristics of the prophet. His message must embody the traditions associated with historical Jerusalem, and he must
represent the community which is the link between past and
future Jerusalem, the remnant, who are in a sense already an
angelic community. He must be a "prophetic wise man," in keeping with the "Hasidic apocalyptic wisdom tradition" and its
understanding of revelation and inspiration. The concept of
apostleship by ἀποκάλυψις, while making him a participant in
Jerusalem's glorious past traditions, frees him from any binding obligations to the new Christian community, the apostles
of the community, and the community's central proclamation of
the earthly, suffering Jesus.[155]

This chapter began by pointing out that there is a
general consistency, in religious propaganda, between the messenger and the message, and the self-understanding of the
emissaries and the religious traditions used to maintain that
self-understanding.[156] Those who spoke of God's δύναμις being
active and present through men in a certain way (that is, in
themselves) maintained careful traditions of past heroes,
divine men in whose lives the divine was manifested in a congruous way.[157]

This phenomenon is demonstrated by the way Socrates,
especially as portrayed in Plato's *Apology*, became a pattern
for various forms of religious propaganda for centuries.[158]
This method of "proclamation by aretalogy" was widely used in
Judaism as well.[159] In fact, there was even a use here of the
"Socratic tradition."[160] The "Hasidic apocalyptic wisdom

tradition," with its particular understanding of revelation
and inspiration, had its own version of "aretalogy." There
was the "praise of the Fathers,"[161] a hagiographic way of
writing history,[162] and the presentation of wise men and
prophets as heroic personalities who authenticated themselves
by an unusual demonstration of the presence of God.[163] Perhaps
the favorite character in these hagiographic histories was
Abraham, who brings to civilization the oldest of all wisdom.[164]

     It is for this reason that the opponents' self-
understanding, as reflected in the tradition of apostle, looks
forward to further theologoumena to be considered. Heroes of
Israel's past figure prominently in the debate in Galatians;
and the tradition of apostle and the self-understanding of the
opponents stand close to circles which cherished particular
images of these heroes, and for particular theological reasons.

CHAPTER SEVEN

THE TRADITION OF ABRAHAM AND
SEED OF ABRAHAM

*The Function of the Tradition
in Galatians*

It has been noticed above that the Stichwort "Abraham"
dominates chapters 3 and 4.[1] This must be for polemical reasons. It is no doubt the opponents who have made Abraham a
central figure in the debate.[2]

The opponents use a tradition in which Abraham reveals
the way to God for Gentiles. To the question, πῶς ὁ θεὸς
δικαιοῖ τὰ ἔθνη; comes the answer, "As He did Abraham" (3:8).[3]
There must be a real concern for the conversion of Gentiles,
even though Paul belittles the motives behind the concern
(4:17, 6:12, 13).[4] As noted above, the opponents are vigorous
and effective missionaries. Abraham apparently provides a
model for their prospective converts, and for themselves.

The way of δικαιοσύνη that Abraham demonstrates for
Gentiles is the way of obedience to the law, and the εὐλογία
τοῦ 'Αβραάμ is to be received by works (3:10-14). When, in
3:15-18, Paul asserts that God gave Abraham the κληρονομία by
ἐπαγγελία, and not by νόμος, it must be because the opponents
have asserted the opposite. Abraham to them is the one who
demonstrates perfect obedience to the law[5] and therefore
demonstrates that Gentiles must keep the law.

This model of Abraham as the one who perfectly obeys
the law suggests that the opponents assert a close relationship between Abraham and Moses. To the question, "Who are the
sons of Abraham?" comes the answer, "Those who follow Moses."[6]
It may be for this reason that, when Paul separates Abraham
from Moses in 3:15-18, he must then go on to answer the question, τί οὖν ὁ νόμος, in 3:19-25. His separation of the two

has created a problem where none existed before.[7] This same
polemical intent shows through in 4:21-31, where Sinai is made
a mountain in Arabia which only engenders bondage--a rather
un-Pauline assessment of the Mosaic covenant.[8] Sinai has an
important part in the argument in which Abraham is at the
centre.

The opposing tradition evidently asserts that those
who follow Abraham and keep the law, even Gentiles, are σπέρμα
'Αβραάμ or υἱοί 'Αβραάμ.[9] These terms play such a central
part in the debate (3:7, 16, 29, 4:5, 22, 26, 31) that they
cannot have been casually introduced. They are bound up with
interest in the κληρονομία which is the legitimate property of
the σπέρμα 'Αβραάμ (3:18, 29; 4:1, 7), perhaps the glories of
the age to come.[10]

The polemical nature of this title is evident from the
way its use differs in Romans.[11] There the term is used in
the context of the Jewish claim of physical descent from Abraham and exclusiveness of salvation as the privilege of the
Jew. So Paul asserts in Rom 4:16, εἰς τὸ εἶναι βεβαίαν τὴν
ἐπαγγελίαν παντὶ τῷ σπέρματι, οὐ τῷ ἐκ τοῦ νόμου μόνον ἀλλὰ
καὶ τῷ ἐκ πίστεως 'Αβραάμ. Here there is some seed of Abraham
ἐκ τοῦ νόμου, an impossible suggestion in Galatians, and one
which would destroy Paul's schematic salvation-historical argument.[12] In Romans 9 the argument of the "children of promise"
(9:8) is used to validate the principle of the remnant (9:27)
--there has always been a people of promise, a nation within
the nation. But in Galatians Christ is the promised seed
(3:16) who comes at a fixed point in time (3:19, 24), and
only after that time does the collective σπέρμα come into
existence (3:29; 3:23, 24). Before Christ the people of Israel
were νήπιοι, under ἐπίτροποι καὶ οἰκονόμοι or the στοιχεῖα τοῦ
κόσμου (4:1-3). Before the coming of the Son (4:4), there was
no sonship in the sense of σπέρμα that receives the κληρονομία
(4:5, ἵνα τὴν υἱοθεσίαν ἀπολάβωμεν).[13] Only in the present
time of redemption in Christ will Paul speak of σπέρμα, υἱός,
and entrance into the κληρονομία. Evidently, in Romans, Paul
addresses Jews who appeal to the title σπέρμα 'Αβραάμ to
exclude Gentiles from redemption. His answer is, There are
two seeds, one of νόμος and one of πίστις. But in Galatians

the question is not that of physical descent at all;[14] it is
an appeal to Abraham as the exclusive way of salvation for
both Jews *and* Gentiles. So Paul takes up this same exclusiveness and reinterprets it.

       This suggests something about the opponents' soteriol-
ogy. For them, a man is designated σπέρμα 'Αβραάμ by law-
righteousness. In 2:14, the whole stress comes to fall on
'Ιουδαϊκῶς ζῆν and 'Ιουδαΐζειν,[15] not 'Ιουδαῖος ἐθνικῶς. Such
stress is reminiscent of the message of John the Baptist in
Luke 3:8 ("Do not . . . say . . . 'We have Abraham as our
father;' for I tell you, God is able from these stones to
raise up children to Abraham") and of some circles within
Judaism which saw themselves as a "purified" Israel. It is
not far from saying that one a Jew by descent is not one of
the σπέρμα 'Αβραάμ to saying a Gentile *is* one of the σπέρμα
'Αβραάμ, if he lives as a "true" Jew and meets all the
requirements of the covenant of Abraham.[16] Such a soteriology
would be consistent with the reform mentality of the opponents,
their separatism, and their upholding of the pre-Christian
traditions of Jerusalem,[17] while flouting the leadership of
the Jerusalem church and the traditions of the earthly Jesus.[18]

       The propaganda regarding Abraham and the law is
intensely appealing to the Galatians, Gentiles though they are.
Under its spell they have apostatised ταχέως (1:6) and are in
grave danger of submitting to circumcision wholesale.[19] This
is so unusual in the Hellenistic world as to call for a particular explanation.[20] Not only must a tradition of Abraham
be sought which encourages a Gentile mission. It must also be
one which makes that mission particularly attractive and compelling to Gentiles.

                    Possible Sources of the Tradition

       Judaism widely portrays Abraham as demonstrating the
way to God for Gentiles. He is himself a גר, a proselyte, the
first to come from heathenism to true religion.[21] In Philo
and Josephus, as well as in other Jewish literature, Abraham
is the first to know and declare the one true God, the Creator,
whom he came to know from the observation of natural

phenomena.[22] Rabbinism declares him to be the father of
proselytes,[23] who leads the whole world to repentance,[24] and
demonstrates God's love for proselytes.[25] He represents a
standard for all proselytes.[26]

It was also widely understood that Abraham's example
was one of perfect obedience to the law. Faith was a work or
meritorious deed,[27] and Gen 15:6 (Gal 3:6) was linked with
Gen 22:15-18 as in the book of James: Abraham was righteous
before God because he kept the law by anticipation and was
perfectly faithful in temptation.[28] For Philo, too, the outstanding characteristic of Abraham was his perfect obedience.[29]
He had his own version of the tradition, based on Gen 26:5,
that Abraham kept all the laws of Moses in anticipation.[30] It
was "unwritten nature," not "written words," which taught him
these commands.[31]

Thus Abraham demonstrated that the proselyte must take
upon himself circumcision, the sign of the Abrahamic covenant,
and obey all the commandments of the law.[32] In all these
respects there is nothing in the opponents' use of Abraham
that does not accord with widely held Jewish teaching.

As well as the tradition itself, it is important to
ask about the function of the tradition; and it is here that
some circles of Judaism may not qualify as prospective sources
of the opponents' theology.

Abraham and his obedience are especially important to
much of Judaism, not for his significance for Gentiles as much
as for the founding of the covenant with Israel.[33] God's
choice of Israel is explained in terms of the meritorious
actions of the ancestors, particularly Abraham,[34] and the
covenant that is made is unconditional.[35] All Israelites have
a share in the world to come because of this covenant and its
meritorious founder,[36] who becomes the basis of the teaching
of *zekut' abot*, the merits of the fathers which are available
to all physical descendants of Abraham.[37] The interest, then,
is in those who are already members of the covenant by virtue
of the obedience of Abraham: Gentiles are dealt with only
sporadically.

Abraham here principally serves the interests of
Jewish exclusivism, as he evidently does in the Jewish

arguments in Romans (see above). In keeping with this, a
proselyte is never called σπέρμα 'Αβραάμ.[38] He may be called
a גר צדק,[39] but he never stands in Israel on equality with
native Israelites and may have no share in the merits of Abraham. Different attitudes towards the Gentiles prevailed in
different circles and at different times,[40] but on the whole
the title σπέρμα 'Αβραάμ was used in the service of Jewish
isolation.[41] Abraham bolstered the Jewish assurance of salvation[42] and contributed to the very opposite of a missionary
understanding.[43] It is doubtful that the opponents' missionary zeal, connected with a traditional understanding of Abraham, could be derived from such sources.

        Over against this exclusiveness based on Abraham there
must be placed on the one hand, the interest of some Jewish
literature in Gentiles, and, on the other hand, a great interest of Gentiles in Judaism.[44] The latter is probably to be
accounted for at least partly by the former. It may be the
treatment of Abraham in such literature that explains the opponents' zeal for both Abraham and for converts--and for the
Galatians' own sudden enthusiasm for the religion of Abraham,
which must certainly be accounted for.[45]

        This Abraham who would appeal to Gentiles is found in
what is commonly called "apologetic" literature, though very
little of it was probably written with the specific intention
of winning converts.[46] Rather, it is given its significant
characteristics because it has adopted "Hellenistic" methods
of propaganda and presentation, especially Hellenistic historiography.[47] Further, the literature is not particularly
"Hellenistic" or "Palestinian" in a geographic sense;[48] its
motifs and theology are common property of a wide segment of
Judaism, including some apocalyptic literature.[49] It is significant, too, that this way of portraying Judaism began to
come to an end after CE 70;[50] and as it did, so did a particular way of portraying its heroes.[51]

        There are certain reasons why this "apologetic" Abra-
ham should be taken into account here. Firstly, there is the
different attitude to history and, therefore, to the heroes
of history, after AD 70;[52] the Abraham of the Rabbinic material
may not altogether be the Abraham of Paul's day.[53] Secondly,

the literary circles to which the opponents' tradition of
apostle has affinities shared this interest in hagiographies
that authenticated a certain self-understanding.[54] And
thirdly, though missionary zeal was not characteristic of any
Jewish circles in particular,[55] a missionary impetus would be
encouraged by the apologetic Abraham, and this Abraham would
make the missionaries and their propaganda more appealing to
Gentiles.

The basis of this "apologetic" writing was the Hellenistic approach to history, now adopted by Judaism, and resulting in a New Jewish interpretation of Greek learning, cults,
and mythology.[56] Abraham was given a leading place in this
interpretation.[57] He was portrayed first as the philosopher-
king, astronomer, and father of all culture. He was forced to
flee Chaldea because his knowledge of cosmic phenomena, and
his deduction from it of the Creator God, infuriated the Chaldeans. His journey to Egypt was in fact a religious quest,
and, while there, he introduced the Egyptians to arithmetic
and laws of astronomy. Thus the sciences travelled from the
Chaldeans to Egypt, whence they passed on to the Greeks.[58] He
was thus the father of all cultures.[59]

The portrayal also rests on a particular understanding
of the relationship between natural and divine law, and law as
the key to cosmic order. Because Abraham understands the
secrets of the universe and God, he has remarkable control
over it. This is demonstrated in his role as inventor, impressive to the Hellenistic interest in technology and technologi-
cal improvement,[60] and his prowess as a wonder-worker and
impressive representative of God,[61] who baffles the Egyptian
priests and terrifies Pharaoh.[62]

In this literature, the "apologetic" Abraham was
closely linked with an "apologetic" Moses. Often the two are
portrayed in parallel terms.[63] As Abraham is portrayed in
terms of Heracles, so Moses is equated with Musaeus and Hermes
and is the teacher of Orpheus.[64] As Abraham is the father of
philosophy, astronomy, and culture, so Moses taught the Egyptians philosophy and cosmology.[65] As Abraham came to understand the secrets of the cosmos and natural law, so God
revealed to Moses the secrets of law and cosmic order.[66] Both

Abraham and Moses are prophets, inspired by God.[67] Moses,
like Abraham, must confront and defeat the Egyptian priests in
a contest of divine powers.[68] It may be that this "apologetic"
equation of Abraham and Moses is connected with the opponents'
association of the two.

This tradition may explain why the opponents should
find it natural to appeal to the Galatians in terms of Abraham.
It may also explain why Gentiles suddenly wish to be called
"sons of Abraham." The widespread Jewish tradition of Abraham
as the one who perfectly obeyed the law is maintained,[69] but
carried even further: "Law," in good Hellenistic fashion,
becomes natural and cosmic law, the essential knowledge for
the true θεραπευτής and philosopher.

It was suggested above that the soteriology the opponents applied to Gentiles may have been the soteriology they
applied to Jews too. In keeping with their reform mentality,
they are insisting that Gentiles live as they insist that Jews
live. However, in Rabbinic soteriology, the obedience of
Abraham functions not as an imperative but as an indicative,
inaugurating an unconditional covenant and providing a wealth
of merit to ensure that a Jew remains in the covenant.[70] This
soteriology is close to John 8:38, whereas the soteriology of
the opponents seems closer to Matt 3:9.[71] Strack and Billerbeck claim some Rabbinic parallels to the Baptist's message,
but they are few and unconvincing.[72] The apocalyptic literature cited above seems much closer, especially 2 Baruch 57 and
58, in which the seer declares that Abraham was justified by
works--and so will Israel be justified, *if* she obeys the law.
Jubilees 23:10 also uses the argument that Abraham was justified by works in a similar imperative fashion, which is not
typical of Rabbinism.[73] The soteriology of John the Baptist--
and of the Galatian opponents--would appear to be closer to
that of such "reform literature" as Jubilees, 2 Baruch, and
4 Ezra,[74] and of such reform movements as the Qumran sectaries,
than to that of Rabbinism.[75]

Conclusions

  In Galatians there is an important tradition about
Abraham which is working in a particular way. Though there
are elements of this tradition that are found widely throughout Judaism, it is more likely to be the "apologetic" Abraham
who provides the impetus for the opponents' mission--and
explains the Galatians' sudden enthusiasm for Abraham-sonship.
This "apologetic" Abraham is known also in apocalyptic
circles:[76] and within this apocalyptic literature is a soteriology based on Abraham which may also be owned by the Galatian
opponents.

  Though it cannot be proven that this "apologetic"
Abraham was the Abraham of the opponents, certain factors suggest that it must be taken into account. As well as those
mentioned above,[77] there is the tradition of apostle, and the
self-understanding which accompanied it, examined above. The
apostle, for the Galatians, must authenticate himself as personally commissioned by God, a powerful representative of the
presence of the divine.[78] In this tradition of Abraham is
"aretalogy" which would authenticate such a self-understanding.
Further, there is much to suggest that the opponents present
Christianity as a mystery, with degrees of perfection.[79] The
Abraham who journeys on his religious quest, and who discovers
the secrets of the cosmos and God, is just the model that such
a religion demands.

CHAPTER EIGHT

TRADITIONS OF LAW

Function of the Law-Tradition
in Galatians

It has been suggested above that, in the total fabric
of Paul's argument, δικαιοσύνη comes to mean cosmic or eschatological deliverance.[1] In that the expression "justification
by faith" stands polemically over against the opponents' "justification by works of law," they must propagate a corresponding doctrine of cosmic deliverance on the basis of a program
of "works of law."[2]

Further, Paul introduces mystery-language into his
polemic on behalf of justification by faith,[3] which, being
dialogical, apparently confronts a mystical understanding of
justification by law. This is reinforced by the way πνεῦμα
is used in what is for Paul a unique way in 3:1-5, suggesting
that he is taking up the opponents' criteria. They are self-
styled πνευματικοί.[4]

Thirdly, the opponents apparently have a tradition
that speaks of "justification by faith (or grace)." They
agree that there is a sense in which the law is ineffective,
and δικαιοσύνη can only result from the δικαιοσύνη θεοῦ. But
once a man is justified by grace, their covenant understanding
demands that a man keep the law, be justified by "works of
law." There is an interplay of law, grace, and covenant, and
various meanings of δικαιοσύνη.[5]

Law and Abraham

Abraham reveals for the opponents that justification
is by law; that promise and law are complementary, and inheritance is by law; that the Mosaic covenant is a reaffirmation

115

of the Abrahamic covenant; and that the law provides the way
for one to become σπέρμα 'Αβραάμ.[6] The opponents have a strong
sense of consistency in all Israel's past saving history: each
covenant is a reaffirmation of past covenants.[7]

It is possible that the Abraham tradition that was
operating for the opponents was one that justified them in
seeing themselves as exclusivist and exalted above their congregations, having fellowship with angels and heavenly powers,
as well as being able to work wonders,[8] demonstrate their possession of the Spirit, and lay claim to esoteric, cosmic
knowledge.

Law and Moses

The centrality of Mosaic law for the opponents is
revealed by 3:17, διαθήκην προκεκυρωμένην ὑπὸ τοῦ θεοῦ ὁ μετὰ
τετρακόσια καὶ τριάκοντα ἔτη γεγονὼς νόμος οὐκ ἀκυροῖ, εἰς
τὸ καταργῆσαι τὴν ἐπαγγελίαν. Its unique function for them
is revealed by Paul's unique negative attitude towards it.
He cannot even bring himself to name Moses.[9] The most explicit
reference to him is in 3:19-20 (μεσίτης).[10] And Paul even
turns this into a derogatory title: the μεσίτης represents
only angels, and not God.[11]

That this is the intention of the verse is supported
by the context. Law and Moses are dealt with in a careful
sequence of argument that runs from 3:6 to 4:11,[12] and the
turning point of the whole sequence appears to be in 3:15-22,
which focuses on two personalities, Abraham and the μεσίτης.
Paul evidently has his eye on the opponents' self-claims,
their tradition of apostle as one who receives his gospel via
unmediated ἀποκάλυψις from God, and their tradition of Moses
and Abraham. This last is in keeping with another Jewish
tradition which appears in various circles, in which Moses'
ascent on Sinai is presented in "glorified" terms: Moses com-
munes with angels, is given a crown of light, and receives all
the secrets of heaven.[13] The opponents probably present him
as the supreme mystagogue. Then Paul appears here to be playing the opponents' claims for the Abraham-gospel against their
claims for the Moses-gospel. A true prophet or apostle must

have a direct message from God (agreed). Abraham was given
the promise directly by God (3:16-17, the διαθήκη προκεκυρωμένην ὑπὸ τοῦ θεοῦ), and there is no mention of a μεσίτης
(agreed). But Moses was a μεσίτης, and he was therefore only
spoken to by angels. So the Moses-gospel, unlike the Abraham-
gospel, has *not* come directly from God.[14] It was added (προστιθέναι), interrupting the truly heavenly Abraham-gospel or
faith-gospel.[15] This picks up the polemic of 1:6-9, where
Paul asserts that there can be only one gospel, and that an
angelic gospel can never displace that one gospel. The
Abraham-gospel is of an entirely different quality from the
Moses-gospel, and Abraham, not Moses, is the supreme mystagogue.

In keeping with this contrast of the two mystagogues
in 3:15-22, and leading up to it, Paul in 3:6-14 contrasts
law and faith as two ways of life.[16] His argument is really
very simple. He uses Hab 2:4 in a polemical way to assert
that δικαιοσύνη (life) can only be ἐκ πίστεως, therefore it
cannot be by law.[17] It is simply not in the nature of law to
be a means of δικαιοσύνη. There appears to be a contrast here
between Rom 7:10 (ἡ ἐντολὴ ἡ εἰς ζωὴν αὕτη εἰς θάνατον) and
Gal 3:21 (εἰ . . . ἐδόθη νόμος ὁ δυνάμενος ζῳοποιῆσαι, ὄντως
ἐκ νόμου ἂν ἦν ἡ δικαιοσύνη).[18] The abruptness of this contrast is explicable in terms of the contrast of the two mystagogues.[19]

In 3:15-22 itself is an unusually negative contrast
of the two covenants, the Abrahamic and the Mosaic.[20] The
promise to Abraham is compared to an already ratified treaty
or covenant to which nothing can be added (3:15-17).[21] Hence
law must be concerned with a completely different question
(τῶν παραβάσεων χάριν, 3:19),[22] and law and promise must be
antithetical (εἰ γὰρ ἐκ νόμου ἡ κληρονομία, οὐκέτι ἐξ ἐπαγγε-
λίας [3:18], paralleling the antithesis of law and faith with
respect to life in 3:11, 21).[23] In 4:21-31 these two covenants
(ἅτινά ἐστιν ἀλληγορούμενα. αὗται γάρ εἰσιν δύο διαθῆκαι
[4:24]) are opposites in every respect (παιδίσκη and ἐλευθερία,
σάρξ and ἐπαγγελία, δουλεία and ἐλευθερία, σάρξ and πνεῦμα),
which is rather strong even for Paul's writings.[24] Again, such

a contrast is explicable in terms of the particular contrast
of the two personalities who epitomise the covenants.[25]

The next pericope (3:23-29) is also understandable in
terms of this contrast. The argument against law here is a
simple historical one: ὁ νόμος παιδαγωγὸς ἡμῶν γέγονεν εἰς
Χριστόν, ἵνα ἐκ πίστεως δικαιωθῶμεν (3:24). Law came 430
years after the promise (3:17) and functions only εἰς Χριστός
(3:24). Only after this historical time period of law is
faith again possible (ἐλθούσης δὲ τῆς πίστεως οὐκέτι ὑπὸ παι-
δαγωγόν ἐσμεν [3:25]). This construction of salvation-history
is itself unique;[26] it results in charging the negative nature
of the age of law only to the law itself, the specific purpose
for which it was given (3:19), and its own inherent nature
(3:21).[27]

Again, the completely negative and "tyrannical" nature
is explicable from the contrast of the two mystagogues. The
revelation that each one receives reflects the nature of its
source. Moses' revelation comes from angels and is therefore
an enslaving revelation, which is negated when God resumes
the purpose of His own life-giving revelation to Abraham in
the work of the Messiah.

The historicising argument against the law climaxes
in the stressing of the historical event of the death of Christ,
in the next pericope (4:1-7). It may be that Paul must stress
the historical nature of both law and Christ because the opponents have a tendency to mythologise both law and Christ, just
as they have a tendency to eternalise the law with their
dogma of covenant and reenactment.[28]

This exegesis of the central argument of the *probatio*
suggests that Paul heavily rests his case on the contrast of
the two figures, Abraham and Moses. It has been suggested
that the figure of Abraham which plays an important part in
the opponents' propaganda is a certain "apologetic" Abraham.
The traditional methods of propaganda, along with Paul's sustained attack on the person of Moses, suggests that the opponents boasted of a Moses who, like their Abraham, was a "hagiography for a cult," an Abraham-type Moses. Jewish "apologetic"
did portray Abraham and Moses in parallel terms[29]--terms that
were very appealing to the Hellenistic world and Hellenistic

concepts of religion and divine men.[30] This appeal of the
divinely powerful Moses was connected with Jewish law and was
what made it appealing. Moses demonstrated such superior cosmic powers because he possessed unique insights into law--
cosmic law.[31] From Paul's argument, it is evident that Moses
and Law are being portrayed in parallel terms. This suggests
that it is a cosmic portrayal of law, accompanying an apologetic "Moses," that is partly the reason for the Galatians'
apostatising (1:6).

Finally, it must be asked, What specifically is "Law"
in the opponents' law tradition? It is clear that Paul
asserts that the opponents observe less than the "whole law"
(6:13, 5:5).[32] Each apparently charges the other with inconsistency. The opponents say Paul is inconsistent in his *rejection* of law, because he preaches circumcision.[33] Paul says the
opponents are inconsistent in their *acceptance* of law, because
they observe some but not all of the law.[34] "Works of law"
appears to mean, in Paul's letters, a "random selection" of
commandments from Israel's legal tradition,[35] perhaps especially cultic and ceremonial commandments.[36]

This is consistent with the way that, in Galatians,
only certain precepts of the law are singled out, these having
to do with calendrical observance and circumcision.[37] But
this does not mean that either Paul or his opponents think in
terms of a division between moral and ceremonial law.[38] The
opponents would admit that those things Paul says they have
failed to observe are also fully "law" (6:13), and their traditions of Abraham and Moses stress law as a totality. Nor
does Paul direct his attack only at specific precepts in question, but first deals with law in principle,[39] law as
demand.[40] When Paul calls the law παιδαγωγός (3:24), he is
speaking of the "whole law."[41]

The issue, therefore, is law as law, law in principle.
But the issue of law in principle is being debated in terms
of what law in principle has become in the light of the opponents' specific and selective demands--in terms of the "Tendenz" of this selectivity. This "Tendenz" is in two directions
in particular: the direction of differentiation and separatism,[42] and the direction of calendrical prescriptions, of

law as cosmic order. These were the terms in which Jewish law
was often understood and accepted by the Hellenistic world.[43]
But in apocalyptic literature the law of Moses is particularly
understood as the law of cosmic order.[44]

Law and the στοιχεῖα τοῦ κόσμου

Attention must now be directed to the relationship
between the law and the στοιχεῖα τοῦ κόσμου. It has been
shown above that the analysis of genre and structure have
implications for the place of the expression in the whole
scheme of Paul's argument against justification by law: 4:8-11
is not a sudden diversion from the question of the Galatians'
adoption of the program of the intruders. The unity of the
letter does not allow divisions into errors of Galatians and
errors of intruders. Three further considerations are now
called for.

Firstly, δικαιοσύνη in Galatians comes to mean cosmic
or eschatological deliverance,[45] and the eschatological terms
κόσμος and αἰών play an essential role in defining δικαιοσύνη
in this way. Therefore the word κόσμος should not be allowed
to fall out of the expression στοιχεῖα τοῦ κόσμου. Bandstra
states correctly that the meaning and function of κόσμος is
crucial in determining the meaning of this last phrase.[46]

Secondly, both here and in Colossians there is a unique
use of στοιχεῖον. In Heb 5:12 and 6:1 the word is best translated "first principles" and is neither positive nor negative.
2 Pet 3:10 refers by στοιχεῖον to the material elements of the
universe, again in a neutral sense. But the term in Galatians
(and Colossians) has a decidedly negative sense. It is not
enough to say that the στοιχεῖα are merely "temporary and
ineffectual for salvation."[47] They enslave (δουλοῦν [4:3]);
and in the parallels between the στοιχεῖα τοῦ κόσμου of 4:3,
the ἐπίτροποι καὶ οἰκονόμοι of 4:2, and (through the parallel
of στοιχεῖα τοῦ κόσμου of 4:3 and the experience of being ὑπὸ
νόμος [4:5]) the παιδαγωγός of 3:24,[48] the στοιχεῖα τοῦ κόσμου
are equated with decidedly coercive powers. They are not
"temporary or ineffectual for salvation," or neutral in the
sense of Heb 5:12 and 6:1; their period of domination is one

of hopeless enslavement, during which all mankind is held
fast under lock and key by a jailor (3:23, φρουρεῖν, συγκλεί-
ειν).[49]

    Thirdly, allowance must be made for the uniqueness of
Paul's reference to historic Israel in Galatians. In 4:3
Israel was under the στοιχεῖα τοῦ κόσμου and in slavery, just
as in 4:24 Sinai bears children for slavery.[50] But in 4:8, 9
Paul parallels οἱ φύσει μὴ ὄντες θεοί[51] to the στοιχεῖα τοῦ
κόσμου. The latter become the equivalent of pagan dieties,
and the striking word πάλιν (used twice in 4:9) clearly relates
the service of the στοιχεῖα τοῦ κόσμου to the Galatians' pagan
past.

    But this same πάλιν reveals Paul's meaning to be that
the Jews, from Moses to Christ, worshipped οἱ φύσει μὴ ὄντες
θεοί.[52] Judaism and Paganism alike are nothing but "pre-
Christian religion."[53] Elsewhere, Paul says Jews have "much
advantage" (Rom 3:2) because they possess the oracles of God:
that adherents of law will be fellow-heirs with those who
inherit by faith (Rom 14:16); and that historic Israel is
blessed abundantly because to her belong ἡ υἱοθεσία καὶ ἡ δόξα
καὶ αἱ διαθῆκαι καὶ ἡ νομοθεσία καὶ ἡ λατρεία καὶ αἱ ἐπαγγελίαι,
ὧν οἱ πατέρες (Rom 9:4-5). Israel has priority in the history
of redemption (Rom 11:17-24).[54]

    Paul can speak negatively of Israel's experience else-
where, e.g., Rom 9:30-33,[55] but the negative stress is because
of Israel's rejection of the offer of grace which was always
present along with the law (Rom 9:32, 10:5-13, 1 Cor 10:1-11,
etc.). However, in Galatians grace has fallen completely out
of Israel's history, and there is only a stark periodization:
an era of law followed by an era of grace (3:23, 24).[56]

    It is not the expression στοιχεῖα τοῦ κόσμου that
creates the negative tone of the portrayal. Rather, the
expression is caught up into a particular negative fabric of
argument. It seems no coincidence that Paul's only letter to
speak of Israel in this fashion also speaks of her bondage to
the στοιχεῖα τοῦ κόσμου which becomes a bondage to φύσει μὴ
ὄντες θεοί. Thus there is in Galatians a uniqueness in speaking of justification as deliverance from the κόσμος; a uniquely
negative use of στοιχεῖα; a unique equation of historic Israel

and paganism; and a uniquely negative way of speaking of the
law. This complex of expressions must be allowed their holistic force, and it is within this holistic complex that the
expression στοιχεῖα τοῦ κόσμου must be interpreted.[57]

     The place of 4:1-11 in the argument of chapters 3 and
4 should be reviewed.[58] The crucial phrase here is νῦν δὲ
γνόντες θεόν, μᾶλλον δὲ γνωσθέντες ὑπὸ θεοῦ, πῶς ἐπιστρέφετε
πάλιν ἐπὶ τὰ ἀσθενῆ καὶ πτωχὰ στοιχεῖα, οἷς πάλιν ἄνωθεν δουλεύειν θέλετε (4:9). By γνόντες θεόν, μᾶλλον δὲ γνωσθέντες
ὑπὸ θεοῦ, Paul evidently refers to the experience he placed
at the beginning of the *probatio*--the Galatians' acceptance of
Christianity. There he used terms of initiation into and perfection in a mystery religion (ἐνάρχεσθαι and ἐπιτελεῖν, 3:3),
and the suggested irony is, You were initiated into one religion, and are seeking perfection in another, and can therefore
only be called ἀνόητοι, people who are impervious to the deep
secrets of religion: you may have received the Spirit εἰκῆ.
The same pattern recurs here in 4:9. The expression γνόντες
θεόν, μᾶλλον δὲ γνωσθέντες ὑπὸ θεοῦ has important parallels
in Hellenistic religion, where it refers to experience of the
divine through gnosis, the highest level of religious awareness.[59] ἐπιστρέφειν (4:9) therefore denotes a complete apostasy from the deep things of religion, as does the sequence of
beginning and ending in 3:1-5. And again, Paul laments that
his labors in initiating the Galatians into the mystery of
Christianity may have been εἰκῆ (4:11). So here, as in 3:1-5,
are the sequence of beginning and ending, the mystery terms
that add force to the sequence, and the lament, fearful to
the mystes, that all may have been εἰκῆ. In this case, 4:8-11
returns to the primary cause of the dispute dealt with in the
probatio--the Galatians' acceptance of an álien religion.

     Paul elaborates the precise point at which this apos-
tasy is taking place: ἡμέρας παρατηρεῖσθε καὶ μῆνας καὶ καιροὺς καὶ ἐνιαυτούς (4:10).[60] There are striking Jewish parallels to this formulation, especially in Eth Enoch and other
apocalyptic literature.[61] In this apocalyptic law-tradition,
the orders of creation become identified with the Torah, and
knowledge of the former safeguards the latter.[62] These parallels tend to confirm the suggestion based on genre and

structure analysis--it is because of the new religion which
the Galatians have adopted, especially in terms of cultic festivals, that Paul says they are returning to the worship of
the στοιχεῖα.

    That the opponents provided the precedent for this
equation is further suggested by the tradition that connects
angels with the giving of the law that appears in 3:19.[63] They
used the tradition obviously to enhance the law,[64] and Paul has
turned it on its head. Therefore the way Paul stresses personal powers in connection with the law, and speaks of angels
in connection with the giving of the law, seems to be directly
related. Although Reicke may move too quickly in identifying
the angels of 3:19 directly with the στοιχεῖα,[65] it would seem
that Paul speaks of these angels as belonging to a larger class
called στοιχεῖα--and that the opponents have provided him with
the precedent for this language.

    The relationship of Gal 4:1-11 to Colossians 2 must
next be examined, as these are the only two passages in the
New Testament to use the expression στοιχεῖα τοῦ κόσμου.[66]

    Christology plays an important role in the polemic
against the Colossian heresy. The letter stresses that in
Christ κατοικεῖ πᾶν τὸ πλήρωμα τῆς θεότητος σωματικῶς, at
every point of His career, and particularly on the cross.[67]
In the context, there is a confrontation of the powers of the
universe (ἀρχαί καί . . . ἐκουσίαι [2:10, 15]) and Christ,[68]
the powers competing for the worship due to Christ. This
worship of the powers is referred to as θρησκεία τῶν ἀγγέλων
in 2:18, heightening the personification of these cosmic
forces.[69] In 2:8 and 2:20 these ἀρχαί, ἐξουσίαι, and ἀγγέλοι
are summed up as στοιχεῖα τοῦ κόσμου.[70] Thus this expression,
in the Colossian debate, stands for the cosmic powers and
angels who are competing for the lordship and πλήρωμα[71] that
belongs only to Christ.

    The opposing teaching is a φιλοσοφία (2:8), having
its own παράδοσις that has been received through mysterious
vision (2:18). It is this φιλοσοφία and παράδοσις that is
attacked by the subordination of all στοιχεῖα to Christ. The
implication, then, is that the expression στοιχεῖα τοῦ κόσμου
belongs to the heresy itself.[72]

When the heretics' festivals are attacked (ἑορτῆς ἤ
νεομηνίας ἤ σαββάτων [2:16]) it is because they are intimately
connected with the veneration of the στοιχεῖα τοῦ κόσμου. As
in Galatians, the sign of the periodic cycles of nature is
especially related to the word κόσμος in the phrase στοιχεῖα
τοῦ κόσμου.[73]

It is more than coincidental that two heresies that
propagate calendrical festivals both come to attract the
expression στοιχεῖα τοῦ κόσμου.[74] In Colossians the term is
clearly occasional and must belong to the heretics themselves
--offering support for the contention that it does also in
Galatians. This Colossian heresy of worship of the στοιχεῖα
has its Jewish features, and its own version of veneration of
the law. And the strongly personal as well as cosmic character of the στοιχεῖα must be significant for the meaning of the
term in Galatians.

The history of religions evidence for the meaning of
the term will now be examined. It should be borne in mind
here what is being sought. Firstly, the Galatian opponents
have evidently laid themselves open to the equation of their
religion with the Galatians' pagan past because their law-
tradition is bound up with an interest in the cosmic elements,
cosmic order, and angels. They do not necessarily worship the
elements, but this suggestion, along with that of personification of the elements and equation of them with angels, is
present.

Secondly, the Galatians, as ex-pagans, are expected to
immediately recognize Paul's twist of the opponents' position
out of their own pagan past; they must know a δουλεία to στοιχεῖα which is a worship of θεοί in a real sense. Thus, two
kinds of external parallels will be relevant. The Jewish
parallels will be considered below. They must be a complexity
of all the factors that are found together in the law-tradition
as it has been sketched so far, and need only provide the suggestions necessary for the dialogical twist of 4:8-11 to work.
However, the pagan parallels, which will be considered here,
should reveal a real worship of the στοιχεῖα, which provides
an analogy according to which Judaism can be represented in
propaganda as devotion to στοιχεῖα τοῦ κόσμου.

The relevant sources have already been competently
presented in several places and need not be exhaustively reproduced here.[75] However, in the light of Delling's assertion
that, on the whole, στοιχεῖον in the ancient texts means "basic
materials," and that it is unlikely that the term was used in
Paul's day in the sense of "spiritual forces,"[76] some of the
evidence should be examined again.

The doctrine of the four elements, from which all
visible things proceed, goes back to Empedocles, Plato, and
Aristotle.[77] The stoa, too, took over the doctrine of the
four στοιχεῖα from which the cosmos arises.[78] It is evidently
a development of this doctrine that becomes the speculative
cosmology of the mystery religions, where men can obtain freedom from εἱμαρμένη through the power of the deity, which is
greater than that of the elements of the stars.[79]

Philo polemicizes against those who worship the elements as though they were gods,[80] as he polemicizes against
the doctrine of εἱμαρμένη.[81] This evidence strongly suggests
that the practice of worship of the στοιχεῖα was well established in the first century, as does the even more virulent
criticism of second century writers.[82]

But there is further evidence that must be considered.
Bultmann has observed that the same concern for cosmology and
εἱμαρμένη as in the mysteries appears in more "gnostic" systems.[83] Here, however, the stars and cosmic bodies establish
this grip of man in fate.[84] Delling admits a close connection
in the texts between the elements and the stars.[85] Stoicism
since Posidonius taught that destiny is controlled by the
heavenly bodies.[86] It becomes evident that these "gnostic"
cosmological systems, with their own doctrine of εἱμαρμένη,
are also a development of the stoic doctrine of the στοιχεῖα.[87]

This equation of στοιχεῖα with stars, at a time early
in the first century, and criticism of the worship of stars at
the same time, must be further evidence for a conception of
στοιχεῖα as personalised powers, controlling man's fate, in
Paul's day. The cosmological systems themselves attribute
great power to these heavenly bodies. Poimandres, perhaps one
of the earliest cosmologies,[88] portrays man in slavery to
εἱμαρμένη and the planetary gods. That such cosmologies must

have existed very early in the first century is now strongly
suggested by several of the Nag Hammadi tractates, which give
evidence of a development from pre-Christian to Christian
gnosticism.[89] Thus these widespread evidences of speculation
regarding the power of the stars and planets and their control
of man's fate, probably leading back to the first century,
supports Dodd's contention that " . . . in Philo's day the
sun and moon and other heavenly bodies were regarded in certain
circles as διοικηταὶ τῶν συμπάντων."[90] There should be no
objection to the position that the στοιχεῖα, in the Paganism
of Paul's day, were regarded as personal, potent powers dom-
inating the lives of men, and it is out of such a backbround
that the Galatians probably understand Paul's dialogical twist
of the opponents' own propaganda. This suggests that the
opponents' own law-tradition must itself be open to such a
dialogical twist.

                    *   *   *

     In conclusion, the threads of this argument must be
drawn together to illuminate the significance of the phrase
στοιχεῖα τοῦ κόσμου for the opponents' law tradition.
     The phrase belongs in a pattern of argument in which
Paul speaks in a unique way of justification, the στοιχεῖα,
Israel, and the law. The phrase στοιχεῖα τοῦ κόσμου does not
give the argument its uniqueness, but must be taken up into
this uniqueness, and must carry a connotation consistent with
the argument as a whole, which is particularly negative regarding Judaism and the law. Exegetical considerations reveal how
the passage (4:8-11) is an integral part of Paul's attack on
the intruding theology. Chapter 4:10 reveals the precise
point at which the charge of worship of the *stoikeia* is earned.
And these religious observances have probably been introduced
by the opponents (in fact, they may in particular reveal what
the opponents understand by "law"). The phrase itself probably
belongs to the opponents, as a comparison with Colossians suggests; and this comparison also indicates that the *stoikeia*
are personal powers, competitors for the worship of Christ.[91]
The pagan evidence of the worship of the *stoikeia* indicates

the sort of concerns (*heimarmene*, *stoikeia* and the stars,
cosmic order, etc.) that the opponents' law-tradition is open
to have attached to it. When this law-tradition is held up to
such a mirror out of a pagan past, this is what the Galatians
see. Thus Paul's use of the expression στοιχεῖα τοῦ κόσμου is
related in a particularly close way to his attack on the opposing law-tradition and indicates a great deal about the law-
tradition itself.

Conclusions for the Law-Tradition
as Functioning in Galatians

Law is seen operating as part of a program of cosmic
deliverance, couched in mystery language, and especially
attached to Moses, who is the supreme mystagogue (probably a
Moses in the style of the apologetic Abraham) who receives
the law by heavenly revelation. It is a law-tradition that
calls forth an unusually negative treatment from Paul. The
period of bondage under law is because of the nature of law
itself. Law is dealt with in principle. But it is law in
principle as indicated by the "Tendenz" of the opponents'
selectivity--that is, exclusivism and calendrical observance.
This, in fact, is how the Hellenistic world often understood
Jewish law.

Bondage to the law is presented as bondage to the
στοιχεῖα τοῦ κόσμου, not only in the Galatians' present apostasy, but also in Israel's past history. It is the opponents'
law-tradition that makes possible this analogy of Israel's
past history and Pagan worship of *stocheia* as gods. When the
stocheia are conceived in such terms, history-of-religions
evidence reveals that concerns of fate, cosmic order, et
cetera, are present--and this in itself reveals something of
the intruding law-tradition.

Possible Sources of the Law-Tradition

Gnosticism

When Paul writes to the church at Corinth, in which
"gnosticising" principles are at work,[92] he is able to put

"gnostic" language to work,[93] retain an openness to the work
of the Spirit, and refuse to place the church under a nomistic
principle,[94] but at the same time he incorporates important
correctives into his teaching that prevent their being
exploited by the enthusiasm for *sophia* and *gnosis* in the community.[95] But in Galatians he also uses language that has
been productive in Gnosticism (3:19-21, 4:8-11 in conjunction
with 4:1-7; see below) and has used no corrective. It would
be wrong, in the light of Paul's other letters and the second-
century conflict between Gnosticism and the church, to assume
that Paul was a Gnostic.[96] It is much more logical to assume
that Gnosticism was not present in Galatia.

        The suggestion of Gal 3:19 is that the law has come,
not from God, but from angels. But this is Paul's twist of
the opponents' position. They have connected the giving of
the law and angels in a way that exalts the law.[97] This makes
their concept of Jewish law a very un-Gnostic one.[98] The same
dynamic is involved in 4:10: Paul can equate the new religion
with a return to the worship of the elements because the new
religion evidently has a high view of the elements of the uni-
verse--again, very un-Gnostic.[99]

        Later Gnostic use of Paul's arguments in Galatia
should also be considered. Paul in the second century became
the "Gnostic apostle," and the early church never attempted to
use the arguments of Galatians against Gnostics.[100] Gnostic
tractates themselves, such as the Valentinian Gospel of
Philip[101] which makes particular use of Galatians,[102] reveal
that it was precisely the passages of Galatians that deal with
nomism that are taken up, giving Paul the reputation of the
"Gnostic apostle."[103] If "Gnosticism" is a useful criterion
in the assessment of Galatians, it can only demonstrate that
Gnosticism was not an issue in the Galatian context.[104]

Jewish Law and Hellenistic Wisdom

        The way in which the law-tradition is working in
Galatians suggests that parallels should be sought in the
literature of the "larger Hellenistic movement of higher wisdom
by revelation.[105] There was here a connection of wisdom and

the doctrine of creation, so that wisdom became the basic
principle in the ordering of the cosmos.[106] Further, wisdom
was identified with law, a development that began perhaps with
Sirach,[107] so that there is a direct relationship between the
laws of the cosmos and the laws of God.[108] At the same time
there was a tendency for God to become transcendent and
abstract, with a resultant growth in "middle beings" who
interposed between God and man--both in Palestine and in the
Diaspora.[109] Finally, this movement, with its doctrine of
revelation and inspiration, was the one to which the tradition
of apostle, examined above, belonged.[110] Some of the circles
which shared in this development, and the way in which they
shared in it, will now be examined.

Philo

Philo presents Abraham and Moses in terms of the same
basic pattern. Moses is one of the greatest heroes of the
Jewish past, to be followed and imitated by the true worship-
per of God.[111] He is a prophet who speaks not of himself but
of God.[112] He is god and king of the whole race.[113] He, too,
turns from paganism to worship the true God; and he, too, is
a great astrologer, understanding the secrets of the cosmos.[114]
In fact, he is the supreme mystagogue, who receives the ultimate revelation of God's law.[115]

Because the law of nature and the law of God are
closely identified, so, too, are the law of God and the one
who receives this revelation of the law.[116] He can speak of
the divine character of Moses.[117] In this man there is a combination of mortal and immortal.[118] Therefore, there is an
unbreakable harmony between the law and order of the cosmos
and the moral law. the torah.[119] In addition, the divine-
human figure, Moses, because of his identification with this
law, exercises power over the cosmos--and the *elements of the
universe*.[120] Regarding the στοιχεῖα, Philo seems to take an
ambivalent position, on the one hand acknowledging their role
in law and cosmic order, yet, on the other, warning against
the worship of them.[121]

There is the same ambivalence in his treatment of
astrology. It is an essential part of the knowledge of God,
and the founders of the religion of Israel were the greatest
astrologers.[122] But on the other hand he condemns any worship
of the stars or fate.[123] One gets the impression that Judaism
as he presented it laid itself very much open to the charge
of being nothing but adoration of the cosmos.[124] Especially
in his very favorable portrayal of the θεραπευταί and their
attention to the sun, the seasons, et cetera,[125] must he empha-
size that they do not do what in fact they appear to do--wor-
ship the heavenly bodies and εἱμαρμένη. Josephus has his
Essenes do exactly that.[126] In fact, there is much to suggest
that, on the popular level, Israel's religion was practised in
terms of magic and astrology.[127]

Thus these traditions of Moses, cosmos, and law, as
they are found in Philo, could possibly account for some
aspects of the opponents' "law-heresy." With the Therapeutai
is the suggestion of a bridge between Philo and Palestinian
piety; and, in fact, it will become evident that much of this
law-tradition does not only belong to Philo, but is found in
other bodies of Jewish literature.[128]

Josephus

Josephus also identifies Abraham and Moses closely, as
has been seen above. Perhaps more than in Philo, Moses is the
impressive representative of God who can overcome all opposition by his miraculous prowess.[129] This impressiveness in the
natural order is intricately bound up with his association
with law.[130] This is because the law of God is directly concerned with nature, the fruitful earth, the peaceful sea, et
cetera.[131] The ten words written by God are a heavenly letter
making possible a εὐδαίμων βίος,[132] because the purpose of the
law is to promote life, both physical and spiritual.[133] In
keeping with this, the Temple is understood in cosmological
terms, as in Philo. It depicts the order of the four cosmic
στοιχεῖα.[134] Because the Tabernacle is a symbol of the
universe, these must be the laws of the God of the universe.
The Jews follow a cosmic law-code.[135]

Apocalyptic Literature

In this literature, as in Josephus and Philo, Moses is the supreme mystagogue, and Sinai is a mystical ascent and occasion of revelation of the secrets of the universe.[136]

In keeping with the wisdom traditions in which the literature shares, there is a mystical correlation of Torah, the order of the cosmos, the righteousness of Israel, and the ultimate fate of man.[137] It has been noted above that calendrical piety was central to apocalyptic; and evidently for good reason. In 1 Enoch the law and order of the cosmos is matter for "essential revelation" (chaps. 72-79); and especially must the righteous be told the alternations in the movement of the heavenly bodies.[138] The fates of men are linked, in these eschatological schemes, with the order and movement of the cosmos.[139] The two laws, the law of order and of creation, and the Torah, come to be identified as one.[140] Moses the lawgiver fits into this role. The laws given to him are especially the laws of cosmic order and of the secrets of the universe, and the way out of cosmic disorder.[141] They are essential to those who would fellowship with the angels and the "middle beings."[142] The concept of the law of Israel as universal law which, in Philo and Josephus, leads to heroic portrayals of Israel's leading figures, here leads to the demand for perfect obedience to calendrical law.[143]

This intensification of the demands of the law[144] leads to a heightened sense of the remnant, which is both fully obedient and fully predestined to salvation.[145] Further, in keeping with the wisdom movement and its understanding of revelation and inspiration,[146] righteousness and wisdom are identical, and the first and basic redemptive gift to the righteous is wisdom.[147] The law is heavenly and esoteric. True insight into the law must be a heavenly gift,[148] and, conversely, heavenly insight or wisdom comes only to those who search out the Torah.[149] Thus the law is couched in mystery-language, and the "righteousness of the law" can be conceived as participation in a mystery.[150] It could be referred to as "nomistic enthusiasm." The keeping of the law brings Lady Wisdom.

There are even angelic guardians of the law.[151] There
seems to be a relationship here to the Pagan concept of στοιχεῖα. The four archangels may take the place of the four elements;[152] and angels, elements, astral bodies, and their functions appear interchangeable.[153] In later literature in which
the same traditions are taken up, the "elements" are described
as beings who appear to be persons, and who are the cosmic
rulers of the darkness of this age.[154] Some of this literature shows striking parallels to material from Qumran.[155]

Here is a law-tradition which shows a close correlation to the one functioning in Galatia. There is a radical
nomism. Law is couched in mystery language, and the one who
has insights into the law is one who is granted personal revelations from heaven; and the Torah comes to be identified
with cosmic law and order. There is a vital relationship
between calendrical piety and the righteousness of the righteous; and righteousness, or entrance into the mysteries of
the law, is with a view to participating in the cosmic ordering of history and securing a place in the age to come.[156]
Angels have an important role in the administration of the law,
and the Pagan concept of στοιχεῖα seems to be passing over into
concepts of the role of angels.[157] This literature shares
views of revelation and inspiration with "apologetic" literature;[158] and with respect to law, the role of Moses here is
close to his "hagiographic" role in that literature. It is
not impossible that the opponents have combined the cultic
function of heroes in "apologetic" Judaism with the above
aspects of Torah tradition in apocalyptic literature.[159] In
fact, this would be expected if the traditions of apocalyptic
Judaism were taken into an apologetic setting--such as a missionary campaign to the Gentiles.

Qumran Literature

Qumran literature, too, shares in and even intensifies
some of the characteristics of the "hasidic wisdom tradition."[160] A sharpening of the demands of the law accompanies
an expectation of an imminent apocalyptic end.[161] But this
intense preoccupation with the law, and a consciousness of

being a righteous remnant of Israel,[162] in fact leads to a
break between the community and the geographical focus of
Israel's law, Jerusalem.[163] This simultaneous zeal for law
and rejection of the temple led to both modifications in law
observance[164] and an idealisation of Jerusalem.[165]

Part of this sense of sharpening of the law is a sense
of a continuity in the covenants of God. "Sinai was itself
but a rearticulation of that which God had previously made
. . . with Abraham, Isaac, and Jacob."[166] Thus the "New Covenant"[167] of the sectaries was an intensification of the eternal covenant that had been constantly reaffirmed with Israel.[168]

Here, in keeping with the "wisdom" tradition, law is
a mystery[169] and can only be fully understood through heavenly
revelation.[170] This heavenly revelation, in turn, is given to
the one who devotes himself to the law,[171] and it constitutes
one a member of the eternal communion of the nonmortal beings
of the celestial realm.[172] The hasidic teacher of the law
receives almost a missionary commission.[173]

There is, further, a vital connection between the law
and order of the cosmos and the law given to men.[174] The
intense desire of the community to live according to the structure of the universe[175] is revealed in the concern to observe
a particular festal calendar.[176] A life according to the
Torah, corresponding to the laws of creation and the course of
history, is only possible with the correct calculation of time
revealed by God.[177] The "exact interpretation of the law"
becomes in particular the exact observance of the calendrical
festivals according to the community's own reckoning,[178] and
the "New Covenant" is identified constantly with the correct
interpretation and observation of the festivals.[179] This preoccupation with cosmic order is especially evident in that the
"hidden things" that are "revealed" to the obedient in their
quest to understand the law are the Sabbaths, festivals, et
cetera.[180] It is not surprising that some have found in these
texts close parallels to Gal 4:10.[181]

The Qumran sectaries gave angels an important place in
the ordering of the cosmos, drew close connections between
angels and heavenly bodies, and saw a strong astral influence
in the lives of men.[182] Particularly interesting are the

references to the apparently angelic/astral figure, the "Prince
of Lights."[183]   Because the cosmos is so ordered by these spiritual powers, there is a close connection between man's observance of cosmic order and his fellowship with the angels.[184]
Hence observance of "God's truth," or His law, of which an
essential part is calendrical observance,[185] becomes for
another reason a participation in a mystery.[186]   There is
mounting evidence of the practice of astrology in Qumran,[187]
which must belong with this cosmic concern. There is the same
ambivalence here as in Philo: the warnings of Jubilees were
not heeded.[188]

        This community also had a great concern for righteous-
ness--a concern which shows both continuity and contrast with
Paul's argument for righteousness by faith in Galatians.[189]
The sectaries speak of God's righteousness in two principal
senses: the perfection of God in contrast to the sinfulness
of man,[190] and God's work of pardon or cleansing of man[191]
through משפט (justification) by the צדקה (righteousness) of
God.[192]   Man's righteousness is spoken of in three ways: the
covenantal sense of the community as the righteous elect;[193]
the unrighteousness of man before God and the need of cleansing
and justification by His mercy or grace;[194] and, significantly
for this study, human righteousness by works of law.[195]   The
aim of God's grace is always consistent with His repeatedly
confirmed covenant, and the man who is justified by grace will
then be justified by his law obedience.[196]   Being righteous
involves doing the law. This is the condition of remaining
elect.[197]   The doctrine of justification by grace is accompanied by a standard of obedience far stricter than that of
the rabbis.[198]

        In conclusion, there is here a sharing of various tra-
ditions regarding the law with other literature (law and cosmic order, the law as a mystery, etc.), though several strands
are strengthened. There is a vigorous awareness of the community as both separated from the rest of humanity and also
taken up into the fellowship of divine beings. Because of the
break with the geographical centre of the law, there is both
modification and idealization of law.

In at least one strand of law-tradition in the documents,[199] the "new covenant" is associated especially with the
calendrical and cultic feasts. There is a close connection
between these last and the orders of creation. The intense
interest in the calendar is part of an intense interest in the
governing forces of the cosmos and a desire to live in harmony
with the cosmos.

There is an emphasis on the grace of God and, at the
same time, an understanding of covenant in terms of continuity
which places alongside justification by grace a justification
by law and a demand for perfect obedience to law. This concern for justification is in the context of a search for deliverance from mortality and the cosmos.

Conclusions

In all of the above traditions there is evidence of
certain law-traditions that are held as common property--in
particular, the law as the basis for cosmic order, the law as
that which ensures harmony between man and his cosmos, and a
relation between the law and angels or powerful spiritual
forces in the universe. Law is conceived as a mystery, and
Judaism as a mystery religion.

This common core of law-traditions is strikingly
parallel to the law-tradition evidently held by the opponents,
which becomes apparent in the mystery language of 3:1-5 and
4:8-11, the connection between law and angels in 3:19 and
between the false gospel and angels in 1:6-9, the relation
between law and cosmic order evidently behind 4:8-11, and the
reference to calendrical piety. It is a law-tradition which
matches the way law is dealt with in Galatians as a principle,
but as a principle in terms of the selective "Tendenz" of the
opponents, with their stress on calendrical law.

It is therefore a law-tradition which can explain how
the opponents' law teaching, while not advocating the adoration of the στοιχεῖα as gods, is yet very much open to a
propaganda attack which makes it analogous to pagan devotion
to the στοιχεῖα. Philo perhaps struggles against just such
an equation of his law-tradition with Pagan astrology and

veneration of cosmic forces; and his law-tradition is shared
in many respects with apocalyptic and Qumran traditions regarding the law and cosmic order, which are also open to such an
analogy. This illuminates the dynamic involved in the way
Paul brings the στοιχεῖα into the argument. The opponents
evidently exalt the στοιχεῖα and their place in the mainte-
nance of lawful cosmic order. Paul parallels them to the
στοιχεῖα that the Pagan Galatians have served in the past,
making them--and therefore the law they enforce--enslaving
instruments that come not from God but from the forces of evil.
Judaism is suddenly just another pre-Christian religion, and
Israel's past history is analogous to Pagan worship of στοιχεῖα. The Galatians have begun with one religion but are now
seeking initiation into another--which is really the one they
left when they first became Christians.

        Apart from these common law-traditions, some of the
particular emphases of the Qumran documents appear to be significant, such as the intensification of the law, the identification of the law especially with the sacred calendar (both
also in apocalyptic literature), the assumption that all the
Old Testament covenants are consecutive reaffirmations of one
eternal covenant, and the different definitions of righteousness, so that a righteousness by grace apart from works is
held to alongside a righteousness by works.

        Besides these emphases of Qumran, the propaganda
technique of apologetic literature (as in Philo and Josephus),
and the portrayal of Moses as a religious hero, appear to be
particularly congruous with the opponents' self-understanding,
their evident exaltation of Moses as the supreme mystagogue
(see on 3:15-20), and equation of Abraham and Moses (where
Paul has apparently accepted their first religious hero, Abraham, and rejected the second).

        There would seem to be good reason for suggesting that
the opponents have combined traditions similar to those of
Qumran with those of the "apologetic" tradition.[200] Firstly,
they are congruous,[201] and much of their law-traditions
appears to be common property. Secondly, the Qumran literature is not apologetic. It would be expected that apologetic
techniques would be used if ever such a law-theology were

presented to Pagans. Qumran reveals how far a nomistic community can go in making law a cosmic mystery. Apologetic
literature reveals the method that may have been used to make
this Jewish law-mystery appealing to Gentiles. And thirdly,
in Qumran, too, the tradition of the religious hero appears.
In the Genesis Apocryphon is found the same impressive Abraham
as in the "apologetic" literature.

        This law-tradition suggests how Paul can charge the
nomists with failure to keep the "whole law." The opponents
evidently understand law particularly as calendar observance,
perhaps even in the sense that the Qumran community does.[202]
Josephus closely equates the observance of Jewish law throughout the world with the observance of the Sabbath and Jewish
festivals;[203] and other ancient authors associate Jewish law
especially with these observances.[204] It is possible that, in
their combination of apocalyptic and apologetic traditions of
law, the opponents have taught the Galatians only those aspects
of law that fit readily into the cosmological and mystical
understanding of law. Thus Paul refers to this law-tradition
in terms of mystery rites, and to Judaism in terms of mystery
religion and a devotion to the στοιχεῖα. It leads only to a
failure to keep the "whole law."

CHAPTER NINE

THE TRADITION OF THE SACRAMENTS

By "sacrament" will be meant here "an act which by
natural means puts supranatural powers in effect,"[1] and the
two sacraments considered here will be circumcision and baptism. There is little debate that the latter can be called a
"sacrament":[2] and though the *Encyclopaedia Judaica* asserts
that the former cannot be,[3] Goodenough appears correct when he
observes that, because of its function, the term "sacrament"
should be applied to circumcision too.[4] The significant question here is the function of circumcision, and of baptism, in
the theology of the opponents.

The Function of the Tradition
in Galatians

Circumcision

The necessity for circumcision in the opponents'
scheme has been pointed out above and becomes even more evident when the unusual nature of Paul's attack on circumcision
is considered. Unlike 1 Cor 7:17-24, where circumcision
becomes one of the ἀδιάφορα,[5] Paul here says not only "you
need not be circumcised," but "you *must* not (5:2-4)."[6] In
Rom 2:25-29 he can say περιτομὴ . . . ὠφελεῖ ἐὰν νόμον πράσσῃς;
but in Gal 5:2-4 he says ἐὰν περιτέμνησθε Χριστὸς ὑμᾶς οὐδὲν
ὠφελήσει, and you are cut off from Christ. It was commented
above that in Romans 2 Paul brings together physical and spiritual circumcision as was done by Philo and the Qumran sectaries;[7] but in Galatians he will not even discuss spiritual
circumcision or use the argument that Christianity is the true,
spiritual circumcision, as in Col 2:11-13 and Phil 3:3. This
suggests that the opponents themselves were propagating the

139

necessity of both physical and spiritual circumcision and the
indissoluble connection between the two.[8]

The opponents are Christians and hold to a justification by faith, which is followed by a justification by works--
which, from Gal 5:2-4, is epitomised by circumcision (ἐὰν
περιτέμνησθε, Χριστὸς ὑμᾶς οὐδὲν ὠφελήσει . . . κατηργήθητε
ἀπὸ Χριστοῦ οἵτινες ἐν νόμῳ δικαιοῦσθε). As Christians, they
undoubtedly practice a baptism that makes effectual for them a
"justification by faith" (as is suggested by the way 2:16-21
develops the meaning of baptism). But it is probably a baptism
which is only a beginning initiatory rite to be followed by
further, advanced rites.[9] As Genesis portrays their hero Abraham, the order of salvation is faith, then circumcision; so, in
their propaganda, the order of salvation for Gentiles is probably baptism, then circumcision.[10] This would help explain
Paul's reluctance to argue from Abraham's circumcision, as he
does in Rom 4:11. In Rom 4:1-2, Paul states that Abraham first
believed and was then circumcised--and makes a sound argument
for the priority of faith. But the opponents' position may
have been exactly that of Rom 4:11, speaking of Abraham, καὶ
σημεῖον ἔλαβεν περιτομῆς, σφραγῖδα τῆς δικαιοσύνης τῆς πίστεως
τῆς ἐν τῇ ἀκροβυστίᾳ, stressing circumcision as the sign of
the Abrahamic covenant (which, as seen above, they made con-
tiguous with all covenants). This would explain why Paul in
Galatians is fearful of mentioning the circumcision of Abraham
at all, or the "spiritual" circumcision of the Christian.[11]

The Galatians' evident sudden attraction to circumcision is as unusual as is Paul's uncompromising attack on it.
Acceptance of circumcision by Gentiles in the Hellenistic
world must have been exceedingly rare,[12] and it was *not* among
those features of Judaism to which Gentiles were attracted.[13]
The older Sibyllines require washing only, not circumcision,
for Gentile converts,[14] and Diaspora Judaism desired to make
Gentiles only "Noachides" or "God-fearers," not complete
Jews.[15] The Hellenistic world regarded circumcision as a bar-
baric rite,[16] a criticism that Jewish propaganda was sensitive
to.[17] In fact, it may be that Gal 5:12 picks up the Galatians'
earlier attitude to circumcision: ὄφελον καὶ ἀποκόψονται οἱ

ἀναστατοῦντες ὑμᾶς.[18] If so, their sudden attraction to it is
even more paradoxical.

It is evident, therefore, both from Paul's "violent
reaction"[19] to circumcision, and the Galatians' highly unusual
enthusiasm for it, that it not only occupied an essential
place in the opponents' scheme but probably functioned with all
the power of a sacrament--and a climactic sacrament, at that.

Baptism

It has been argued above that in Gal 3:27-29 baptism
is not suddenly introduced for no reason, but has been in Paul's
thinking all along. In fact, 2:19-20 and 3:1-5 are polemically
developing the significance of baptism; and again, in 5:24, he
returns to the subject of the eschatological significance of
the rite.[20] Whereas, in Paul, baptism usually clarifies the
new life in Christ, here it clarifies justification, and therefore the radical baptism statement of 3:26-29 is summarizing
Paul's argument regarding justification. And as δικαιοσύνη in
Galatians comes to mean eschatological deliverance from the
κόσμος or present evil age,[21] so it is being claimed that baptism makes effectual for the believer this eschatological deliverance. In the statement of 3:27-29, Paul claims a sacramental realization of eschatological deliverance without
reservation. He appears to border on enthusiasm.[22]

But it must be asked, Whose sacramental theology is
this? It appears very much that it is that of the opponents--
that Paul has taken over this sacramental understanding, which
they applied to circumcision among other things, and applied
it to baptism. The central polemic of the letter sets justification by faith over against justification by works of law.
This becomes the setting of baptism (2:19-20, 3:1-5, 26-29,
5:24) over against circumcision (5:2-4, where circumcision
epitomizes justification by law). The mystery-language that
Paul uses in 3:1-5 to polemically explore the significance of
the Galatians' baptism has been examined above. Paul is
asserting that that which the opponents see only as an initiatory rite at the beginning of the Christian life actually
conducted the Galatians into the climax of the Christian

mystery. If they cannot see this they can only be called
άνόητοι, and the whole mystery has been εἰκῇ. That which the
opponents say is only a beginning, Paul says is both beginning
and ending.

In Colossians there may be another instance of a
canonical writer making claims made for circumcision and
applying them to baptism. There is no question that the book
is polemical and constantly takes up the catchwords of the
heretical "philosophy," particularly in 2:4-23 where the discussion on περιτομή occurs.[23] The "philosophy" could be
labelled "enthusiastic," as it offers its devotees a way of
sharing in the πλήρωμα of the deity and the universal powers.[24]
One of the means by which the devotee shares in the πλήρωμα is
evidently by περιτομή (2:11-13).[25] There are several reasons
why this is most likely to be a literal περιτομή.[26] Firstly,
the phrase ἐν ᾧ καὶ περιετμήθητε περιτομῇ ἀχειροποιήτῳ is best
explained as a polemic against a περιτομή χειροποίητος. The
passage refers to circumcision in three ways. The author of
Colossians and the heretics both agree that Gentiles, before
conversion, were νεκροι . . . (ἐν) τοῖς παραπτώμασιν καὶ τῇ
ἀκροβυστίᾳ τῆς σαρκὸς (2:13); the opponents propound as a solution to this an enthusiastic περιτομή which Colossians calls
χειροποίητος;[27] and Colossians offers, instead of this, baptism
as περιτομή ἀχειροποίητος and περιτομή τοῦ Χριστοῦ. Several
have noted the fundamentally negative connotations of χειροποίητος as something made by man, over against something that
can only be a work of God.[28] The strictures of the "philosophy"
that are condemned in 2:16, 21-23 are physical enough and are
offered as ways of dealing with problems of σῶμα and σάρξ
(2:23). The philosophy itself apparently speaks of περιτομή
as ἀπέκδυσις τοῦ σώματος τῆς σάρκος (2:11).[29]

Secondly, doubts about the literalness of circumcision
rest largely on assessments of the degree to which the philosophy is "Gnostic." Lohse and others have disagreed with
Schmithals by positing that circumcision among Gnostics was
only figurative, never literal.[30] But here it must be noted
that the heretical philosophy, in its assertions about the
στοιχεῖα τοῦ κόσμου, regarded them as benevolent divine powers,
though it still retained a dualism between the visible and the

higher world.[31] It is therefore clear that there is not here
the radical dualism of some later Gnosticism.[32] If this is
the case, the nature of circumcision should not be judged by
the "spiritualizing" of the rite in later Gnostic writings.
The debate seems to be thrown back to the language of 2:11-13
itself, where the suggestion is strong that the rite was a
physical one. And if this is the case, then in Col 2:11-13
the claims made on behalf of an "enthusiastic" circumcision
are taken over and applied to baptism.[33]

Returning to Galatians, the particular language in
which ecclesiology is expressed in 3:26-29 seems significant.
In 1 Cor 12:12-13 the same baptismal formula is used[34] with
the idea of ecclesiology expressed in terms of σῶμα, which
plays an important role throughout the letter and is probably
connected with the Corinthians' own enthusiastic theology.[35]
But just as Paul develops a σῶμα-ecclesiology in 1 Corinthians,
he develops a σπέρμα-ecclesiology in Galatians, using the same
baptismal formula. As the σῶμα-ecclesiology seems to be intimately related to the Corinthian theology, so the σπέρμα-
ecclesiology is clearly related to the Galatian opponents'
propaganda (see the polemical development of the idea of υἱός
or σπέρμα 'Αβραάμ that begins in 3:6 and continues through to
4:21-31). This suggests further that as Paul portrays the
function of baptism in Christianity, he has taken over the
opponents' own claims--especially for that which they put in
place of baptism, circumcision.

It is in fact to be expected that Paul should utilize
the sacramental theology of his opponents, since this is the
typical way in which he argues. Elsewhere, he develops the
significance of baptism by taking over the sacramentalism of
those he is addressing and pushing it to conclusions which
accord with his scheme,[36] or modifies it in a way that takes
up sacramental expectations and twists them at certain points.[37]
This makes it the more likely that he is doing something similar here in Galatians.

In conclusion, it appears that, in Gal 3:26-29, Paul
has taken up the opponents' sacramental theology and played it
against them, and so has been able to place the final objective
offered to the Galatians (the mystery of 3:1-5, which they have

not yet entered into, but are about to, 4:21, 5:2-4) and
placed it in the Galatians' past. If he is doing so, and is
applying to baptism what the opponents claim for circumcision,
and, in linking it to a sperma-ecclesiology, is even taking
over the opponents' terminology, it may be that in 3:27-29
Paul is taking over almost entirely a formula that was widespread in early Christianity and was for the opponents a cultic
confession which they associated with their sacrament of circumcision.[38]

Possible Sources of the Tradition

Circumcision

        The attitude of Diaspora Judaism to circumcision as a
requirement for Gentile converts has already been considered.
It is unlikely that this stream of Judaism would make demands
on Gentiles like those of the opponents. Palestinian Judaism,
on the other hand, was much more insistent on circumcision of
converts.[39] In the Maccabean age, circumcision became in
Palestine something worth dying for,[40] and once Jews gained
the upper hand there was compulsory mass circumcision.[41] The
Herod family had a strict attitude to the rite,[42] and in
Josephus' account of the conversion of Izates, it was a Palestinian Jew who insisted on circumcision.[43]
        Paul will not use in Galatians the argument of physi-
cal and spiritual circumcision that he does in Romans--suggest-
ing that the opponents themselves speak of the rite in these
two senses. Philo speaks of physical and spiritual circumcision and knows of Jews who advocate spiritual circumcision
alone.[44] But despite his attempt to appeal to the Hellenistic
world, he defends the rite (though he gives "rationalistic"
reasons for it)[45] and insists that the two senses of circumcision be held together.[46] The Qumran tractates, too, speak
of figurative circumcision[47] and obviously insist on the
necessity of both senses.[48]
        Philo, Qumran, and Paul all stand over against later
Rabbinic Judaism with its disinterest in the figurative understanding of circumcision.[49] On the other hand, it seems

correct to postulate Gnosticism's rejection of literal circumcision.[50] It is only by saying that Paul has misunderstood
the opponents at this point that Schmithals is able to call
them Gnostics.[51]

The particular language of 3:1-5 and 4:1-11, and the
law-traditions and apostle tradition examined above, indicate
that the opponents presented Judaism as a sort of cosmic mystery, and the law as the practical means of entering into the
mystery of the cosmos. If circumcision epitomized their system of works of law, then it must have been presented in a way
that was consistent with that system. There is in fact evidence that circumcision was given a mystery-role.

Jubilees, which takes the stricter Palestinian view
of circumcision,[52] says that the rite is necessary, at least
in part, because the angels are created circumcised. Circumcision then is in imitation of the angels.[53] In 2 Baruch,
proselytes enter into all the good of the age to come because
they submit to circumcision.[54] Schmithals may be correct in
seeing "traces" of this interpretation in Col 2:9-19.[55] Goodenough presents further significant evidence. In the Jewish
ceremony that was in use until the eighteenth century, there
are features that are best explained by a very old association
of circumcision with the sun and the zodiac, just as the rite
seems to signify fertility in some way.[56] And in Odes of
Solomon 11 there is a hymn to the circumcision of the heart,
probably to accompany the performance of the physical rite,
which recalls the initiation hymn of Apuleius' *Metamorphoses*
Book 11.[57]

There are further reasons why, from the side of the
Galatians themselves, Judaism's supreme rite should come in
the form of a powerful mystery initiation. Firstly, Judaism
itself was presented to the Hellenistic world as a mystery.[58]
And secondly, circumcision, functioning in this mystery setting
as the final rite of initiation and that which separated the
initiated from the uninitiated, became a powerful sacrament
that gave right to take part in the full service of and fellowship with God.[59] So although the impetus to circumcise, as
well as the particular way in which circumcision functioned
as a mystery for the opponents, probably came from a more

Palestinian provenance, ready acceptance of the rite in these
terms was perhaps prepared for among the Galatians because of
their own experience of Judaism.

In summary, it has been suggested that a circumcising
mission such as had appeared in Galatia is much more likely to
have come from Palestine; the literal-figurative language of
circumcision is found in both Philo and Qumran; circumcision
is presented in some Palestinian literature as imitative of
angels; in Colossians there is evidence of an "enthusiastic"
Jewish-Christian circumcising movement which must be countered
by an "enthusiastic" baptismal theology, and a model of "putting off" and "putting on"; Goodenough presents evidence of
Judaism that saw circumcision as a mystery-rite; and Judaism
in the Hellenistic world laid the foundation for an understanding of circumcision as a final initiatory rite. All of this
provides background for the evident way in which Paul in Galatians claims for baptism what the opponents are claiming for
circumcision; and it provides the background, too, for a more
careful analysis of the form and terminology of Gal 3:28.

Baptism

The way in which Paul is using baptism will be considered firstly in terms of a comparative form-analysis of
Gal 3:27-28, 1 Cor 12:13, and Col 3:10-11.

Gal 3:27-28	1 Cor 12:13	Col 3:10-11
εἰς Χν. ἐβαπτίσθητε,	εἰς ἕν σῶμα	ἐνδυσάμενοι τὸν
Χν. ἐνεδύσασθε.	ἐβαπτίσθημεν	νέον (ἀνθ) τὸν
		ἀνακαινούμενον
		. . . κατ'
		εἰκόνα . . .
οὐκ ἕνι 'Ιουδαῖος,	εἴτε 'Ιουδαῖοι	οὐκ ἕνι "Ελλην
οὐδὲ "Ελλην, οὐκ	εἴτε "Ελληνες	καὶ 'Ιουδαῖος,
ἕνι δοῦλος οὐδὲ	εἴτε δοῦλοι	περιτομὴ καὶ
ἐλεύθερος, οὐκ	εἴτε ἐλεύθεροι	ἀκροβυστία, βάρ-
ἕνι ἄρσεν καὶ	. . .	βαρος, Σκύθης,
θῆλυ·		δοῦλος, ἐλεύθε-
πάντες γὰρ ὑμεῖς	πάντες ἕν πνεῦμα	ρος, ἀλλὰ πάντα
εἷς ἐστε ἐν Χ.	ἐποτίσθημεν.	καὶ ἐν πᾶσιν Χ.

These verses have been examined by Meeks, Jervell,
and Macdonald, among others, who have concluded that there is

here a creedal formula, a rather fixed form, whose life-
situation in the church is the liturgy of baptism.[60] If this
is the case, an analysis of the use of the form in Colossians 3
and 1 Corinthians 12 should help in understanding the use of
the form in Gal 3:28.[61]

In Colossians, the formula by no means stands out from
its context.[62] It appears in the midst of motifs coming from
baptismal paraenesis[63] and should therefore not be separated
from 2:11-13,[64] where Colossians evidently takes up the claims
of the opposing philosophy and applies them to baptism.[65] As
the indicative and imperative of the letter are so bound up
with baptism, and as baptism is so polemical in that it interprets the claims of the opponents,[66] it is logical to suppose
that the formula of 3:9-12 is part of the polemical situation
and that these verses represent one interpretation of the
formula, over against that of the opponents.[67]

In 1 Corinthians, too, the saying is very "contextual"
and is being used as part of the debate, one interpretation of
the saying being stood over against another.[68] If this is so
in Colossians and 1 Corinthians, a similar relation between
form and function could be expected in Galatians.

Part of the context of both Colossians and 1 Corinthians is the debate over the precise meaning of "putting off"
and "putting on" (see references to Colossians above; and also
φορεῖν and ἐνδύειν in 1 Cor 15:49, 53). Therefore, the question of "putting on" (ἐνδύειν) in Galatians 3:28 should also
be expected to be part of a contextual debate.[69] It has
already been noticed above that the ecclesiology language in
both 1 Cor 12:13 and Gal 3:28 is contextual (see above on σῶμα
and σπέρμα; and the "slave-free" element in the saying is also
contextual in Galatians, in comparison with 4:21-31, etc.).
If the language of the formulae in these instances is contextual, it is reasonable to assume that the formulae themselves
are contextual.

There are significant expressions in all the sayings
and their contexts which suggest a tradition based on Genesis
1-2. Both Ephesians[70] and Colossians refer to the παλαιὸς
ἄνθρωπος and the καινὸς ἄνθρωπος, κατ᾽ εἰκόνα τοῦ κτίσαντος
αὐτόν (Col 3:10), and τὸν κατὰ θεὸν κτισθέντα (Eph 4:24).

Colossians stresses the fact that Christ is εἰκὼν τοῦ θεοῦ,
and 1 Corinthians speaks of εἰκὼν τοῦ χοϊκοῦ and εἰκὼν τοῦ
ἐπουρανίου.[71] It has already been noted that in all instances
this language echoing Genesis 1-2 is "contexual." However,
Gal 3:28, by a change of comparative expressions (from οὐκ ἔνι
. . . οὐδὲ to οὐκ ἔνι . . . καί) deliberately echoes LXX Gen
1:27 (ἄρσεν καὶ θῆλυ ἐποίησεν αὐτούς).[72] It is to be expected
that this Genesis-language, which belongs to the "urzeit-
endzeit" pattern in which redemption is the return to an
original condition,[73] is contextual in Galatians also, and even
more so because of this striking modification.

        This suggests some conclusions for form and function
in Galatians. In the Pauline churches, there was apparent
widespread concern with the interpretation of a tradition,
drawing on Genesis 1-2, and its relation to baptism. This
concern and interpretation of this tradition appears to have
belonged in Galatia too. 1 Corinthians shows that there were
sharply different interpretations of the tradition; and Colossians suggests a situation in which the tradition was worked
out in terms of circumcision and opposed by the same tradition
worked out in terms of baptism. Only in Galatians and Colossians is there a concern with the στοιχεῖα τοῦ κόσμου. In
Colossians the opponents seek to share in the glory of the
στοιχεῖα through a ritual system of speculative Judaism. In
Galatians, too, there is a concern for Jewish ritual; "law"
and "works of law" are understood in selective terms, and
traditions are operative in which there is a concern for
fellowship with angels (also in Col 2:18), bound up with
interest in the στοιχεῖα. As the formula in question was
evidently part of the "context" of Colossians (as well as
1 Corinthians), it is suggested that in Galatia, too, the
formula belongs to the context of the debate, and the Genesis-
tradition is bound up with the claims of the opponents.

        To clarify the formula and its function further, the
sayings above should be related to close parallels that appear
both in the Fathers and in Gnostic literature.[74] The best
examples of these sayings are in 2 Clem 12:1-2, the Gospel of
the Egyptians (Clem Alex *Stromata* 3. 13. 92, *NTA*, 1:168), the

Gospel of Thomas 22 (*NHL*, 121), and the Gospel of Philip 67.
29-36 (*NHL*, 141).[75]

Gos Egypt	Gos Thom	2 Clem	Gos Phil
The Lord said, When you have trampled on the garment of shame, and when the two become one and the male with the female neither male nor female . . .	Jesus said to them, When you make the two one, and when you make the inside like the outside, and the outside like the inside, and the above like the below, and when you make the male and the female one and the same, so that the male not be male nor the female female . . .	For the Lord Himself . . . said: When the two shall be one and that which is without as that which is within, and the male with the female neither male nor female . . .	[The Lord] said, I came to make [the things below] like the things [above, and the things] outside like those [inside. I came to unite] them in that place

        Certain characteristics of these sayings are signifi-
cant for understanding the canonical versions of the tradition.[76] For most of them, the context is a concern for the
future state.[77] In all of them, a return to the primordial
androgynous state is a necessity for ultimate redemption.[78]
This corresponds to the stress on the "one" in the canonical
sayings.[79] All the sayings have a version of "putting off,"[80]
which is found in the saying in Col 3:9 and is inferred in
Gal 3:28. All refer to the dissolution of male and female,[81]
a concept found in the canonical sayings only in Gal 3:28.
The context of these noncanonical sayings, too, is an interest
in Genesis 1-2 and a speculation on the future state in terms
of urzeit and endzeit.[82] Concerning life-situation and function, the examples in the Gospel of Thomas and the Gospel of
the Egyptians appear to refer to baptism,[83] but not those in
2 Clement and the Gospel of Philip.[84] Here, as in the New
Testament, there is apparently evidence of a variety of

interpretations of baptism, and its relationship to the future
androgynous state.[85] And it is significant that the saying-
tradition itself is not heterodox at this time: it can be
quoted in 2 Clement as an accepted saying of the Lord.[86]

The common elements in each instance of the saying,[87]
the allusions to (but not quotations of) Genesis 1-2,[88] and
the parallels to the canonical sayings which are at the same
time not quotations of any one of them,[89] suggest that both
canonical and noncanonical examples of the sayings-formula go
back to a common independent tradition, whose life-situation
in Christian circles was concern for the attainment of the
original androgynous condition and whose connection with baptism was a subject of debate.[90]

In order to get behind this debate in the New Testament, and in Galatians in particular, sources of concern for
unification of opposites should be briefly examined. Leach
speaks of formulations of unification of opposites, including
the opposites of male and female, in "every myth system."[91]
Particularly, Christianity's symbolization of a reunified
mankind may have reflected aspirations of society and religion
around it. The shrine of Agdistis in Philadelphia offered,
through cultic means, a way of dissolving the differences
between "household slaves," "men and women, bond and free."[92]
In most of the Oriental and Egyptian mysteries, the cult provided a way of setting aside social distinctions.[93] Some
offered a cultic exchange of sexual roles through initiation.[94]
The philosophical schools, too, strove for a community experience in which there was a "unity of all rational being--the
gods, men, and women."[95] And of course Judaism had its Adam-
speculations, in which distinctions of race and sex were dissolved.[96] It was characteristic of these attempts at new community in the face of the breakdown of πόλις, φρατρία, and
θίασος[97] that myth and social structure were intimately related.
There could be no credible achievement of new structures, and
breakdown of old, without some concrete realization in cultus
of the mythological ideas for humanity.[98]

All of this suggests that the traditions reflected in
the formula under discussion, and even the formula itself,
probably had a wider context than early Christianity;[99] and

the symbolic achievement of unification could have been by
rites other than baptism.

The "male-female" element in the saying, and the myth
behind it, should also be explored.

As mentioned above, phenomenologists have observed an
interest in the opposite sex roles, and resolution of these
opposites, in "every myth system."[100] Very often the myth of
a bisexual progenitor of the human race, common in the Hellenistic world, was involved.[101] However, the sayings under consideration come from a context in which such a myth has become
bound up with interpretations of Genesis 1-2.[102] This process
is evident in at least two writers of Diaspora Judaism.[103]
Much has already been written on Philo's treatment of the two
creation accounts,[104] in which the ἄνθρωπος of Genesis 1,
created in the εἰκὼν θεοῦ, was ἄφθαρτος, ἀσώματος, οὔτ' ἄρσεν
οὔτε θῆλυ, whereas the ἄνθρωπος of Genesis 2 consisted of σῶμα
καὶ ψυχή, and was φθαρτός, though he too at first was one and
enjoyed μόνωσις.[105] The taking of the rib from Adam in Genesis
2 was the separation of the sexes and the destruction of this
μόνωσις,[106] which resulted in the fall of concupiscence and
the resultant clothing in "coats of skin," the body or "garment
of flesh."[107] It is for this reason that this ἄνθρωπος is now
a mixture of corruptible and incorruptible, body and soul.[108]
Death was the separation of soul and body, whereby the soul
returned to its place of origin and original unity.[109] This
is illustrated in the experience of Moses, who, in his pil-
grimage from earth to heaven, exchanging mortality for immor-
tality, "resolved his twofold nature of soul and body into a
single unity, transforming his whole being into νοῦς."[110]
This is a return to the condition of the first ἄνθρωπος of
Genesis 1.[111]

However, this soteriological restoration of the state
of μόνωσις can be experienced in the present through the true
φιλοσοφία, or the study of the scriptures, and the Jewish
rites, which in Philo become the most potent of mysteries.[112]
The Therapeutai have achieved this heavenly experience,[113] and
it is significant that they have also succeeded in breaking
through the social roles of male and female.[114]

There are suggestions of this myth in the romance,
Joseph and Asenath.[115] Here Asenath removes her old, black
garment;[116] receives an unction of incorruption and is renewed
and made alive once more;[117] puts on her ancient robe of marriage, her "first robe";[118] is introduced into the "mysteries
of God";[119] and is told to take off her veil because ἡ κεφαλή
σού ἐστιν ὡς ἀνδρος νεανίσκου.[120]

However, this speculation should not be confined to
Diaspora Judaism. For the Rabbis, too, Adam was created
androgynous,[121] and the two sexes resulted when Eve was taken
from Adam.[122] The "robes of skin" of Gen 3:21, the physical
body, replace the lost image of God.[123] There is also the use
of Gen 1:26 to refer to the converted man, the "new man." In
Num R. 11. 2 Abraham the proselyte is also made new, probably
by circumcision.[124] The Rabbis also share in the tradition
of the mystic ascent of Moses on Sinai, in which he received
a crown of light and was reclothed with the lost image of
Adam.[125] Moses' ascent became the paradigm for the Jewish
mystical experience.[126]

In apocalyptic literature, too, the future state of
the righteous is a return to the original Adamic state. They
will be reclothed with the "garments of glory" which Adam lost
in the age to come.[127] Moreover, just as Adam was associated
with the angels in the beginning,[128] so, in the future age,
the righteous will be like the angels.[129] Apocalyptic literature reveals certain definite ascetic tendencies,[130] and the
future angelic state is of course a sexless state.[131] It is
significant for this study that, in the apocalyptic hope of
the future angelic state, the spiritual resurrection body is
compared to the stars.[132]

It has been shown above that these same speculations
concerning Adam and androgyny made their way into the writings
of the Fathers.[133] They also appear in an un-Christianised
form in the Gnostic work Poimandres,[134] which probably predates
the Christian Gnostic forms of the myth.[135] Here there are
suggestions that initiates experienced a mystical resolution
of the fallen condition[136] through γνῶσις, liturgy, or even
sacraments.[137] Then, a little later, the same myth appears in

the Syrian Gospel of Thomas and the Valentinian Cassianus and
the Gospel of Philip.[138]

The conclusion must be that the original tradition
behind the unification sayings was widely known; that it was
deeply embedded in Judaism and Jewish speculations on Genesis
1-2; and that, connected with the tradition, there were ritual
or cultic means of experiencing a return to the condition of
the ideal ἄνθρωπος--which were certainly other than Christian
baptism.

Some of these factors about the tradition make its
suggested role in the debate in 1 Corinthians even more convincing.[139] It casts light on the concern with angels in
1 Corinthians 11, along with problems resulting from confusion
of sexual roles[140] and the preoccupation with speaking in the
tongues of angels in 1 Cor 13:1. It explains the confusion
over the questions of the body, sex, and marriage, in chapters
5-7.[141] The argument in 1 Corinthians 15 now becomes clear;
when Paul says ὁ πρῶτος ἄνθρωπος ἐκ γῆς χοϊκός, ὁ δεύτερος
ἄνθρωπος ἐξ οὐρανοῦ (15:47), he is reversing an enthusiastic
soteriology based on speculations regarding the two men of
Genesis 1-2.[142] This discussion of the resurrection in 1 Corinthians 15 also suggests some intrusion of apocalyptic ideas
of the future angelic state. Paul must discuss the fact that
there are σώματα ἐπουράνια καὶ σώματα ἐπίγεια (15:40), that is,
that astral bodies are involved in the resurrection.[143] Thus
a formula similar to the baptismal unification-saying examined
above is probably involved in the Corinthian conflict,[144] which
Paul has taken up and reinterpreted in a particular way, in
conjunction with a σῶμα-ecclesiology.[145] This would explain
why the "male-female" element has been left out of the saying
in 1 Corinthians. It is exactly a self-understanding which
claims to have attained the androgynous state which is plaguing
the Corinthian church.[146] It is significant, too, that, just
as the underlying mythical tradition was not the property only
of Hellenistic Judaism, as forms of it appear in rabbinic and
apocalyptic literature, so, here in 1 Corinthians, there are
suggestions of the interests of both Hellenistic and apocalyptic circles. That which Philo attained by φιλοσοφία and
mystical Jewish rites, the Therapeutai and the hermetists

attained by cultus and ritual, and the apocalyptists hoped
they would attain in the future by "works of law," the Corinthians believed they had already attained in baptism.

Some conclusions can be drawn at this stage. If the
myth of creation, fall, and restoration based on Genesis 1-2
was widely known in Judaism and was part of the dialectic in
Corinth, it may well have been known by the Galatian opponents.
If mythical resolution of the fall condition was experienced,
in various circles, other than by baptism, the Galatian opponents, too, may propagate a resolution through means other
than baptism. In Colossians, there is an enthusiastic-nomistic
use of various "Jewish" ceremonies, climaxed and epitomized by
"circumcision," propagated in terms of "putting off" and "putting on," a scheme which Colossians has taken over dialec-
tically. The unification-formula here is so "contextual" that
it was probably used by the circumcising heretics. Only Colossians and Galatians refer to the στοιχεῖα τοῦ κόσμου. In Colossians the opponents seek, by their ritual, to share in the
glory of the στοιχεῖα; in Galatians, the opponents are interested in fellowship with angels and apparently refer to their
program of "works of law" in mystery-terms.[147] This offers
support for the suggestion that a similar dialectic is involved
in Galatians. Confirmation is offered by the direct correlation of Gal 3:28 (ἄρσεν καὶ θῆλυ) with the LXX of Gen 1:27,
that breaks with the rest of the formula, indicating a particular relevance of the ἄνθρωπος of Genesis 1 to the situation.
Further, the very contextual σπέρμα-ecclesiology is juxtaposed
with the baptism-saying, which itself uses the unusual Χριστὸν
ἐνεδύσασθε.[148] Also to be taken into account is the suggestion
that the particular structure of the argument in Gal 3:6-26 is
a polemic against a projection of Moses as the chief mystagogue, and of his Sinai ascent as a consorting with angels;[149]
and the mystery-terms in which the opponents apparently present
their program in Gal 3:1-5.[150] All this suggests that, in
Galatians, there is a polemical intent behind Paul's use of
the language of Gal 3:28 and that he has taken this language
from the opponents.[151]

The noncanonical sayings quoted above raise another
question which may have further implications for the opponents'

sacramental tradition. In every one of these instances, the
saying is introduced as a saying of the Lord.[152] This is not
to say simply that the saying was a saying of Jesus;[153] but
this strong association with Jesus must be accounted for, and
it may throw light on some of the baggage that perhaps travels
with the unification saying.

A clue to the process in which the unification-saying
came to be a dominical saying appears in Clement's debate with
Cassianus and his followers. In *Stromata* 3. 6. 47-48, the
unification-saying is clearly linked with Matt 22:30 (ἐν γὰρ
τῇ ἀναστάσει οὔτε γαμοῦσιν οὔτε γαμίζονται, ἀλλ' ὡς ἄγγελοι ἐν
τῷ οὐρανῷ εἰσιν). It is interesting that this dominical saying
shows striking similarities to the basic elements of the
unification-saying. The reference is to the resurrection, and
the verse implies a future sexless state, which Jewish tradition understood as an angelic state.[154] Cassianus and his
followers were evidently seeking such an angelic state.[155]

There is good reason to believe that this very synoptic
saying, or its historical antecedents, was also involved in the
Corinthian controversy, where the androgyne-tradition apparently played an important role. Several have noticed that,
in Corinth, a crucial issue was the interpretation of various
sayings of Jesus,[156] and that the treatment of these sayings
by the Corinthians was very similar to their treatement in
Q.[157] D. L. Balch has now pointed out that this is apparently
true also for certain dominical sayings concerning marriage.[158]
It appears, from 1 Cor 7:10, 25, that the Corinthians were
claiming that there was a saying of the Lord demanding that
couples should separate, and that Paul was forced to deny
this.[159] Further, the two verbs γαμεῖν and γαμίζειν, one of
which is exceedingly rare, occur together not only in 1 Cor
7:36, 38, but in a series of synoptic sayings dealing with
marriage and putting away of wives (Luke 20:35 = Matt 22:30 =
Mark 12:25; Luke 17:27 = Matt 24:38). The Corinthians are
apparently making a particular use of these words of the
Lord.[160] It is significant, then, that there is evidence to
suggest that Q interpreted these sayings in an ascetic sense,
so that the call to the kingdom was a call to separate from
one's wife.[161] One of these sayings, Luke 20:35 and parallels,

was the saying concerning the resurrection, marriage, and the
angelic state. The Corinthians are apparently treating the
dominical sayings regarding the angelic state and marriage as
Q does, just as they treat the dominical sayings regarding
wisdom and signs as Q does. This coincides with the confusion
in Corinth regarding baptism and resurrection, the body, sexual
roles, et cetera,[162] in which confusion the tradition of unification and androgyny is involved.[163]

     The suggested conclusion is this. In Corinth, early
in Paul's ministry, and later, in the second century, in the
debate with Cassianus, the unification tradition is associated
with the dominical saying, Matt 22:30 and parallels, which
speaks of the resurrection and the future, angelic state.[164]
This may be, then, the way the unification saying came to be
circulated as a saying of the Lord.

     This in turn suggests some of the "baggage" that may
be travelling with the unification-saying in Galatia: it is
evidently bound up with concern for the attainment of the
future, angelic state. It has already been suggested that, in
the Pauline churches, the unification-saying was being used
polemically to support different interpretations of baptism.[165]
In all these cases, there was a simultaneous interest in
attainment of the angelic state.[166] The early concern behind
the transmission of the unification-saying, then, was not
simply baptism, but attainment of the angelic state; and the
transmission of the saying as a baptism-saying was only one
interpretation of an earlier sayings-complex, one assertion of
the way the angelic state was actualised in the present. The
divided opinion over the efficacy of baptism for the realization of androgyny continued into the second century.[167] And
it may even have been Paul who first suggested that androgyny
was attained in baptism--and who, by doing so, helped to
trigger off the sexual confusion of the Corinthians.[168]

     It appears, then, that the unification-saying is being
used polemically in Gal 3:28, against a competing interpretation in which the angelic state was purported to be actualized
in some other way--that is, by a sacramental system based on
Jewish calendrical laws, climaxed and epitomized by circumcision.

Conclusions

The implications of the above rhetorical analysis
should continually be borne in mind. Galatians is throughout
a dialogical response to an offending theology which is now
owned by the Galatians themselves.[169] Then the suggestions of
sacramentalism against which Paul argues, even the expressions
in 3:28, will probably be associated with the opponents' program.

Further, baptismal statements run throughout the
letter[170] in such a way that baptism, the concretion of the
argument for justification by faith, stands over against circumcision, which comes to epitomize the program of works.[171]
Paul refutes the opponents by filling out the meaning of baptism.[172] His answer to the opponents, then, is a sacramental
answer: justification conforms to the shape of the eschatological Christ-event into which one is brought by faith and
baptism.[173]

The stress on the significance of baptism itself indicates the stress the opponents place on circumcision. For
them it is indeed a sacrament, that which works the miracle of
salvation.[174]

This all suggests that, in 3:27-29, Paul has not left
his main argument.[175] Rather, in this formula and its language
can be seen yet another way in which he argues for justification by faith by developing the significance of baptism. In
this case, then, this language, and the "baggage" that travels
with it, is another indication of the essence of the whole
debate in Galatia, and of that which the opponents hope to
accomplish by their "sacrament."

The significance of this language and its "baggage" is
evident in four ways. Firstly, a form-analysis of Gal 3:28
and other New Testament parallels points to an underlying tradition which draws on Genesis 1-2 in propagating a bisexual
progenitor of the human race, a fall from androgyny to division
of the sexes, and redemption as a return to the primordial
state.[176] Gal 3:28 in particular appears to be picking up a
traditional saying, because of the change of verb tenses and
because of a distinct break in the pattern of the saying by

which the last phrase, ἄρσεν καὶ θῆλυ, et cetera, is made to
conform precisely to LXX Gen 1:27.[177] The association of the
saying with a σπέρμα-ecclesiology, itself extremely contextual,[178] suggests further that the saying itself is being
used contextually.[179]

Secondly, when later Christian instances of the formula are examined,[180] it is seen that the saying typically
operates in a polemical setting, in which competing interpretations of baptism (or of some other rites over against baptism, as in Colossians and the Gospel of Philip) are placed
over against each other. Thus the life-setting of the saying
is not simply baptism, but attainment of the resurrection condition of primordial androgyny and the angelic state.[181]

Thirdly, the concept of unification of opposites, and
of a return to a primordial condition of androgyny, was found
to exist in a wide variety of pre-Christian contexts--includ-
ing Jewish contexts.[182] And along with the myth were means of
realizing ritually (or sacramentally) the soteriological goals
of the myth: φιλοσοφία and mystic Jewish rites in Philo,
ritual among the Therapeutai, "works of law" in apocalyptic
Judaism, communion with God on Sinai in the case of Moses in
later Jewish speculations, and γνῶσις and liturgy in Poimandres.[183] This further suggests that the opponents could have
attached the myth to some Jewish rites, in particular, circumcision;[184] and that Paul in Galatians has taken up their
claims and used them for his own purposes--as in fact is done
in 1 Corinthians and Colossians.[185]

Fourthly, the persistent circulation of the unification-
saying as a saying of the Lord suggests that the form of the
saying known in Christian circles grew out of a situation in
which Matt 22:30/Luke 20:34-36 was seen to be congruous with
the mythical speculations based on Genesis 1-2. This association appears in the circles of Cassianus, but was evidently
made as early as 1 Corinthians, if not earlier. The primary
concern, again, appears to be, not merely the meaning of baptism, but the cultic attainment of the angelic state. This
was precisely the future hope of apocalyptic circles, and it
seems also to play a role in 1 Corinthians.

All of this, then, helps to illuminate the use the
opponents make of their sacrament of circumcision. It is
presented as the climactic sacrament, the completion of the
mystery in which the Galatians became novices by baptism,[186]
which "puts off" the condition of the flesh and subjection to
earthly powers,[187] and "puts on" the original Adamic glory,
making one a companion of angels and heavenly powers (στοιχεῖα).

Paul's way of arguing here would then be consistent
with the way he argues sacramentally elsewhere, taking up the
sacramental assumptions of his opponents and putting them to
his own use.[188] The substance of his argument would also be
consistent with the way he answers the intruding theology,
throughout the letter, by presenting justification as cosmic
deliverance, and freedom from the enslaving powers of the present evil aeon.[189] It would be consistent, too, with the indications that the opponents present their law-program as a
mystery, which itself works cosmic deliverance and brings
fellowship with angels.[190] It also explains Paul's unusual
treatment of circumcision in Galatians, and the Galatians'
unusual acceptance of the rite.[191] The opponents probably
come from circles such as the Essenes, where baptism was much
less than a final, once-for-all sacrament. They also probably
present circumcision as imitative of angels, in keeping with
the tradition of Jubilees; and they may have affinities with
the heretics of Colossae, who also represent an "enthusiastic"
circumcising movement seeking fellowship with angels.

Paul has probably stressed the social consequences of
the unification-saying by inserting οὐκ ἔνι 'Ιουδαῖος οὐδὲ
"Ελλην, οὐκ ἔνι δοῦλος οὐδὲ ἐλεύθερος. This addition, no
doubt part of the aspirations connected with the myth
already,[192] is used in the canonical sayings not only to
counter threats to the community resulting from religiously
heightened distinctions between circumcised and uncircumcised.[193] The opponents may even have used this phrase, too,
in keeping with the Jewish tradition about the unity of mankind
in Adam.[194] They may have said that circumcision removes the
distinction not only between Jew and Gentile, but between male
and female, human and angelic. Their mystic-nomistic rite was
that which brought in anticipation a realization of the future,

mythical roles of humanity, therefore making possible a change
in societal roles,[195] and bringing into being the "remnant,"
the covenant people, the σπέρμα 'Αβραάμ.[196]   But Paul asserts
that it is in baptism that identification with Christ, the
true σπέρμα 'Αβραάμ, has been realized.[197] The ultimate intention of the true, heavenly religion is then fulfilled.[198]   The
demand for circumcision, then, far from bringing about the
"remnant," the covenant people, is dividing them, taking them
only backwards into pre-Christian religion.[199]

        There is an indication here of the opponents' Christol-
ogy. They have a place for Jesus in their system, but it is
only a preliminary place. Baptism into Christ makes one a
novice, as was Abraham when he had faith. One must then
advance to the heart of the mystery through circumcision and
the observance of calendrical law. Jesus was given a function
within a much larger scheme of "law as the cosmic rule of
God."[200] In this scheme he has no chance of surpassing the
significance of Moses and Abraham.

        The opponents must also have a particular eschatology.
The inclusion of the provocative element, ἄρσεν καὶ θῆλυ, shows
that they (and the Galatians) must be less than enthusiasts in
the Corinthian sense, where Paul expresses an "eschatological
reservation" by eliminating the "male-female" element of the
saying. But in Galatia, attainment of the angelic state, and
the final resolution of the sexes, still lies in the future.
Law-obedience is the means of achieving this goal, and those
who are on the way, brought into fellowship with all the powers
of the universe through the sacraments epitomized and climaxed
by circumcision, proleptically achieve fellowship with the
angels and taste a little of the sexless state. Here, then, it
is the opponents who have the "eschatological reservation" as
far as baptism is concerned, and Paul who portrays baptism into
Jesus in terms of "realized eschatology."[201] In fact, it may
have been Paul's "enthusiastic" baptism-statement here which
contributed to the Corinthian excesses.[202]

        The Galatian opponents, like the Corinthians, are
"enthusiasts."[203] Both embrace theologies which are forms of
wisdom speculation,[204] both threaten the social unity of the
church, and both reject the cross, in theology and experience.

But the Galatian opponents are "nomistic" enthusiasts, like
the Colossian heretics, and perhaps the opponents behind 2 Corinthians.[205] Wisdom-speculations and enthusiasms could apparently express themselves through a variety of eschatologies.
For the Corinthians, the final eschatological event is behind
them; for the Galatian opponents, it is still before them.

Robinson has noticed the difference between the "opponent" in 1 and 2 Corinthians,[206] which causes Paul very much
to alter his approach, so that "the position he assumed in
2 Corinthians was to some extent parallel to that of his opponents in 1 Corinthians."[207] He now "so emphasizes realized
eschatology as to sound reminiscent of the heresy of baptismal
resurrection he himself combatted in 1 Corinthians."[208] His
position in Galatians is very similar to this last. While the
opponents of 2 Corinthians can be called "enthusiasts,"[209]
they are unquestionably nomists, proclaiming the indissolubil-
ity of the old and new covenants,[210] the salvific value of the
Moses-tradition, and their own impeccable Israelite "pedi-
gree."[211] Their nomistic enthusiasm has led them to fail to
appreciate the realized eschatology in God's deed in Christ--
as is true, too, for the Galatian opponents.

Finally, this portrayal of the opponents' sacramentalism is consistent with traditions dealt with already, such as
the tradition of apostle, traditions of revelation and inspiration in which vision and ecstasy are the confirmation of the
prophetic wise man, the tradition of Abraham as one of the
great heroes of Israel's religion and as the epitomy of the
Gentile who comes to God, and traditions in which Judaism is
a mystery religion, Jewish law is the key that opens up the
secrets of the cosmos and brings fellowship with the angelic
rulers of the universe, and Moses is the supreme mystagogue
who, on Sinai, becomes angelic and even divine, receiving
again the lost "glory" of Adam.

CHAPTER TEN

ETHICAL TRADITIONS

It has already been noticed that some construct the
theology of the opponents from the ethical portions of the
letter, considered almost in isolation,[1] or else they see two
groups behind the letter, principally on the grounds that the
nomism of the opponents in the early portions of the letter
cannot be matched with the apparent moral laxity of the recipients of the second portion.[2] Both such theories encounter
great problems because of the unity of the letter,[3] the way
the letter, in both its major sections, expounds the meaning
of baptism,[4] and the theological and literary questions of the
form and function of paraenesis in Paul's letters[5]--all of
which suggest, in fact, that the last chapters of Galatians
are integral to the whole argument of the letter and are
answering the same intruding theology as the earlier chapters.[6] This is further indicated by the way each of the
three parts of the *refutatio* begin with an indicative statement;[7] the use of the antithesis of σάρξ and πνεῦμα as two
antithetical powers, and two life-possibilities, in both chapters 3-4 and 5-6;[8] and the way the Galatians are addressed in
both sections of the letter as πνευματικοί, probably using the
self-designation of the opponents themselves, who are nevertheless under a spell (βασκαίνειν), deceived (πλανᾶν). Both
sections of the letter appear to be called forth by the one
attempt to be πνευματικοί.[9]

Further, there are reasons for expecting that Paul
will here use, to an extent, the ethics of the opponents themselves. Paul typically does so in his paraenesis.[10] The
subtlety of a rhetorical *refutatio* suggests that this will be
the case.[11] And thirdly, the suggested dynamic behind Gal
3:28[12] indicates that the opponents are claiming to be community apostles[13] who are establishing the new community of

God, the remnant, or σπέρμα 'Αβραάμ, in which their sacrament
brings a breakdown of traditional social structures, and a
realization in anticipation of the future, mythical roles of
humanity (no Jew or Greek, male or female, etc.).[14] Thus the
community ethics in the paraenesis can be expected to be the
opponents' own, the paraenesis itself functioning as a refutation of their community claims. Because in fact the new idyllic
relationships between members of the community have not come
about, the opponents' claims to be community apostles, bringing God's last remnant into existence, must be false.[15]

         One further aspect which is essential for an under-
standing of the nature of the ethical traditions which are
here dealt with, and the way in which Paul deals with them,
is the sudden appearance, here in the ethical section, of the
unique expression νόμος τοῦ χριστοῦ. Several have noticed
this puzzle at the end of Galatians. Whereas, in the early
chapters, Paul radically rejects the religion of law in unusually harsh terms, in the last two chapters the religion of law
returns again--though now it is the "law of Christ." This
last is νόμος in the real sense (6:2). The Spirit allows no
moral laxity,[16] and the law of retribution has returned in a
real sense (6:7-8).[17] Any attempt to fit the ethical passage
into Paul's overall argument must be able to explain this dialectical treatment of νόμος.

              The Function of the Ethical Traditions
                        in Galatians

         The ethical chapters are built around Paul's use of a
particular form, and it is suggested here that the passage as
a whole is best approached through an analysis of this form.[18]
         There is general agreement that Gal 5:19-23 belongs
to the form of a catalog of virtues and vices,[19] which is
widely attested both within the New Testament[20] and outside
it.[21] The form appears to be dualistic in its essential
nature,[22] climaxing in threat of destruction or promise of
salvation.[23] The life situation of the form seems to be, in
many instances, initiation into a community;[24] and correspond-
ingly, its function tends to be hortatory, stressing the
separation of the community from the world.[25]

The relationship of this form to the "two-way scheme"[26] is often not made clear.[27] However, the latter is at least as old as the virtue- and vice-catalogs,[28] and comes to share in so many features of them, especially the essential dualism,[29] that the two can be treated, for all essential purposes, as the one form. As far as Gal 5:19-23 is concerned, therefore, it seems correct to speak of the dualistic form of the two-way scheme or virtue- and vice-catalog, which is both paraenetic and propagandistic in intent.[30]

The dualism of the form itself matches well with the dualism inherent in the argument of Galatians, evident in the language of the two ages or two worlds, the antithesis of σάρξ and πνεῦμα, and other stark contrasts such as the age of law and the age of grace, Jerusalem below and Jerusalem above, et cetera. It would seem to be no coincidence, then, that 5:19-23 has a particularly dualistic construction. The "ethical" portion of the letter, as well as the "dogmatic," seems to be debating the same dualistic thought world.

As noted above, Paul's real meaning is seen, not simply in his use of forms and traditional material, but in his particular modification of them.[31] This typical Pauline modification appears in 1 Cor 6:11, which follows a virtue- and vice-form in 6:9-10. Here Paul concludes, καὶ ταῦτά τινες ἦτε. ἀλλὰ ἀπελούσασθε, ἀλλὰ ἡγιάσθητε, ἀλλὰ ἐδικαιώθητε ἐν τῷ ὀνόματι τοῦ κυρίου Ἰησοῦ Χριστοῦ . . . , probably a reference to the Corinthians' baptism.[32] Here the essential newness in Paul's ethic becomes apparent. It lies not in new forms of ethical behavior,[33] but in a decisive shift in the division of the ages. In Christ, the new age has already arrived, the Spirit has come, the new man has already appeared.[34] So the Corinthians, by virtue of their baptism into the community or "body of Christ," have already been separated finally from those who have no part in the kingdom of God, and have already become righteous, holy, et cetera.[35] Christian ethics are eschatological ethics, the ethics of life truly turned to the future for the first time,[36] as becomes clear in 1 Cor 6:12-20, where Paul goes on to exposit the consequences of the eschatological holiness now present in the "body of Christ."[37]

There is the same modification in Galatians 5. Verse
17 portrays a dualism of flesh and spirit in terms of a mythical struggle between two great powers, for whom man is only
an involuntary arena.[38] There is no possibility for any third
position. Man must be a subject of one power or the other.
In terms of this typical apocalyptic understanding of the
world, 5:19-23 then takes up this dualism and contrasts the
irreconcilable hostility of these two powers in terms of
ethics.[39] For those who do the ἔργα τῆς σαρκός (5:19) there
remains only the typical climax of the catalog form, the
assurance of damnation: οἱ τὰ τοιαῦτα πράσσοντες βασιλείαν
θεοῦ οὐ κληρονομήσουσιν (5:21). But in place of the corresponding climax of bliss at the end of the catalog of virtues,
there is the unique Pauline modification: οἱ . . . τοῦ χριστο-
τοῦ ['Ιησοῦ] τὴν σάρκα ἐσταύρωσαν σὺν τοῖς παθήμασιν καὶ ταῖς
ἐπιθυμίαις (5:24). The aorist ἐσταύρωσαν most probably refers
to baptism,[40] as does 1 Cor 6:11. This again shifts the
dividing of the ages and gives the form an intensified indicative sense. Christians, because joined to Christ in baptism,
have already died to the sphere and power of σάρξ. As an
inevitable way of existence, the flesh was eliminated when
they were incorporated into Christ.[41] What the dualistic
scheme typically referred to as promise has now become a historical reality, and the catalog now functions to proclaim the
freedom of the Christian.[42]

It is for this reason that the catalog, at the heart
of the ethical section, must be taking up the main thrust of
the letter, going back to the baptismal statement of 2:19-20
and continuing the polemic of chapters 3 and 4 on behalf of
the liberty of faith.[43] It is because Christ has brought in
the eschatological aeon of the Spirit that it is unthinkable
for a Christian to exist in the grasp of σάρξ.[44] And because
this is an eschatological argument, it is also a Christological argument. Paul's argument for justification by faith,
and his argument for ethics, have the same Christological base.
Nothing can be added to the believer's justification by faith,
because in faith--that is, in baptism--he is conducted into
the finished work of Christ.[45] So, just as "baptism is the
dedication of the new life," so also "the new life is the

appropriation of baptism."[46] Here, as in 1 Corinthians 6,
because Gal 5:24 is a baptismal statement, ethics become
eschatological ethics, the other side of the eschatological
declaration of righteousness by faith[47]--the continuation of
Paul's "sacramental" answer to the opponents.[48]

     Though there is an indicative sense here, the typical
paraenetic function of the form is also present. One can
speak of an "imperatival indicative."[49] Paul proclaims that
the Christian *does not* live in the sphere of the flesh--because
the Galatians *do* live in the sphere of the flesh (5:13-15).
The catalog is the indicative on which the imperative is based:
but it is also imperative in that it makes clear which of the
two antithetical powers it is under which the Galatians are
now living,[50] thus calling them to live under another power.

     As well as modifying the eschatological perspective
of the form, Paul also typically modifies the contents of the
form, adapting it to particular circumstances.[51] On the basis
of statistical analysis, Wibbing has suggested the modifications in Galatians 5.[52] For the vices,[53] the first five and
the last two belong together as a "family" (πορνεία, ἀκαθαρσία,
ἀσέλγεια, εἰδωλολατρία, φαρμακεία; and then finally μέθαι,
κῶμοι), forming an *inclusio* around eight vices that particularly relate to community life (ἔχθραι, ἔρις, ζῆλος, θυμοί,
ἐριθεῖαι, διχοστασίαι, αἱρέσεις, φθόνοι). It is this central
cluster that seems to be directed to the Galatian situation,[54]
particularly διχοστασίαι and αἱρέσεις.[55] In this list, then,
it is the libertinistic vices that are the traditional ones:
contextuality, that is, Paul's thrust at the Galatians, is at
the point of love in the community.

     The list of virtues also shows contextuality. ἀγάπη
is not merely one virtue among many; and the following virtues
are not grounded in the Greek virtue-ideal.[56] They are fruit
(singular) of the Spirit, not separate individual traits of
character. Love embraces and includes all the other virtues
which follow.[57] These virtues put into ethical terms the *life*
of the community of the new age, the life of the Spirit.[58]

     These suggestions regarding contextual modification of
virtue and vice-lists tend to be confirmed in the ethical topoi
of Galatians 5-6, and the way they are related to the lists.

It is typical for Paul to modify the indicative precisely at
the point at which the indicative is to be expanded in the
imperative.[59] It is significant, then, that it is with the
subject of love in the community that the ethical topoi are
especially concerned.[60] In the heart of Gal 5:1-12, the first
imperative passage growing out of an indicative statement,[61]
appears the maxim, ἐν γὰρ Χριστῷ 'Ιησοῦ οὔτε περιτομή τι ἰσχύει
οὔτε ἀκροβυστία, ἀλλὰ πίστις δι' ἀγάπης ἐνεργουμένη (5:6). The
three verses following the next indicative statement (5:13),
are completely taken up with the maxim ἀγαπήσεις τὸν πλησίον
σου ὡς σεαυτόν.[62] And after the final part of the imperative
inclusio around the double catalog, the call to love in the
community is taken up immediately (μὴ γινώμεθα κενόδοξοι,
ἀλλήλους προκαλούμενοι, ἀλλήλοις φθονοῦντες[63] [5:26]), and
continues to be the dominant subject of the topoi (ἀλλήλων τὰ
βάρη βαστάζετε, [6:2]; ὡς καιρὸν ἔχομεν, ἐργαζώμεθα τὸ ἀγαθὸν
πρὸς πάντας, μάλιστα δὲ πρὸς τοὺς οἰκείους τῆς πίστεως [6:10].
The dynamic relationship between Paul's indicative and imperative thus become clear. The indicative/imperative nature of
the double catalog perfectly accords with the *inclusio* at
either end.

        λέγω δέ, πνεύματι περιπατεῖτε καὶ ἐπιθυμίαν
        σαρκὸς οὐ μὴ τελέσητε (5.16)
        εἰ ζῶμεν πνεύματι, (5.25),
        πνεύματι καὶ στοιχῶμεν

and the topoi which expand it. The life of the new age, the
life of freedom from the σάρξ and freedom in the πνεῦμα, is a
life of love in the community in concrete terms.[64]

        The function of the ethical passage in Galatians can
now be made clear. There is both tradition and modification
in the lists, suggesting that they are functioning as both
indicative and imperative. They are taking up well known
ethical standards, probably many of them the standards of the
opponents themselves. But whereas, traditionally, both lists
ended with a promise, now only the vice-list does. The virtue-
list climaxes in a declaration of the arrival of the new age.
The community standards that the opponents lived with only in
a tension of law-righteousness and future hope, Paul declares
are now to be lived with in a tension of eschatological "now"

and "not yet." The lists have become for Paul an indicative
which lifts Christian ethics to an entirely new plane.

And yet there is also imperative force to the double
catalog. Paul has infiltrated the description in ethical
terms of the godless, the "world," the sphere of σάρξ, with
the shortcomings of the Galatians themselves, in their attempts
to be πνευματικοί. Suddenly they both appear on the same level,
eradicating the difference between "secular" and "religious"
vices. The sin of failure to live in love in the community
becomes just as deadly as all the wickedness of the "world"
and shows that one is in the grasp of σάρξ. The traditional
climax in threat of damnation intensifies this shocking transvaluation of values: the Galatians themselves stand on the
wrong side of this eschatological dualism. In this ethical
description of who the Galatians are--and are not--there is
inherent the call to them of whom they are to be. The virtue-
list, the description of the life of the eschatological community, functions in the same way, for it is certainly not a
mirror-image of the Galatians. And the revolutionary indicative statement in 5:24 itself intensifies the imperative function of the catalog. The pronouncement of the establishment
of the new creation is itself a call to live out the new creation.[65] But there is an irony in this pronouncement too. It
is the height of folly to live under the power of σάρξ, as the
Galatians are doing in their harsh, exclusivist behavior, now
that the σάρξ has been defeated in Christ. To do so only
means that the new age, the age of the Spirit, has come εἰκῇ.[66]

The double catalog and the ethical topoi are therefore
inseparable in function and content. If the catalog carries
on the argument of the earlier chapters against the apocalyptic-
dualistic heresy of works of law, then the ethical topoi do too.
As the double catalog takes up the well known ethical values of
the opponents, modifies them at significant points, and proclaims these as the values of the new age into which the Galatians have already been established by faith and baptism, so
the ethical topoi take up traditional values which belong
within the ethical propaganda of the opponents themselves, but
which their intruding theology has demolished. On their own
terms, Paul declares the intruders and those who follow them

to be on the "dark" side of the dualistic scheme, the side of
the damned, threatened by their own law of sowing and reaping.
What makes it suddenly so much more serious is that this is the
new age, when God's people are already justified, have already
crucified the flesh, and have been delivered from the necessity
of living under the dominion of σάρξ--when the mystery, far
from having only commenced, has actually been consummated, so
that the catalog of virtues stands now not under a promise but
a proclamation of fulfillment. Foolish Galatians indeed![67]

Possible Sources of the Ethical Tradition

        Because of the dualistic nature of the argument of
Galatians, it is no coincidence that Paul has chosen to carry
on his argument here in terms of a dualistic form, the virtue-
and vice-catalog. It is therefore logical to look firstly for
parallels to this form itself and to look for dualistic life-
situations which would foster such a form.
        External parallels to the complete double catalog are
quite rare.[68] Wibbing traces it to Qumran,[69] and Kamlah to
Iran.[70] Possibly both are right, in that the dualism of Qumran, along with Jewish apocalyptic dualism generally, suggests
some Iranian influence.[71]
        The instance outside the New Testament of a form most
closely approximating that used here by Paul is in 1 QS 3-4.[72]
Its structure is as follows:[73]

3:13-14	the life-situation of the catalogs: initiation into the community or instruction of novices
3:16-24	the deterministic structure of the two classes of mankind[74]
3:25-4:1	introduction to the virtue catalog[75]
4:2-6	the virtues of those who live by the Spirit of truth[76]
4:6-8	the climax of the virtue-list, the promise of salvation[77]
4:9-11	the vices of those who live by the Spirit of error

> 4:12-14   the climax of the vice-list, the threat of
>   damnation
> 4:15-18   the present situation of the evil age[78]
> 4:18-23   the hope of purification for the righ-
>   teous.[79]

It is interesting that an essential part of this future
hope in 4:18-23 is the restoration of the כבד אדם, that which
Adam lost in the fall.[80]

There is a striking continuity and contrast between
1 QS 3-4 and Galatians 5. As in Galatians, the catalog is
placed in a dualism overruled by two antithetical powers.[81]
The vice-list is climaxed by a similar threat of damnation.
In both, there is a tension of indicative and imperative.[82]
Both call the initiate to walk (περιπατειν/הלך) in a particular
way.[83] But in Galatians, the time of salvation, the time of
the Spirit, has already come: the flesh has been crucified,
and one need no longer live under its domination. There is a
strikingly similar dualism but a radically different eschatological tension.[84]

If such a form, with its attendant eschatology and
ethic, were part of the context of Galatians, then Paul's
polemic has a particular point, and his use of the form is a
sharp thrust at the opponents' whole scheme. He agrees with
their ethic and agrees that it is an eschatological ethic. But
for this reason, it can only be realized in the new age--which
has in fact come to pass in Christ and in the community of
those who have been crucified with Him.[85] The eschatology
which Paul answers when he argues for justification by faith[86]
appears to be very close to the eschatology of 1 QS 3-4--and
to the eschatology which Paul opposes here in the ethical section. If this is so, Paul's answer is also a Christological
answer. The Christology Paul opposes when he declares that
justification conforms to the "shape" of the completed work
of Christ appears to be the Christology he opposes here, where
Jesus has a place in a scheme which still retains Qumran's
despairing dualistic estimation of the age in which the
believer lives. Here in the ethical section, Christology
would continue to be the heart of Paul's answer to the opponents.

A comparison of the contents of the catalogs in Galatians 5 and 1 QS 3-4 also yields significant results. Six of
the vices enumerated by Paul are also in the Qumran catalog,[87]
whereas a much higher proportion of the virtues have possible
parallels.[88] It would seem that Paul's vices belong more to
the common Greek ethical tradition than do his virtues, which
may be his way of continuing the traditional function of the
form by breaking any correspondence between virtues and vices.
Because the virtue-lists are much more reflections of the self-
understanding of the community,[89] it is significant that his
virtues should so closely approximate those of Qumran. Both
see the community in the same ideal terms.

If the contents of 1 QS are the ethics of the opponents,
then Paul's modification of the vice-list is also significant.
He raises to serious heights the failure to live out love in
the community; and this very ethic is at the heart of the Qumran catalog, "Abounding love for all who follow the truth."[90]
Such an ethic could be expected to be owned by community-
apostles who claim that their sacraments bring in the present
a realization of the mythical goals of humanity, no "Jew or
Greek," "male and female," et cetera.[91]

At the point where Paul apparently modifies form and
content there are significant parallels to the catalogs of
1 QS. The opponent is to be sought, not among libertines, but
among nomistic, dualistic sectarians: " . . . it is not impossible that Paul was drawing on a didactic tradition within
Judaism which is represented for us in one of its forms in
the Scrolls."[92]

Consideration must now be given to possible sources
for the ethical topoi which are inseparably connected to the
catalogs. There are two significant clues to begin with: the
opponents are Christians, as well as Judaisers, and evidently,
have an important place for Jesus in their scheme;[93] and Paul
comes to characterize his ethic (which has evidently been to
a large extent taken over from the opponents) as the "law of
Christ" (6:2).

There seems to be good evidence that, in Pauline
paraenesis, "reminiscences of the words of the Lord Jesus
Himself are interwoven with traditional material,"[94] suggesting

that "it was the words of Jesus Himself that formed Paul's
primary source in his work as an ethical διδάσκαλος."[95]   It is
important to note that these words of Jesus function, not as
specific quotations, but as a basis for interpretation and
application to some specific situation.[96] For instance,
Robinson has demonstrated that this occurs in 1 Cor 4:5-13,
where "sayings that occur in free variation" in a wide spectrum
of Christian paraenetic materials[97] are again functioning in
terms of an interpretation that is directed to a specific
situation.[98] Here is a contextual interpretation of material
that, from other sources, is known to be held together in a
tradition of "sayings of the Lord."

It is for this reason that it is not adequate to
exclude the possibility of an underlying tradition of sayings
of Jesus for any Pauline paraenetic passage, simply because
there are no formal quotation or introductory formulae.[99]

Further, there should be an examination of the function in Christian literature of the dual catalog, and the
ethical topoi which were usually associated with it.[100] It is
typically either a frame for ethics[101] or an integral part of
a paraenetic passage.[102] Several have noted that the ethical
topoi which are taken up into the catalog, in the Pauline
epistles, reflect to a significant degree the ethical teachings
of Jesus.[103] This becomes even more pronounced in Did 1-6 and
Barn 18-21. Not only are there suggestions of a "common catechetical cluster" in early Christianity;[104] there are also
hints that this cluster was typically associated with, or
placed into the frame of, a "two-way" scheme. There is the
suggestion of an association of this latter form and ethical
topoi based on the sayings of Jesus.

Thirdly, there must be some reasonable explanation for
the puzzling expression "the law of Christ."[105] There is a
closely parallel expression in 1 Cor 9:21, where Paul says
Jesus-believers are μὴ ὢν ἄνομος θεοῦ ἀλλ᾽ ἔννομος χριστοῦ,
closing a passage where he also "has occasion to refer to certain maxims belonging to the tradition of the teaching of
Jesus."[106] This suggests that such ἐπιταγαί and διατάγματα
as are referred to in 1 Corinthians (7:6, 25 and 9:14) "are
conceived as in some sort constituent elements in the 'law of

Christ.'"[107]   If this is so in 1 Corinthians, then the expression νόμος τοῦ Χριστοῦ raises the same possibility in Galatians,[108] which is not to be tested simply by looking for cita-
tions of sayings recorded in the gospels.[109]

Even on this last basis, Alfred Resch was able to find
some significant parallels between Galatians and the synoptics,
although his whole endeavor suffers from exaggeration.[110] However, when the ethical chapters of Galatians are compared with
other passages in early Christian literature that consist of
free variations of ethical topoi associated with the form of
a two-way scheme, the results appear more significant.[111]

Several conclusions stand out from such a comparison.
There are in all cases certain typical subjects (humility,
community love, care, and sharing;[112] teachers and the taught;
forgiveness of erring community members; warnings against
judging, associated with reminders of the future judgment; the
demand for love for a neighbor, who is likely to be a worst
enemy). In all of them (setting Galatians aside for the
moment) there are attempts to relate these topics to sayings
of Jesus, even though there may be no specific quotes for some
topoi (i.e., 1 Clem 13:1, 3). All of them give evidence, not
just of quotation, but of interpretation in a particular context. There may even be "dubbed-in" quotations for which
there is no known parallel.[113] All show a tendency to combine
what are separate quotations in the synoptics.

This comparison reveals that there are some rather
explicit parallels between synoptic sayings of Jesus and some
of the central topoi in Galatians 5-6.[114] However, it also
suggests that the place of sayings of Jesus in these chapters
may be even more prominent than these rather explicit parallels
indicate. Several of the topoi show a proximity to *interpretations* of sayings of Jesus in other paraenetic passages using
a two-way scheme.[115] In the light of the typical way in which
early Christian literature treated sayings of Jesus, the comparison suggests, then, that Galatians 5-6 is an interpretation of the same ethical traditions that are behind these
other passages--that is, "sayings of Jesus."

This can be seen in another way, too. The dual catalog was shown to be imperative precisely at the places where

form and content were modified; and because of the dynamic of
indicative and imperative in the passage, the ethical topoi
relate directly to these modifications. But the modifications
of the catalog form are in terms of love in the community,
which turns out to be the recurring subject of the topoi,
too[116]--which are anchored in Gal 5:14, probably a saying of
Jesus. Thus the whole paraenetic passage can be seen as an
interpretation of the saying behind Matt 22:34-40 and parallels,
expanded with the aid of other sayings of Jesus, particularly
the ones behind Matt 18:15-20 and Matt 11:28-30. The two chapters, then, stand under the heading of the "law of Christ" and
are a development of the dominical saying recorded in 5:14.[117]

    This is not only consistent with the probable sense
of the parallel expression ἔννομος Χριστοῦ in 1 Cor 9:21, as
well as the typical way in which Paul bases his paraenesis on
sayings of Jesus; it is also consistent with the overall dialogue with the opponents. In the dual catalog, Paul evidently
takes over the ethics of the opponents and defeats them on
their own grounds.[118] But the catalog and the topoi are
inseparable. So, in the topoi too, Paul evidently takes up
the ethics of the opponents.[119] If, then, the topoi are owned
by the opponents, and if these topoi are based on sayings of
Jesus, then the opponents themselves must have an interest in
sayings of Jesus,[120] and the expression νόμος τοῦ Χριστοῦ may
be their own.[121] It probably epitomizes the connection they
see between Jesus and the law. Given their other traditions,
and the way they are functioning in the opponents' theology,
this connection would have functioned for them in two ways in
particular. Jesus would have been seen as a law-giver after
the style of Moses, who, through heavenly revelation, was able
to communicate the particularities of the secrets of the cosmos; He would have been made a dispenser of wisdom-sayings in
keeping with the hidden wisdom embodied in the law. And secondly, He would have been placed in a stream of powerful
representatives of covenant-law,[122] so that he eternalized the
law, especially the Mosaic law, or law in terms of their selective tendencies. He would have been understood as leading the
remnant to keep the law in a new, deeper sense; He would have
been a reauthentication of Moses. Hence the opponents no

doubt spoke of a νόμος τοῦ Χριστοῦ in a way that made Christ
a second Moses, who, because of the tradition of reauthentication of the covenants, could not rise above Moses.[123] By the
"law of Christ" the opponents would have understood the precepts of Jesus, interpreted within the framework of the law of
Moses.

The opponents' interest in Jesus, and in the "law of
Christ" in this sense, is understandable in terms of traditional Jewish expectations regarding the Messiah, some of
which may have particular proximity to the debate in Galatians.
In a wide spread of Jewish literature, the coming Messiah is
to have his new Torah,[124] and Qumran materials are among such
literature.[125] If Jewish schemes dividing history into the
age of Tohuwabohu, the age of Mosaic law, and the age of the
Messiah, are to be taken into account,[126] they only reinforce
the expectation that the Messiah was to bring fulfillment of
the law of Moses in a deeper, renewed sense.[127] Such traditions may help to understand how the opponents can preach both
Jesus and the law, and how Paul can turn from rejecting a religion of law to speaking suddenly of the "law of Christ."[128]

Is such a movement, heretical and yet attached to the
sayings of Jesus, at all likely? There is much to suggest
that it is. Coming from various directions, several have concluded that "the most original gattung of the Jesus-tradition"
was the "*Logoi Sophon*," "which, in the canonical gospels,
became acceptable to the orthodox church only by radical critical alteration . . . achieved by Matthew and Luke through
imposing the Markan narrative-kerygma frame upon the sayings
tradition represented by Q."[129] Not only so, but the gattung
"*logoi sophon*" apparently had certain inbuilt heretical tendencies such as a "gnosticising proclivity," which could take
legalistic directions.[130] As for Q itself, both the form and
the content of the collection may have had particular Christological aims, dispensing with the passion or presenting suffering only in a heroic manner;[131] and eschatologically, it
may have paid most attention to the *coming* kingdom of God.[132]
Already it has been suggested that the debate behind Gal 3:28
may have involved a particular understanding of sayings of
Jesus.[133] And in a wider frame, too, it is possible to say

that, as Paul takes up the ethical topoi of Galatians 5-6
closely conntected with sayings of Jesus, he is taking up the
ethics of the opponents themselves and defeating them on their
own ground.

The opponents are an early Christian movement, with
an important place for Jesus; and yet they reject the full
eschatological significance of the Christ-event[134] and the
concrete personal implications of the cross.[135] From Galatians 5-6 it appears that they are an ethical movement, even
a reform movement. But from the particular way in which Paul
has modified the form of the dual catalog, they see themselves
as living still in the present evil age. Their hope must lie
in the future kingdom of God. This eschatology immediately
infers also a particular Christology. It denies that the
Christ-event has divided the ages and that the death of Christ
has brought deliverance from the present evil age.

Such ethics, eschatology, and Christology are in perfect accord with a belief that acceptance of Jesus brings a
justification by faith to which must be added a justification
by works of law--a justification by faith which is the beginning of a covenant relationship that must then be maintained
by a δικαιοσύνη ἐξ ἔργων νόμου. If there is a "low" Christology, and no eschatological dividing of the ages, then the
ancient covenant dispensation is still in force. It is the
one Christology and eschatology that Paul must answer firstly
by a proclamation of justification without works of law--and
finally by a proclamation of the totally new ethic that is
the other side of the defeat, in Christ's death, of the power
of the σάρξ.[136] Justification is an eschatological doctrine,
and ethics become eschatological ethics.

One last thing should be said. Paul has not, here in
Galatians, so enthusiastically stated the Christian's freedom
from the law that he reaches excesses and can never speak
again so boldly.[137] He has not removed all suggestion of
external compulsion and specific ethical precepts, putting in
their place the law of the Spirit as a sort of "inward and
nonpropositional guidance."[138] The ethical passage of the book
returns to particularity and contextuality,[139] a real sense of
"law," in two ways. Firstly, the modifications of the catalog

form are especially directed at shortcomings in behavior
attributable to the intruding theology. They are "imperatives" in the real sense, demands that are expected to be
carried out. Secondly, the ethical topoi, which are inseparably connected with this contextual modification, are themselves an interpretation of a larger ethical tradition; they
not only represent a particular application of that tradition
but also infer and bring into play the whole tradition.[140]
"Law" has returned in full force.[141] The difference between
the opponents and Paul is not that of law versus no law, but
of law identified with Moses in a particular sense versus law
identified with the person of, and attached to, Christ; and
of law as a way of entering the new age versus the law for
one who is already, in Christ's deed, in the New age and for
whom, for the first time, there is the possibility of fulfillment of eschatological demands.

Conclusions

An essential part of early Christian theology was
meditation on Jesus and his sayings[142]--meditation using various frames in which Jesus-traditions were placed and coming to
diverse conclusions.[143] Paul's own letters represent certain
directions which such meditations could take[144] as do the gospels themselves.[145] The Galatian opponents, too, are Christians and have an evident interest in Jesus and His teachings.[146]
In the ethical section of Galatians Paul gives yet another
interpretation not only of Jesus' sayings but--because he
builds this interpretation on the assertion that the new age
has arrived in Christ--of Jesus Himself. This stands over
against the opponents' own interpretation of Jesus' sayings,
which also grows out of an understanding of Jesus.

This assessment of the dialogue involved in Galatians
5-6 offers an explanation of the sudden appearance of the
unusual expression "the law of Christ." It would seem that,
in the Galatian context, "maxims which formed part of the
traditions of the sayings of Jesus are treated as if they were
in some sort elements of a new Torah."[147] The subtlety is
that an analysis of the usual sources for Paul's paraenesis,

the form of the two-way scheme and its connection with the
ethical topoi of the chapters, possible Jewish traditions that
provide a precedent for the expression "law of Christ," and
the typical function of a rhetorical *refutatio* all suggest that
the expression and the maxims belong to the opponents. This is
in a frame in which the Mosaic covenant is mythologized as the
highest form of wisdom, and Jesus is merely the last of wisdom's
spokesmen. The opponents have brought to Christianity their
frame of sectarian Judaism and have placed Jesus and His teachings in that frame.

Paul, then, must find a way of negating the frame and
all its consequences, while retaining Jesus and His teachings.
In the earlier chapters he takes Jesus out of the sequence of
great heroes of the law by making the law an interim period,
and the line of salvation a line that runs directly from Abraham to Christ. He historicises Jesus, stressing the cross in
history and eschatology, so that he can speak of the arrival
in the present of the new age. He is then ready to defeat the
opponents on their own grounds, in terms of Jesus and His
teachings.

This would explain why Paul can move so abruptly from
speaking of being imprisoned under the "whole law" (ὅλον τὸν
νόμον [5:3]) to speaking of fulfilling "all the law" in the
life of the Christian (ὁ πᾶς νόμος [5:14]; ἀναπληρώσετε τὸν
νόμον τοῦ χριστοῦ [6:2]; and the references to νόμος in 5:18,
23). The force of the two ways in which Paul speaks of law
must be preserved; and in this way a correct assessment of the
ethical section safeguards the understanding of the dogmatic
section. Paul battles against the "whole law" in principle.
But it is law in principle in terms of the "Tendenz" of the
opponents' selectivity, and of their assertion of the cosmic
and soteriological significance of law, which brings one into
all the blessings of the age to come. There are certain indications of this in the "dogmatic" section itself; but it is
confirmed by the way in which, in the "ethical" section, Paul
comes to speak positively of "law."

It is for this reason that the paraenetic passage of
Galatians belongs with the whole argument. In both chapters
3-4 and 5-6 Paul is developing the significance of baptism.

Both sections go back to 2:15-21, the believer's death to the
law in the death of Christ, and the elaboration of righteousness as "life" which has one unchanging quality from beginning
to end. The ethical passage, which, at its heart, places the
Christian under the new imperative, is the converse side of
that righteousness which is life which is first taken up in
2:15-21.[148] In both sections, then, Paul is dealing with the
one problem, the one intruding theology. The "biting and
devouring" (5:13-15) which epitomizes an ethical breakdown
among the Galatians as serious as any "worldly" sins, arises
out of the intruders' program of nomistic perfection and
spirituality (ὑμεῖς οἱ πνευματικοί [6:1])--the same program
which results in a hierarchic exclusivism and a boasting of
converts, and the cruel rejection of Paul himself.[149] The
ethical section is an important commentary on the opponents'
program, theology, spiritualism, self-understanding, and
ecclesiology.

          Paul can here speak of fulfillment of law in the
Christain life (5:14), and of this life as one in which law
can find no shortcoming (5:23). But only when Jesus and His
"law" are taken out of the frame of law in terms of cosmic
redemption, that is, law in terms of the "Tendenz" of the opponents, can "the will of God revealed in the Christian" be
"identical with the demand of the law."[150] Only when the
lordship of Christ over the aeons and the cosmos is established
--only when the lordship of Christ over law is established--
does the "eschatological" ethic, the fulfillment of the "whole
law," become a real possibility.[151] Only in the new freedom
of the Spirit, the "new creation,"[152] is there the possibility
of realizing the command's intention to bestow life.[153]

          Paul is saying to the opponents, "Even your ethic
breaks down, for the very reason that it is an eschatological
ethic. You have not acknowledged the eschatological work of
Christ, and for you there can be no fulfillment. The very
thing you preach most against has happened, and you have fallen
subject to σάρξ." In this sense the paraenetic section is a
rhetorical *refutatio*, the final argument against the intruding
theology. The heresy is not a perfection of that religion
into which the Galatians were conducted by their baptism, the

religion of πνεῦμα (3:1-5). It is a retrogression into the
antithetical existence, the existence of σάρξ. Paul is refut-
ing the opponents' case in terms of their own ethos, claiming
the debate has been won, demanding damages and compensation--
the return of the community to the freedom of the Spirit.

Table 1

A Comparison of Galatians 5-6 with Ethical Traditions Associated with a
Two-Way Scheme, and Possible Synoptic Parallels

Rom 12-15	Synoptics	Gal 5-6	Did 1-5	Barn 18-21	Clem
12:3 Don't think of self more highly than--ought 12:6 Do not be haughty . . . never be conceited	Matt 5:5 Blessed are the meek.154	6:3 If anyone thinks he is something when he is nothing, he deceives himself.	3:9 Thou shalt not exalt thyself, nor let thy soul be presumptuous.154	19:3 Thou shalt not exalt thyself, but shall be humbleminded in all things.	1 Cor 13:1 Let us . . . be humbleminded . . . putting aside all arrogance and conceit . . . 13:3 let us . . . walk in obedience to His (Jesus') hallowed words, and let us be humbleminded.155 1 Cor 13:2 As ye are kind, so shall kindness be shown you.156
12:10 Love one another with brotherly affection: outdo one another in showing honor. 12:16 Live in harmony with one another.	Lk 6:27 καλῶς ποιεῖτε. Matt 11:28-30 the φορτίον of the Messiah.157 Matt 23:4 the Scribes and Pharisees who lay on others	6:2 Bear one another's βάρη. 6:5 Bear your φορτίον158 6:9 Let us not grow weary in well-doing (καλὸν ποιοῦντες.) 6:11 Let us	4:8 Share everything with thy brother.	19:8 Thou shalt share all things with thy neighbor.	

Table 1 (Continued)

Rom 12-15	Synoptics	Gal 5-6	Did 1-5	Barn 18-21	Clem
12:11 Never flag in zeal.	φορτία Βαρέα.158	do good to all, especially household of faith.159			
12:7 He who teaches, in teaching.	Lk 6:40 The teacher and the taught.	6:6 Let him who is taught share with him who teaches.	4:1 Remember . . . him who speaks the word of God to thee, and thou shalt honor him as the Lord.	19:9 Thou shalt love as the apple of thine eye all who speak to thee the word of the Lord.	
12:18 As far as possible, live peaceably with all. 15:1 We who are strong ought to bear with the failings of the weak, and not to please ourselves.	Matt 6:12 As we forgive our debtors. Lk 6:37 Forgive, and you will be forgiven. Matt 18:15-20 Church order.161	6:1 Anyone overtaken in a trespass, you who are spiritual should restore him in a spirit of gentleness.161	3:8 Be thou longsuffering, and merciful and guileless, and quiet, and good. 4:3 Thou shalt not desire a schism, but shalt reconcile those who strive.	19:12 Thou shalt not cause quarrels, but shalt bring together and reconcile those that strive.	1 Cor 13:2 Forgive, that you be forgiven. 1 Cor 13:1 The words of the Lord Jesus which he spoke when he was teaching gentleness and long-suffering.160
14:10 Why do you pass judgment on your	Lk 6:37 Judge not, and you	6:1 Look to yourself, lest you too		19:10 Thou shalt remember the day	1 Cor 13:2 As you judge,

Table 1 (Continued)

Rom 12-15	Synoptics	Gal 5-6	Did 1-5	Barn 18-21	Clem
brother? For we shall all stand before the judgment seat of God.163 14:13 Let us not judge one another any more . . . judge this . . . rather . . . no stumbling block in another's way.	will not be judged; condemn not, and you will not be condemned.	be tempted. 6:7ff. As a man sows, so shall he reap.		of judgment day and night.162	you will be judged.162
13:8 Love one another; for he who loves his neighbor has fulfilled the law . . . love is the fulfilling of the law. (πεπλήρωκεν)	Matt 22:34-40 and parallels love your neighbor as yourself. Matt 5:17 πλη-ρoῦν Matt 5:43 love neighbor . . . enemy.	6:2 Bear one another's burdens, and so fulfill the law of Christ (ἀνα-πληρόσετε) 5:14 For the whole law is fulfilled in one word, Love your neighbor as yourself, (πεπλήρωται)	1:2-5 Way of life . . . love God . . . neighbor . . . bless those who curse you . . . Love those who hate you.	19:4-5 Thou shalt not bear malice against thy brother . . . thou shalt love thy neighbor more than thy own life.	2 Cor 13:4 Love your enemies and those who hate you.

Table 2

A Selection of Parallels between Galatians
and the Synoptic Sayings of Jesus
Suggested by D. Alfred Resch[164]

Galatians	Synoptics
2:20 τοῦ υἱοῦ τοῦ θεοῦ . . . παραδόντος ἑαυτὸν ὑπὲρ ἐμοῦ	Matt 20:28, Mark 10:45 ὁ υἱὸς τοῦ ἀνθρώπου . . . ἦλθεν . . . δοῦναι τὴν ψυχὴν αὐτοῦ λύτρον ἀντὶ πολλῶν
5:21 οἱ τὰ τοιαῦτα πράσ- σοντες βασιλείαν θεοῦ οὐ κληρονομήσουσιν	Matt 25:34 κληρονομήσατε τὴν . . . βασιλείαν
6:1 ἀδελφοί, ἐὰν καὶ προ- λημφθῇ ἄνθρωπος ἔν τινι παραπτώματι, ὑμεῖς οἱ πνευματικοί καταρτίζετε τὸν τοι- οῦτον	Matt 18:15, Luke 17:3 ἐὰν δὲ ἁμαρτήσῃ ὁ ἀδελφός σου, ὕπαγε ἔλεγξον αὐτὸν μεταξὺ σοῦ καὶ αὐτοῦ μόνον
6:1 σκοπῶν σεαυτὸν	Luke 11:35, Matt 6:23 σκόπει οὖν μὴ τὸ φῶς τὸ ἐν σοὶ σκότος ἐστίν
6:2 καὶ οὕτως ἀναπλη- ρώσατε τὸν νόμον τοῦ Χριστοῦ	Matt 22:40 ἐν ταύταις ταῖς δυσὶν ἐντολαῖς ὅλος ὁ νόμος κρέμαται καὶ οἱ προφῆται
6:5 ἕκαστος γὰρ τὸ ἴδιον φορτίον βαστάσει	Matt 11:30 τὸ φορτίον μου ἐλαφρόν ἐστιν
6:7-8 The Judgment-saying	Matt 13:24-30 Parable of the Harvest
6:9 καιρῷ γὰρ ἰδίῳ θερί- σομεν	Matt 13:30 καιρῷ τοῦ θερισμοῦ

CONCLUSIONS

The Unity of Galatians and Its Argument

This thesis began by positing the unity of Galatians
and its argument firstly on the basis of methodological considerations. The defensive statements of the letter, which
come mostly from the "historical" passages, cannot account for
the opponents' theology. The direct charges that Paul answers
in Galatians do not explain the most distinctive passages of
the letter.[1] A quest for the opponents based on the mirror-
image of the defensive statements is inadequate. Further,
the whole letter is polemical, and yet only brief verses refer
to the opponents themselves.[2] Then again, references to the
opponents are not references to the opponents' theology. Paul
does distinguish between the Galatians and the opponents, but
not between the Galatians' and the opponents' theology.
Rather, his handling of their theology is bound up with the
structure of the letter as a whole.[3] Finally, the Galatians
are treated as a homogeneous community. If there are any
threats, the whole community is in danger of acceding to
them.[4] Along with this, the only commonly used indicator of
two groups behind the letter (either Galatians and opponents
separately [Jewett and Hawkins],[5] or two "parties" of Galatians [Gunter, Bruce, etc.]),[6] the ethical passage, raises
other complex issues such as use of ethical traditions,[7] making it unacceptable for this purpose. The letter resists subdivision based on its final section, and the same concerns
appear in every part.[8]

Thus the dialogical nature of Galatians stands out.
It is a letter motivated by an intruding, offending theology,
yet it addresses the theology almost exclusively by addressing
the congregation that has been "bewitched" by the intruders.

The unity of the letter was further explored in terms
of genre analysis. From a comparison of Galatians with other

Pauline letters,[9] a comparison of Galatians with extra-Biblical
literature giving evidence of a similar purpose and structure,[10]
and an examination of certain indicators within the letter
itself (especially the *conclusio* and *prooemium*),[11] it was suggested that Galatians belongs to the literary genre of apologetic speech.[12] This has important implications for the relationship of the parts of the letter to each other. The
prooemium (1:6-10), which functions as a *causa*, reveals that
it is the Galatians, and their acceptance of the opponents'
propaganda, not merely the opponents themselves, who have
called forth the letter. The Galatians are in a sense the
opponents; and as this passage stands at the head of the
letter, the whole letter will dispute the *Galatians'* acceptance
of the *intruders'* false gospel, and its consequences.[13]

The *propositio* (2:15-21) picks up the climax of the
narratio in 2:14 and elaborates the issue to be determined in
terms of that which is agreed upon and that which is particularly in dispute. Then the whole debate comes to hinge on two
understandings of righteousness by faith--one about which there
is agreement and one about which there is disagreement. A
noticeable shift in language from 2:16-18 to 2:19-20 not only
puts the issue in the most relevant form but looks forward to
the rest of the argument that is to follow.[14]

The clear break in structure and language, in 3:1-5,
indicates that a new division begins here--in rhetorical terms,
the *probatio*, the central argument against the offenders and
their central argument, running from 3:1 to 4:31. Of this
division, 3:1-5 stands apart as an *interrogatio*, the bridge
from the concluding climax of the *propositio* into the precise
way the writer wishes to conduct the *probatio*. Here again,
the point in dispute, righteousness by faith, is put into significant terms. For the rest, certain striking themes run
through the whole *probatio*: Abraham, the (Mosaic) law, slavery, freedom, sonship, et cetera.[15]

In rhetorical terms, 5:1-6:10 would be expected to
function as a *refutatio*, the final destruction of the adversaries' argument.[16] In this case it is integrally connected
with what has preceded, and is still addressing the same
problem--the Galatians' acceptance of the intruders' theology.

Further, a *refutatio* would conclude the debate by appealing to
norms to which even the opponents had to agree. As the passage
is in the style of ethical exhortation, then, these must be the
ethics of the opponents themselves.[17] Paul is attacking an
ethos that is owned by the opposition, with standards that
belong to the opposition.

In addition to the internal indicators that Galatians
belongs to the genre of "apologetic speech," the letter, when
analyzed in terms of this genre, unfolds in a way that is consistent with the evident unity that has been demonstrated
already. Genre-analysis indicates the sense in which Galatians is dialogical, dialogical to what extent, and dialogical
with whom. It is a dialogue especially with Galatians who
have accepted the theology of the intruders.

These conclusions regarding the unity of the letter
were then confirmed by an examination of internal indicators
of structure which at the same time sought to establish an
outline of the opponents' position and the essential issues
being disputed.

The opening and closing elements of the letter (1:1-5,
6:11-18) show striking modifications of Paul's epistolary
practice, indicating that he has here incorporated items
essential to the debate. The issue of apostle is inseparable
from the issue of the gospel and throws light on the effici-
ency and authoritarianism of the opponents, confirming the
way the Galatians are completely "under their spell."[18] The
stress in the letter on the relationship between apostolicity
and doctrine supports the assertions about the unity of the
letter. Perhaps even more important, prescript and postscript
both indicate the essential place of Christology and eschatology. Justification is to be understood as cosmic deliverance,
entrance into the new age, and participation in the new
creation.[19] Paul's debate, carried on by elaborating the
meaning of justification, is carried on by elaborating Christology, and the eschatology derived from it.[20] And these
opening and closing elements introduce or tie off an important
antithesis (which, in diatribe style, summarizes the debate),
freedom and slavery. The implication is that the central term
in the debate, δικαιοσύνη, is being expounded in terms of this

antithesis.   In Galatians, justification is particularly freedom from all enslaving powers.[21]   In these parts of the letter
Paul also stresses the cross in both theology and experience.
Unlike Paul's other letters, there is little mention of the
resurrection.   The cosmic deliverance of justification is
elaborated instead in terms of crucifixion.[22]

The *causa* (1:6-10) sets forth the central feature of
the heresy--μετατιθέναι, abandonment or desertion--beginning
one way and ending another.   In a way that is consistent with
apologetic speech, the *causa* is restated throughout the whole
letter.   In every section (1:6-10, 2:15-21, 3:1-5, 4:8-11,
and 5:16-24), and in different terms (ἐνάρχεσθαι and ἐπιτελεῖν,
ἐπιστρέφειν, καταλύειν and οἰκοδομεῖν, μὴ πείθειν, τὴν σάρκα
σταυροῦν and ἐπιθυμίαν τὴν σάρκα τελεῖν), the one reason behind
the whole letter is reaffirmed--the treacherous embracing by
the Galatians of the opponents' theology.[23]

The *propositio* in 2:16-21, in many ways the heart of
the letter, sharpens the issue of beginning and ending in
theological terms.   Terminology, syntax, et cetera, indicate
that the opponents themselves accept a justification without
works of law.   The heresy is essentially a Christian one, and
Paul here, in his polemical formulation of justification by
faith without works of law, is not leveling a criticism at
Judaism itself.   Paul and the opponents part company when
justification by faith becomes more than just a starting-
point, to which must be added a justification by works of
law.   By moving from aorist to continuous tenses, and from
"legal" to mystical and existential language, justification
for Paul becomes the equivalent of life, a continuous identification with Christ, and faith becomes an attitude that characterizes all of life, from beginning to end.   This move also
places the debate in the context of the significance of baptism and the Christian's participation in the death and resurrection of Christ.   Whereas Paul usually uses baptism to
discuss the new life of the Christian, he uses it here to
clarify the meaning of justification.   The two have become
equivalent.   Paul's answer to the opponents is a sacramental
answer and is therefore a Christological answer: justification
corresponds to the present lordship of Christ and can therefore

be in no sense added to.   Because it is a Christological
answer, it is also an eshcatological answer.   To refuse it is
to say "Christ died in vain," that is, that the cross does not
mark the dividing of the ages (4:4-5).[24]

This significance of baptism, and the definition of
justification that grows out of it, runs throughout the whole
letter (2:16-21, 3:1-5, 3:27-29, 4:5-6, and 5:24), and becomes
the essence of Paul's answer to the opponents.   This links the
theological and ethical portions of the letter together.   Both
justification and ethics are dealt with by expounding the significance of the new creation that the Christian enters in
baptism; and both justification and ethics take on the shape
of Christology and eschatology.   This again confirms the above
conclusions based on methodology and genre analysis.

The *interrogatio*, in 3:1-5, introduces further significant language as it opens up the central argument of the
letter, again by examining the meaning of baptism.   The Galatians are twice called ἀνόητος, often meaning an uninitiate,
one who stands outside the mysteries of religion.   They are
ἀνόητοί because they have been bewitched (βασκαίνειν), cast
under a spell by the intruders.   The essence of their foolishness is made apparent by the play on ἐνάρχεσθαι and ἐπιτελεῖν,
words often denoting the beginning and completion of religious
ceremonies or mysteries, possibly coming from the opponents
themselves.   The Spirit came to them at baptism, and the Spirit
is the eschatological sign of the completion of religious
initiation.   Then their new attempt at completion (ἐπιτελεῖν)
cannot be a progression in the religion they accepted at baptism, but must be an entirely different religion.   If, then,
at baptism they entered the religion of πνεῦμα, they must now
be returning to a religion of σάρξ.   This is why they are
ἀνόητοι.   They have returned to the standing of one who was
never initiated into the true mysteries of religion.   Not only
is this elaborating the *causa*; it is also elaborating the way
in which the opponents themselves have presented their nomistic
program--as a completion (ἐπιτελεῖν) of a mystery of which
baptism is only an initiation (ἐνάρχεσθαι).[25]

The antithesis of σάρξ and πνεῦμα is then taken up
throughout the rest of the letter, climaxing in chapters 5 and

6, where, in their ethos, the Galatians are again charged
with having fallen under the domination of the power of σάρξ,
which is so serious because the new age of Spirit, and deliverance from σάρξ, has already arrived (5:16-24).[26]

An analysis of chapters 3 and 4 reveals that the
argument between 3:1 and 4:11 is being held together by the
device of the "mot crochet." The whole piece is an integral
argument, and both 3:1-5 and 4:8-11, functioning as restatements of the *causa*, lament that the Galatians' experience may
have been εἰκῆ.[27] The controversial section (4:8-11) has not
fallen out of the argument but is intimately bound up with the
attack on the offending theology.

One of the conclusions thus arrived at is that the
chapters dealing with method, genre, and structure hold
together and tend to confirm each other. Galatians throughout
is a dialogical response to opponents; in theological terms,
the Galatians are identified with the opponents, and the whole
letter is written against a single theological complex. The
other conclusion is that these indications of unity and structure allow a preliminary hypothesis regarding the theology of
the opponents.[28]

The Traditions of the Opponents

If the letter holds together in this way, if these
various pieces in Paul's argument are all directed at one
offending theology, and if that theology is as sketched out
above, then who are the opponents? The attempt to uncover
possible sources for such a theology--sources in which the
different elements or theologoumena of the letter would be
congruous--is at the one time a testing of the hypothesis
already arrived at and a further filling out of that hypothesis. There appears, in fact to be an inner consistency and
coherence in the theologoumena and the way they are functioning in the letter.

The opponents' tradition of apostleship is one in
which there is a programmatic demand for ἀποκαλύψεις, the
content of which must be divulged, and, at the same time,
there is a reverence for certain traditions associated with

Jerusalem and a scorning of the Jerusalem leadership of the church. The suggestion that the source here is Gnosticism must be dismissed.[29] It is much more likely to be apocalyptic Judaism.[30] This apostle-tradition belongs with a particular self-understanding,[31] which itself would encourage certain "hagiographies" of religious heroes[32]--thus looking forward to some of the other theologoumena to be considered.

A tradition centering in Abraham is evidently important to the opponents. Not only is he a keeper of the law,[33] but in certain circles he is a basis for an appeal to Gentiles[34] and a basis for a reform-nomistic soteriology which applied to Jews as well as Gentiles.[35] Although this Abraham belongs especially in "apologetic" literature, the categories of literature must not be made too rigid. The "apologetic" Abraham appears also in some "apocalyptic" literature,[36] and certainly the "nomistic" Abraham belongs here. Further, this particular "Abraham" matches well with the tradition of apostle and the self-understanding associated with it.

Central to the opponents is a cluster of traditions associated with the law. Law to them must be a way of cosmic deliverance, the dialogical counterpart to Paul's presentation of justification as cosmic deliverance.[37] They also hold to a sense of "justification without the works of the law."[38] Their special reverence for law is tied up with their presentation of Moses as the chief mystagogue, making the Mosaic covenant the highest form of revealed religion.[39] "Law" to both Paul and the opponents is the "whole law," but it is the "whole law" in terms of a selectivity in the demand for observance of the law that focuses on circumcision and calendrical feasts.[40] And it is a law-tradition which, while it may not own to worship of the στοιχεῖα τοῦ κόσμου, lays itself open to a propagandistic analogy between its own program and Pagan στοιχεῖα--religion as practiced by the Galatians before they became Christians.[41]

Again, it is the law-traditions in apocalyptic literature which most closely match these characteristics. This literature fills out further the probable law-tradition of the opponents, where law was conceived as that which brought one into harmony with the cosmos and gave one power over it.[42]

It was a knowledge of law that could come only by revelation;
and both the medium and the contents of this revelation lifted
one into angelic company.[43] There was such an interest in
calendrical piety, and such a close association between the
Mosaic law, the secret order of the cosmos, and angelic inter-
mediaries that this law-tradition could have been open to the
charge that it was nothing other than a counterpart of the
Pagan worship of the στοιχεῖα.[44]

    As Paul's answer to the intruding theology is essen-
tially a sacramental answer, sacrament can be assumed to be
playing a central role in the debate. As well as making circumcision essential to salvation, the opponents apparently
understand the rite in a unique way, judging by Paul's unique
attack upon it.[45] It is associated with an understanding of
Judaism as a mystery religion, has unusual appeal to Gentiles,
and may be said to be imitative of angels.[46] In one of the
climaxes of the letter, Paul makes baptism its dialogical
counterpart. What the opponents say is to be achieved by
circumcision, Paul says is already achieved by baptism.[47]
This in itself is consistent with the *causa* of the letter:
the religion is one of beginning and ending, novitiate and
final initiation, where baptism is the beginning initiation,
and nomistic sacraments, epitomized by circumcision, are the
climax.[48]

    Counterparts to this understanding of circumcision,
far from being found in Gnosticism, appear in apocalyptic and
mystical Judaism, and perhaps receive encouragement from
"apologetic" portrayals of Judaism.[49]

    The exact role played by the sacraments in the theology
of the opponents becomes even more apparent when the baptismal
formula of 3:28 is examined more carefully. The opponents are
Christians, as well as Judaizers. The use of this form here
and in other literature suggests that it may have been first
introduced into Galatia by the opponents themselves, in connection, not with baptism, but with their own sacramental program.[50] If so, the concern behind the formula may have been
a sacramental realization of the angelic state--again, a concern of apocalyptic literature,[51] and one that matches well

with the peculiar traits of their presentation of circumcision,
as well as the theologoumena examined previously.

The ethical passage of the letter, chapters 5 and 6,
figures prominently in the debate regarding the unity of the
letter, and therefore is particularly relevant for understanding the program of the opponents. Here there was first an
examination of the form and content of the double catalog and
of Paul's modification of these two.[52] It was concluded,
firstly, that the ethical passage continues Paul's argument of
2:15-21, is based on baptism, is in terms of σάρξ and πνεῦμα,
as in 3:1-5, and has the same thrust as the repetitions of the
causa: the Galatians have again placed themselves under the
power of σάρξ, the power whose hold was broken in baptism.
Paul indeed is probably here conducting the debate in the
opponents' own ethical terms and is showing that, in their own
reckoning, their program has failed.[53] Secondly, the closest
parallels to the form and content of the double catalog are
again in apocalyptic literature, this time in Qumran
writings.[54]

An examination of the topoi associated with the double
catalog revealed that they are inseparable from the former and
are again probably the topoi of the opponents. The possibility that sayings of Jesus are involved here is consistent with
the treatment of 2:16-21, which stressed that the heresy is a
Christian heresy, that it has an important place for Jesus in
its scheme (who, in the light of their law-traditions, is
probably made a dispenser of nomistic sayings about law and
cosmic order), and has a concept of faith. The topoi therefore accord with the dialogical function to be expected of
this passage--a refutation of the opponents on their own
grounds.[55]

In conclusion, the examination of the theologoumena
reveals that it is indeed possible that one intruding theology
has called forth the whole book. Further, there is consistently one probable source for this theology--apocalyptic and
sectarian Judaism, especially circles associated with Qumran.[56] At the same time, there may have been a drawing on
the propaganda methods of "apologetic" Judaism, although so

often the traditions are common property. Along with these,
there is the other important source of early Christian tradition.

It is when Galatians is understood dialogically, as a
response to a single opponent, that it becomes possible to draw
together the various theologoumena, called for by the particular passages of the letter, and find their inner consistency.

The Theology of the Opponents

From an examination of the above theologoumena, certain probable characteristics of the opponents' theology stand
out.

As has been shown above, Christology is evidently
central to the letter. Paul refers to it at several important
places (i.e., 1:4, 4:4-5, etc.), and the opponents, too, probably have a central place for Jesus.[57] Their gospel is another
gospel, with another Jesus. Because of their traditions of
law, et cetera, He is probably a Jesus who is powerful to
enable the law to be kept, a Jesus who glorifies the old
covenant-dispensation.[58]

There is a subtlety in the Jesus of the opponents.
On the one hand, they probably preach a glorious Jesus who
accords with their tradition of apostle and their self-
understanding, a Jesus who becomes another hagiography to
stand alongside those of Abraham and Moses, a Jesus who is a
powerful representative of God. This is revealed in the way
he must be to them a cross-less Jesus, as Paul must stress the
cross, in theology and experience.[59] The Jesus of the Galatians may have been very similar to the Jesus of the opponents
in 2 Corinthians,[60] "A power-laden glorious miracle-worker,
much as in the signs source (of John), whose earthly ministry
could well be epitomized by comparing his glory with that of
Moses, as in 2 Corinthians 3."[61]

Yet at the same time this glorious Jesus is not the
eschatological revelation of God. The opponents' doctrine of
justification no doubt conforms to their Christology: it is
a justification which must be added to, because Jesus to them
has not brought in the new age, and the law-covenant remains

the most glorious revelation of God. Jesus is probably made
one of a series of mighty representatives of God--and in this
way, is not able to surpass the significance of Abraham and
Moses.

So Paul must proclaim *both* the humanness, weakness,
and cursedness of Jesus (3:13, 4:4-5) *and* the eschatological
finality of Jesus, who has brought the new age, the new creation (1:4, 6:12-14). Paul's Jesus is at the same time less
and more than the Jesus of the opponents.

For both Paul and the opponents, eschatology conforms
to the "shape" of Christology.[62] Their eschatology is not
that of the "Hellenist enthusiasts,"[63] as is plain from Paul's
use of the unification-saying in 3:28.[64] It is Paul who
stresses realized eschatology, especially in his use of the
baptism-tradition: the age of the Spirit is now (3:1-5), the
climax of religion is already attained (3:28), and the possibility of life under the power of σάρξ has been removed for
the Christian (5:24). Even Paul's answer regarding the law
is an eschatological one. From the perspective of the cross,
it can be seen that the age of law is the age of curse, an
age that has now been brought to an end.[65] There is even
modification of Paul's typical "eschatological reservation"
in Galatians. The form of eschatology so conforms to Christology that the new age has come while the old age remains, and
the new age is only present in Christ. Outside Christ, the
only possibility is to live in the old age. However, Paul
adds little "reservation" to the nature of existence in Christ
(5:16-25). In this respect, his eschatology is similar to
that in 2 Corinthians.[66]

All the indications are, then, that the opponents
preached something much less than a realized eschatology.
Their message was probably centered in the coming kingdom of
God, and even their enthusiastic sense of fellowship with
angels only contributed to their nomistic reform program.[67]

Ecclesiology, too, for both Paul and the opponents,
grows directly out of Christology. The Christology of the
opponents would seem to have two consequences in particular
here. Firstly, their glorious Jesus fixes attention on the
individual in a competitive sense, which results in a

hierarchical, schismatic ecclesiology which glorifies the
intruding apostles.[68] It is coupled with a remnant concept,
so that as law-keeping more and more brings fellowship with
angels and the higher powers of the universe, it separates
the law-keeper more and more from those around him. The
glorious Jesus is fragmenting the community. Secondly, the
less than eschatological Jesus of the opponents, who has not
yet divided the ages, means that this angelic remnant *must be*
a law-keeping remnant, adding justification by works to their
justification by faith, thereby becoming a bridge between the
covenant-traditions of the Jerusalem of the past and the Jerusalem of the future.[69] The glorious Jesus makes the opponents
part of the heavenly Jerusalem. The less than eschatological
Jesus makes them keepers of all the traditions of the earthly
Jerusalem.

It is for this reason that the heresy has been referred
to above as a "nomistic enthusiasm."[70] It is enthusiastic as
it grows out of traditions of the glorious apostle and the
glorious Jesus; but it is nomistic, because Jesus has not yet
divided the ages. Long ago, Lightfoot proposed that Paul was
everywhere confronting a movement that was distinct from the
Jerusalem apostles, a Judaising movement which took two
forms--a Gnosticising form (evident in 1 Corinthians) and a
Pharisaic form (appearing in Galatians). However, these two
forms of the one movement only became distinct in the second
century (becoming libertine Gnosticism and ascetic Jewish
Christianity).[71] This general proposition now requires some
modification (for instance, it has been suggested above that
the Galatian opponents are not Pharisaic;[72] and Gnosticism
was more usually ascetic than libertine[73]); but it also may
contain a great deal of truth. Others since have found a
"Gnosticising" movement in 1 Corinthians, and different,
nomistic opponents in 2 Corinthians.[74] And yet, in many ways,
the characteristics of these two movements are not as distinct
as they later became in the second century. So it is possible
to speak of a "Gnostic coloring" to the opposition in Galatia,
while not ignoring its nomism.[75] In fact, the law-tradition
itself could be called "Gnostic" in a sense--though not in
the second-century sense.[76] It is perhaps this "Gnostic

coloring" which gives the opponents their enthusiastic bent.
Here is a time, then, when enthusiasm is not at all separated
from nomism, but is its natural companion.[77] It is in this
sense, too, that the heresy in Galatia apparently stands in
proximity to that in Colossae.[78]

Given the dialogical nature of Galatians, it is significant that Paul's answer to the Galatians is basically a
sacramental answer. His eschatology, as well as being shaped
by Christology, is also shaped by sacrament: the new age is
come, but the old age still exists; and only those are in the
new age who are in Christ, by faith and baptism. This is not
a sacramentalism. Baptism does not bring one into the new
age inevitably. Rather, the sacrament becomes the basis for
the imperative;[79] and in Galatians, the call is to not allow
the sacrament to have been εἰκῇ. It would seem that Paul is
able to present such a forceful argument for the eschatological nature of Christian existence because he can take up the
opponents' own assumptions about the efficacy of sacrament.
These assumptions are revealed in a particular understanding
of circumcision, which apparently completes that which was
begun by baptism.[80] Their sacramental goal appears to be consistent with their traditions of apostle, ecclesiology, et
cetera. They are seeking the attainment of the angelic
state.[81] In keeping with contemporary understandings of the
realization of change in societal roles, the opponents perhaps
believe that they experience proleptically, in their sacrament,
something of the angelic condition.[82] In all of this, they are
adding "justification by works"[83] to their "justification by
faith:"[84] their sacrament, too, takes on the shape of their
Christology and eschatology.

Far from there being, in the Galatian context, no
relationship between the doctrine of justification by faith
and ethics,[85] the ethical argument of 5:1-6:10 carries on the
argument of justification by faith.[86] Both are ways of looking at the finality of Christ's work, and the new age into
which the Christian has been brought. For this reason, there
is one argument in both the antinomistic and ethical portions
of the letter, which is based on baptism, and goes back to
2:16-21. In the ethical portion, then, Paul is not disputing

anti-nomians but nomists, ethical supermen whose system is
perhaps illustrated by 1 QS 4. Ethics are seen as the
believer's part in the struggle between two dualistic powers
--a struggle which still looks forward to its final eschatological outcome.

Paul responds to this program, in effect, by saying
that this approach to ethics has led to a breakdown of ethics.
He puts all ethical maxims on one level,[87] and shows, on the
opponents' own grounds, that they are living on the basis of
the old age, not the new age. In fact, one cannot fulfill the
ethics of the new age unless one enters the new age.

The ethical topoi illustrate the place given to Jesus
by the opponents regarding ethics. He was perhaps a dispenser
of wise law-sayings, a lawgiver after the style of Moses, who,
through revelation, could communicate the secrets of the cosmos.
He was probably given a place in a frame of covenant-theology,
so that he became only a reauthentication of Moses. But he had
not brought the believer into the new age. The opponents may
even have used the expression νόμος τοῦ Χριστοῦ,[88] in view of
some of the expectations of the Messiah and his law in apocalyptic circles.[89] But because of the frame in which Jesus
was placed, this law of Christ could only be a reauthentication of the law of Moses.[90]

Paul must reject the frame in which Jesus has been
placed, while retaining Jesus as an ethical authority. This
perhaps explains the unique expression, "law of Christ," and
its dialogical function. There is, in chapters 5 and 6, a
real return to law-language,[91] which is a part of Paul's total,
dialogical response to the opponents. Jesus is an ethical
authority only when it is clear, from 2:16-4:31, that He is
the bringer of the new age. This means that ethics have a
firm base only when justification is by faith, apart from
works of law--that is, when justification corresponds to the
lordship of Christ.[92]

Paul's Response: Justification by Faith

In Galatians, justification by faith is a polemical
doctrine,[93] and epitomizes Paul's whole answer to the

opponents. Every section of the letter grows out of 2:16-21, where justification is being radically defined as life.[94] Because of the central place of Christology, justification conforms to the lordship of Christ; and because eschatology grows out of Christology, justification is the equivalent of eschatological deliverance. Justification is not only a point at the beginning of life, but takes in the whole of life: it is the life of the new age.[95] In Galatians, anthropology hardly enters the discussion:[96] rather, justification is spelt out in terms of Christology, eschatology, and sacrament. It is spelt out in terms of sacrament, because it is by the sacrament that the believer is established "in Christ."[97] It is absolute and cannot be added to, because Christ is absolute and has finally brought in the new age.[98] The doctrine stands over against a justification by faith plus works, where law is understood as the secret of cosmic order, the means of rising above mortality, the knowledge of salvation--that which will bring in the new age.

Because justification by faith is sacramentally defined and is the equivalent of the new life, ethics are the other side of justification.[99] Perhaps the heart of the ethical passage is 5:24, where Paul modifies a known form in an unexpected way--in terms of baptism, and the arrival in the present of the new age.[100] This is only the continuation of the debate begun in 2:16-21.

In terms of the present discussion, then, it could be said that, in Galatians, justification is a gift, because it is by faith, which is not a work but the end of works, and trust in the work of God.[101] Justification is all a part with the new life, the life of the Spirit, brought about by God's decisive act in Christ.[102] Justification here comes to mean all that the opponents mean by justification by faith *plus* justification by works of law. It would appear that it is Paul himself who is fusing the forensic and ethical/relational senses of δικαιοῦν/δικαιοσύνη.[103]

So Paul develops "justification" or "righteousness" in a particular way in this polemical situation. But how "Pauline" is this particular exposition? This must be settled by a much wider examination of Paul's uses of the word-group.

And yet, for all its contextuality, the development in Galatians may be not "un-Pauline." The expression "Righteousness
of God" in Romans 1-3, inseparable from the gift or declaration of "righteousness" or "justification" in these chapters,
seems to refer to the power and action of God, as well as His
rightness and His fidelity to what He has promised.[104] Paul's
argument in Romans may divide not at the end of chapter 5 but
the end of chapter 4,[105] in which case Paul in Romans 5-8 is
continuing to present the subject of "justification" with
which he began in 3:21-26,[106] and "righteousness by faith"
again becomes a Christological/eschatological doctrine, "freedom from sin and death" that is found in conjunction with life
in the Spirit.[107] The doctrine in Galatians stands very close
to the doctrine as it is presented in Romans 5-8. This may in
fact be the "real Paul."[108]

INTRODUCTION

[1]For example, F. F. Bruce, "Galatian Problems: 5. Galatians and Christian Origins," *BJRL* 55 (1973):284. "Galatians is the most 'Pauline' of all Paul's letters."

[2]For Ferdinand Christian Baur, Galatians revealed the central conflicts in the early church, and the protagonists were Paul and the other apostles. So, *Paul, His Life and Works*, 2 vols. trans. E. Zeller (London: Williams and Norgate, 1875), 1:113, 129-30. Rudolf Bultmann also sees Paul in Galatians in conflict especially with Palestinian Christianity. So, *Theology of the New Testament*, 2 vols. trans. Kendrick Grobel (New York: Scribners, 1951), 1:63-64, 108-9.

[3]So, Johannes Munck, *Paul and the Salvation of Mankind*, trans. Frank Clarke (Atlanta: John Knox, 1977), p. 56. Because Galatians is one of the "controversial" texts, this is not the place to begin to assess Paul's theology.

[4]John W. Drane, "Tradition, Law, and Ethics in Pauline Theology," *NovT* 16 (1974):167-78; and the conclusion reached by John Gale Hawkins, "The Opponents of Paul in Galatia" (Ph.D. dissertation, Yale University, 1971), pp. i, 343-53.

[5]Drane, "Tradition," p. 177.

[6]J. C. O'Neill, *The Recovery of Paul's Letter to Galatians* (London: SPCK, 1972), p. 9, etc., following the earlier theories of van Manen and others. See below, p. 11. O'Neill asserts that "if Paul was a coherent, argumentative, pertinent writer, Galatians as it now stands cannot have been written by Paul, for it is full of obscurities, contradictions, improbable remarks, and nonsequiturs; but, if Galatians was not written by Paul, it is too obscure and disjointed, and at the same time too urgent and compelling, to have been written by a compiler. Nobody could have written Galatians but Paul; yet the Galatians we possess is not entirely Paul's." A crucial assumption behind O'Neill's failure to hold Galatians together is that it was written against "orthodox" Judaism. So he would modify passages on law and Judaism, completely omit the στοι-χεῖα-passage (4:1-3, 8-10), and emend references to apostleship.

[7]Hans Joachim Schoeps, *Paul. The Theology of the Apostle in the Light of Jewish Religious History*, trans. Harold Knight (Philadelphia: Westminster, 1961), pp. 65-77, 171-83, 213-17. More recently, E. P. Sanders, *Paul and*

Palestinian Judaism (Philadelphia: Fortress Press, 1977), has
stressed the gulf between Paul and Tannaitic religion.

[8]Helmut Koester, in *Trajectories through Early Christianity*, by James L. Robinson and Helmut Koester (Philadelphia:
Fortress Press, 1971), pp. 144-47.

[9]John J. Gunther, *St. Paul's Opponents and Their Background*, Supplements to Novum Testamentum, 35 (Leiden: Brill,
1973):294; Heinrich Schlier, *Der Brief an die Galater*, Kritisch-
exegetischer Kommentar über das Neue Testament (Göttingen:
Vandenhoeck und Ruprecht, 1951), pp. 133-37.

[10]See below, pp. 91-92.

[11]Helmut Koester, "Paul and Hellenism," in *The Bible in
Modern Scholarship*, ed. Philip J. Hyatt (Philadelphia: Fortress Press, 1968), p. 192, notes, " . . . scholars are looking for a particular polemical situation in which Paul,
prompted by opponents, was enticed to discuss theories so
alien to his thought as those proposed in the epistle to the
Romans."

[12]Gunther, *Opponents*, p. 61; see also below, pp. 17-18.
on Schmithals and Marxsen.

[13]For an approach to the New Testament from the perspective of the opponents, see, for instance, Joseph B. Lightfoot, *Epistle to the Galatians* (London: Williams and Norgate,
1892), pp. 292-374; Walter Bauer, *Orthodoxy and Heresy in
Earliest Christianity*, trans. Philadelphia Seminar on Christian Origins (Philadelphia: Fortress Press, 1971), passim;
Walter Schmithals, *Paul and the Gnostics*, trans. John E.
Steely (Nashville: Abingdon, 1972), passim; C. K. Barrett,
"Paul's Opponents in 2 Corinthians," *NTS* 17 (1970-71):233-45,
and "Pauline Controversies in the Post-Pauline Period," *NTS* 20
(1972-73):229-54; and further literature below, pp. 10-30.
Lightfoot, *Galatians*, p. 334, citing the example of Luther as
an illustration of this principle, noted, "Luther renouncing
the Pope for idolatry and Luther rebuking Carlstadt for icono-
clasm writes like two different persons. He bids the timid
and gentle Melanchthon 'sin and sin boldly'; he would have cut
off his right hand sooner than pen such words to the antinomian rioters of Münster."

[14]See, for instance, the method advocated by E. P.
Sanders, "Patterns of Religion in Paul and Rabbinic Judaism:
A Holistic Method of Comparison," *HTR* 66 (1973):455-78; and
Paul, pp. 12-24.

[15]On Galatians as literature, see Adolf Deissman, *Light
from the Ancient East*, trans. L. R. M. Strachen (London:
Hodder and Stoughton, 1911), pp. 290-302, 409; D. J. Selby,
Toward an Understanding of St. Paul (Englewood Cliffs, NJ:
Prentice-Hall, 1962), pp. 235-41; Robert W. Funk, *Language,
Hermeneutic, and Word of God* (New York: Harper & Row, 1969),
pp. 257-72; Hans Dieter Betz, "The Literary Composition and
Function of Galatians," *NTS* 21 (1975):353-79; and other sources
below, pp. 31-45.

[16]As defined by William G. Doty, *Contemporary New Testament Interpretation* (Englewood Cliffs, NJ: Prentice-Hall, 1972), p. 167; and Stephen H. Travis, in *New Testament Interpretation*, ed. I. Howard Marshall (Grand Rapids: Eerdmans, 1977), p. 153.   See further below, p. 31.

[17]Doty, *Interpretation*, p. 56, refers to it as the attempt to "evaluate the significance and influence of the larger units of the materials, the genres."   See also Frederick Veltman, "The Defense Speeches of Paul in Acts: Gattungsforschung and Its Limitations" (Th.D. dissertation, Graduate Theological Union, 1975), pp. 251-52, and further literature below, p. 32.

[18]See the description and identification of this genre below, pp. 42-46.

[19]See further description and sources, below, pp. 43-46.

[20]See the list of apocalyptic literature in David Syme Russell, *The Method and Message of Jewish Apocalyptic* (London: SCM Press, 1964), pp. 37-38.   Of Jubilees he says, "Jubilees is not, strictly speaking, an apocalyptic book; but it belongs to the same milieu" (p. 54).   Because this thesis is more concerned with the ideas in the milieu than with a precise definition of apocalyptic, it seems justifiable to refer to Jubilees as apocalyptic literature.   Gene L. Davenport, *The Eschatology of the Book of Jubilees* (Leiden: Brill, 1971), pp. 5-9, after noting the difficulty of distinguishing between apocalyptic and prophetic eschatology, claims that there are both prophetic and apocalyptic elements in Jubilees.

[21]These two definitions of apocalyptic are found, for instance, in Philip Vielhauer, NTA, 2:582, and Doty, *Interpretation*, p. 165.   The concern of the dissertation is not to isolate the ideas of this literature, but rather to explore some of the traditions held in common with other Jewish sources.   On this sharing of traditions, see Russell, *Method*, pp. 24-27, and further literature below, pp. 91-92, 101.

[22]See Bultmann, *Theology*, 1:4-11.   Because the stress here falls on "last things," it is possible to speak of God's saving deed in Christ as eschatological occurrence (so Bultmann, ibid., 1:43, 306, 329, etc.; and Herman Ridderbos, *Paul. An Outline of His Theology*, trans. John R. de Witt [Grand Rapids: Eerdmans, 1975], pp. 44-53), and the church as the eschatological community (Bultmann, ibid., 1:37-42 etc.).

[23]See Ridderbos, *Paul*, pp. 40-41, who notes in Paul's writings a tension between "realised" and "futurist" eschatology.

CHAPTER ONE

THE IDENTITY AND THEOLOGY OF THE OPPONENTS

[1]The anti-Marcionite prologue is quoted in W. G.
Kümmel, *Introduction to the New Testament* (Nashville: Abingdon, 1975), p. 229. Bruce, "Christian Origins," p. 254,
quotes the Marcionite prologue. It is interesting that, in
the second century, Hegessipus says that there was no Gnosticism in Paul's time, Eusebius, HE 3. 32; yet, by the fourth
century, Epiphanius makes the Galatian culprit the Gnostic
(or Jewish-Christian?) Cerinthus, *Panarion* 28. 2. 3, as does
Jerome a little later, perhaps following him. See the material cited in Schmithals, *Paul*, pp. 36-38. But note the discussion of this same material in A. F. J. Klijn and G. J.
Reininck, *Patristic Evidence for Jewish-Christian Sects*
(Leiden: Brill, 1973), pp. 6, 8, 12, 19, who conclude that it
is practically worthless.

[2]*To Diognetius* 4 (ANF, 1:26).

[3]Irenaeus *Against Heresies* 4. 2. 7, quoting Gal 2:24
(ANF, 1:465).

[4]Justin *Dialog with Trypho* 11 (*PG*, 6:497): νόμος δὲ
κατὰ νόμου τεθεὶς τὸν πρὸ αὐτοῦ ἔπαυσε . . . αἰώνος τε ἡμῖν
νόμος καὶ τελευταῖος, ὁ Χριστὸς ἐδόθη, ...

[5]Bauer, *Orthodoxy*, p. 199.

[6]Irenaeus *Against Heresies* 3. 13. . (ANF, 1:436),
against Marcion's claims for Paul's superior apostleship; and
5. 35. 2 (ANF, 1:565-66), on Gal 4:26 and the heavenly aeon,
Jerusalem.

[7]Elaine H. Pagels, *The Gnostic Paul* (Philadelphia:
Fortress Press, 1975), p. 157; and, for example, the Gospel
of Philip. Irenaeus found it necessary to reclaim Paul from
the heretics, *Against Heresies* 4. 41. 4 (ANF, 1:525).

[8]See Georg Strecker's introduction to Kerygmata Petrou,
NTA, 2:108.

[9]Pagels, *Paul*, pp. 101-6; Gos. Phil. 17, 47, and 95
(*NHL*, 132, 134, 149).

[10]John Calvin, *The Epistles of Galatians, Ephesians,
Philippians, and Colossians*, trans. T. H. L. Parker (Grand
Rapids: Eerdmans, 1973), pp. 4-7, 14, 115-16.

[11]Martin Luther, *Commentary on Galatians*, trans.
Theodore Graebner (Grand Rapids: Zondervan, 1953), p. 9.

[12]Henry Hammond, *A Paraphrase and Annotations upon All the Books of the New Testament*, 7th ed. (London: Tho. Newborough and Benj. Tooke, 1702), pp. 517, 537-52. He proposes circumcised Gnostics, preaching circumcision to Gentiles, opposed by both Peter and Paul, and sees these same opponents in 1 Timothy 5-6, and Ignatius' *Magnesians* and *Trallians*. They belong with Simon Magus, Menander, Basilides, the Nicolaitans, etc.

[13]Johann L. von Mosheim, *Institutes of Ecclesiastical History*, 4 vols. (London: Longman, Brown, Green, et al., 1845), 1:107-29.

[14]Edward G. Burton, *An Enquiry into the Heresies of the Apostolic Age* (Oxford: Collingwood, 1829), pp. 102, 120-45.

[15]Baur, *Paul*, 1:113, 119-30. More recently, a similar position on the opponents has been taken by S. G. F. Brandon, "The Crisis of 70 AD," *Heythrop Journal* 46 (1947-48): 222-23; and James L. Blevins, "The Problem in Galatia," *Review and Expositor* 69 (1972):449-58.

[16]See Strecker, *NTA*, 2:103-6.

[17]Bruno Bauer, *Kritik der paulinischen Briefe* (Berlin: Hempel, 1852; reprint ed., Aalen: Scientia Verlag, 1972), 1:5-6, 118-29. Baur's "four genuine Pauline epistles" are all assigned to the second century.

[18]W. B. van Manen, "Marcions Brief van Paulus aan de Galatiërs," *Theologisch Tijdschrift* 21ste Jaargang (1887):382-404, 451-533. This writer reads little Dutch and has relied heavily on interpretations of this article in J. C. O'Neill, *The Recovery of Paul's Letter to the Galatians* (London: SPCK, 1972), and others. O'Neill regards van Manen's work favorably and uses the latter's analysis of Marcion's version of Galatians (reproduced on pp. 497-533 of his article) as a basis for his own emendation of the text of the letter.

[19]See, for example, Helmut Koester, "Häretiker im Urchristentum als theologisches Problem," in *Zeit und Geschichte: Dankesgabe an Rudolf Bultmann zum 80. Geburtstag*, ed. E. Dinkler (Tübingen: J. C. B. Mohr, 1964), p. 62.

[20]Albert Schweitzer, *The Mysticism of Paul the Apostle*, trans. W. Montgomery (London: A. and C. Black, 1912), pp. 75-100, 182-87.

[21]Hans Lietzmann, *An die Galater*, HNT 10, 3rd ed. (Tübingen: Mohr, 1932), pp. 38-46.

[22]Joseph B. Lightfoot, *St. Paul's Epistle to the Galatians* (London: Macmillan, 1866), p. 284. See the entire essay, "St. Paul and the Three," pp. 284-370.

[23]William M. Ramsay, *A Historical Commentary on St. Paul's Epistle to the Galatians* (London: A. and C. Black,

1899), pp. 258, 326-71, 394-95. He equates the founding of
the Galatian churches with Paul's first visit to Lystra, Anti-
och, and Iconium, which he also equates with the accounts of
Acts 13 and 14 (p. 327). The "South Galatia Theory" tends to
favor a third Jerusalem party as the opponents: it puts the
Galatian churches in the province of synagogues and intense
Jewish activity. Another alternative is that of Kirsopp Lake:
The opponents were local Jews. See Gunther, *Opponents*, p. 1.

[24]Schoeps, *Paul*, pp. 65-77. He agrees with Baur
regarding the importance of the Ebionites and the central
place of the Clementine romance as a source for early Christian conflicts. See Strecker, *NTA*, 2:104.

[25]Though there is a basic disagreement between them:
Schoeps' position is close to Schweitzer's.

[26]But can Pharisees, Galatian opponents, and Ebionites
all be so simply equated? See, for instance Strecker, *NTA*,
2:104-5. The Ebionisms in the Clementines may be interpola-
tions, etc. Also Gunther, *Opponents*, p. 20: the Ebionites
and Paul's opponents cannot be the same, as the former reject
animal sacrifices, the Temple, and many Old Testament books
and prophets; and 67-73: Paul's opponents are not from "normative" Phariseeism, but are closer to Jewish sectarian legalism (Qumran) and apocalyptic Jewish-Christianity.

[27]This, to Schoeps, explains why Galatians comes after
Acts 15 and yet does not mention it. He differs with Ramsay.
Here it is Paul, not the Judaisers, who reject the decree.
But in both cases, the decree is part of the problem Paul
faces. Schoeps reiterates a point of Schweitzer's: Acts 15
deals with law by formulating specific, pragmatic precepts,
whereas Galatians rejects the idea of law in principle. See
Schweitzer, *Mysticism*, pp. 75, 80.

[28]Schoeps, *Paul*, pp. 171-83, 213-17. His criticism
of Paul's treatment of law is drawn mainly from Galatians 3
and 2 Corinthians 3; and Romans 5, 7, and 10:4 are interpreted
in terms of these first texts. But is this legitimate, where
Paul confronts opponents in the former texts and not in the
latter?

[29]For instance, Richard N. Longenecker, *Paul, Apostle
of Liberty* (Grand Rapids: Baker, 1964), pp. 212-17; Herman N.
Ridderbos, *The Epistle of Paul to the Churches of Galatia*
(Grand Rapids: Baker, 1953), pp. 16-18; and Donald Guthrie,
New Testament Introduction (Downer's Grove: Inter-Varsity,
1976), pp. 466-68. Gunther, *Opponents*, pp. 314-17, takes
this general position, though he sees a basically united anti-
Pauline movement coming out of sectarian Judaism, witnessed
by such texts as Ascension of Isaiah, Jubilees, the Qumran
documents, Philo's Therapeutai, etc. It is mystic-apocalyptic,
ascetic, non-conformist, syncretistic Judaism, close to the
Essenes.

[30]Some put Acts 15 after Galatians, following a "South
Galatian" theory that dates Galatians very early. But Acts 15
still reveals the parties in conflict.

[31]F. F. Bruce, "Galatian Problems" 3. The "Other"
Gospel, *BJRL* 53 (1971):253-71.

[32]Here Bruce both follows Schweitzer (the concept of
spheres) and disagrees with him on law as a principle in Galatians. Schweitzer's position on law seems to have more support.

[33]For instance, Hans Conzelmann, *An Outline of the
Theology of the New Testament* (New York: Harper & Row, 1968),
pp. 200-214; Werner Kümmel, *Introduction to the New Testament*
(Nashville: Abingdon, 1975), pp. 209-302; and Hans D. Betz,
"Geist, Freiheit und Gesetz. Die Botschaft des Paulus an die
Gemeinden in Galatien," *ZTK* 71 (1974):78-93.

[34]Gunther, *Opponents*, p. 10--a representative statement. It is often held that Paul deals with two fronts simultaneously. The "libertine" is either an errant Pauline Christian or a hypothetical creation of legalist objectors to Paul's
gospel.

[35]Ernst G. Hirsch, "Zwei Fragen zu Galater 6," *ZNW* 29
(1930):192-97; and Wilhelm Michaelis, "Judaistische Heidenchristen," *ZNW* 30 (1931):83-89.

[36]Munck, *Paul*, pp. 87-134.

[37]Ibid., p. 70.

[38]Taken as implying that the opponents themselves are
only now being circumcised.

[39]Munck here heightens a problem raised by William D.
Davies, *Paul and Rabbinic Judaism* (London: SPCK, 1977), pp.
62-84, 95-97--Paul's great sympathy for Judaism. After his
own Gentile missions, he, like Philo, returned to Jerusalem
to worship as an orthodox Jew. How can this attitude, and
Romans 9-11, be reconciled with Galatians 3-4? We do not
solve the problem by ignoring Acts. And how can Gal 5:3, 4 be
reconciled with Acts 16:3? Galatians seems to differ from
both Romans and Acts.

[40]On the basis of Genesis alone, the opponents may be
more exegetically correct than Paul about the congruence of
faith, circumcision, and obedience to the commandments of God.
John W. Drane, *Paul, Libertine or Legalist?* (London: SPCK,
1975), p. 28.

[41]Paul's apostleship is attacked: the Galatians suppose he has kept some vital teaching from them and has not
preached the same message as the Jerusalem apostles.

[42]Robert Jewett, "The Agitators and the Galatian
Congregation," *NTS* 17 (1971):199. The Judaisers circumcise
the Galatians, not themselves.

[43]Jewett, "Agitators," pp. 198-99; Koester, *Trajectories*, pp. 143-44.

[44]Jewett, "Agitators," p. 198; see Gal 4:17.

[45]That is, how to deal with the letter and the heresy as a unity.

[46]Munck asserts that the centre of Paul's theology is a message of salvation: first the Gentiles are to be saved, then the Parousia will come, then Israel will be converted. His opponents reversed the first and third stage. See the criticism in Koester, "Hellenism," p. 192.

[47]There may be evidence of spontaneous Judaising among Gentile Christians. Ignatius *Philadelphians* 6:1 (ANF, 1:82) speaks of a Judaism taught by the uncircumcised. See also the appendix by Strecker in Bauer, *Orthodoxy*.

[48]Wilhelm Lütgert, *Gesetz und Geist: eine Untersuchung zur Vorgeschichte des Galaterbriefes* (Gütersloh: Bertelsmann, 1919).

[49]An objection to this theory must lie in the work of Drane, "Tradition," where the totally different approach of Paul in Galatians and 1 Corinthians is pointed out. Would Galatians ever answer a libertine? But against Drane, would it create Corinthian libertinism?

[50]James H. Ropes, *The Singular Problem of the Epistle to the Galatians* (Cambridge, Mass.: Harvard University Press, 1929).

[51]Jewett contradicts it by placing the persecution in Judea, not Galatia; see below, pp. 16-17.   Lütgert saw the circumcision campaign as a means of coming under the state protection of *religio licita*, *Gesetz*, pp. 96-106.

[52]Bruce, "The Other Gospel," pp. 254-72. Drane, *Paul*, p. 87, sees two groups within Galatians, although he also wants to say that Paul here meets a hypothetical Jewish objection (pp. 81-82).

[53]Betz, "Geist," pp. 78-93.

[54]However, "pneuma" holds Paul's argument together, rather than separating it into two answers to two different opponents: Koester, "Gnomai," p. 145. Betz, ibid., also fails to account for the real nomism in the opponents, in that they insist that circumcision is vital for salvation. See Dieter Georgi, *Die Geschichte der Kollekte des Paulus für Jerusalem* (Hamburg: Herbert Reich, 1965), p. 35.

[55]Richard N. Longenecker, *Paul, Apostle of Liberty* (Grand Rapids: Baker, 1964), p. 216; Gunther, *Opponents*, pp. 112-13. Gunther here says Paul actually agrees with his opponents regarding ethics, but refutes their charge of "cheap grace."

[56]*Die urchristliche Verkündigung im Streit zwischen Paulus und seinen Gegnern nach dem Galaterbrief* (Regensburg:

Friedrich Pustet, 1971). He is to be included here because, though he rejects any two-front theory (pp. 131-62), his understanding of paraenesis removes the paraenetic section of the letter from the discussion of the identity of the opponents.

[57]That is, they are Jewish-Christians from Palestine (pp. 76, 102, 235). They attack Paul's gospel as illegitimate because it does *not* agree with that of the Pillars (p. 233). Eckert relies heavily on Galatians 1-2 for defining the opponents (pp. 230-33), and has not seen the "historic" rather than "historical" function of these chapters and the way that the overall argument suggests that they be used.

[58]Eckert dismisses the suggestion that a "syncretistic" form of Judaism is involved. The mention of the στοιχεῖα τοῦ κόσμου, and the equation of Judaism with Paganism, in 4:3-11, is explained rather by the radical and ironical way in which Paul argues, and his subjective involvement in the Galatian situation (pp. 23-24, 91-93, 127-28). The dualistic nature of the argument is also to be explained by Paul's tendency to see everything in "black and white" (p. 25--despite the uniqueness of the dualistic argument in Galatians). As far as the law is concerned, he also dismisses the suggestion that an intertestamental theology of law is in question (pp. 114-23).

[59]Following Dibelius' definition of paraenesis (pp. 149-50).

[60]Ibid., p. 232.

[61]Ibid.

[62]Jewett, "Agitators," pp. 198-212; that is, their circumcising mission authenticates them as loyal Jews.

[63]A similar situation is pictured by Eduard Schweizer, "Christianity of the Circumcised and Judaism of the Uncircumcised," in *Jews, Greeks, and Christians: Religious Culture in Late Antiquity*, ed. Robert Hammerton-Kelly and Robin Scroggs (Leiden: Brill, 1976), pp. 245-60. The heresy is a pythagorised Judaism, using the Mosaic law to achieve ascent of the soul through the στοιχεῖα. Parallels are in Apuleius, Philo, and Colossians, and the heresy is ascetic, not libertine.

[64]Why does this mission appear in Galatia? Are the opponents only pragmatic? Why are Gentiles so enthusiastic for circumcision?

[65]Which he set out to do. He himself notes the unity of the letter and the way Paul deals with the Galatians as a homogeneous group. The paraenetic sections answer questions raised by nomism; and 5:1, 13 address the same group.

[66]Rudolf Bultmann, *Primitive Christianity in its Contemporary Setting*, trans. Reginald Fuller (New York: Thames and Hudson, 1956), pp. 189-208.

[67]Ibid., p. 190, on Gal 3:19, 4:3, 9: Paul uses "mythological concepts derived from Gnosticism."

[68]Ibid., pp. 191, 193, 202, etc.

[69]Ibid., p. 208. In his *Theology*, 1: 164 he states, "side by side with positive influence from Gnosticism we also find rejection of it." However, he saw the central portion of Galatians, chaps. 3-4, as dealing with the problem of Jewish legalism. See *Theology* 1:164-66 on affinities between Christianity and Gnosticism (both radical religions of redemption); and 260-65 on the legalistic nature of Judaism. He did not try to characterize a specific Galatian opponent.

[70]Walter Schmithals, *Gnosticism in Corinth*, trans. John E. Steely (Nashville: Abingdon, 1971) and, specifically on Galatians, *Paul*, pp. 8-66.

[71]So, too, Jewett, "Agitators," p. 212, assumes that these rites are not Jewish. However, see the evidence below, pp. 122-23. Schmithals at least sees that the calendrical rites are a part with the circumcising program, and Jewett's case is weakened by separating them. But when it is seen that Gnostic circumcision is highly unlikely (below, pp. 142, 144-45), it makes it probable that both are very Jewish.

[72]G. Stählin in *Die Religion in Geschichte und Gegenwart*, 7 vols., 3rd ed., s.v. "Galaterbrief"; Schlier, *Galater*, pp. 11-16; and Georgi, below, p. 20.

[73]All of above. Stählin and Conzelmann say they must be of Jewish descent, based on the parallels in 2 Cor 11:21-22, Phil 3:2-6.

[74]See Robert McL. Wilson, "Gnostics--in Galatia?" *Studia Evangelica* 4 (1968):358-67; Hans Conzelmann, *1 Corinthians*, trans. James W. Leitch, Hermeneia (Philadelphia: Fortress, 1975), pp. 14-15; Helmut Koester, "The Purpose of a Polemic of a Pauline Fragment," *NTS* 8 (1961-62):317-32.

[75]Willi Marxsen, *Introduction to the New Testament*, trans. G. Buswell (Philadelphia: Fortress Press, 1968), pp. 50-58. If he makes the opponents Gnostics, he must follow Schmithals and say that Paul did not understand them.

[76]He has removed all objectivity by saying that Paul did not understand his opponents (Jewett, "Agitators," p. 199; Georgi, *Kollekte*, p. 35). He has not done justice to the struggle against nomism in the letter (Georgi, ibid.); Gnostics never seem to regard circumcision as essential to salvation, and may condemn it (Jewett, ibid., and below, p. 142. His own theory has broken up the unity of Galatians, as he defines the opponent from only chaps. 1-2 and 5-6 (Georgi, ibid.); and he has misunderstood the anti-Pauline movements as a whole (Conzelmann, *1 Corinthians*, pp. 14-15, Pagels, *Paul*, pp. 162-64).

[77]They disagree with Bultmann in some respects.
Pharisaic Judaism is less legalistic, and Paul's concerns are
more genuinely Jewish. Pre-Christian Gnosticism has a much
less definite shape than Bultmann gave it, and more connections with sectarian and apocalyptic Judaism. Hellenistic
influences on Paul are more in terms of Hellenistic Judaism,
or Judaism that has come in contact with mystery religions.
There is a difference here from Jewett, Gunther, Schweizer,
etc. The syncretistic elements in Galatians are integral to
the opponents' system.

[78]Frederick C. Crownfield, "The Singular Problem of
the Dual Galatians," *JBL* 64 (1945):491-500.

[79]Koester, "Gnomai," pp. 144-47. Paul's answer is
more Rabbinic than the position of the heretics themselves.
A partial agreement with Davies, *Paul*, 112-46, on Christ as
the New Torah.

[80]Against Schmithals' position on Galatians 3 and 4.

[81]Koester here picks up Schmithals' point. Galatians
5 seems to confront Gnosticizing enthusiasts.

[82]The sources that have been used here are a passage
from an article entitled "Einwände und Exegetische Anmer-
kungen," in Ernst Wolf, ed., *Christentum im Atombombzeitalter*
(Munich: Kaiser, 1959), cited in Hawkins, "Opponents," pp.
53-54 (unfortunately the original source was not available);
Kollekte, pp. 34-38; and circulated notes from the class,
"Theology of the New Testament," Harvard Divinity School,
Spring, 1977.

[83]Referring to 3:1-3 (the criteria of the opponents
themselves), 5:18, 5:25-6:1, etc.

[84]*Kollekte*, p. 35: "Vorläufer einer Gnosis, wie sie
dann später im Kolosserbrief und in den Ignatianen bekampft
wird."

[85]They have room for "faith" in their scheme, which
to them is a deepened understanding of the law. However,
they see Paul's doctrine of "righteousness by faith" as a
summons to lawlessness (5:1-15).

[86]The heretical nomos-tradition goes back to the
Wisdom of Solomon and other wisdom literature and is not to
be understood in terms of Rabbinic casuistry. For them, law
is not only Jewish law, but the law of the world in general.
It could even be called "syncretistic," holding together Jewish and heathen revelation-traditions.

[87]Thus the opponents had a particular Christology:
Christ stood in a long line of law-preachers and was himself
the conclusive revelation of law. The expression "law of
Christ" belongs to the opponents.

[88]Baptism into Christ is set forth in an undisputed
way in Gal 3:27.

[89]The opponents' stress on circumcision is evident
from 5:2-4, 6-13.

[90]The opponents were perfectionist and ascetic, but
they had no time for the "bourgeois" ethic of Paul, as set
forth in Galatians 5-6.

[91]*Kollekte*, pp. 15-21. In 2:6 Paul gives a polemical
corrective to the opponents' claims about the Jerusalem
authorities.

[92]Ibid., pp. 35-36.

[93]The opponents were seeking to relate early Christian and Jewish traditions.

[94]E. Earle Ellis, "Paul and His Opponents," in *Christianity, Judaism, and other Greco-Roman Cults. Studies for
Morton Smith at Sixty*, ed. J. Neusner (Leiden: Brill, 1975),
pp. 282, 292.

CHAPTER TWO

OPPONENTS AND METHODOLOGY

[1]Koester, "Hellenism," pp. 192-93.

[2]Ibid., p. 193.

[3]Ibid., pp. 192-93.

[4]See Koester, *Trajectories*, pp. 114-36. He begins
with a historical and geographical analysis of early Christian
movements, and the theologies that first existed in the earliest centers of Christianity. Careful attention is paid to
literary forms, and the functions they played in these early
movements. The New Testament is then interpreted out of this
reconstructed context. A similar method is used by Dieter
Georgi, *Die Gegner des Paulus im 2. Korintherbrief* (Neukirchen-
Vluyn: Neukirchener Verlag, 1964). He begins with a reconstruction of the history of religions background, in particular apologetic Judaism and its concerns.

[5]Koester, "Hellenism," p. 194.

[6]Munck, *Paul*, pp. 85-87.

[7]For instance, Drane, *Paul*, p. 79: ". . . since the
epistle is our only evidence for the Galatian heresy, any
valid impressions of its character must in the nature of the
case be based on an exegetical understanding of the epistle
itself."

[8]Drane, ibid., pp. 5-59, builds much of his case on
the differences within Paul's letters (i.e., between Gal 1:11
and 1 Cor 15:3, Gal 3:18-26 and Rom 8:12-17, and Gal 5:6 and
1 Cor 7:19).

[9]Munck, *Paul*, pp. 55-56.

[10]Munck interprets Galatians in terms of several of his
own unique themes, i.e., Paul's apostolic consciousness, and
the absence of any Jewish-Christian mission to Gentiles.

[11]Joseph B. Tyson, "Paul's Opponents in Galatia,"
NovT 10 (1968):241-54.

[12]Tyson finds essentially six charges: Paul's
apostleship derives from a human authority; he had frequent
contact with the Pillars, and is their subordinate, trying to
please them; the Pillars require circumcision; Paul preaches
circumcision; physical descent from Abraham is required for
justification; and circumcision is necessary in Christianity.

[13]Tyson can find no way of saying what is obvious--
that the opponents preach a "Christian" gospel in which justification and life are attained on the basis of both law and
faith; that is, he cannot clearly relate Gal 3-4, the heart
of the letter, to the opponents' theology.

[14]Franz Mussner, *Galaterbrief*, Herders Theologischer
Kommentar zum Neuen Testament, vol. 11 (Freiburg: Herder,
1974), p. 13.

[15]They refer probably to the historical trappings
which were only supportive of the opponents' real theological
thrust. See below, pp. 44, 49-51.

[16]Munck, *Paul*, pp. 95-96, discussing Gal 2:3.

[17]Gunther, *Opponents*, pp. 14-15.

[18]For example, see 3:29 as a repetition of the claim,
"We are Abraham's offspring."

[19]For example, 3:19-22. But Gunther may assume here
more unity within Paul's letters than in fact exists.

[20]For instance, Paul's reinterpretation of πνευματικοί,
6:1-10.

[21]See below, pp. 163-70, on 5:19-23.

[22]Mussner, *Galater*, p. 13, finds catchwords in 1:18
(Paul learnt his gospel from Jerusalem), 2:1 (Paul had to lay
his teaching before the Jerusalem authorities), 2:2, 6 (οἱ
δοκοῦνται), 2:6 (Paul paid a tax to Jerusalem), 2:11 (in
Antioch, Peter was right), 2:17 (one who does not keep the law
is a servant of sin), 3:7 (we are the true sons of Abraham),
3:19 (God Himself gave the law), 3:21 (righteousness comes by
the law), 4:26 (Jerusalem is our mother), 5:2 (circumcision
is necessary for salvation).

[23]Mussner summarises the opponents' teachings as follows: they demand a Jewish law piety (4:21, 5:4 etc.); they promote circumcision (5:2, 6:12); they advocate calendrical piety and worship of the στοιχεῖα (4:8-11: which is not derivable from his catchwords); Paul's "gospel" does not correspond to that of the "Pillars" (1:1-12, 2:2-10), Jerusalem is the true place of the Messianic salvation (4:21-31). Also essential to the debate, but missing from the catchwords, are the opponents' criticism of the Jerusalem apostolate, their own place for faith, ethical considerations, etc.

[24]Claus Bussmann, *Themen der paulinischen Missionspredigt auf dem Hintergrund der spätjüdisch-hellenistischen Missionsliteratur* (Bern: Herbert Lang, 1971), p. 22, refers to lexical arguments (hapaxes, words used in unusual ways, grammatical constructions), literary arguments (style, parallels, etc.), and logical arguments. On the basis of a larger frame of reference, Jewett, "Agitators," pp. 196-218, finds several catchwords that are contradictory to Mussner's, suggesting that the opponents claim that Paul is on their side, that he too is zealous for the law (1:14), and Paul has always preached circumcision (5:11). In fact, the argument for a catchword in 3:19 may point in the opposite direction from the one suggested by Mussner.

[25]This is the place given to catchwords in methodology in E. Earle Ellis, "How the New Testament Uses the Old," in I. Howard Marshall, ed., *New Testament Interpretation* (Grand Rapids: Eerdmans, 1977), pp. 201, 203-8, and in Bultmann's work, referred to below, pp. 41-42.

[26]"Gnosticism" is one of those ambiguous words of modern scholarship. Perhaps the most adequate brief definition is the one formulated at the Messina Colloquium: ". . . a coherent series of characteristics that can be summarised in the idea of a divine spark in man, deriving from the divine realm, fallen into this world of fate, birth, and death, and needing to be awakened by the divine counterpart of the self in order to be finally reintegrated. . . . This gnosis of Gnosticism involves the divine identity of the knower (the Gnostic), and known (the divine substance of one's transcendent self), and the means by which one knows (. . . a revelation-tradition . . .). See Ugo Bianchi, ed., *Le Origini dello Gnosticismo, Colloquio di Messina 13-18 Aprile 1966* (Leiden: Brill, 1967), p. xxvi.

[27]Hans Jonas, "Delimitation of the Gnostic Phenomenon--Typological and Historical," in Bianchi, *Gnosticismo*, p. 100.

[28]See above, pp. 17-18.

[29]See above, pp. 15-17, on explicit and implicit two-front theories.

[30]See Georgi, *Gegner*, pp. 23-25, on the different direction of attack in 2 Cor 6:14-7:4 and 2 Corinthians 10-13; and a different opinion, though still making a distinction between intruders and congregation, C. K. Barrett, *A Commentary*

on the Second Epistle to the Corinthians, Harper's New Testament Commentaries (New York: Harper & Row, 1973), pp. 243-46.

[31]For instance, Phil 3:2-21.

[32]For instance, τινές, 1:7; τις, 1:9, 3:1, 4:17, and 5:7; ὁ . . . ταράσσων ὑμᾶς, . . . ὅστις ἐὰν ᾖ, 5:10; οἱ ἀναστατοῦντες ὑμᾶς, 5:12; ὅσοι θέλουσιν εὐπροσωπῆσαι ἐν σαρκί, 6:12.

[33]Jewett, "Agitators," p. 210, noting Paul's reference to agitators (1:8-10, 5:12, 6:12-13) separate from his references to the congregation, (3:1-5, 4:8-16, 5:7-8).

[34]Mussner draws attention to the verbs used in these verses: θελεῖν, 1:7, 4:17, 6:12 and 13; ἀναγκάζειν, 6:12; ἀναστατοῦν, 5:12. The opponents are forcing their teaching on the Galatians.

[35]See the note on the teachings of the opponents, above, p. 216, note 23.

[36]See above, pp. 25-26, on Tyson's method and its weaknesses.

[37]See the references to Dibelius, Funk, Furnish, etc., and the way in which Paul's ethics are both traditional and contextual, below, p. 54.

[38]Lütgert assumed that 3:6-29 was against legalists, and Ropes said it was against libertines. See above, p. 15.

[39]Especially when the question of apostleship is brought into the argument. Is it used to debate those who reject the Jerusalem tradition (libertines), or those who exalt it (legalists)? These appear not to be two distinct options, but a unitary complex that runs through the whole letter.

[40]That is, law, Spirit, and flesh (3:1-5 as well as 5:13-24 and elsewhere in the paraenetic section, 6:1, 2, 7-8). Jewett, "Agitators," pp. 196-98.

[41]Typified by his revolutionary assertion that law promotes παραβάσεων (3:19). Apparently, being "in sin," "in the flesh," and "under the law" are synonymous. See Sanders, "Patterns," pp. 470-78.

[42]Victor Paul Furnish, *Theology and Ethics in Paul* (Nashville: Abingdon, 1968), pp. 68-69: Paul's ethics are not confined to the so-called paraenetic sections in his letters, which cannot be neatly divided into doctrine and ethics.

[43]Jewett, "Agitators," p. 198. He notes further that Gal 1:6, 3:1-5, and 5:7 imply that all the Galatians had equally accepted the opponents' propaganda.

[44]Jewett himself must be criticised here: he rejects
the idea of two parties among the Galatians, but retains the
two theological and ethical extremes of the two-front theorists, thus still inevitably pulling the letter apart.

[45]See Jewett, "Agitators," and Hawkins, "Opponents,"
referred to above (pp. 31-33). They represent most recent
attempts to make distinctions within Galatians.

[46]Jewett finds such suggestions in 4:8-10, 6:1, 7-8.

[47]He claims that, on the basis of 5:16-24, immorality
and Hellenistic libertinism exist in the congregations.

[48]Because the peculiar Pauline expression, "works of
law," which appears only in Galatians 2 and Romans 3 (but
which is probably close in meaning to other expressions such
as "works" and "righteousness by works") is always in the
context of selections of Jewish law, especially circumcision
and calendar-feasts. So the calendar feasts of 4:10 are
probably part of the program of circumcision. At least
Schmithals seems more consistent here.

[49]See below, p. 145. Even Jewett admits this, "Agitators," p. 198.

[50]See below, pp. 122-23.

[51]See below, pp. 121-22. The unusual treatment here
of Israel and its religion, even for Paul, must be accounted
for.

[52]See below, p. 121, and the striking use of πάλιν
twice in Gal 4:9.

[53]See above, p. 16. Note the homogeneity of the Galatian churches, the same concerns in the theological and paraenetic sections of the letter, and the way the letter as a
whole appears to address one problem.

[54]See 1:6-9, 3:1-5, 5:2-4, 6:12-15. The letter indicates that the Galatians as a whole had accepted the opponents' propaganda--even circumcision!

[55]See above, p. 17, on Hawkins, "Opponents."

[56]Hawkins, "Opponents," pp. 1, 4, etc.

[57]He attempts to begin his exegesis of the letter
from Gal 6:12-13 (p. 86)--one of the most controversial texts
in the book

[58]Hawkins, "Opponents," p. 2.

[59]Ibid., pp. 79-84. Note his high evaluation of Justin
and the other Fathers. But see the criticisms of the early
Fathers' understanding of Galatians, above, p. 9, and of
the assessments of the later heresiologists, p. 145.

[60]See the brief survey in the introduction to
tradition-analysis (pp. 91-92); and the following treatment
of various passages (pp. 122-23, etc.).

[61]It is this uncertainty that lies behind the explicit
and implicit two-front theories, Schmithals' gnostic theory,
and, more recently, the approaches of Jewett and Hawkins.

[62]See above, pp. 26-27.

[63]For instance, Munck must admit that he really
starts from outside the text, because of the "controversial"
nature of the letter (see above, p. 24); and the approaches
of Mussner and Tyson, fastening onto indications in the text
of controversy, charge and countercharge, etc., fail to
explain some of the most obvious thrusts of the intruders
(see above, pp. 25-26).

[64]This need for holistic control is especially the
case in the face of the breakdown of traditional categories
for classifying Judaism (see below, pp. 91-92).

[65]By "genre," this thesis will mean the "larger forms"
of literature such as gospel, epistle, etc. See William G.
Doty, *Letters in Primitive Christianity* (Philadelphia: Fortress Press, 1973), p. 53; and William A. Beardslee, *Literary
Criticism of the New Testament* (Philadelphia: Fortress Press,
1970), p. ix, who speaks of the "larger forms of whole books,"
the equivalents of genres. He also notes "the significance of
structure or form for meaning" (p. iv).

[66]Beardslee, ibid., p. 1: "If a work of literature
is to be understood, it must be placed in some kind of larger
framework; it must be tested in one way or another."

[67]As is suggested below, pp. 37-39.

[68]See above, p. 24.

[69]Frederick Veltman, "The Defense Speeches of Paul in
Acts: Gattungsforschung and Its Limitations" (Th.D. dissertation, Graduate Theological Union, 1975), p. 252.

[70]See above, p. 27.

[71]See above, p. 27.

[72]See above, p. 28.

[73]See above, p. 28.

[74]In a similar way, Bultmann speaks of the tasks of
historical investigation and interpretation of the text. See
Theology, 2:251: "Neither exists, of course, without the
other, they stand constantly in a reciprocal relation to each
other. . . ."

[75]On the inescapable circularity when dealing with
text and context, see also William G. Doty, *Contemporary New
Testament Interpretation* (Englewood Cliffs: Prentice-Hall,
1972), p. 62.

[76]Beardslee, *Criticism*, pp. iv-v, notes that literary
criticism is to be used in conjunction with form- and
redaction-criticism.

[77]See Veltman, "Defence Speeches," pp. 251-52, and
below, p. 43, on flexibility within the genre under consideration.

[78]Veltman, ibid., p. iv.

[79]Beardslee, *Criticism*, p. 2, includes under the head
of "literary criticism" both the examination of small literary
details and analysis of the overall structure of the work and
its parts. This differs from literary criticism in the older
sense, that is, the historical study of authorship, date, and
sources (ibid., p. 6). See also Doty, *Interpretation*, pp. 55-
56. Since this dissertation was defended, Professor Hendrikus
Boers kindly sent to me, upon request, three papers in which
he discusses Betz's attempt to analyze Galatians in terms of
"macro-structure" ("The Structure and Meaning of Galatians,"
"Gen 15:6 and the Discourse Structure of Galatians," and "The
Structure of Galatians: Rhetorical or Text-linguistic Analysis"). He offers many valuable insights which, unfortunately,
cannot now be utilized in this dissertation. But certain of
his statements on method should here be noted. He points out
that Betz's work, properly called "form-critical," seeks to
determine the outline of Galatians, and hence its meaning, by
moving from the unit of meaning of the largest scale to those
of smaller scale. Of Betz's work, he suggests that "The mold
of the apologetic letter is too determinative" ("Gen 15:6,"
p. 15), and he is not able to approach the text of Galatians
except in terms of this structure. This dissertation par-
tially agrees with such a criticism, and seeks to guard
against it, firstly, by noting flexibility in the genre of
apologetic speech itself, and secondly, by extending the task
of genre-analysis (in the terms of Beardslee and Veltman) to
include analysis of indications of structure of smaller scale.
Boers admits that his own semantic analysis is "heavily
dependent on intuition" (Gen 15:6," p. 24); and would probably
acknowledge that such a method needs the external control of
"given conventional forms in which meaning is brought to
expression" ("Gen 15:6," p. 4), that is, genre- and form-
analysis. To a large extent Betz and Boers share a "common
endeavor" ("The Structure of Galatians," p. 1)--"What is
fundamentally important is that we are both persuaded that
there is no way in which a text such as Galatians can be
interpreted properly without taking into consideration its
structure" ("The Structure of Galatians," p. 3). This conviction lies also behind this present work.

[80]Günther Bornkamm, "The Heresy of Colossians," in
Fred O Francis and Wayne A. Meeks, eds., *Conflict at Colossae*
(Missoula, MT: Scholars Press, 1975), p. 123.

CHAPTER THREE

GALATIANS AND LITERARY GENRE

[1]Beardlsee, *Criticism*, p. 4.

[2]Betz, "Composition," p. 353.   James A. Fischer, "Pauline Literary Forms and Thought Patterns," *CBQ* 39 (1977): 209, also notes that the body of the Pauline letter has as yet escaped diagnosis.

[3]For example, Gustav Adolf Deissmann, *St. Paul; a Study in Social and Religious History*, trans. William E. Wilson (London: Hodder and Stoughton, 1926), pp. 13-14; and John Lee White, *The Form and Function of the Body of the Greek Letter* (Missoula, MT: Scholars Press, 1972), passim.

[4]Funk, *Language*, p. 170.

[5]White, *Body*, pp. 74-75; Betz, "Composition," p. 357; Ralph P. Martin, *New Testament Foundations: A Guide for Christian Students*, 2 vols. (Grand Rapids: Eerdmans, 1978), 2:243.

[6]For convenience, the disputed Pauline letters will be left out of consideration.

[7]Doty, *Letters*, p. 70.

[8]Funk, *Language*, p. 254.

[9]Doty, *Letters*, p. 70.

[10]Ibid.   Ralph P. Martin, "Approaches to New Testament Exegesis," in I. Howard Marshall, ed., *New Testament Interpretation* (Grand Rapids: Eerdmans, 1977), p. 232, notes that there is here a recurring pattern that has bewildered the commentators.

[11]Robert W. Funk, "The Form and Structure of 2 and 3 John," *JBL* 86 (1967):424-30.

[12]Martin, *Foundations*, 2:247, summarizing much recent scholarship, notes that Paul's letters were an extension of his person, mediating the apostolic presence and charged with apostolic power, building a lively bond between himself and his congregations.

[13]See the discussions in Otto Michel, *Der Brief an die Römer* (Göttingen: Vandenhoeck und Ruprecht, 1955), pp. 25, 337; Amos N. Wilder, *Early Christian Rhetoric* (London: SCM, 1964), p. 42; and Doty, *Letters*, p. 29.   Several suggest that Paul has combined the customary Greek χαίρειν and the Hebrew שלום: see Beda Rigaux, *The Letters of Paul* (Chicago: Franciscan Herald Press, 1968), p. 168.

[14]Paul Schubert, *Form and Function of the Pauline Thanksgivings* (Berlin: Alfred Topelmann, 1939), passim; Rigaux, *Letters*, p. 170, suggests that these thanksgivings are adaptations of the ברך יהוה of Ps 144:1 etc., and use a literary framework known from Qumran and elsewhere.

[15]Conzelmann, *1 Corinthians*, p. 6.

[16]Funk, *Language*, p. 257, and especially Schubert, *Thanksgivings*, pp. 71-82. See 1 Cor 1:4-9.

[17]1 Cor 1:10, Philem 8, etc.

[18]Gal 1:11, Rom 1:13, 2 Cor 1:8, Phil 1:12, etc. See Jack T. Sanders, "The Transition from Opening Epistolary Thanksgiving to Body in the Pauline Corpus," *JBL* 81 (1962): 352-62.

[19]See Rigaux, *Letters*, p. 171, who has five classifications of autobiography, some rather strained. His main examples are 1 Cor 16:5-9, 2 Cor 7:5, Rom 1:11-14, Phil 1:12-16, Rom 15:17-21, and Gal 1:11-2:14.

[20]See Funk, *Language*, pp. 264-72, on Rom 15:14-33, 1 Thess 2:17-3:13, etc., and his thesis of the "presence of apostolic authority and power."

[21]Betz, "Composition," p. 376, seems correct in saying that either paraenesis is poorly defined as "special caveats often in the form of proverbs either loosely strung together or simply following one another without connection" (Martin Dibelius, *From Tradition to Gospel*, trans. Bertram L. Woolf [New York: Scribner, 1965], p. 238); or what we have in Paul's letters is not paraenesis, when compared to James.

[22]Funk, *Language*, p. 270; White, *Body*, p. 70.

[23]Rigaux, *Letters*, p. 168, noting diversity and individuality within the letter genre itself.

[24]It has a letter-opening, 1:1-3, a prooemium, 1:4-9, and a concluding greeting. See Conzelmann, *1 Corinthians*, p. 6.

[25]Which does not at all stand in the paraenetic tradition, Funk, *Language*, p. 272. He notes that 1 Cor 5-15 is unique in the Pauline corpus.

[26]See Conzelmann, *1 Corinthians*, p. 7.

[27]Barrett, *2 Corinthians*, pp. 21-25; Funk, *Language*, p. 273.

[28]That it is: Funk, ibid., p. 272, and literature.

[29]Ibid., p. 269.

[30]See Jacob Jervell, *Imago Dei: Gen 1:26 im Spätjuden-tum, in der Gnosis und in den paulinischen Briefen* (Göttingen: Vandenhoeck und Ruprecht, 1960), pp. 232-33, for the way paraenesis in this letter takes over the scheme of the oppo-nents, and grows out of the polemical claims that are made for baptism.

[31]Rigaux, *Letters*, p. 168.

[32]Conzelmann, *1 Corinthians*, p. 7. The two differ too: Romans approximates more closely the structure of a tract, Rigaux, *Letters*, p. 168.

[33]That is, Galatians has no opening, thanksgiving, or travelogue, and the closing is unusually polemical. See Funk, *Language*, p. 268.

[34]Funk, ibid., p. 269, admits that the structural vari-ation raises the question of the relation of the letters to each other and to letter "form."

[35]This applies especially to any predictable arrange-ment of the body of the Pauline letter. See Doty, *Letters*, p. 42, and Fischer, "Literary Forms," p. 209.

[36]For instance, 1 Corinthians has letter characteris-tics, but its structure is explained on other grounds.

[37]Doty, *Letters*, p. 42.

[38]Gustav Adolf Deissmann, *Bible Studies*, trans. L. R. M. Strachan (Edinburgh: T. and T. Clark, 1901), pp. 3-59, distinguished between "epistles" (Literary productions) and "letters" (spontaneous, personal, and unaffected). Paul wrote true "letters," which were dashed off quickly, with no coherent, logical structure to their argument.

[39]Disagreement comes from, for example, Wendland, Conzelmann, Funk, White (see below, pp. 39-40), Martin, *Foundations*, 2:243.

[40]Paul Wendland, *Die hellenistisch-römisch Kultur in ihren Beziehungen zu Judentum und Christentum. Die Urchrist-lichen Literaturformen* (Tübingen: J. C. B. Mohr, 1912), p. 344: "Aber die Grenzlinie zwischen echtem Brief und litera-rischem Epistel darf nicht zu scharf gezogen werden." He rejects Deissmann's association of Paul's letters with papyri. Cicero wrote two types of letters, one more "literary" (*Ad Fam* 14. 21. 4 [LCL Cicero *Ad Fam* 3, 313-14]; *Ad Att* 4. 15 [LCL Cicero *Ad Att*, 3, 307]), but both are "letters." The letters of Seneca are genuine letters, but also literary.

[41]Conzelmann, *1 Corinthians*, p. 6, notes that Clement is an artistic literary creation, but also a genuine letter.

[42]Selby, *Paul*, p. 239. Wendland, *Literaturformen*, p. 346, notes that there are the same variations among Paul's

letters, that is, between for instance Philemon and Romans, as
among the letters of Cicero and Epicurus, where some are
intended for private consumption, others for publication.
Paul's letters depart from the model of the private letter
more and more as they are intended for wider circulation: the
letter that stands furthest from Philemon in this sense is
Galatians.

[43]Funk, *Language*, p. 256. The Sitz of "paraenesis"
is a vexed question (see above), but it is not a typical part
of nonliterary letters.

[44]Ibid., p. 252, quoting Weiss. If Deissmann is correct, "the Pauline letters at least will continue to be conceived as salutation, thanksgiving, and closing, with virtually anything in any order thrown in between."

[45]See Conzelmann, *1 Corinthians*, above, and the significance of Wisdom and existential questions for the structure of 1 Corinthians.

[46]See Rigaux, *Letters*, pp. 165-99, for various literary factors evidently at work in Paul's writing, such as
kerygmatic formulations, use of scripture, rhetoric, apocalyptic, prose and hymnic rhythm, paraenesis, etc. See also,
for instance, the influence of the techniques of "Spät-
judentum" on such passages as Rom 1:18-31. See Hans Lietzmann, *An die Römer*, HNT 8 (Tübingen: J. C. B. Mohr, 1934),
pp. 31-33, and Günther Bornkamm, *Early Christian Experience*,
trans. Paul L. Hammer (New York: Harper & Row, 1969), pp. 50-
51.

[47]On Paul's use of diatribe style, see Rudolf Bultmann, *Der Stil der paulinischen Predigt und die kynisch-stoisch
Diatribe* (Göttingen: Vandenhoeck und Ruprecht, 1910), passim;
and Hartwig Thyen, *Der Stil der Jüdische-Hellenistischen
Homilie* (Göttingen: Vandenhoeck und Ruprecht, 1955), passim.
Paul's style is more akin to popular philosophy, i.e., the
diatribe, than to the language of the common Egyptian letters.
Portions of his letters are not "epistolary" at all, but are
dominated by diatribe style, Bultmann, *Stil*, pp. 64-72.

[48]See note 38 above.

[49]White, *Body*, p. 3. Later, on p. 68, he says Deissmann was wrong in "his proposal that the common letter tradition was the literary genre to which the Pauline letter
belongs."

[50]Ibid., pp. 7-66, especially p. 65. "The body (of
the letter) usually has three discrete sections: body-opening,
body-middle, and body-closing." His subsequent analysis of
Galatians (pp. 79-111), in which he assumes that the letter-
body is 1:6-5:12, based on transitional devices culled from
the papyri, seems to slide over other studies on body-opening
transitions such as Sanders, "Transition," pp. 348-62.
Fischer, "Literary Forms," p. 210, criticizes the artificiality
of the use of transitional devices from the papyri.

[51]Wendland, *Literaturformen*, p. 349.   There is no necessary connection between Paul's work and the terms and suppositions of letters.

[52]Plato, *Epistle 7*, in Loeb, *Plato*, trans. R. B. Bury, 7 vols. (Cambridge, Mass.:   Harvard University Press, 1946), 7:463-565.   Bury notes that the epistolary features are merely a literary device: the work is an apology and manifesto in epistolary form.   Arnaldo Momigliano, *The Development of Greek Biography* (Cambridge, Mass.:   Harvard University Press, 1971), pp. 60-61, calls it an "apologetic letter" and the first auto-biographical letter.

[53]*Isocrates*, trans. George Norlin, 3 vols. (Cambridge, Mass.:   Harvard University Press, 1948).   Any epistolary features are minimal.

[54]Doty, *Letters*, p. 3.

[55]See above, p. 39.

[56]Seneca, *Epistulae Morales*, trans. Richard M. Gummere, 3 vols. (Cambridge, Mass.:   Harvard University Press, 1953). There are the briefest epistolary features.   George Kennedy, *The Art of Persuasion in Greece* (Princeton, NJ: Princeton University Press, 1963), pp. 293-98, notes that Stoic rhetoric was dominated by dialectic.   The thought of the speech was the speech, and would produce its own natural and good expression. He cites Cato: "*rem tene, verba sequentur*."   This domination of the structure by style is evident in Seneca and Pliny.   But Seneca's letters are still letters.

[57]Doty, *Letters*, p. 7, commenting on Seneca's letters to Lucilius--"the letter type farthest from the private inti-mate letter."

[58]Doty, *Letters*, p. 8.   Again, epistolary features are minimal.   Martin Hengel, *Judaism and Hellenism*, 2 vols. (London: SCM Press, 1974), 1:110, referring to the Jewish epistles in the Hellenistic period (the Letters of Jeremiah, 2 Macc 1:10-2:18, letters in the Apocalypse of Baruch, the Letter of Aristeas, and the letters of Solomon in Eupolemus), notes that they are not much more than "an expansion of the exchange of messages."

[59]Many other letter-writers could be referred to. The definitive collection of Greek epistles is R. Hercher, *Epistolographi Graeci* (Paris, 1873).   Most of the Cynic epistles in this collection have now appeared in uncritical form in A. J. Malherbe, *The Cynic Epistles* (Missoula: Scholars Press, 1977); and of these, the letters of (pseudo)-Heracleitus in critical form in Harold Attridge, *First-Century Cynicism in the Epistles of Heracleitus* (Missoula: Scholars' Press, 1976).   The letters in these last two collections show a close relationship to popular philosophy and the rhetoric influenced by such philosophy.   The epistolary features are minimal, and the structure is dominated by the subject-matter in diatribe style.   See Attridge, ibid., p. 12 (on the relation between

diatribe and rhetoric), and Bultmann, *Stil*, p. 20. The main
contributions for the New Testament are in style (diatribe)
and form (haustafeln, virtue and vice lists, etc.). See
Malherbe, ibid., pp. 1, 14, 28.

[60]Wilder, *Rhetoric*, p. 39; and Doty, *Letters*, p. 15.

[61]Cicero sees the letter as speech in written medium,
Ad Att 8. 14. 1 (LCL, 2:163); 9. 10. 1 (LCL, 2:225-26); 12. 53
(LCL, 3:107); and Quintillian writes that letters should be in
the style of a dialogue, *Oratoria* 9. 4. 19-20 (LCL, 3:517).

[62]Veltman, "Defense Speeches," p. 252, after his
examination of the various media in which speeches occur, concludes, ". . . speeches, letters, and stories, were common
stock-in-trade items available to every writer."

[63]For instance, the regret at mistreatment of the
letter. See Demetrius, *On Style*, trans. W. R. Roberts (London:
Cambridge University Press, 1902), ## 229, 231 (pp. 175-76).

[64]A. J. Malherbe, "Ancient Epistolary Theorists," *Ohio
Journal of Religious Studies* 5 (1977):3-17, assesses the place
of letter-handbooks in letter-writing and notices the tendency
of letter-teaching to fall into the hands of rhetoricians.

[65]Bultmann, *Stil*.

[66]Thyen, *Stil*.

[67]The main sources used by Bultmann are Seneca and
Epictetus.

[68]Such as οὐκ οἶδας, τί οὖν, ὁρᾶτε, μὴ γένοιτο, the
α-privative, etc.

[69]The relation of cynic-stoic literature to rhetoric
is somewhat contradictory. There is a rejection of oratory,
rules of rhetorical structure, etc.; and yet small-scale
rhetorical devices are used frequently. See Bultmann, *Stil*,
pp. 20-24.

[70]The best examples of the dialogical diatribe are
Rom 2:1-29, Romans 6, Romans 10, 1 Cor 7:18-24, 1:20-25, and
3:5-9.

[71]Though it seems strange to say that Paul was not
personally acquainted with the situation in Corinth.

[72]Bultmann, *Stil*, p. 67.

[73]Thyen, *Stil*, p. 41. The diatribe does not dominate
the structure of Paul's letters, as it does for the cynics and
stoics.

[74]For instance, Gal 2:14, 17 (using μὴ γένοιτο),
3:1-5, 19, 21 (again, μὴ γένοιτο), 4:9, 16, and 21. But of
these, 3:1-5, 4:9 and 21 clearly have in focus the Galatians
themselves, and not some conjectured opponent.

[75] See above, pp. 40-41.

[76] Betz, "Composition," pp. 353-79. Betz's excellent
commentary has now of course appeared (Hans Dieter Betz, *Galatians* [Philadelphia: Fortress Press, 1979]), though too late
to be used in this dissertation. He takes further his analysis
of the literary composition and function of Galatians (pp. 14-
25). Though there are naturally ways in which his work differs
from the present one, it appears to be supportive of many positions taken here.

[77] J. Weiss, *Beiträge zur paulinischen Rhetorik*
(Göttingen: 1897); Rigaux, *Letters*, pp. 176-78; Doty, *Letters*,
pp. 50-51; J. P. Sampley, "Before God, I Do Not Lie," (Gal 1:
20). Paul's Self-Defense in the Light of Roman Legal Praxis,"
NTS 23 (4, 1977):477-82. To be noted are the warnings of such
classicists as Wendland (Literaturformen, p. 344: 'der paulinischen Briefe . . . sie ursprünglich nicht Literaturprodukte
im strengsten Sinne gewesen sind . . .") and Wilder (*Rhetoric*,
p. 44: "In comparison with Greco-Roman models . . . none of
the New Testament writings could be identified as "literature"
as then understood . . .") against applying classical canons
too rigidly.

[78] Betz, "Composition," pp. 354-55. See also above
p. 225, note 52, for the comment of Bury and Momigliano.

[79] Momigliano, *Biography*, p. 60.

[80] Ibid., pp. 58-62, 93-101, where the development of
this literary genre is traced.

[81] Ibid., pp. 58-59. Momigliano notes that some of
the most influential apologetic speeches were "never uttered,"
that is, they were speeches in literary form only.

[82] Kennedy, *Persuasion*, p. 5: once oral literature
became written, speech did not lose the special significance
it had, either in form or in substance. And p. 270: rhetorical forms were always closely related to literary forms.

[83] *Plato*, LCL, 1:61-146.

[84] Werner Jaeger, *Paideia: The Ideals of Greek Culture*,
trans. Gilbert Highet, 3 vols. (Oxford: Basil Blackwell,
1947), 3:133. Momigliano, *Biography*, p. 59, calls it a "fic-
tional speech."

[85] James Jerome Murphy, ed., *Demosthenes' On the Crown*,
trans. John H. Kearney (New York: Random House, 1967).
Momigliano, *Biography*, p. 58, notes that the speech belongs
in the stream of autobiography to which the apologetic letter
belongs. It was originally an apologetic speech before a
court of law: in written form, it became a model copied
repeatedly. See Kennedy, *Persuasion*, pp. 332-36.

[86] *Isocrates*, LCL, 2:181-366.

[87]Jaeger, *Paideia*, p. 133, who speaks here of a "mixture of forms," and a refinement of rhetorical skill. It
pretends to be what was said in lawsuit.

[88]Momigliano, *Biography*, p. 59.

[89]Cicero *Brutus*, LCL, 10:68-144. Momigliano, *Biography*,
p. 60, notes the Socratic influence on Cicero through Isocrates.
See below, pp. 105-6, for the way in which Plato's Socrates
influenced Jewish apologetic literature.

[90]Veltman, "Defense Speeches," pp. 79-202, has analyzed
the reports of defense speeches in the historiography of the
Greeks (Polybius, Dionysius of Halicarnassus, and Appian),
Romans (Livy, Q. Curtius Rufus, and C. Cornelius Tacitus), and
Jews (1 and 2 Macc, Josephus, and Philo), as well as such
speeches in Greek and Latin romance, in an attempt to determine the genre of the defense speech in such literature.

[91]Ibid., p. 74, noting the "close association of historical composition and oratory," with primary and secondary
sources. That historians intentionally edited the speeches
they reported, to present them as models of oratory, is
clearly suggested by Quintillian *Oratio* 9. 4. 18 (LCL, 3:515):
" . . . in the speech inserted by historians we may note something in the way of balanced cadences and antitheses."

[92]Cicero *Oratore* distinguishes between historiography
and oratory, noting that the two have different styles, aims,
and criteria: 2. 15. 62-622 (LCL, 1:243-49).

[93]Veltman, "Defense Speeches," p. 250, concludes that
the speeches in historiography are not numerous, are often
incomplete, and are not rhetorically complex; in fact, it is
difficult to define a genre of defense speech in historiography
with any precision.

[94]Betz, "Composition," pp. 357-58.

[95]Donald Lemen Clark, *Rhetoric in Greco-Roman Education* (New York: Columbia University Press, 1957), p. 25:
rhetoric was primarily intended for law-courts; and Kennedy,
Persuasion, p. 11. The basic rhetorical speech applies best
to judicial oratory. See Cicero *Oratore* 1. 10. 44 (LCL,
1:35). Note that law, politics, and oratory come together.
Ad Herennium 1. 2, referring to the scope of rhetoric, speaks
especially of "law and citizenship."

[96]Cicero *Oratore*, 1. 11. 45-47, claims that oratory is
to be used in philosophy and science as well as law, that is,
politics (LCL, 1:35-43); and Quintillian *Oratio* 2. 21. 3 states
that "the material of rhetoric is composed of everything that
may be placed before it as a subject for speech" (LCL, 1:357).

[97]So, Demosthenes' *De Corona* is an apologetic speech
before a court of law (Momigliano, *Biography*, p. 58);
Isocrates blends forensic oratory with his self-defense and
autobiography (Jaeger, *Paideia*, pp. 132-33); and Plato's

Apology has a forensic setting.   Veltman, "Defense Speeches,"
p. 64, remarks that apologetic speech is a category of forensic
speech.

[98]Beardslee, *Criticism*, p. 3.   See above, p. 31, on
the terms "genre" and "larger form."

[99]This is the method adopted by Veltman, "Defense
Speeches," passim.

[100]Demosthenes' *De Corona* probably conforms most
closely to the textbook structure of rhetorical speech, dividing into *prooemium* (1-8), *narratio* (10-52), *probatio* (60-109),
confutatio (160-296), and *peroratio* (297-324).   See Murphy,
Demosthenes, pp. 137-44.   Kennedy, *Persuasion*, pp. 229-32,
analyses the speech almost identically, and speaks of a "traditional pattern."   The same structure is basically discernible
in the other examples, though the bulk of Isocrates' speech is
probatio, and *confutatio* is difficult to distinguish; and in
Cicero's *Brutus*, diatribe style begins to dominate the *probatio*.   Theory demanded flexibility (Quintillian *Oratio* 7. 1.
12 [LCL, 3:13]) and there was careful attention to the
quaestio or speech situation (ibid., 3. 5. 5-18 [LCL, 1:399-
407]).   It could be of two kinds, *infinita* (general discussion)
or *finita* (concerned with particular persons or cases).   It
could also be designated forensic (judicial), epideictic
(demonstrative), or deliberative (discussion of policy).   Similarly, *Ad Herennium* 1. 2. 2 (LCL, 5).

[101]The texts used here will be those of Cicero, (*De
Oratore* and *De Inventione*) in his prime about BCE 75-63; the
supposedly anonymous *Ad Herennium*, dated about 81 BCE and
followed closely in classical and postclassical times; and
Quintillian (*Institutio Oratoria*), who belongs in the first
century CE, coming at the close of a great period and summing
it up.   See Clark, *Rhetoric*, pp. 70, 14.

[102]For instance, Cicero makes the speech have four
parts by including *partitio* with *narratio*, and treating *con-
firmatio* and *confutatio* under one category (*Oratore* 1. 4
[LCL, 3:313]).   See Clark, *Rhetoric*, p. 70.

[103]*Ad Herennium* 1. 3. 4 (LCL, 9).

[104]*Ad Herennium* distinguishes two kinds of openings:
the direct opening, or *prooemium*, and the subtle approach, or
ephodos (1. 4. 6 [LCL, 11-12]).   There were four methods of
making the hearer well-disposed (1. 4. 8 [LCL, 15]), and
where there was no need to gain attention, a direct opening
or *prooemium* could be used.

[105]Cicero *Oratore* 2. 30. 132 (LCL, 1:293), also
called *exordium*.

[106]*Ad Herennium* 1. 9. 14-15 (LCL, 25-27): it should
have three qualities, brevity, clarity, and plausibility.   It
should only cover those facts necessary to the case; the
shorter it is, the easier it is to follow; and it is best to
follow chronological order.

[107]Quintillian *Oratoria* 4. 2. 31 (LCL, 2:67).

[108]*Ad Herennium* 1. 3. 4.

[109]Cicero *Inventione* 1. 22. 31-32. 33 (LCL, 63-67).

[110]Quintillian *Oratoria* 4. 4. 1-4. 5. 26 (LCL, 2:131).

[111]For instance, *Ad Herennium* 1. 10 17:   Orestes killed his mother (agreed); but did he have a right to (disagreed)?

[112]Quintillian *Oratoria* 4. 4. 1 (LCL, 2:131).

[113]*Ad Herennium* 1. 3. 4.

[114]Cicero *Inventione* 1. 24. 34 (LCL, 69).

[115]See the details summarized in Clark, *Rhetoric*, p. 147.

[116]Quintillian 4. 2. 79 (LCL, 2:93).

[117]*Ad Herennium* 1. 3. 4 (LCL, 9).

[118]*Ad Herennium* 2. 30. 47-2. 31. 50 (LCL, 145-41); Quintillian 6. 1. 1-9 (LCL, 2:383-94).

[119]For instance, into recapitulation, emotional appeal, and refutation.   See Quintillian 6. 1. 1-2 (LCL, 2:393-85); Cicero *Inventione* 1. 52. 98-1. 53. 30 (LCL, 147-53); and *Ad Herennium* 2. 30. 47 (LCL, 145).

[120]*Ad Herennium* 2. 30. 47 (LCL, 145):   "The summing up gathers together and recalls the points we have made . . . and we shall reproduce all the points in the order in which they have been presented, so that the hearer . . . is brought back to what he remembers."

[121]See above, note 102.

[122]Kennedy, *Persuasion*, p. 7.

[123]Clark, *Rhetoric*, p. 59.   He notes that the Hellenistic pattern of education was well established in Rome by the mid-second century BCE and was extended to Gaul and even Britain by the end of the first century CE, according to Juvenal (*Satire* 14. 110 [LCL, 297]).

[124]Kennedy, *Persuasion*, p. 270.   Hengel, *Judaism*, 1:69, notes that education was mainly devoted to the dominant fashions.

[125]Kennedy, *Persuasion*, p. 332:   "This rhetorical μιμήσις or imitation, in which one studied an author and tried to reproduce his style, became such a major interest of teachers of rhetoric that in later Hellenistic times it tended to overshadow everything else."   See, for example, Quintillian on imitation, *Oratoria* 10 (LCL, 4:75-122).

[126]Hengel, *Judaism*, 1:65.

[127]Ibid., p. 66.

[128]Josephus *Ant* 12. 119.

[129]Hengel, *Judaism*, 1:67.

[130]The prohibition of Jews from the gymnasium in Alexandria in 41 CE led the way to a Jewish rebellion and eventual annihilation of the Jewish Diaspora in Egypt, 115-117 CE, ibid., p. 68.

[131]Philo *Spec Leg* 2. 230; *Som* 61. 129-30.

[132]Philo *Spec Leg* 2. 230; *Ebr* 49; *Som* 1. 3-6.

[133]Hengel, *Judaism*, 1:102: the Greek literature of Palestine gives evidence of training in rhetoric, though not used against Hellenistic civilization; and 81, the dialectic form of instruction of Rabbinic Judaism, with its sequence of question and answer, could almost be called Socratic and shows the influence of Greek rhetorical schools.

[134]Strabo *Geography* 16. 2. 29 mentions four famous writers from Gadara, among them "Theodorus the rhetor of our days" (i.e., BC 63-19 AD).

[135]Ibid., 14. 5. 13: "The people of Tarsus have devoted themselves so eagerly, not only to philosophy, but also to the whole round of education in general, that they have surpassed Athens, Alexandria, or any other place that can be named where there have been schools and lectures of philosophers. . . . Further, the city of Tarsus has all kinds of schools of rhetoric."

[136]Selby, *Paul*, p. 126.

[137]Koester, "Hellenism," p. 187.

[138]J. P. Sampley, "Before God, I Do Not Lie," (Gal 1:20). "Paul's Self-Defense in the Light of Roman Legal Praxis," *NTS* 23 (1977):477-82; significant here because law was conducted in terms of rhetoric.

[139]See the references above, note 77; and Rigaux, *Letters*, p. 178, for further bibliography.

[140]Rigaux, *Letters*, p. 178, considers the whole of Romans and Ephesians to reveal rhetorical structure.

[141]The use of rhetoric has been seen in 1 Cor 1 and 2 (Munck, *Paul*, p. 153; Conzelmann, *1 Corinthians*, pp. 39-48), Rom 15, 2 Cor 8-9, 1 Thess 2:15, 5:4-12 (Rigaux, *Letters*, pp. 179-80; Bultmann, *Stil*, pp. 74-76).

[142]The speech of Tertullus in Acts 24, only briefly reported, opens with a *captatio benevolentiae* (Veltman,

"Defense Speeches," p. 213, discussing 24:2-3) that conforms
to the direct opening built upon goodwill of *Ad Herennium* 1.
4. 6 (LCL, 13), which goes on to say, "From the discussion of
the person of our hearers goodwill is secured if we set forth
the courage, wisdom, humanity, and nobility of past judgments
they have rendered . . ." (1. 5. 8 [LCL, 17]). 24:4-6 can be
understood to be the *causa* (p. 91, above), and 24:8 is a brief
conclusio. Paul's reply is also briefly recorded. It opens
with a *captatio benevolentiae* (Veltman, ibid., p. 215), then
has a brief *narratio*, 24:11-13 (above, p. 44), a *divisio*, 24:
14-16 (above, p. 44), and the beginnings of a *probatio*, 24:17.
However, from here on the speech structure dissolves (Veltman,
ibid., p. 215). The more complete speech of Acts 26 has a
prooemium that is a *captatio benevolentiae*, 26:2-3 (Veltman,
ibid., p. 218), followed by a *causa*, 26:4-8. Then there is a
narratio (26:9-18), a *divisio* (26:19-23), and evidence that
the speech was then interrupted, 26:24. As far as it continues, then, it follows classical structure.

[143]F. J. Foakes Jackson and Kirsopp Lake, *The Beginnings of Christianity*, 4 vols. (London: Macmillan and Co.,
1933), 4:213, understand Acts 17:22-31 to be a trial or
defense speech. Timothy D. Barnes, "An Apostle on Trial,"
JTS 20 (1969):407-19, has more recently examined the evidence
in favor of this assessment, pointing to such things as the
powers and functions of the Ἀρεἰος Πἀγος and the use of ἐπι-
λαμβάνεσθαι. Ernst Haenchen, *The Acts of the Apostles* (Philadelphia: Westminster, 1971), p. 517, points to indications
in the speech and its context that there is an attempt at
reminiscence of Socrates and his defense, such as references
to the ἀγορα, the Ἀρεἰος Πἀγος, ξἐνα δαιμονἰα, etc.

[144]Martin Dibelius, *Studies in the Acts of the
Apostles*, trans. Mary Ling (New York: Scribner, 1956), pp.
27-30, and Paul Schubert, "The Place of the Areopagus Speech
in the Composition of Acts," in *Transitions in Biblical
Scholarship*, ed. J. Coert Rylaarsdam (Chicago: University
of Chicago Press, 1968), pp. 251-68, both draw attention to
the structure of the speech, an introduction (or *prooemium*),
17:22, 23 (including a *causa*, 17:23), followed by an exposition in three themes, 17:24-29, and a conclusion or *peroratio*,
17:30-31. Schubert, pp. 257, 261, draws attention to rhetorical features within the speech, as does Eduard Norden, *Agnostos
Theos* (Stuttgart: B. G. Teubner, 1956), pp. 10-56.

[145]Norden, *Agnostos Theos*, pp. 10-11, draws attention
to the parallels between the end of the Areopagus speech and
Hellenistic apologetic missionary speeches such as those in
Poimandres, Odes of Solomon, the Kerygma Petri, etc.

[146]Barnes, "Apostle on Trial," pp. 418-19, sees no
anomaly between the conclusion from the evidence he presents,
that is, that the speech is a trial or defense speech, and
the obvious apologetic or hortatory tendency of the conclusion
of the speech.

[147]See below on the paraenetic portion of Galatians,
and the suggestion that a forensic *refutatio* has here been

adapted to the "speech situation," so that it performs a hortatory function, p. 54.

[148]Momigliano, *Biography*, p. 62, suggests that the "Platonic precedent" reappears in Paul; and Clark, *Rhetoric*, p. 142, writes that the rhetorical canons as they appear in *Ad Herennium* guided many of those who addressed the public in writing--Demosthenes and Cicero in their speeches, and Seneca --and Paul--in their letters.

[149]See above, pp. 28-29.

[150]So, Funk, *Language*, p. 272, quoted above, p. 39. Lightfoot, *Galatians*, p. 63, notes that "The epistle of Galatians is especially distinguished among St. Paul's Letters by its unity of purpose. The Galatian apostasy . . . is never lost sight of from beginning to end."

[151]See above, p. 41.

[152]Sampley, "Self-Defense," p. 478, suggests that rhetoric should be especially applicable to Galatians, where Paul is both defending himself and making countercharges.

[153]Paul uses the curse elsewhere only in 1 Cor 16:22, at the end of a letter.

[154]Betz, "Composition," p. 334, who notes the use of the curse by Demosthenes in *De Corona* 324. Quintillian discusses the place of the curse in the forensic speech in *Oratoria* 4. 1. 20-22 (LCL, 2:17).

[155]See Sampley, "Self-Defense," pp. 477-82, and Quintillian, 5. 6. 1 (LCL, 2:165), who states that the oath was a sign of bad faith unless the same privilege was allowed to the opponent. Paul in effect does this in 4:14-15, "I bear you witness that, if possible, you would have plucked out your eyes and given them to me."

[156]Note how Tertullus rests his case in Acts 24:8. Quintillian *Oratoria* 6. 1. 3 (LCL, 2:385) says that an effective conclusion is to pretend to wonder "what hope the accuser can have after the manner in which we have refuted all the charges brought against us." A concluding type of appeal may be made in several places in the speech (ibid., 6. 1. 53; *Ad Herennium* 2. 30. 47).

[157]Both BAG and H. D. Betz, "στίγμα," *TDNT*, 6:663-64, follow LS in translating στίγμα as a tattoo, mark, etc. BAG notes Hierod., Carm. Aur. 11, p. 445 Mull., where στίγματα are the scars left by the rod of discipline. The word is used in the NT only at Gal 6:17.

[158]See 2 Cor 1:5, 8, 4:10, 6:4-6, 11:23-26, and Col 1:24.

[159]See Gal 2:20 in conjunction with the above texts; and Mussner, *Galater*, p. 417.

[160]Ibid., p. 418. LS refer to Gal 6:17 as a meta-phorical use of στίγμα.

[161]Sampley, "Self-Defense," pp. 477-82; Betz, "Com-position," p. 329, gives examples. Quintillian *Oratoria* 6. 1. 21 (LCL, 395-97) states that " . . . the defendant . . . his worth, his manly pursuits, the scars from wounds received in battle, his rank and the services rendered by his ancestors, will all commend him to the goodwill of the judges."

[162]Betz, "Composition," p. 327.

[163]Kümmel, *Introduction*, p. 294; Mussner, *Galater*, p. 43. It is clearly different from Rom 1:1-7, 2 Cor 1:1-9, and other introductions to Paul's letters. This section of the epistle will be discussed further below.

[164]See, for example, the manner in which the speaker concludes in Demosthenes' *De ,Corona*, Socrates' *Apology*, and Isocrates' *Antidosis*, etc.

[165]See above, p. 44, on the way a *conclusio* could be subdivided, with references. For the different emotional appeals that were appropriate in this part of the speech, see Quintillian *Oratoria* 6. 1. (LCL, 2:383-94).

[166]The remarks of the commentators are well summarized by Mussner, *Galater*, pp. 53-54.

[167]Funk, *Language*, p. 270.

[168]See above, p. 44, on the types of *exordia*. Gal 1:6-11 conforms closely to the "direct opening" of *Ad Herennium*, where the attention of the audience is assured.

[169]Compare Rom 1:8-17, 1 Cor 1:3-9, 2 Cor 1:3-5, Phil 1:3-6, Col 1:3-4, 1 Thess 1:2-4. See the comments of Mussner, *Galater*, p. 53.

[170]Betz, "Composition," p. 359, refers to the use of θαυμάζειν in *exordia* by Demosthenes, Plato, Isocrates, etc.

[171]Lightfoot, *Galatians*, pp. 65-66.

[172]See above, p. 229, note 102, noting that Cicero in-cluded *partitio* with *narratio*. In fact, *partitio* and *narratio* in Galatians are both connected and separate in a way suggested by the texts.

[173]Its seriousness is indicated by the fact that, in verses 6-9, the nominal or verbal form of εὐαγγέλιον is used five times. The preacher of a false εὐαγγέλιον is placed under a double curse. The source of the disturbance is clearly a Christian heresy, a false εὐαγγέλιον. See Mussner, *Galater*, pp. 59-62.

[174]The force of θαυμάζειν has been noted above, p. 48. Paul is astonished partly because it has all happened ταχέως.

[175]Sampley, "Self-Defense," p. 478.

[176]It has already been noted above that Paul writes
as a missionary (Wendland, above, p. 40) and as an apostle
(Martin, above, p. 38). He does not write merely to theological issues or to theologians but to churches. It must be the
Galatians themselves who have called forth the letter. Sampley,
"Self-Defense," pp. 477-82, notes that, according to legal
theory, the privilege of the oath was offered to the opponent.
However, in ·the example of this that he cites from Galatians,
4:15-16, the privilege is offered to the Galatians. This confirms that the Galatians are at once judge, jury, and offending
party.

[177]As proposed by Drane, *Paul*, pp. 137-39, who makes
the letter an attack on three false doctrines, one dealt with
in each of chaps. 1-2, 3-4, and 5-6.

[178]The *causa* is in the second person plural: the
Galatians are considered as one group. Lightfoot, *Galatians*,
p. 63, notes that "The sustained severity of this epistle is
an equally characteristic feature with its unity of purpose."

[179]See *Ad Herennium* 1. 9. 14-15 (LCL, 25-27) on the
function of the *narratio*. Quintillian *Oratoria* 4. 2. 11 (LCL,
2:55) says the facts should here be presented as simply as
possible.

[180]J. T. Sanders, "Paul's 'Autobiographical' Statements in Gal 1-2," *JBL* 85 (1966):335-43, comparing Gal 1:11-17
and 1 Cor 15:1,3, which appear contradictory.

[181]Quintillian *Oratoria* 4. 2. 31 (LCL, 2:67).

[182]Against Drane, *Paul*, pp. 137-39, and others who see
Gal 1-2 as dealing specifically with apostleship.

[183]Lightfoot, *Galatians*, p. 64. He notes that the
letter both begins (1:1-5) and ends (6:11-18) with two main
themes in juxtaposition--Paul's apostolicity and the validity
of his gospel.

[184]Sampley, "Self-Defense," p. 478, noting the significant place at which Paul's oath occurs in 1:20--Paul is
saying that, in Jerusalem, he saw only Cephas and James.

[185]Drane, *Paul*, pp. 13-14.

[186]See below, pp. 69-78.

[187]See Kümmel, *Introduction*, pp. 300-1; and Schmithals,
Paul, pp. 8-66.

[188]See below, pp. 58-59.

[189]Quintillian *Oratoria* 7. 1. 12 (LCL, 3:13). See,
for instance, how Cicero, in his *Brutus*, begins with a *narratio*

that deals with a general history of the teaching of rhetoric,
not the specific events that have occasioned the charges and
his reply.

[190]Munck, *Paul*, p. 100.

[191]Quintillian *Oratoria* 4. 2. 132 (LCL, 2:121).

[192]This is why the exact positions of the opponents
cannot be decided from the historical portion of the letter;
against Tyson and others, above, pp. 25-26.

[193]See above, p. 44.

[194]See above, pp. 44-45.

[195]See above, p. 44, and references.

[196]For instance, Ernest de Witt Burton, *A Critical and
Exegetical Commentary on the Epistle to the Galatians*, ICC p.
lxxii, summarizes 2:15-21 as the "continuation and expansion
of his address at Antioch so stated as to be for the Galatians
also an exposition of the gospel which he preached."

[197]This assertion will be examined more carefully
below, pp. 69-78.

[198]Noting the adversative δὲ and the μὴ γένοιτο of
2:17 and the polemical change from ἁμάρτωλος to παραβάτης in
2:17-18. See below, pp. 71-73.

[199]Quintillian *Oratoria* 4. 4. 1 (LCL, 2:131).

[200]The structure and language of 2:15-21 will be
examined more carefully below, pp. 73-77.

[201]It is significant that the diatribe style is used
most frequently in these chapters: 3:1-5, 19, 21, 4:9, 16,
21.

[202]Betz, "Composition," p. 370. On the *interrogatio*,
see Quintillian *Oratoria* 5. 7. (LCL, 2:171-90), and *Ad Herren-
nium* 4. 15. 22 (LCL 283).

[203]*Ad Herennium*, ibid., states that the most impressive
interrogation reinforces the argument just delivered, in this
case Gal 2:15-21 and Paul's particular statement of justification.

[204]Quintillian *Oratoria* 5. 7. 31 (LCL, 2:187).

[205]Thus the question of the presence and power of
πνεῦμα and δυνάμεις (3:2, 5) directly carries on the argument
about the way of justification; and the experience of the
Galatians referred to here (whatever that might be: see
below, pp. 78-82) is an essential part of Paul's answer
about the way of justification.

[206]Betz, "Composition," p. 372, with reference to the use of the topos περὶ φιλίας in speeches and letters. See Quintillian *Oratoria* 5. 11. 41 (LCL, 2:295).

[207]See further below, p. 59.

[208]Betz does not consider that Galatians may have a *refutatio* and tries to explain this passage rhetorically as paraenesis by claiming examples of paraenesis in rhetorical literature. However, the sole example he cites (Seneca, Epistle 76) is unconvincing. It belongs to Stoic diatribe literature, which used rhetorical techniques but not a rhetorical structure (see above). Bultmann speaks of a hortatory or imperative tone in diatribe literature, but not paraenesis (*Der Stil*, pp. 32-34). The rhetorical handbooks make little or no allowance for paraenesis.

[209]*Ad Herennium* 2. 30. 47 (LCL, 147). See above, p. 46.

[210]See above, p. 46.

[211]See the criticism of Dibelius' definition above, p. 222, note 21.

[212]Above, p. 28, quoting Jewett, "Agitators," pp. 196-98. It is significant, too, that both 5:1-12 and 5:13-6:10 are bound together by the exhortation to ἀγάπη (5:6, 6:14-15, 5:22).

[213]See the reference to Quintillian *Oratoria* 7. 1. 12, above, p. 229, note 100, and the need for attention to the *quaestio* or speech situation.

[214]Perhaps analogous to Hellenistic missionary propaganda, which used rhetorical techniques, but followed the presentation of the main argument with ethical exhortation. See Norden, *Agnostos Theos*, pp. 10-11.

[215]Clark, *Rhetoric*, p. 210, refers to the oratorical procedure of showing that the case under consideration comes as a minor premise under a large generalization or major premise: all temple robbers should be prosecuted; this man has robbed a temple. Quintillian *Oratoria* 5. 13. 17 (LCL, 2:321) states that it is sometimes an orator's duty to make it appear that an opponent's argument is really favorable to his own client.

[216]Doty, *Letters*, pp. 37, 57-58, refers particularly to virtue and vice lists and "rules for the household." It is the use of these forms which led Dibelius to his definition of paraenesis, above, p. 222, note 21, with its stress on tradition.

[217]Furnish, *Ethics*, pp. 71-72, notes that Paul "does not seek to distinguish between the content of his ethical advice and (his readers'), but supports his own exhortations by relating them to what, on other grounds, his readers are already willing to acknowledge." This is especially apparent

in Galatians, where, Paul says, the "works of the flesh" are
φανερά. He sees Christian tradition in Paul's exhortations in
1 Cor 7:10-40, 14:37, 1 Thess 4:15 (dominical traditions),
1 Cor 11:23 (liturgical traditions), 1 Cor 15:3-11 (παρα-
δίδοναι, παραλαμβάνειν), Phil 2, Rom 1:3-4, 1 Cor 11:2 (customs in the churches), etc.

[218]Doty, *Letters*, p. 57; Rigaux, *Letters*, p. 197.   To
this extent, Dibelius is correct.

[219]Doty, *Letters*, p. 38; Furnish, *Ethics*, p. 84.   It
is the subtle modification of vice-lists, etc., that is the
genius of Paul's ethic.

[220]Ibid., p. 84.   Paul was not a wandering street
preacher but an apostle, and his ethics reflect this function.
There is a contextuality and concrete relevance to his ethics.
He does not leave the identification of "good" and "evil"
deeds to the congregations' imaginations.   In Galatians, for
example, Paul "describes concretely" how the exhortation to
love is fulfilled.   To this extent, Dibelius was wrong.

[221]Funk also questions Dibelius' assumption about the
general rather than specific nature of Paul's paraenesis,
noting that use by Paul of traditional material does not mean
he no longer has a specific situation in mind.   Paul's customary method of argument is to adapt traditional material in
a particular way.   To resolve the question, it is necessary
to consider (1) the way in which paraenesis is set in the
letter as a whole; (2) the way the traditional material has
been framed in the context; and (3) Paul's disposition to
traditional language.   See *Language*, pp. 270-71.

[222]Bultmann, *Stil*, p. 30, and Quintillian and Cicero,
quoted above, p. 40.

[223]See Beardslee referred to above, p. 43.

[224]See above, p. 45, on the place of rhetoric in
Palestine; and the place of the Socratic tradition in Palestinian Jewish literature, below pp. 105-6.

CHAPTER FOUR

INTERNAL INDICATIONS OF STRUCTURE

[1]In accordance with the definition of and procedure
for literary criticism suggested by Beardslee, above, p. 32.

[2]Building on the suggestion of Bultmann above, p.
41, that Paul's writings are influenced by diatribe, an important element of which is the antithesis.   See also Kennedy,
quoted above, p. 225, note 56.

[3]The epistolary features of Galatians are almost all
confined to these passages: and because of this, they are
profitably analyzed in terms of epistolary practice. See
above, pp. 47-48.

[4]White, *Body*, passim; Fischer, "Literary Forms," pp.
209-23.

[5]Fischer, "Literary Forms," pp. 209-23.

[6]Bultmann, *Stil*, pp. 97-98.

[7]Ibid., pp. 74-75. See also Ernst Käsemann, *An die
Römer*, HNT 8a (Tübingen: J. C. B. Mohr, 1974), pp. 131-33;
and Egon Brandenburger, *Fleisch und Geist* (Neukirchen-Vluyn:
Neukirchener Verlag, 1968), pp. 45-49, on the antithesis of
σάρξ and πνεῦμα in Galatians.

[8]Following to a limited extent the procedure of John
Bligh, *Galatians* (London: St. Paul Publications, 1969), who
assumes that the letter is a large chiasm. Betz, "Composition," p. 353, seems correct when he remarks that the "commentary genre is at present not the most creative format within which to work," that is, a simple verse-by-verse treatment
of a document quickly loses touch with its vital dynamics.
Sanders, *Paul*, pp. 12-23, also writes of the necessity of a
"holistic" method.

[9]See the references above, p. 38, to Rigaux, Schubert,
etc. Note, for example, how Romans expands Rom 1:2-6, and
1 Corinthians expands 1 Cor 1:2.

[10]Paul here uses a typical epistolary salutation
(sender, addressee, greeting) and material that is apparently
traditional (ἀπόστολος, θεοῦ πατρὸς τοῦ ἐγείραντος αὐτὸν ἐκ
νεκρῶν, 1:1; χάρις . . . καὶ εἰρήνη; κυρίου Ἰησοῦ Χριστοῦ
τοῦ δόντος ἑαυτὸν ὑπὲρ τῶν ἁμαρτιῶν ἡμῶν, 1:3-4; ᾧ ἡ δόξα,
1:5: Mussner, *Galater*, pp. 36, 43). The significant thing
is the way Paul adapts these conventions and this material.

[11]Compare the phrase θεοῦ πατρὸς τοῦ ἐγείραντος αὐτὸν
ἐκ νεκρῶν, 1:1, with ἐγήγερται τῇ ἡμέρᾳ τῇ τρίτῃ κατὰ τὰς
γραφάς, 1 Cor 15:4, which is called a piece of παράδοσις
(1:3).

[12]1 Cor 1:1, Rom 1:1, Phil 1:1.

[13]See above, p. 49, on the importance of εὐαγγέλιον
in the *causa*. Stählin, "Galaterbrief," p. 1188, notes that in
1:1 Paul says he is not a "man's apostle"; in 1:11 he says his
gospel is not a "man's gospel." In Galatians, "the source of
the apostolate automatically passes judgment on what is taught,"
Schmithals, *Paul*, pp. 19-26.

[14]See above, pp. 52 and 59, on the importance of the
section περὶ φιλίας, 4:12-20.

[15]See above, p. 50.

[16]Georgi, *Kollekte*, pp. 35-38. Wherever possible, Paul stresses agreement between himself and the other apostles (2:2, 6), and his gospel is testable by the Jerusalem gospel (2:2).

[17]Schmithals, *Paul*, pp. 19-26, notes particularly the different understanding of the relation between apostleship and authoritative doctrine held by the opponents and the Jerusalem church.

[18]See below, p. 66.

[19]A final conclusion must wait until the nature of the revelation-tradition in the Galatian context has been more fully examined: see below, Chapter Six. At this stage it can be said that, in circles with strong doctrines of "vertical" revelation and inspiration, there was also a strong cherishing of traditions of succession. So, Hengel, *Judaism*, 1:136.

[20]Also to be examined more carefully below, pp. 96-97.

[21]The opponents obviously have their own traditions, such as scripture and its interpretation, traditions of Abraham, Moses, law, Jerusalem, etc.: see below, pp. 96, 156, etc. Paul is being charged with denying the authentic Jerusalem tradition, 2:11-14, 4:26; and the opponents are by no means open to a free interchange of ideas, however directly they have come from heaven. They have called Paul a heretic and turned the Galatians away from him and his gospel (1:10, 4:12-20).

[22]See the texts immediately above, and the significance in rhetorical terms of the passage περὶ φιλίας, 4:12-20, above, p. 52. The Galatians' treatment of Paul is introduced in 1:6-10. This passage, and the communities' treatment of Paul, combines with other factors to suggest that the opponents themselves make apostolic claims: see below, pp. 93-94.

[23]See above on the passage περὶ φιλίας and its implications: the opponents have taken over the community and have not just brought in new teachings. On community apostles, see Georgi, *Gegner*, pp. 41-42.

[24]That is, service of the στοιχεῖα τοῦ κόσμου, days, months, etc., Gal 4:8-11: see Jewett and Hawkins, above, pp. 15-17.

[25]For instance, Gal 2:17. See below, p. 119, on the opponents' charge against Paul of inconsistency: they say he rejects law but preaches circumcision.

[26]Conzelmann, *Theology*, p. 81; Robert McLachlan Wilson, *The Gnostic Problem* (London: A. R. Mowbray, 1964), p. 79, who calls it a "Jewish Torah tradition" based on Isa 37:19 etc.

^{27}As claimed by Jewett and Hawkins: see above, pp. 29-32.

^{28}See above, p. 58.

^{29}Mussner, *Galater*, p. 51.

^{30}For instance, σοφία οὐ τοῦ αἰῶνος τούτου (1 Cor 2:6), compared with σοφία τοῦ κόσμου τούτου (1 Cor 3:19); see also 1 Cor 5:10, 7:31, and Eph 2:2; and Sasse, "αἰών," *TDNT*, 1:203-5.

^{31}See 2 Enoch 66:6, 7, 43:3, 65:8, 61:2, etc.   Sasse, ibid., p. 206, gives further examples from 2 Baruch, and also 4 Ezra, where *saeculum*, *mundus*, and *tempus* are all equivalents.

^{32}See, for instance, Eph 2:2; κατὰ τὸν αἰῶνα τοῦ κόσμου τούτου, κατὰ τὸν ἄρχοντα τῆς ἐξουσίας τοῦ ἀέρος.

^{33}See 2 Cor 4:4 ὁ θεὸς τοῦ αἰῶνος τούτου, compared to 1 Cor 2:6 οἱ ἄρχοντες τοῦ αἰῶνος τούτου; Sasse, "κοσμέω," *TDNT*, 3:892.   An expression that stands very close to this Pauline tradition is Col 2:20, εἰ ἀπεθάνετε σὺν χριστῷ ἀπὸ τῶν στοιχείων τοῦ κόσμου, τί ὡς ζῶντες ἐν κόσμῳ δογματίζεσθε; see Eduard Lohse, *Colossians and Philemon*, trans. William R. Poehlmann and Robert J. Karris (Philadelphia: Fortress Press, 1971), pp. 3, 115-18; Bligh, *Galatians*, p. 71.

^{34}Mussner, *Galater*, p. 51.

^{35}Bligh, *Galatians*, p. 77.   Wrede placed the doctrine of justification in Galatians under the heading, "Christ and Redemption from the Powers of the Present World," quoted in Ulrich Wilckens, *Rechtfertigung als Freiheit* (Neukirchen-Vluyn: Neukirchener Verlag, 1974), p. 86.

^{36}Mark 10:30, Luke 16:8, 20:34, Mark 3:29, Matt 12:32; in Paul, Rom 12:2, 1 Cor 1:20, 2:6, 8, 3:18, 2 Cor 4:4.   See also 1 Enoch 48:7, 71:15, 2 Enoch 66:6, 7, 43:3 (Sasse, "αἰών," *TDNT*, 1:203-5, and Sasse, "κοσμέω," *TDNT*, 3:883).   In apocalyptic literature, cosmology and eschatology are intimately related.   Categories of time and space cross each other: this age is the abode of sin, etc. (2 Enoch 66:6, 4 Ezra 4:11, 1 Enoch 48:7), and the new age will bring a new κόσμος.   Compare Rom 8:28-32.   "Normative" Judaism had a much more positive view of the cosmos.

^{37}So, 3:1-5 continues the argument of justification in 2:16-21, but now in eschatological terms, that is, in terms of the reception of the Spirit.   "This gift of the Spirit has a cosmical significance, for it shows that men are not entirely under the sway of the powers of this world, but may be brought into living contact with God Himself," Duncan, *Galatians*, p. xliii.   See also Brandenburger, *Fleisch*, p. 49, on the eschatological significance of the reception of the Spirit at baptism.   Further, at the heart of the *Probatio*, the proof of 2:16-21, is the crucial eschatological statement of 4:4, 5, ὅτε δὲ ἦλθεν τὸ πλήρωμα τοῦ χρόνου, ἐξαπέστειλεν ὁ θεὸς τὸν υἱὸν αὐτοῦ . . . ἵνα τοὺς ὑπὸ νόμον ἐξαγοράσῃ. . . . Koester, *Trajectories*, p. 146.

[38]Paul here claims that, in Christ, the eschatological reservation typical of two-way schemes in Jewish apocalyptic has been dissolved. See below, pp. 165-67.

[39]They apparently make Christ a teacher of the covenant, somewhat like the Teacher of Righteousness in the Damascus Document: below, p. 177, on the place the opponents give to Jesus in the succession of Israel's teachers of the law.

[40]1 Cor 12:13 and Col 3:10-11. See below, pp. 146-48.

[41]For instance, the Gospel of the Egyptians, the Gospel of Thomas, 2 Clement, and the Gospel of Philip. See below, pp. 149-51.

[42]It would seem to be a similar interpretation of baptism that Paul encounters in Romans 6 and especially the enthusiastic context of 1 Corinthians 11. See below, pp. 153-54.

[43]Gal 1:8, 3:19, 4:14. See below, p. 103.

[44]On circumcision in the opponents' theology, and its connection with their interest in angels, see below, pp. 144-46.

[45]As was done, for example, by the Qumran community: 1 QS 5:1, 9:14, 1 QH 1:15, 10:22, 16:16. It was commonly held by all of Judaism that the law, given on Sinai, existed from all eternity and was to exist to all eternity: Strack-Billerbeck, 1:244-45; George Foot Moore, *Judaism in the First Christian Centuries of the Christian Era*, 2 vols. (New York: Schocken Books, 1971), 1:263-66.

[46]Schoeps, *Paul*, p. 171, referring to the scheme of Sanh. 979, Ab. Zara 9a, and Jer. Meg. 70d, of 2,000 years of Tohuwabohu, 2,000 years of Mosaic law, and 2,000 years of the era of the Messiah. He claims that this is partly the basis of Paul's theology of law. He depends heavily on Schweitzer, *Mysticism*, pp. 188-90, and the assumption that apocalyptic had no place for the law in the Messianic era, because of the supramundane nature of the Messianic kingdom.

[47]William David Davies, *Torah in the Messianic Age and/or the Age to Come* (Philadelphia: Society of Biblical Literature, 1952), pp. 3-4; Jacob Jervell, "Die offenbarte und die verborgene Tora," *ST* 25 (1971):90-108; Sanders, *Paul*, pp. 478-80.

[48]See Moore, *Judaism*, 1:265-67; Jervell, "Tora," pp. 90-108; William David Davies, *The Setting of the Sermon on the Mount* (Cambridge: Cambridge University Press, 1966), pp. 147-56. The last two references relate the tradition to Jewish texts which discuss a "new torah."

[49]But Paul's polemical intent makes the scheme mean for him the opposite to its meaning for the opponents. Nor

do the opponents mean, if the scheme is a dialogical answer
to one of theirs, that there was no law in the era of Abraham
(see below on Abraham as the perfect example of one who kept
the law, pp. 248-50), or that Jesus has brought an end to the
law.

[50]Gal 6:2. On the Jewish law-traditions that the
expression suggests, see below, pp. 175-76, and the place the
opponents give to Jesus among the great law-teachers of Israel.

[51]This is the conclusion of Jervell, "Tora," pp. 106-8.
God through the Messiah will give a new law in the sense that
both the torah and Israel will be perfectly renewed, and the
new age will be one in which the law is spontaneously fulfilled.
Davies, *Sermon*, p. 156, holds that in the Messianic age the law
will be better understood and better enforced than ever before.

[52]2 Bar 3:32-4:1 speaks of the law which abides for
ever; 1 Enoch 99:2 speaks of the "eternal law." See also
2 Bar 48:23-24, 84:2-4, and 4 Ezra 7:60-61 etc. See Davies,
Torah, pp. 14-15 and Sanders, *Paul*, pp. 478-80.

[53]See CD 1:11, 6:11, etc., and Fitzmyer, in Solomon
Schechter, *Documents of Jewish Sectaries*, prolegomenon by
Joseph A. Fitzmyer (New York: Ktav Publishing House, 1970),
p. xii; Davies, *Sermon*, pp. 147-48, concludes that the expression "new covenant" does not mean an anullment of the old
covenant, and the aim of the sect is to return to Moses (CD
3:13, 19, 15:8-10).

[54]Philo, *Vit Mos* 2. 43-44, Sib Or 3:719, 757.

[55]See above, p. 49, on the *causa* (1:6-10) and the
prominence of εὐαγγέλιον. The opponents are gospel-preachers.

[56]Marie Joseph Lagrange, *Saint Paul; Epitre aux
Galates* (Paris: J. Gabalda, 1950), p. xxxi; Koester, *Trajectories*, p. 146. It is for this reason that Schoeps must be
wrong. The opponents accept Jesus, probably as messianic in
some sense; but they see his coming as authenticating law, not
eradicating it. See especially the portrayal of the Teacher
of Righteousness in 1 Qp Hab 1:1-2:10, 6:12-8:3, CD 6:11, who
teaches how to live by the law and the covenant. In Wisd
2:12-20, 5:1-7 he is opposed to wicked men who do not recognize the covenant. This teacher is an apocalyptic figure,
arising at the end of the days. See J. A. Ziesler, *The Meaning of Righteousness in Paul* (Cambridge: Cambridge University
Press, 1972), p. 92; and Fitzmyer, in Schechter, *Sectaries*,
pp. xii-xv.

[57]Schoeps, and Schweitzer, must be wrong further, in
that Paul himself does not argue that the coming of the Messiah
brings the cessation of the law. This misunderstands the whole
endeavor, on the part of both Paul and the opponents, to maintain consistency in the revealed will of God. Both claim that
what now obtains in Christ is perfectly consistent with the
period of law: and Paul asserts that he is consistent because
the period of the law was a period of bondage and condemnation

(which has no counterpart in Jewish literature, Sanders, *Paul*,
p. 479). For Paul, the new, Messianic era is not a radical
break in salvation-history, but is perfectly consistent with
it, because the promise passes from Abraham to Christ. The
law falls out of salvation-history because if one could be
righteous by the law, Christ need not have died (2:21). This
is vastly different from saying the Messiah has come, and the
previous salvific order is now done away with. See Sanders,
Paul, pp. 483-84.

[58]On the criticism of Jerusalem Christianity by the
opponents, see above, p. 94. And on the criticism of "normative" Judaism in the Damascus Document, see Fitzmyer, in
Sectaries, p. xv. Apocalyptic reform teachings are taken up
into Christianity in the Testament of the Twelve Patriarchs,
so that Jesus Himself becomes the renewer of the law, in the
context of the general apostasy of Judaism.

[59]5:3 and the charge that they do not keep the law.
See p. 64.

[60]Schrenk, "δίκαιος," *TDNT*, 2:190. Paul has not
abandoned the definition of the righteous man as the one who
fulfills the law (Gal 5:14), but only in Christian freedom
from the law can he conduct himself according to the divine
norm.

[61]See above, p. 41, on Bultmann and diatribe style.

[62]Lightfoot, *Galatians*, p. 73, notes that ἐλευθεροῦν,
"to deliver," and cognates, strikes the keynote of the epistle.
The gospel is a rescue, an emancipation from a state of bondage
(4:9, 31; 5:1, 13). In Galatians, the redemptive act in
Christ is especially the freeing of man.

[63]Mussner, *Galater*, p. 543. 5:1 lays the basis for
the argument of 5:2-10, and 5:13 for the argument that follows.
But see how the indicative/imperative structure holds the two
together. See above, p. 53.

[64]That is, freedom from sin (6:18, 22, 8:2, 21); freedom with respect to righteousness (6:20); free from the law
(7:3). See Brandenburger, *Fleisch und Geist*, p. 55.

[65]Mussner, *Galater*, p. 342, calls this a "dativ des
Zieles," where freedom is the final goal of all redemption.

[66]Rom 5:20-21, and 1 Cor 15:56. In Galatians there
is an absence of the antitheses of law-sin-flesh/Christ-grace-
Spirit of Romans (Rom 5-6). See Brandenburger, *Fleisch und
Geist*, p. 55; Käsemann, *Römer*, p. 131; and Schlier, "ἐλεύθερος," *TDNT*, 2:496-97.

[67]See the progression in 3:22-23: Scripture consigned
all things to sin . . . we were confined under the law, kept
under restraint.

[68]Even in 3:10-14, the stress does not fall on the
inability of man in sin to meet the law's obligations. That

suggestion is there (3:10), but the stress comes to fall on
the polemical use of Hab 2:4--the law cannot justify, because
justification is by *faith*. This is a very different use of
Hab 2:4 from that in Rom 1:17. See Sanders, *Paul*, p. 483.

[69]See Betz, "Composition," p. 359. Gal 6:11-18 is
fully integrated with the rest of the letter. Jewett, "Intruders," p. 200, suggests that the opponents' aims will appear
here most clearly.

[70]A *conclusio* was often divided into parts (see above,
p. 44); and Gal 6:11-17 seems in fact to divide into these
parts, though in a different order (p. 48).

[71]See Stählin *Galater*, p. 1188; and against Drane,
Paul, pp. 16 etc., who minimises the place of circumcision in
the Galatians' program because it appears most clearly in
5:2-6:10. He has misunderstood the literary function of the
various passages. Mussner, *Galater*, p. 346, notes that Paul
refers to circumcision not as an individual act but as an
institution, that is, as a part of the program of the offending theology.

[72]Where it becomes the equivalent of justification by
law (μαρτύρομαι δὲ πάλιν παντὶ ἀνθρώπῳ περιτεμνομένῳ ὅτι ὀφει-
λέτης ἐστὶν ὅλον τὸν νόμον ποιῆσαι. κατηργήθητε ἀπὸ Χριστοῦ
οἵτινες ἐν νόμῳ δικαιοῦσθε [5:3-4]), and brings to a conclusion the debate begun in 1:6-10 and 2:16-21 (justification by
faith rather than by works of law). See above, p. 102,
on Paul's appeal for a decision in 5:10, probably coming after
his most powerful argument in the case.

[73]See especially Jewett, "Intruders," p. 198, who says
the intruders introduced it for expediency; and Betz, "Geist,"
pp. 78-80, who says they introduced it to check a problem of
"the flesh." See also the Review of Literature.

[74]See below, p. 139, on the striking contrast between
Gal 5:2-5 and 1 Cor 7:19 (almost identical in many ways),
where circumcision is one of the ἀδιάφορα; and between Gal
4:10-11 and Rom 14:5-6, where Paul takes the side of the
weaker (probably Jewish-Christian) brother. In the latter he
says, Observe whatever day you like: here he says, You
observe days . . . I've labored over you in vain!

[75]Mussner, *Galater*, p. 348, concludes "Die ganzen
theologischen Darlegung des Apostels in Gal. hatten keinen
rechten Ruckhalt in der konkreten Situation in Galatien, wenn
dort von den Gegnern nicht die Heilsnotwendigkeit der gesetz-
lichen Lebens, wozu die Beschneidung wesentlich gehört,
gelehrt worden wäre."

[76]Kuhn, "προσήλυτος," *TDNT*, 6:730, notes that Josephus
has really only one "success story" about the conversion of a
Gentile to Judaism and the requirement of circumcision--the
king Izates (*Ant* 20. 41-42). See below, pp. 144-45, on circumcision.

[77]Jewett, "Intruders," pp. 206-7. But when Paul speaks of breakers of law, he means those who transgress in concrete terms. For instance, see Romans 2 and 7, where the breaking of the law is concrete transgression, not, as Bultmann has asserted, the "Leistung" of law-keeping (*Theology*, 1:308-9). See the criticisms of Wilckens, *Freiheit*, pp. 78-80.

[78]See 3:15-29, and the treatment of this passage below, pp. 263-70, 276-77. In Galatians, Israel and the law are in no sense a *praeparatio evangelica*.

[79]This is the only occurrence of the word in the New Testament. On the basis of Josephus *Ant* 20. 139 (τὰ 'Ιουδαί- ων ἔθη μεταλαβεῖν), *Apion* 2. 210 (ὑπὸ τοὺς αὐτοὺς ἡμῖν νόμους ζῆν ὑπελθεῖν), *Ant* 20. 38, *Bell* 2. 463, and Esther 8:17, K. G. Kuhn, "προσήλυτος," *TDNT*, 6:732 defines it as "to live in strict accord with all Jewish customs and commandments." Where law keeping is in such literal terms, it steps outside the discussion to speak of law breaking in some different sense. There is no hint of this last in Galatians.

[80]This is not to say that by law Paul means only the cultic law in Galatians. In chapters 3 and 4 he considers law as principle, and certainly takes in the law of Sinai. See the discussion below, pp. 116-20. There is a selectivity in the opponents' law keeping, and Paul is pointing to a logical weakness in their program.

[81]Palestinian Judaism taught that the one who wished to come over to Judaism had to accept circumcision and submit to the law in its entirety. See Kuhn, "προσήλυτος," *TDNT*, 6:739. Thus the Pharisees of Acts 15:5 appear orthodox: ἐξανέστησαν . . . τινες τῶν ἀπὸ τῆς αἱρέσεως τῶν Φαρισαίων πεπιστευκότες, λέγοντες ὅτι δεῖ περιτέμνειν αὐτοὺς παραγγέλειν τε τηρεῖν τὸν νόμον Μωϋσεως.

[82]So, Mussner, *Galater*, p. 347, concludes that there is a clear difference between the theology of Paul and the Pharisaic Judaisers of Acts 15, on the one hand, and the Galatian opponents on the other. It is not only acceptance of Christ that has led Paul to call the opponents less than lawkeepers. The Judaisers of Acts 15 have also accepted Christ, but still insist on circumcision *and* the law.

[83]It will be argued below that 2:19-20 refer to baptism, in which the Christian comes to share in all that has been accomplished in the Christ-event. Throughout the letter, baptism is referred to in terms of crucifixion (2:19-20, 5:24 see below). Hence this last reference to crucifixion is also probably referring to baptism, and it is in this way that Paul brings his defense to a close. This emphasises the Christological/sacramental nature of his argument throughout.

[84]Ernst Käsemann, *Perspectives on Paul*, trans. Margaret Kohl (Philadelphia: Fortress Press, 1969), p. 73, writes that Paul's doctrine of justification, with the doctrine of the law that belongs to it, is ultimately his interpretation of Christology. See also Ridderbos, *Paul*, pp. 52-56,

and Sanders, *Paul*, pp. 474-82, on the Christological character
of Paul's eschatology.

[85]Rom 6:1-11, Phil 3:9-11, 1 Corinthians 15, Col 3:1-4.

[86]In Gal 2:19 Paul says Χριστῷ συνεσταύρωμαι. Christ
lives in Paul, but it is the Christ who "gave Himself for me."
In 3:1 he reminds the Galatians that, in his preaching, before
their eyes 'Ιησοῦς Χριστὸς προεγράφη ἐσταυρωμένος. But from
this message someone ὑμᾶς ἐβάσκανεν. In fact, the false gospel of circumcision κατήργηται τὸ σκάνδαλον τοῦ σταυροῦ (5:11).
And in the imperative the Galatians are reminded of the fact
that οἱ τοῦ Χριστοῦ ['Ιησοῦ] τὴν σάρκα ἐσταύρωσαν (5:24).

[87]See Quintillian *Oratoria* 4. 1. 73 (LCL, 2:47: it
is possible to give the force of the *exordium* to other parts
of the speech, to continually remind the judge of what the
chief issue is), and 3. 11. 26 (LCL, 1:353: there is need to
continually keep attention on the subject "lest . . . we
should let our weapons drop from our grasp"). See also 4. 1.
53, 72 (LCL, 2:35, 45).

[88]See above, p. 51, authorities cited on the way the
narratio ends where the issue to be determined begins, so
that 2:14 is in principle the issue in Galatians. So,
Wilckens, *Freiheit*, p. 87, and Betz, "Composition," p. 361.

[89]On 'Ιουδαΐζειν, see above, p. 64.

[90]On the subtle change from ἁμαρτωλός in 2:17 to
παραβάτης in 2:18, see below, p. 72.

[91]See above, p. 52 on 3:1-5 as an *interrogatio*, an
examination of the witnesses, so that the Galatians' past
experience, and the language in which it is referred to
(πνεῦμα and δύναμις), is essential to the case.

[92]On the reception of the Spirit at baptism, see Acts
2:38 (where it has eschatological significance), 10:44-48
(where the order of the Spirit and baptism is reversed), and
11:17, 18, 19:1-7 (where the significance of the reception of
the Spirit by the Gentiles for their admission to the church
is indicated). See Bultmann, *Theology*, 1:311 on the Spirit
conferred at baptism and its eschatological consequences;
Oepke, "Βάπτισμα," *TDNT*, 1:529-45; Schrenk, "δίκαιος," *TDNT*,
2:206, on 1 Cor 6:11 and the synonymity of justification,
baptism, and reception of the Spirit; and Brandenburger,
Fleisch, p. 49, on Gal 3:27, 1 Cor 10:1-11, and 1 Cor 12:12,
where baptism is connected with pneumatic existence.

[93]This underlies the way δικαιοσύνη is an eschatological doctrine in Galatians.

[94]So, Schrenk, "δίκαιος," *TDNT*, 2:205: "It is because
this impartation determines the whole life of faith that one
can speak of a *state* of justification." See also pp. 208-10
on Gal 3:2, compared to Rom 3:28, showing the equivalence of
the reception of the Spirit and justification. In Romans, the

believer is justified apart from works of law; in Galatians,
he receives the Spirit apart from works of law.

[95]The second person plural is not used in 2:18, 3:15,
and 5:24, but Paul is here arguing in general terms.

[96]This homogeneity of the Galatian churches compares
strikingly with, for example, 1 Cor 1:10-17, 5:1, 2 (let him
who has done this be removed, etc.), 7:10-12 (to the married
--to the unmarried), 8:7-12 (weak and strong), etc.

[97]Rather than defining the meaning of the terms here
from Paul's other letters, especially Romans, and then interpreting the rest of the debate in Galatians by these defined
terms, as done by Wilckens, *Freiheit*, Robert C. Tannehill,
Dying and Rising with Christ (Berlin: Töpelmann, 1967), and
others.

[98]See above, p. 51. The *narratio* ends where the issue
at hand is taken up.

[99]See above, p. 51, on the change of tone in 2:15
which indicates the beginning of a new section.

[100]This is especially apparent from the use of ʹΙου-
δαΐζειν in 2:14. See above, p. 64. Rengstorf, "ἁμαρτωλός,"
TDNT, 1:324, notes that Israel was conscious of being δίκαιος
on the basis of election, which made her essentially different
from the Gentiles, who were equated simply with ἁμαρτωλοί.
The same sense of ἁμαρτωλός is used in 4 Ezra 3:26-36, 7:22-24
etc., where the wicked are those outside the covenant. The
Qumran sectaries were also aware of themselves as the righteous elect (1 QS 4:5, 1 Qp Hab 7:10-12, etc.). See Ziesler,
Righteousness, p. 96, who notes the strong sociological connotation in the word ἁμαρτωλός. Hengel, *Judaism*, 1:73 illus-
trates the seriousness with which Judaism viewed any "attempt
to do away with the result of five hundred years of Israelite
and Jewish history," by adopting non-Jewish life and removing
those marks which particularly distinguished Jews from non-
Jews.

[101]Lightfoot, *Galatians*, p. 113. Paul's opponents
elsewhere were clearly of Jewish extraction (2 Cor 11:22).
See Georgi, *Gegner*, pp. 51-52.

[102]So, Wilckens, *Freiheit*, p. 85; Nils Alstrup Dahl,
Studies in Paul (Minneapolis: Augsburg Publishing House,
1977), p. 95; Käsemann, *Paul*, p. 70.

[103]Ziesler, *Righteousness*, p. 172.

[104]See above, p. 51, on the analysis of 2:15-21 according to the rhetorical genre.

[105]Jürgen Becker, in *Die Briefe an die Galater, Epheser,
Philipper, Kolosser, Thessalonicher und Philemon*, von Jürgen
Becker, Hans Conzelmann, und Gerhard Friedrich, NTD 8 (Göt-
tingen: Vandenhoeck und Ruprecht, 1976), p. 29, notes that

there is no disagreement at this point between Peter and Paul
(pointing to the use of "we"). But as this dialogue is a
"front" for the dialogue between Paul and the opponents (see
above, p. 51), there is probably no disagreement between the
latter here either. Both sides can use the formula. Becker's
reasons for seeing a formula here are syntactical (the complicated structure of the sentence in 2:16) and comparative
(the comparison with Rom 3:28 and perhaps with 3:25-26), as
well as being based on the introductory formula used (see
below). Others who see a formula here are Mussner, *Galater*,
p. 168; Munck, *Paul*, p. 127; and Wilckens, *Freiheit*, p. 88.

[106]Munck, *Paul*, p. 126, referring to εἰδότες ὅτι or
οἴδαμεν ὅτι in Rom 2:2, 3:19, 5:3, 6:9, 7:14, 8:22, 28, 1 Cor
6:2, 3, 9, 8:1, 4; 2 Cor 1:7, 4:14, 5:1, 6; Col 3:24, etc.
Many give the impression of "crystallized traditional material"
(Mussner, *Galater*, p. 168).

[107]Quoting Ps 143:2. Lightfoot, *Galatians*, p. 115,
asserts that the second ὅτι must have the function of introducing a substantiation, otherwise 2:16c is a meaningless
repetition. This means, though, that even 2:16c cannot be
taken as a uniquely Pauline expression, or it would not function as a substantiation.

[108]The words ἐξ ἔργων νόμου are not in the psalm; but
the footnote above suggests that these are not the unique
Pauline addition. He himself has used πᾶσα σάρξ instead of
πᾶς ζῶν, closely paralleling 1 Enoch 81:5, "No flesh is righteous in the sight of the Lord." It should be noted that in
2:16 ἐξ ἔργων νόμου does not function to belittle νόμος, but
in fact exalts it. It stands as the equivalent of "before
Thee" or "in the sight of the Lord." This meshes poorly with
Paul's later argument in Galatians, especially 3:19 and 4:1-11
--suggesting further that Paul is here using a formula the
opponents themselves have introduced.

[109]For instance, Rom 4:6-8, quoting Ps 32:1-2.

[110]There is an abundance of further material. For
instance, 1 QS 1:26, 2:1, 10:11, 11:3, CD 2:4, 1 QH 4:30, 36,
1:6-26, 14:15, 16:11, 7:28, 9:14. Becker, *Galater*, p. 30,
remarks that the coincidence with the language of Galatians
is "no accident." See also Millar Burrows, *The Dead Sea
Scrolls* (New York: Viking Press, 1955), p. 334, who notes
especially the parallel between Paul's language and 1 QS 11:13
(referred to below, p. 134). Matthew Black, *The Scrolls and
Christian Origins* (New York: Scribner, 1961), p. 128, who
assesses the Qumran teaching on righteousness as a continuation of the piety of the psalms and prophets, and a *praeparatio
evangelica*; Dahl, *Paul*, pp. 96-99; Ziesler, *Righteousness*, pp.
85-102; Sanders, *Paul*, pp. 305-12. Wilckens' comment, *Freiheit*, p. 88, that Qumran saw justifying efficacy in the law,
passes over the strong similarity between Qumran and Paul.
There were different senses in which justification was spoken
of. Righteousness meant behavior that remained within the
covenant (Sanders, *Paul*, p. 312; Ziesler, *Righteousness*,

p. 85). But there was also a sense in which righteousness
could never be on the basis of man's work, but only on the
gracious work of God (Sanders, ibid., p. 311; see below,
p. 134). Dahl, ibid., p. 99, seems to be correct when he says
that the essential difference is that Paul has found God's
justifying grace revealed eschatologically in Christ. Justification is "now"; it is "in Christ"; and it is in Christ
alone.

[111]On pre-Christian formulae using justification-
language, see Bultmann, *Theology*, 1:46-47 and "ΔΙΚΑΙΟΣΥΝΗ
ΘΕΟΥ," *JBL* 83 (1964):12-16; Ernst Käsemann, *New Testament
Questions of Today*, trans. W. J. Montague (Chatham: W. and
J. Mackay, 1969), pp. 177-82; Lohse, *Einheit*, pp. 219-44; and
Dahl, *Paul*, pp. 99-101.

[112]Dahl, *Paul*, pp. 100-1, compares 1 QS 3:3-6, " . . .
justified . . . absolved by atonement . . . purified by lustral
waters . . . sanctified . . . cleansed . . . ," and 1 Cor 6:11,
"But you were washed . . . sanctified . . . justified in the
name of the Lord Jesus Christ . . ."--itself an "un-Pauline"
verse. See also David Flusser, "The Dead Sea Sect and Pre-
Pauline Christianity," *Scripta Hierosolymitana* (Jerusalem:
Magnes Press, Hebrew University, 1955), 4:215-66.

[113]It should be noted again that the opponents are
gospel-preachers; see above, p. 49. They have an important
place for Jesus and probably even speak of *faith* in Jesus,
Georgi, *Geschichte*, pp. 34-35; Stoike, "Christ," pp. 95-97.

[114]Duncan, *Galatians*, p. 66, points to the force of
ἐπιστεύσαμεν in 2:16. The subject is Jews who have come to
believe in Christ.

[115]Becker, *Galater*, p. 30. Paul is saying in 2:15-16,
if justification were by the law, we would have remained Jews:
we accepted Christ because we knew that there is no justification by means of law.

[116]Mussner, *Galater*, p. 170. Justifying faith is not
"allerweltsglaube," but faith in Jesus Christ.

[117]Hab 2:4 is used in the *probatio* in 3:11, and it has
ἐκ πίστεως, which is unusual in Pauline language. Lightfoot,
Galatians, p. 115, says the expression is almost heretical,
making faith a meritorious work, as did Judaism. See StrB,
3:186-202.

[118]In the light of the teachings of Qumran, this is
understandable. The sectaries believed in a righteousness
without works of law, on the basis of God's grace alone (above);
but the only way to remain righteous was to do the commandments of God as specified in the covenant. Human righteousness
was by works of law (1 QS 11:17, 1 QH 7:28-31, etc.), and the
man who was justified by grace was then justified by law-
obedience, the condition of remaining elect. See below, p.
134; Sanders, *Paul*, p. 312; and Ziesler, *Righteousness*, p. 85.
Paul and the opponents can agree about the initiation of the

Christian life, but disagree about the covenant laws under
which the Christian is then bound.

[119]BAG 157, with references to Epictetus, as well as
to Rom 3:4, 5, 31, 6:2, 15, 7:7, 13, 9:14, 11:1, etc.

[120]Duncan, *Galatians*, p. 68; see also Becker, *Galater*,
p. 30.

[121]Lightfoot, *Galatians*, p. 116.

[122]Paul is not importing a meaning into the passage
from Romans 2-3 etc., i.e., that Christ by justifying declares
a man to be a sinner in an ethical sense, as in Jewett,
"Intruders," p. 200, who agrees here with Mussner, Tannehill,
and Lightfoot.

[123]Becker, *Galater*, p. 30.   That is, 2:17a picks up
the conclusion of this process of reasoning, not the premise
--that the definition of "sinner" in terms of the historic
distinction between Jew and Gentile is no longer valid.

[124]H. E. Dana and Julius R. Mantey, *A Manual Grammar
of the Greek New Testament* (Toronto: Macmillan, 1927), pp.
289-90.   ἄν is lacking in the apodosis, as well as the apodosis having no augmented verb.

[125]Tannehill, *Dying*, p. 55.

[126]Ziesler, *Righteousness*, pp. 172-73:   " . . . the
whole debate . . . is not about the relative moral achieve-
ments of Jew and Gentiles, but about the fulfillment of the
law in ritual and technical matters. . . .   If you take the
law as your standard, Christians are sinners."

[127]Ziesler, ibid., p. 173.

[128]Ziesler, ibid., p. 174.   He admits that this verse
contradicts his general thesis that the verb form δικαιοῦν
signifies forensic justification, while the nominal and adjectival forms signify relational/moral righteousness.   The word
in 2:17 comes to have this latter sense, because of the other
verbs with which it is used and because of its local reference,
ἐν Χριστῷ.   For a general criticism of Ziesler's thesis, see
Sanders, *Paul*, pp. 487-88.

[129]Lightfoot, *Galatians*, p. 117.   This gives μὴ
γένοιτο its usual force.

[130]Lightfoot, ibid., p. 117, notes the grammatical
difficulties posed by γάρ in 2:18 but gives reasons for treating it here as an emphatic particle.   See also Dana and Mantey,
Grammar, pp. 243-44, especially on Acts 19:35, where γάρ must
be translated "indeed."   Another possibility is that γάρ here
refers back to 2:17a.   Herbert Weir Smyth, *Greek Grammar*
(Cambridge, Mass.:   Harvard University Press, 1974), pp. 637-
42, notes that, if γάρ is attached to μὴ γένοιτο, the expression can be translated "If on the other hand . . . ."

[131]Duncan, *Galatians*, p. 69.

[132]Ziesler, *Righteousness*, p. 173, who gives other authorities.

[133]Lightfoot, *Galatians*, p. 115.

[134]Mussner, *Galater*, pp. 169-70. He goes on to say, p. 186, "Paulus hat seine Gesetztheologie nicht gegen das Judentum entwickelt, sondern gegen seine 'judaistischen' Gegner aus den Reihen der Christen! Er kämpft im Ga. gegen ein christliches Pseudo-evangelium!" That is, Paul is not writing against Jewish merit-theology (Oepke, Wilckens), the impossibility of fulfilling the law (which Paul as a Jew never held to, Philippians 3), etc. "The real sin is not in infringing the law, but in disloyalty to Christ," Ziesler, *Righteousness*, p. 173. Paul here gives an assessment of non-Christian religion only as post-Christian religion.

[135]Note that the opponents have their own understanding of πίστις, above, p. 250, note 113, referring to Georgi, *Geschichte*, pp. 34-35, who suggests that, for them, πίστις amounts to a deepened understanding of the law. They probably also understood faith as a meritorious work, as this is the sense in which it was used to speak of the justification of Abraham. See below, p. 110.

[136]Those who see baptism in 2:19-20 are Mussner, *Galater*, p. 180, Schlier, *Galater*, on 2:19-20, and Ernst Käsemann, *Perspectives on Paul*, trans. Margaret Kohl (Philadelphia: Fortress Press, 1969), p. 8, to name a few.

[137]So, in Rom 6:1-11 he uses ἀπεθάνομεν (6:2, 7), περιπατήσωμεν and συζήσομεν (6:4, 8). See Bornkamm, *Experience*, p. 78; Bultmann, *Theology*, 1:141; James M. Robinson, "Kerygma and History in the New Testament," in Robinson and Koester, *Trajectories*, pp. 30-31; and Furnish, *Theology*, p. 73.

[138]In 2:19 he uses ζήσω, probably an aorist subjunctive; and in 2:20 he uses the present ζῶ. But the life here is qualified: οὐκέτι ἐγώ, ζῇ δὲ ἐν ἐμοὶ Χριστός, etc. The life that follows identification with Christ is an "I, yet not I," contrasting with the finality of the death of Christ.

[139]In this last, 6:8-10 repeats a pattern established in 6:5-7, the one pattern giving the Christological foundation for the anthropological assertions of the other, as the significance of baptism for Christian experience is developed. See Bornkamm, *Experience*, pp. 74-76; and Franz J. Leenhardt, *L'Epitre de saint Paul aux Romains* (Neuchâtel: Delachaux et Nestlé, 1969), pp. 159-62.

[140]Bornkamm, *Experience*, p. 74, 75: "The baptism-event and the Christ-event are not only related to each other in terms of analogy, but are identical with each other."

[141]Ibid., p. 76: "The death which the baptized and
Christ die is only one death, that is, the death of Christ
Himself, and through baptism this death becomes the death of
the believer."

[142]See 1 Cor 1:30, 6:11, Rom 4:25, Titus 3:5-7, etc.,
and Dahl, *Paul*, p. 102. Lohse, *Einheit*, p. 241, notes the
parallels between New Testament baptism-sayings and New Testament justification-sayings.

[143]For instance, 1 Cor 6:11, 10:1-13, Rom 6:1-12. See
Bultmann, *Theology*, 1:142, 309-11; Robinson, "Kerygma," pp.
30-38; and Käsemann, *Römer*, pp. 151-52. Furnish, *Theology*,
p. 174, quoting von Soden: It is Christ's death that is the
sacrament.

[144]Bultmann, ibid., p. 311; and Lohse, *Einheit*, p. 241.
Righteousness and life are only to be found where God's righteousness in Christ is entered into and man as believer stands
in a right relation to God.

[145]That is, 5:6. See the comments above, p. 64.

[146]On reception of the Spirit at baptism, see above,
p. 247, note 94.

[147]See above, p. 52, on the significance of 3:1-5
as an *interrogatio* for the debate about justification. It is
important that the experience of the Spirit here is a "public
fact" (Lütgert, cited in Stoike, "Christ," p. 76), not merely
a private experience--a community-experience which cannot be
denied; see Becker, *Galater*, pp. 32-33.

[148]It has been noticed above that the language of an
interrogatio was to be most relevant to the case being
established. See above, pp. 67-68. So the language of
πνεῦμα and δύναμις is another way of speaking about justification. Thus the progress in the discussion from justification
(2:15-21) to the Spirit (3:1-5) to justification (3:6-14) is
still the one discussion. Paul's stress on the present
experience of the Spirit among the Galatians is an assertion
that justification, in the sense of eschatological deliverance,
has already been realized. See Duncan, *Galatians*, p. xliii.
Baptism is seen to be involved here by Lohse, *Einheit*, p. 243;
Brandenburger, *Fleisch*, p. 49; Lagrange, *Galates*, pp. 56-57,
etc.

[149]Stählin, "Galaterbrief," p. 1189, notes that, in
3:6-22, all the lines of salvation-history end in the death
of Christ; but by the end of the chapter, they now end in
baptism.

[150]If 2:15-21 develops the significance of baptism to
refute the opponents' system of beginning and ending, faith
then works, then it would be natural to end a passage on justification by faith, not works of law, with a return to the
subject of baptism.

[151]If 3:1-5 is a baptism-passage, this is more evident.

[152]Lagrange, *Galates*, pp. 92-93. The theme of union of adopted sons and the natural Son occurs also in Rom 8:10-15. The Aramaic formula "Abba" also suggests a Christian ritual.

[153]Lohse, *Einheit*, p. 235.

[154]See Jervell, *Imago Dei*, p. 234, and many others, cited below (p. 166). Paul here proclaims the eschatologically new ethic of Christianity, which is typically rooted in the indicative brought about by baptism. See also Bultmann, *Theology*, 1:312-13. Others point out the parallels to other baptism-passages such as 1 Cor 6:11.

[155]It speaks of οἱ τοῦ Χριστοῦ, reminiscent of εἰ . . . ὑμεῖς Χριστοῦ (3:29); and τὴν σάρκα ἐσταύρωσαν is reminiscent of Χριστῷ συνεσταύρωμαι (2:19).

[156]Thyen, *Der Stil*, p. 67, notes that Paul's use of ἐγώ here is probably not biographical, but (as in Romans 7 and 1 Corinthians 13) refers to some common experience that can be used as the basis for an argument. This is understandable if Paul is referring to the common experience of baptism.

[157]1 Cor 6:11, 10:1-13, Rom 6:1-12 and, functioning in the same way, Colossians 3-4.

[158]Which accords with the *causa* and its restatements in terms of beginning and ending; and the shift from δικαιοῦν with a declarative sense in 2:16 to δικαιοῦν as an ethical/relational process in 2:17.

[159]Tannehill, *Dying* pp. 54-61. Dying to the law takes place through crucifixion with Christ; so the essential question becomes the function of the law in the crucifixion of Christ. Sanders, *Paul*, pp. 483-85, stresses the Christological-dogmatic basis for the rejection of the law in 3:21 and 2:21. The fact that Christ died reveals that law was never intended as a way of salvation. The argument in 3:10-14 hangs on the dogmatic use of Hab 2:4--righteousness cannot be by law, *since* it is by faith.

[160]Mussner, p. 179.

[161]Bornkamm, *Experience*, p. 77, notes how Paul uses baptism as a sacramental presentation of the Christ-event, in order to lay a basis for Christian existence.

[162]This is consistent with the importance of Christology and eschatology in the prescript and postscript.

[163]Bornkamm, *Experience*, pp. 79-81. There is a finality in baptism. It can only be once, because it unites with the once-for-all death of Christ. Thereafter it becomes the subject of proclamation. The believer's life is the constant appropriation of what has been made true for him in baptism, and he is not initiated into further means of perfection, but is reminded of what his baptism means.

164See above, pp. 59-66, on Christology and eschatology in the prescript and postscript; and a summary on pp. 66-67.

165See above, pp. 15-17, on Lütgert, Ropes, Bruce, Jewett, Hawkins, etc. The basic assumption is that there is a "libertine" problem in Galatia--and a "legalist" cannot be a "libertine." There is a tendency to understand the doctrine in Galatians in terms of Romans.

166For instance, above, pp. 17-18, on Schmithals, whose gnostic reconstruction makes Galatians 3-4 a misunderstanding on Paul's part, and Marxsen, who follows him closely. Gunther, Opponents, p. 61, stressing the cosmology of the opponents, says that they are not at all answered by justification by faith, and that Paul corrects the oversight in Colossians, which is a much better argument against the opponents' theology.

167See above, p. 52.

168Stählin, "Galaterbrief," p. 1189.

169Delling, "βασκαίνω," TDNT, 1:594-95; BAG, "βασκαίνω." This is the only occurrence of the word in the New Testament. A power of falsehood (γόης) has been exercised to do harm to the νους of the Galatians (they are ἀνόητοι).

170Schlier, Galater, p. 83, referring to Polux 8:83, Eurip Iph Aul 1470, 955. BAG notes that Euripedes makes it a sacrificial terminus technicus.

171BAG 302 gives sources where it means to perform a λειτουργία: Philo Som 1. 214, Hdt., Dit., Syll.³1109, 111; or to offer a θυσία, Ep. Arist. 186, Philo Ebr 129, Som 1. 215 etc., Lightfoot, Galatians, p. 134, refers to Herod 2. 63 (θυσίας) and 4. 186 (νηστείας και ὁρτας) and Schlier, Galater, p. 83, notes its meaning of completion or perfection in religion.

172See Lightfoot, Galatians, p. 134.

173Lightfoot, ibid.; Ramsay, Galatians, p. 324, sees them as mystery terms denoting progress from a lower to higher stage. Similarly, Lagrange, Galates p. 60, and Schlier, Galater, p. 83.

174Lagrange, ibid., pp. 59-60; Schlier, ibid., p. 83.

175See above, pp. 67-70, on the causa (1:6-10), and its restatements (2:15-21, 3:1-5, 4:8-11, 5:2-12, 5:16-24) elaborating the one pattern of beginning and ending.

176See above, pp. 67-68, on reception of the Spirit at baptism.

177Bultmann, Theology, 1:332-35; Brandenburger, Fleisch, p. 45; Mussner, Galater, p. 209.

[178]Bultmann, ibid., p. 332. See the place played in
the debate by the terms αἰών (1:4) and κόσμος (6:14), above
pp. 59-66. See Becker, *Galater*, p. 32, on the development
in Galatians from a neutral (1:16, 2:16-20) to an actively
malevolent sense of σάρξ.

[179]Käsemann, *Paul*, p. 26. σάρξ in this apocalyptic
sense is a hostile, active power.

[180]Bultmann, *Theology*, 1:235-39, 332-35; Käsemann,
Paul, pp. 24-25.

[181]Käsemann, *Paul*, p. 26.

[182]It was noted above, p. 253, note 147, that the
experience of the Spirit referred to here was a "public fact,"
a community experience which cannot be denied.

[183]Mussner, *Galater*, p. 209; Lagrange, *Galates*, pp.
59-60.

[184]See BAG 70, with references to the expression,
frequent in religious homilies, ᾧ ἀνόητοι. See 1 Clem 23:4,
2 Clem 11:3, Herm *Man* 10. 2. 1 etc. Behm, "νοέω," *TDNT*,
9:961, interprets the word in Gal 3:3 as "deficient in an
understanding of salvation."

[185]The word has this meaning in Phil *Som* 2. 181 (ᾧ
ἀνόητε), and in *Corp Herm* 1. 23 (τοῖς δὲ ἀνόητοις καὶ κακοῖς
καὶ πονηροῖς). The ἀνόητοι are stood over against those who
respond to the call to religious perfection. Also in Tit
3:3, it is used of men before becoming Christians.

[186]Brandenburger, *Fleisch*, pp. 45-48, notes the way
the antitheses are developed in Galatians, so that ἐν σαρκί,
σάρκινος, and οἱ σαρκικοί are implied as standing out over
against ἐν πνεύματι, πνευματικός, and οἱ πνευματικοί.

[187]Bo Reicke, "The Law and This World According to
Paul," *JBL* 70 (1951):266.

[188]Käsemann, *Paul*, pp. 24-26: σάρξ and πνεῦμα are
in the later passages the same two antithetical apocalyptic
powers.

[189]Brandenburger, *Fleisch*, p. 45, especially on Gal
5:17.

[190]Sanders, "Patterns," p. 468. Grundmann, "ἁμαρτία,"
TDNT, 1:311 notes that the demonic character of sin uses law
to express itself and increase its power. Brandenburger,
Fleisch, p. 45, commenting on the vice-lists of Galatians 5
and Romans 7, points to the radical connection between law,
flesh, and sin.

[191]See above, p. 74, on 5:24 as a baptismal passage,
and p. 78, on the way both dogma and ethics grow out of
2:15-21. The saying in 6:8 (ὁ σπείρων εἰς τὴν σάρκα ἑαυτοῦ

ἐκ τῆς σαρκὸς θερίσει φθοράν, etc.) is also accommodated with
this interpretation, rather than that of Jewett, "Intruders,"
pp. 202-5, who uses this verse to say that in Galatia were some
Hellenistic enthusiasts who believed they would not face the
judgment. It has already been seen that Paul's eschatology
is more enthusiastic that the opponents'; and if the Galatians
themselves were enthusiasts, it was imprudent of Paul to answer
the opponents in this way. Mussner, *Galater*, p. 403, notes
that μὴ πλανᾶσθε (6:7) announces something well-known; and
σάρξ has by now developed the connotation of failure to live
out *agape* towards other members of the community (5:13-14,
6:2, 9, 10). The one who is trying to deceive God (6:7) is
the one who calls himself πνευματικός (6:1-2), as the opponents undoubtedly do (3:1-5), but does not live towards his
brother in love. See below, pp. 168-69, on the imperative
force of the dual catalog (5:19-23).

[192]In the light of the theories of Jewett and Hawkins.
See above, pp. 29-30.

[193]Mussner, *Galater*, p. 244, has posited the unity of
3:19-29 and 4:1-7 on the ground of the themes and the use of
κληρονόμος:

3:19	ἄχρις οὗ ἔλθῃ τὸ σπέρμα ᾧ ἐπήγγελται
4:4	ἐξαπέστειλεν ὁ θεὸς τὸν υἱὸν αὐτοῦ
3:26	πάντες γὰρ υἱοί θεοῦ ἐστε
4:5	ἵνα τὴν υἱοθεσίαν ἀπολάβωμεν
3:23	slavery under the law
4:3	
3:29	held together by the Stichwort κληρονόμος
4:7	

[194]Although there is a contested reading here, it is
not the noun θεός itself that is contested by most variants.

[195]Above, p. 80.

[196]In both pericopes, the Galatians, once having known
God (4:9) or having entered the sphere of πνεῦμα (3:3), are
now turning to the powers of the old κόσμος (4:9) or the sphere
of σάρξ (3:3).

[197]Above, pp. 68-69.

[198]See above, pp. 52 and 59, on 4:12-20 as a passage
περὶ φιλίας, concerned with the way the opponents have taken
over as community-apostles.

[199]See above, p. 81, on the way chapters 3 and 4
begin and end with the contrast of these two antithetical
spheres. In both 3:1-5 and 4:21-31, νόμος becomes an instrument of the sphere of σάρξ.

[200]The scheme of salvation-history in Galatians is
different from the one Paul uses elsewhere: Conzelmann,

Theology, p. 255. In Galatians 3, the period from Abraham to
Moses is missing, to heighten the preeminence of promise. In
Romans 5, there is a sweep from Adam to Moses, and no Abraham
(and in Romans 4, Abraham is placed alongside David to illustrate the witness of the *law* to the gospel). Galatians 3 contrasts law and promise, and Romans 5 contrasts law and sin.

[201]There is a difference in Galatians from both Romans
and Jewish tradition. In Galatians, Abraham is justified by
faith, and there is no mention of his later circumcision; the
covenant is confirmed with the promise, Gal 3:15-22, not with
circumcision. But in Romans 4, Abraham first believes, and
then is circumcised (and his circumcision is the seal of righteousness [4:11]), to prove that righteousness is by faith and
not works. See below, pp. 139-40. Late Judaism used Abraham
as an example of obedience to God's will. He kept the law in
anticipation, and his faith was a meritorious work. See Jub
23:10, or Man 9, 2 Bar 57:2, 58:1. In 1 Macc 2:52, Gen 15:6
is attached to Gen 22:15-18 as in James, to show that Abraham's righteousness was his obedience to God's will. See
StrB, 3:188-94. So Judaism stresses faith as obedience;
Romans stresses faith *and* obedience, in that order; and Galatians stresses "faith alone."

[202]Compare Romans 9-11, where Israel is a part of
salvation-history and the oracles of God are part of its
treasure, to Gal 4:21-31, where Israel is a Hagar-bondage,
brought about by the enslaving Sinai covenant. Rom 4:16 can
speak of the "seed" of both the law and faith; but in Gal
3:16, 19 there is only one seed, the seed of faith; see below,
p. 118, for further differences between Galatians and
Romans regarding law and Israel.

[203]Schlier, *Galater*, p. 134; and Duncan, *Galatians*,
p. 21. Bornkamm, "Colossians," p. 124, notes that there is
an identification between the στοιχεῖα τοῦ κόσμου and the
angels who give the law; and existence under the στοιχεῖα τοῦ
κόσμου is existence under the law (4:5, 3:13, 23).

[204]See for instance, Josephus *Ant* 3. 180, and Philo,
Vit Mos 1. 155-59. Other sources, such as Eupolemus, Artapanus,
and apocalyptic literature are cited below (pp. 111-13). On
the literature itself, see below, p. 92.

[205]Josephus *Ant* 3. 83, Philo *De Opif Mundi*, etc. The
ten words from Sinai are bound up with order in nature and
make possible the εὐδαίμων βίος. See Josephus *Ant* 3. 75, 77,
etc.; and below

[206]There is an evident equivalence of αἰών and κόσμος
(themselves equivalents, as shown above, pp. 59-60) and σάρξ,
when used in the sense of an apocalyptic power. In 6:14, the
believer is crucified to the κόσμος; and in 5:24, those who
are Christ's have crucified the σάρξ. This further strengthens
the suggested connection between 3:1-5 and 4:8-11.

CHAPTER FIVE

INTRODUCTION

[1]See Bornkamm, quoted above, p. 33.

[2]See the method suggested above, pp. 31-33; and the procedures laid down by David Wenham, in *New Testament Interpretation*, I. Howard Marshall, ed. (Grand Rapids: Eerdmans, 1977), p. 140.

[3]In keeping with the method used by Flusser, "Dead Sea Sect," 215-66.

[4]To again use an analogy from Flusser, ibid., p. 217.

[5]So, Robinson, "Kerygma," p. 114: "The traditional categories, such as normative Judaism, Hellenistic Judaism, apocalyptic, gnostic, cultic, etc., are only blinds that cut out the fresh light. . . ." He goes on to state the need for the dismantling and reassembling of categories.

[6]Even Samuel Sandmel, *Philo's Place in Judaism* (Cincinnati: Hebrew Union College Press, 1956), fond of the term "Normative Judaism," would admit to this distinction (p. 28). He calls Philo's writing a marginal, aberrative version of Judaism which existed at a time when there were many versions of Judaism, of which ultimately only Rabbinism and Christianity have survived to our day. On the variety within the Judaism of the New Testament era, see Erwin R. Goodenough, *Jewish Symbols in the Greco-Roman Period*, 13 vols. (New York: Bollinger Foundation, 1965-68), 12:6-21.

[7]See Davies, *Paul*, pp. 6-16; Flusser, "Dead Sea Sect," pp. 215-66, now finds the "Hellenistic Christianity" of Bultmann to be closer to Qumran, and similarly, Joseph A. Fitzmyer, "A Feature of Qumran Angelology and the Angels of 1 Cor 11:10," *NTS* 4 (1957-58):48-58, finds that even a "hellenistic" passage in Paul such as 1 Corinthians 11 shows the influence of Qumran theology.

[8]Robert Henry Charles, ed., *The Apocrypha and Pseudepigrapha of the Old Testament in English*, 2 vols. (Oxford: Clarendon Press, 1913), 2:vii, noted that, in pre-Christian times, apocalyptic Judaism and legalistic Judaism were not at all antagonistic. Only after CE 70 did Judaism disown apocalyptic. Davies, *Paul*, pp. 10-16, finds no evidence of sectarianism in apocalyptic Judaism, and concludes that it arose out of the mainstream of Jewish life. Hengel, *Judaism*, 1:177-91, traces apocalyptic back to the Hasidim.

[9]Hans Dieter Betz, "On the Problem of the Religio-Historical Understanding of Apocalypticism," trans. James W. Leitch, *JTS* 6 (1969):134-56, and others have pointed out that "apocalyptic" is not an isolated and inner-Jewish phenomenon but is a manifestation of Hellenistic-oriental syncretism.

Thus apocalyptic has affinities with Hellenistic oracle-
literature (Betz, "Problem," p. 138; Hengel, *Judaism*, 1:193,
suggests only a casual relationship between Jewish apocalyptic
and Iranian religion, as all extant Iranian apocalypses are
rather late, and a closer relationship between Egyptian and
Palestinian apocalyptic), and there are close affinities
between Hellenistic-Jewish wisdom literature and Jewish apocalyptic.

[10]See Reicke, "The Law," p. 259, on the similar law-
tradition in Philo and in apocalyptic; Betz, "Problem," pp.
155-56 on the great interest of both Philo and Josephus in
the Essenes--probably because the latter belong within Hellenistic piety. Both Davies, *Paul*, p. 8, and Hengel, *Judaism*,
1:228, note the extent to which Philo and the Rabbis share
cosmologies and other traditions.

[11]U. Wilckens, "σοφία," *TDNT*, 6:498-511; Davies,
Scrolls, pp. 167-69; and Hengel, *Judaism*, 1:228-32 on the
place of σοφία in pseudepigraphical apocalyptic literature,
Qumran literature, and Gnosticism. We can now, in the Nag
Hammadi library, see the heavy influence of Jewish apocalyptic
on Gnosticism.

[12]Georgi, *Gegner*, pp. 42-54, lists as "apologetic"
literature Theodotion, Eupolemus, Aristeas, Artapanus, Aristobulus, Philo, Josephus, 2 and 4 Maccabees, and wisdom
literature, especially the Wisdom of Solomon.

[13]Hengel, *Judaism*, 1:70, notes that this literature
"served only exceptionally . . . to defend Judaism to the
outside world; rather, it met the particular needs of a Greek-
speaking Jewish readership with an intellectual interest."
See also V. Tcherikover, "Jewish Apologetic Literature Recon-
sidered," *Eros* 48 (3, 1956):169-93.

[14]In, for instance, the Genesis Apocryphon: see
Theodor H. Gaster, *The Dead Sea Scriptures* (New York: Anchor,
1976), p. 352; Carl. R. Holladay, *Theios Aner in Hellenistic
Judaism* (Missoula, MT: Scholars Press, 1977), p. 235, comments that "apocalyptic Judaism offers some of the best
examples" of "apologetic" treatment of Israel's heroes.

[15]See above, p. 260, note 10, on the place of the
Essenes in Philo and Josephus. Their piety has a great appeal
to "Hellenists."

[16]See above, p. 72 (quoting Lightfoot, Mussner, etc.).

CHAPTER SIX

THE TRADITION OF APOSTLE

[1]Because the deity is held to be present in the emissary from God, the emissary himself is part of the "message"
about God. Rengsdorf, "ἀπόστολος," *TDNT*, 1:398-448, shows

that, in Hellenistic usage, ἀποστέλλειν is used to unite the
sender and the sent: the emissary from Rome is an impressive
concretion of the Empire; the cynic, with his sense of divine
authorisation, becomes, in terms of the Greek concept of the
divinity of the true philosopher, a θεῖος ἄνθρωπος.   In Jewish
tradition, too, the one sent, the שליח, embodies the one who
sends him.   Thus the Rabbinic saying, שלוחו של אדם כמותו.   In
Jewish apocalyptic and wisdom circles, with which this chapter
is particularly interested, "the continuity of the tradition,
like the idea of inspiration, is meant to provide rational
backing for the ancestral heritage, and to support its authority."   So, Hengel, *Judaism*, 1:136.

[2]Schmithals, *Paul*, p. 19.

[3]Drane, *Paul*, p. 13.   This in itself was not a "heretical" position.   The anti-gnostic and pro-Pauline Acts of Paul
has Paul say, "I delivered to you in the beginning what I
received from the holy apostles who were before me, who at all
times were together with the Lord Jesus Christ" (3:4; *NTA*,
2:375); see also Epistula Apostolorum 31-33, where the twelve
initiate Paul into the teachings which they received from the
Lord (*NTA*, 2:213).

[4]So, correctly, Schmithals, *Paul*, pp. 19-20.

[5]See above, pp. 58-59.

[6]Schmithals, ibid., p. 20.

[7]6:3 (εἰ γὰρ δοκεῖ τις εἶναί, and its proximity to the
reference to οἱ δοκοῦντες in 2:6-9), suggests that the opponents apply to themselves the claims they make for the Pillars.
The opponents' boasting of the winning of the Galatians in
6:12-13 also suggests that the principle of 1 Cor 9:1-2 is at
work, that is, converts are a σφραγίς of an effective apostleship.   The same principle is at work even more forcefully in
2 Cor 10-13.   See Georgi, *Gegner*, pp. 40-53; Gunther, *Opponents*, p. 302; Ernst Käsemann, *Die Legitimität des Apostels*
(Darmstadt: Wissenschaftliche Buchgesellschaft, 1956), pp.
23-30, and Lightfoot, *Galatians*, p. 107.

[8]Schmithals, *Paul*, p. 20.   What is more, it must be
apostles who have a weighty claim to authority.   See Käsemann,
Legitimität, pp. 29-30.   See also above, pp. 52 and 59, on the
intruders as "community apostles," based on 4:12-20.   There
were no numerical limits to the office of apostle in the
earliest texts: see 1 Thess 2:7, 1 Cor 4:9, 9:5-6, 12:28,
Rom 16:7; Lightfoot, *Galatians*, pp. 107-9 and Georgi, *Gegner*,
pp. 44-45.

[9]See above, pp. 58-59.

[10]Schmithals, *Apostle*, p. 83, notes how often Jerusalem
occurs in Paul's alibi: 1:17 (he did not go up to Jerusalem);
1:18 (after three years he went up to Jerusalem); 2:1 (four-
teen years later he again went up to Jerusalem); 2:6-10 (he

received a commendation in Jerusalem). Apparently, for the
intruders, Jerusalem is the centre of the true gospel.

[11]See the effort on Paul's part to prove that he has
the authentication of the "Pillars" (2:6-9). The peculiar
references to οἱ δοκοῦντες are probably to be accounted for
by Paul's encounter with extravagant claims for the Pillars
set up by the Judaisers--an "extravagandised" doctrine of the
Jerusalem apostles (Lightfoot, *Galatians*, p. 107)--who are
then exploited against Paul, and on the opponents' own behalf.
See Käsemann, *Legitimität*, pp. 23-30, and Gunther, *Opponents*,
p. 302.

[12]See above, pp. 58-59.

[13]From 2:6-9 it is clear that Paul's commission to the
Gentiles is already past history (even if this passage does
not refer to the Jerusalem council), and the Judaisers,
though great advocates of the Pillars, have ignored it. See
Ramsay, *Galatians*, pp. 258, 326-71, and Lagrange, *Galates*,
pp. lxiv, 18.

[14]See the use of παραλαμβάνειν and παραδιδόναι in
1 Cor 15:1-3.

[15]See Conzelmann, *1 Corinthians*, pp. 258-59, on 1 Cor
15:8.

[16]Cullmann, *The Early Church*, pp. 57-82.

[17]Koester, *Trajectories*, pp. 144-47; and above,
p. 84.

[18]See below, pp. 178-81, on the way the ethical section of Galatians is a final refutation of the opponents'
program: their theology breaks down at the point of life in
the community.

[19]See Schoeps, *Paul*, pp. 82-84. For literature on the
Kerygmata Petrou, see Strecker in *NTA*, 2:102-27.

[20]Schoeps, ibid., p. 68.

[21]Rec 4:35. A thirteenth apostle is as unthinkable
as a thirteenth month of the year. Schoeps, ibid., p. 70.

[22]In the account in Hom 1:13-16, the attack is on
Simon Magus, probably a veiled Paul. See Strecker in *NTA*,
2:103.

[23]Hom 17. 19. 4-7: "But if you were visited by him
for the space of an hour and were instructed by him and thereby
have become an apostle, then proclaim his words, expound what
he has taught, be a friend to his apostles, and do not contend
with me."

[24]Visions can be and usually are the work of demons,
but God talks with friends "mouth to mouth." So, Hom 17. 18.
1-6.

[25] Schoeps, *Paul*, p. 74 (referring to the Ebionite veneration of James and other members of Jesus' family as the authentic channel of tradition, which appears in Rec 1. 68, 3. 74).

[26] Correctly, Strecker, in *NTA*, 2:103-11, who notes for instance the gnostic influence of the syzygy-doctrine of the True Prophet and the anti-Pharisaic exaltation of oral over written tradition. Other objections could be added, such as the distaste for sacrifices and the Temple (Hom 2. 44. 1-2, 15. 2.). The document is not Essene either. See Joseph A. Fitzmyer, "The Qumran Scrolls, the Ebionites, and Their Literature," in K. Stendahl, ed., *The Scrolls and the New Testament* (New York: Harper, 1957), pp. 208-31.

[27] Gal 2:6-10. Paul can say specifically that he saw no apostle besides Peter and James (1:18-20); see Bauer in *NTA*, 2:28-29. There is no concern for the Twelve here as in Acts 1-2 and later Catholic documents such as the Didache, the Syriac Didascalia, the Apostolic Constitutions, etc. See Georgi, *Gegner*, pp. 44-45.

[28] Only by such an extension of office could any footing be found for the pretensions of the false apostles. See Lightfoot, *Galatians*, p. 97. There seems to be a close relationship between the intruders of Galatia and those of 2 Corinthians, the ὑπερλίαν ἀποστόλοι (11:5) where again it is a question of strong apostolic claims. See Gunther, *Opponents*, p. 302. Paul finds his opponents so difficult to counter simply because there is no fixed concept of apostle in the Christian church. So, Georgi, *Gegner*, against Walter Schmithals, *The Office of Apostle in the Early Church*, trans. John E. Steely (Nashville: Abingdon Press, 1969), pp. 28-56.

[29] The opponents would not be likely to use the argument of Hom 17. 4-7: If you are a good apostle, don't argue with Peter. Their own mission suggests that they have done just that.

[30] The logic of the pseudo-Clementines, that God only speaks face to face, leaves no alternative but to receive tradition from the original apostles. But Gal 1:6-9, with its belittling of a message received by angels, seems to have the opponents' claims in view. See Schmithals, *Paul*, p. 29.

[31] This is the only use of the term in the major Pauline epistles.

[32] See R. Meyer, "προφήτης," *TDNT*, 6:817-20, and 825, on the way in which this phenomenon became "strange" in the program of nomistic rationalism which eliminated all movements which did not correspond to the Pharisaic norm.

[33] See Schmithals, *Paul*, p. 29.

[34] See above, p. 27, and references to J. T. Sanders and Drane. It was noted there too that the Galatian opponents themselves, who have set up the criterion of ἀποκαλύψεις, are

extremely interested in tradition. They pay great attention
to scripture and its interpretation, and the traditions of
Abraham, Moses, law, etc. If ἀποκαλύψεις and tradition are
not contradictory for them, we should not make them so for
Paul. In fact, the essence of the charge against Paul is
that he is holding a particular set of Jerusalem traditions
in contempt.

[35]See Conzelmann, *1 Corinthians*, p. 251. Having
quoted the tradition, he goes on to explain how he himself
is involved in it--through Christ's appearing to him. Even
Schmithals, *Apostle*, p. 25, notes that the resurrected Lord
appeared to all the apostles at the time of their call (1 Cor
15:7-8).

[36]Hengel, *Judaism*, 1:136, notes that, in Jewish
circles holding to doctrines of vertical revelation and inspiration, there was also a cherishing of traditions of succession. See below. Drane, *Paul*, pp. 61-62, claims that, in
the Corinthian context, there is respect for tradition, while
in Galatia it is of no consequence. However, this could be
turned around. It could be said that the problem in Corinth
was a flouting of tradition (1 Cor 1:18-2:5, etc.), and that
in Galatia it was an embracing of it.

[37]This last is the source of apostolic authority and
kerygma in countless Gnostic texts, which nonetheless take the
form of revelatory discourse, i.e., the Apocryphon of James,
Apocryphon of John, the Book of Thomas the Contender, the
Dialog of the Saviour, etc. Hornschuh, in *NTA*, 2:86, notes
that there was equal interest in παράδοσις and διαδοχή in both
the Great Church and Gnosticism.

[38]It became a technical term for "what is apostolic."
See W. Bauer, in *NTA*, 2:31; and R. M. Grant, "Two Gnostic
Gospels," *JBL* 79 (1960):5-26. H. B. Gaffron, *Studien zum
Koptischen Philippus-evangelium* (Bonn: Rheinische-Friedrich-
Wilhelms-Universitat, 1969), pp. 70-76, gives the technical
data for the development of the term.

[39]The Gospel of Philip refers to two orders of what
is ἀποστολικός: that held by the Great Church (55. 25-35,
NHL, 134) and that held by the Gnostics ("For the Father has
anointed the Son, and the Son has anointed the apostles, and
the apostles have anointed us" [74. 15-20, *NHL*, 144]). This
Gnostic claim appears specifically in Clement: "They say
that Valentinus was a hearer of Theudas, and Theudas, in
turn, a disciple of Paul." See *Stromata* 7. 17 (ANF, 2:555).
The Gnostic claim to inheritance of the Pauline tradition
appears in the Gospel of Truth, the Epistle to Rheginos, etc.
Ptolemy, the disciple of Valentinus, makes a similar claim to
apostolic tradition in his *Letter to Flora*: ". . . the
apostolic tradition which we too have received by succession.
We too are able to prove all our points by the teaching of
the Saviour." See ANF, 2:86. The Gospel of Philip claims to
stand in the Pauline exegetical tradition (67. 9-14 [*NHL*,
140]).

[40]Papias can say, "I did not think that what was taken
from books would profit me so much as what came from the living
and abiding voice." See Eusebius, *HE*, 3. 39. 4. Hornschuh,
NTA, 2:82-84 cites similar references in Irenaeus, Clement of
Alexandria, and Origen, noting that Clement sometimes even
called it παράδοσις.

[41]So labelled by Georgi, *Gegner*, p. 40.

[42]From a different circle again, see the opening of
the Mithras liturgy, where ἀποκάλυψις is juxtaposed with
παράδοσις.

[43]Schmithals has presented his case more fully in his
book *The Office of Apostle in the Early Church*. He first
denies a direct connection between ἀπόστολος and προφήτης
(pp. 105-9), to discredit any supposed connection between
"orthodox" Jewish tradition and the Christian office. Then
he asserts that the title and office of ἀπόστολος must be
traced back directly to Gnosticism. However, in all the
Gnostic materials he presents, there is no use of the term
ἀπόστολος; and in all Christian Gnostic materials, there is
no apostle of the New Testament era other than the twelve. It
was quite characteristic of both the Great Church and Gnosticism to single out some disciples as preeminent (W. Bauer, *NTA*,
2:42). But within Gnostic literature there is apostolic authority given only to those within the circle of the twelve
(plus Paul). Further, in the Gnostic tractates Pistis Sophia
and the Books of Jeu, the twelve as a body are extremely
highly regarded (Bauer, ibid., p. 40)--as they are not in
Galatians. Schmithals rests heavily on the assumption that
the concept of the twelve apostles originated in Antioch
(unproven); and he ignores the great amount of evidence linking Gnosticism to apocalyptic Judaism (see above, p. 92).

[44]The wide distribution and significance of these
criteria are evident from the way they are applied to Paul
in order to authenticate him as an apostle in Acts 14:8-18,
28:6, and especially 19:11-20, which describe his healing
miracles and his competition with Jewish exorcists. See
Elizabeth Schüssler Fiorenza, "Miracles, Mission, and Apolo-
getics," in Elizabeth Schüssler Fiorenza, ed., *Aspects of
Religious Propaganda in Judaism and Early Christianity* (Notre
Dame: University of Notre Dame Press, 1976), pp. 9-11. See
also Richard E. Oster, "A Historical Commentary on the Missionary Success Stories in Acts 19:11-40" (Ph.D. dissertation,
referring to the traditional picture of the Jewish wonder-
worker in Josephus *Ant* 8. 2. 5, 20. 5. 1, 20. 8. 6 (the last
two references are to apocalyptists); Juvenal *Satire* 6. 547,
and Lucian *Traj* 1173.

[45]Schmithals, *Paul*, p. 30; also Gunther, *Opponents*,
pp. 300-2. There are several close parallels between the
intruding theologies of Galatians and 2 Corinthians: both
exalt the Mosaic covenant; both make powerful apostolic claims;
both proclaim "another gospel" (2 Cor 11:4), and both set
store by ἀποκαλύψεις.

[46]To be placed alongside the opponents' claims as
"community-apostles." See above, p. 59.

[47]Probably the opponents' criteria. See Mussner,
Galater, p. 29, and above, p. 52.

[48]So Paul begins the *narratio* with Ἠκούσατε . . .
(1:13). See above on the significance of this, in conjunction
with the expected function of a rhetorical *narratio* (pp. 49-
51). Paul is here giving no new information. This is confirmed by a form analysis of the accounts of Paul's "call."
Munck points out the use of the one literary form, an Old Testament prophetic call (particularly modelled on the calls of
Deutero-Isaiah and Jeremiah), in Acts 9:15-19, 22:6-11, and
26:12-18, on the one hand, and Gal 1:11-16, on the other. See
Paul, pp. 13-35. This suggests that the tradition of understanding Paul's call in this way was a long and well established
one. See also Mussner, *Galater*, p. 69. Schmithals, *Apostle*,
p. 31, notes that, even by the time of 1 Corinthians, ἀποκάλυψις and ὅραμα have become technical terms for this event,
based on 1 Cor 9:1, 15:7-8.

[49]Schmithals, *Paul*, p. 30.

[50]In terms of popular expectations of those who
received ἀποκάλυψεις, Paul pointedly revealed very little of
the content of these revelations. He no doubt wishes to mini-
mise any question of impartation of hidden knowledge in his
revelations and to make this criterion irrelevant for the question of his apostolic rights. So, Munck, *Paul*, p. 35; and
Schmithals, *Apostle*, pp. 25-27. Paul took strong steps to
prevent his own extraordinary experience from being organically
linked with his apostolate. See Rengsdorf, "ἀπόστολος," *TDNT*,
1:440.

[51]Schmithals, *Paul*, p. 30. The apostle has to preach
himself as a pneuma-self (2 Cor 4:5, 10:12), and may not with-
hold his ecstasy from the community (2 Cor 5:11, 13) but must
produce the ecstatic σημεῖα τοῦ ἀποστολοῦ as proof of his
apostolate. See also Schmithals, *Apostle*, pp. 32-40. Paul
uses ἀποκάλυψις and ὅραμα to refer to his "call" (Gal 1:12,
16; 1 Cor 9:1, 15:7-8), but the opponents understand something
quite different by these terms and are not satisfied with the
recounting of the Damascus experience. So Paul is pushed to
divulge the ὀπτασίαι καὶ ἀποκαλύψεις κυριοῦ of 2 Cor 12:1-10.

[52]See 1 Cor 1:18-24, 2 Cor 13:4, and above, p. 94.
For Paul, there is a consistency between medium and message. The true apostle, who preaches the crucified as the
power and wisdom of God, himself is a spectacle of human weakness and foolishness. See below, p. 173, on 1 Cor 4:8-12;
and below, p. 98, on the human weakness of Paul in Galatians.

[53]So, strongly, Gal 1:15, 3:1, 4:4. See Martin
Hengel, *Crucifixion* (Philadelphia: Fortress Press, 1977),
pp. 86-90.

[54]Though Christian tradition does more frequently,
Gal 1:15-16 is the only place that Paul himself refers to his
apostolate in these terms. See Schmithals, *Apostle*, p. 56.

[55]K. H. Rengsdorf, "ἀπόστολος," *TDNT*, 1:441-48. שלח
is often used in connection with the call of a prophet, as in
Isa 6:8. 3 βασ 14:6 uses ἀπόστολος as a translation of שלח;
and 1 βασ 4:6 in Aquila equates שלח and ἀπόστολος, as does
Symmachus' rendering of Isa 8:2.

[56]Did 11:3 speaks of ἀπόστολοι καὶ προφῆται and dis-
cusses the apostle in terms of the "true prophet." Clement
Hom 11. 35 equates the two, as does Origen, *Celsus* 6. 9, and
Tertullian *de Pudicitia* 21; see Rengsdorf, ibid.

[57]There is a vertical dualism (2:5-7), the concept of
the church as the temple of God (2:19-21), which has significant parallels in other circles (see below), and a democratiz-
ing of revelations (1:17-19). In Colossians, so close in many
ways to this letter, the false φιλοσοφία shares the above tradition of revelations, claiming to possess special παράδοσις
and basing the content of its teaching on mysterious vision.
So Bornkamm, "Colossians," p. 126.

[58]See 1 Cor 13:2 (ἐὰν ἔχω προγητείαν καὶ εἰδῶ τὰ
μυστήρια πάντα καὶ πᾶσαν τὴν γνῶσιν . . .). The language used
here seems to be closely related to the central issue behind
1 Corinthians. Flusser, "Dead Sea Sect," p. 249, notes that
Paul here takes up the language of the opposition. This
verse connects προφήτεια with μυστήρια and γνῶσις: but Paul
attempts to separate prophecy from these phenomena, and to
understand it in terms of proclamation of the word (1 Cor
14:1-5, 23-25).

[59]It is interesting that Acts, which portrays Paul's
apostleship somewhat in terms of the opposing criteria, also
portrays Paul especially as one who makes prophetic predic-
tions (20:22-23, 21:10-13, 27:22-26 etc.). In his letters,
he claims the prophetic gift, but with a different understanding of prophecy--as proclamation of the word (1 Cor 14:6,
etc.). See R. Meyer, "προφήτης," *TDNT*, 6:848.

[60]See above, p. 59.

[61]That the opponents seek to exclude the Galatians
from the law-free gospel (Burton), from Paul and the Gentile
church (Zahn, Lietzmann, Oepke), from Christ and His grace
(Lightfoot, Schlier), from fellowship with the original community (Lagrange), or from fellowship with the apostles
(Mussner, *Galater*, pp. 310-11).

[62]See above, p. 94. Paul vigorously fights against
a view that would fragment this relationship (Gal 2:1-2 and
1 Cor 3 and 9). See Conzelmann, *1 Corinthians*, pp. 71-72,
151-53.

[63]See above, p. 94, quoting Schmithals, *Apostle*,
p. 83.

[64]See above, p. 93.

[65]For instance, Mussner, *Galater*, p. 327: "Damit
entreisst der Apostel den Gegnern ihr Schlagwort und reklamiert
es für die ohne Werke des Gesetzes Glaubenden." Also Schlier,
Galater, 159-61.

[66]For a brief summary, see Hengel, *Judaism*, 1:84,
referring especially to Menippus in the fourth century and
Alexandrian literature in the third BCE. He posits that
Jewish apocalyptic literature largely took over this genre
of heavenly and hellish journeys.

[67]For instance, the Ascension of Isaiah, Hermes *Vis*
1. 1. 3-4, etc.

[68]For instance, in Irenaeus, *Demonstratio* 9, the
Epistle of the Apostles 6, and Clement of Alexandria, *Strom*
4 (ANF 2:508-13).

[69]As well as the more Gnostic versions of this tradition in, for example, the Apocryphon of John, On the Origin
of the World, etc., Gnosticism has produced apocalypses which
show a heavy dependence on Jewish apocalypses, such as the
Apocalypse of Paul, two apocalypses in the Name of Jesus, and
the Dialog of the Saviour. George W. Macrae, commenting on
the Apocalypse of Adam, notes that it not only depends heavily
on Jewish apocalyptic tradition. It also has no explicitly
Christian themes and may be a transition document between
Judaism and Gnostic apocalyptic (*NHL*, 246). Further on the
close connection between apocalyptic Judaism and Gnosticism,
see George W. Macrae, "The Jewish Background of the Gnostic
Sophia Myth," *NovT* 12 (1970):97-112, and James M. Robinaon,
NHL, 7.

[70]For examples of the heavenly vision, see 1 Enoch
chaps. 12, 17, 36, 71; and Test Lev chap. 2. Jean Danielou,
The Theology of Jewish Christianity, trans. John A. Baker
(London: Darton, Longman, and Todd, 1964), has demonstrated
that many theologoumena that appear in the Fathers, in
Gnosticism, and in the apocalyptic New Testament apocrypha
can be traced back to apocalyptic Judaism. See especially
chaps. 1 and 2, and pages 173-78. Hengel, *Judaism*, 1:204-5,
comments on the importance of the heavenly journey in apocalyptic. There is a need to stress the spatial as well as
the temporal elements of the literature.

[71]Hengel, ibid., 1:202: "The apocalyptic Hasidim
ground their "wisdom" in a claim to direct divine revelations." Also Oepke, "καλύπτω," *TDNT*, 3:563-92.

[72]See Hengel, ibid., 1:206; Russell, ibid., pp. 187-
94; and Meyer, "προφήτης," *TDNT* 6:820-22.

[73]Russell, *Method*, pp. 127-37, has argued that this
characteristic does not mean the apocalyptist has a lesser
sense of being a visionary. Pseudonymity was probably used
because the apocalyptist wrote with an overwhelming sense of

identification with the seer himself; because the apocalyptist
had a sense of contemporaneity with the seer, sharing the same
visionary experiences; and because the appropriation of a name
was understood as an extension of personality.

[74]Hengel, *Judaism*, 1:205, suggests that, in each of
these cases, this was because of the "collective authority" of
the Spirit at work in the community.

[75]Danielou, *Theology*, p. 174. 4 Ezra and 2 Baruch
know of only three heavens: the multiplication to seven
heavens seems to belong to later Christian modification of
Jewish apocalypses. 2 Enoch 8 speaks of paradise in the third
heaven, although in chaps. 11-36 Enoch travels on to the tenth
heaven. Paradise is in the third heaven in Apoc Mos 37:5. In
the α-recension of Test Lev 3:1-4 there are only three heavens,
but in the β-recension there are seven.

[76]As well as the Christian portions of 2 Enoch and
Test Lev, see Ascension of Isaiah, the Gospel of Peter, and
the Apocalypse of Peter.

[77]For instance, Irenaeus, *Demonstratio* 12. 761, Clem
Alex *Stromata* 4. 25. 159, and the Epistle of the Apostles
chapter 17, referring to the Ogdoad, which is the κυριακή.
Danielou, *Theology*, p. 176, proposes that this suggests a
dependence on Plato, *Republic*, 11. 616b, which speaks of
seven heavens and an eighth, and other Hellenistic literature.

[78]The Origin of the World and the Sophia of Jesus
Christ both refer to the Ogdoad, probably using the same
Hellenistic traditions as the Fathers. See Hans Jonas, *The
Gnostic Religion* (Boston: Beacon Press, 1958), p. 43. Valentinian Gnosticism is fond of ten heavens, perhaps showing
Stoic influence (i.e., the Apocryphon of John). The Gospel
of the Egyptians has twelve heavens, Eugnostos the Blessed
refers to 360, and Basilides refers to 365: Jonas, ibid.,
p. 44. It is interesting that the Nag Hammadi tractate the
Apocalypse of Paul (*NHL*, 239-41) combines and takes up Gal
1:15-16 and 2 Cor 12:1-4, building on Jewish apocalyptic, and
has Paul journey on from the third heaven to the fourth, and
then to the tenth.

[79]The rabbis speak of the four who entered Paradise:
Ben Azzai, Ben Zoma, Aher, and R. Aquiba (Hagigah 14b). On
the third heaven as paradise, see StrB, 3:531-33. Philo took
his heavenly journeys. See *Spec* 3. 1-3, "I had no base or
abject thoughts . . . but seemed always to be borne aloft into
the heights with a soul possessed by some God-sent inspiration,
a fellow-traveller with the sun and moon and the whole heaven
and the universe. . . ."

[80]Hengel, *Judaism*, 1:205. He notes, ibid., pp. 228-32,
that the Qumran community shared the "Hasidic wisdom tradition"
of apocalyptic literature, as well as showing a great interest
in collecting apocalyptic literature.

[81]See Isaac Rabinowitz, "'PESHER/PITTARON': Its Biblical Meaning and Its Significance in the Qumran Literature,"
RQ 8 (1972-75):219-32, who has demonstrated, from an examination of six principal "Peshers" of the community (1 QpHab
12:1-10, 6:8-12, 5:1-8, 4 QpHos^a 2:8-14, 4 QpNah 3-4, 2:1-2,
and 4 QPss^a 37:1-2, 2:4-5), that the title does not simply
mean "interpretation" or "commentary," but a presaging of an
emergent reality, tightly closed up in scripture, which
requires disclosure by one endowed with special "revelatory"
skills.

[82]Rabinowitz, "PESHER/PITTARON," p. 231.

[83]Helmer Ringgren, *The Faith of Qumran*, trans. Emilie T.
Sander (Philadelphia: Fortress Press, 1963), p. 114. See, for
instance, 1 QS 9:17, 1 QH 6:26-27, 14:13. Hengel, *Judaism*,
1:221-22, comments on the central significance in Qumran of
that group of concepts which probably possessed the greatest
importance for Essene theology, the concepts of knowledge,
insight, and wisdom (although the terms דעת and שכל are
favored over חכמה and חכם).

[84]For instance, CD 11:3, "For He from the well-spring
of knowledge has made His light to burst forth, and mine eyes
have gazed on His wonders; and the light that is in my heart
has pierced the deep things of excellence" (Gaster).

[85]For instance, 1 QH 12:10 refers to God as the "God
of knowledge" and proclaims, "Behold, for mine own part, I
have reached the inner vision, and through the Spirit Thou
hast placed within me, come to know Thee, my God" (Gaster).

[86]1 QH 1:10-16. See below on understanding law in
Qumran.

[87]For instance, 1 QS 11:6-9, "Through His mysterious
wonder light is come into my heart . . . a virtue hidden from
man, a knowledge and subtle lore . . . these has God bestowed
on them He has chosen, . . . He has given them an inheritance
in the lot of holy beings, and joined them in communion with
the sons of heaven (בני שמים; note the similarity to Eph 1:3,
and 2:19 [συμπολῖται τῶν ἁγίων]; see Gaster, *Scriptures*, p.
235), to form one congregation, one single communion, a fabric
of holiness. . . ." Supernatural knowledge also brings communion with the בני שמים, and a share in the lot of the Spirits
of knowledge, in 1 QH 3:19-24. In 1 QH 6:12-14 they need no
intermediary between themselves and God and are answered
directly out of His mouth. See further, Meyer, "προφήτης,"
TDNT, 6:823.

[88]See above, p. 97.

[89]Meyer, "προφήτης," *TDNT*, 6:813-14. Zech 13:6 may
in fact suggest lively ecstatic-prophetic activity; Psalm 74
may be dated at the time of the Exile, and have nothing to
say about postexilic prophecy; 2 Bar 85:3-4 is probably
referring to the dogma of a canonical period of salvation,

as in Josephus *Apion* 1. 41, and in fact 2 Bar 48:34-37 suggests charismatic phenomena at the destruction of the Temple.
1 Macc 4:46, 9:27, 14:41 can be read to understand that
prophecy was active again in Israel under the leadership of
John Hyrcanus--just as Josephus, *Ant* 13:299 attributes to him
"the rule of the nation, the office of high priest, and the
gift of prophecy."

[90]Ibid., p. 816. The Rabbinic tradition "aimed at
restricting the rise of legitimate prophecy to an ideal classical period in the past" and managed to hold together with
difficulty two opposing remnants of the continuation of
prophecy, the בת קול (StrB, 1:127, 133) and the "wise men."

[91]For instance, *Heres* 295-365 on the patriarchs as
prophets.

[92]He describes prophecy as an ἔκστασις of the ἐνθου-
σιῶν and θεοφόρης which can even be called a μανία, where the
divine presence of God must entirely displace the rational
(*Heres* 265). Though this suggests Platonic concepts of inspiration, there are Jewish elements, such as connection of
prophecy with contemplation of scripture (*Som* 2. 252), and
veneration of the exegete as the true prophet.

[93]*Ant* 13. 299.

[94]*Ant* 17. 41-44. There are other ecstatic-prophetic
manifestations in earliest Rabbinic Judaism, such as the
activities of Gamaliel 2, Samuel R. Akiba, R. Meir, R. Simon b.
Jochai: see Meyer, "προφήτης," *TDNT*, 6:823-24. However, by
the end of the century such activity was becoming "strange"
to official Judaism, ibid., p. 825.

[95]*Ant* 15. 373-75.

[96]Ibid., 17. 346-47.

[97]*Ant* 13. 311-12.

[98]*Ant* 15. 379.

[99]*Bell* 2. 159. Hengel, *Judaism*, 1:240, suggests that
this makes Essene prophecy differ considerably from that of
the Old Testament.

[100]*Bell* 2. 159, 136. This literature may not have been
completely "orthodox," as the last reference links this prophecy with miraculous healing based on inquiry into the secret
properties of roots and stones. The "holy books" may have at
least included apocalyptic writings and perhaps astrological
and magical writings too. Some aspects of this description are
reminiscent of Philo's θεραπευταί in *De Vita Contemplativa*.

[101]Hengel, *Judaism*, 1:240.

[102]*Bell* 3. 350-51.

[103]Ibid., 1:228-32; and 217, Jewish apocalyptic was a part of a larger Hellenistic movement of higher wisdom by revelation.

[104]Ibid., pp. 134, 206. See also Russell, *Method*, pp. 187-94.

[105]Russell, ibid., p. 187. Munck, *Paul*, p. 31, notes the way the new prophetic message is authenticated in 1 Enoch 14:8-16:4--there is a bright light, the sight of the Lord on the throne, divulgence of heavenly secrets, and the command to prophesy, in clear imitation of Old Testament models. There is also a striking contrast to Paul, in that there is much more attention to the divulgence of what was seen on the heavenly journey.

[106]Hengel, ibid., pp. 206, 136. Georgi, *Gegner*, pp. 122-23, notes that, in the New Testament period, apocalyptist and prophet were associated together. Essenes, Zealots, and Pharisees all had their prophets. On the Zealot prophets, see Josephus *Bell* 2. 258, *Ant* 20. 97, 168. These apparently were messianic prophets who promised to work wonders and signs, always analogous to the great events of Israel's past salvation history.

[107]See Hengel, *Judaism*, 1:136; and below, pp. 105-6.

[108]See Hengel, ibid., pp. 229-32, and below.

[109]While exercising certain cautions. There is the undecided relationship between the Qumran community and the Essenes (see Fitzymer, in Schechter, *Sectaries*, pp. 15-16). The description of the Essenes in Philo, Josephus, and Hippolytus is not always easy to square with the Qumran texts. Milik has proposed as a solution four different kinds of Essenes--those in Qumran, the "mother community," those in Damascus (CD: though the name may be metaphorical), those in the towns and villages of Palestine, and the θεραπευταί of Egypt. And there is the difficulty of the general question of prophecy in Qumran. See Meyer, "προφήτης," *TDNT*, 6:826 (but now see Hengel, *Judaism*, 1:207).

[110]See, for example, Ringgren, *Qumran*, pp. 197-98, and the discussion of the messiah(s) in Qumran. Gaster, *Scriptures*, p. 63, suggests that 1 QS 9:8-11, "Until the coming of the Prophet and of both the priestly and lay messiah" may refer to the prophet of Deut 18:18, the forerunner of the two messiahs.

[111]Ibid., p. 183. See 1 QpHab 2:8, 7:4. He, like Paul, sees himself as chosen from the womb in analogy to Jeremiah and Deutero-Isaiah (1 QH 9:29-32).

[112]Ringgren, *Qumran*, p. 168.

[113]Ringgren, *Qumran*, p. 168.

[114]Ibid., p. 167.

[115]In Essenism, Hasidic wisdom becomes saving knowledge, eschatological saving knowledge for both the individual and the community. See Hengel, *Judaism*, 1:228. Here "revelation" is direct inspiration (ibid., p. 222).

[116]Wherever ten members are present, there shall be a "man who searches in the law" to inform the group of what he has found (1 QS 6:6-7, 8:11-12). The whole community exists for the task of safeguarding the true exposition of the law (CD 6:1-11). See Gaster, *Scriptures*, p. 6.

[117]Gaster, ibid., p. 299. See the references in Josephus above, p. 271, notes 93-100.

[118]So, divine revelation is needed, even if one is to know the mysteries of the divine revelation in scripture (1 QH 12:11-13). פשר is in fact a correlative of רז. See Rabinowitz, above, p. 100, and Gaster, *Scriptures*, p. 299. There is a close association of such terms as "knowledge" and "understanding" with "reveal," "enlighten," "appear," and, above all, רז and סוד. See Hengel, *Judaism*, 1:223.

[119]See the association of wisdom, knowledge, the secret, etc., above.

[120]Hengel, *Judaism*, 1:136 notes that a collection of psalms from 2 Q makes even David a *soper* filled with "an understanding and enlightened spirit" who composed all his 4050 psalms "in prophetic inspiration."

[121]Hengel, ibid., 1:207; Russell, *Method*, pp. 164-73.

[122]In distinction from other Jewish apocalyptic tradition. See above, p. 100.

[123]StrB, 3:22, 532, 573, 796. These seem often to be lingering traces of more apocalyptic language. See Strathmann, "πόλις," *TDNT*, 6:528-29.

[124]It belongs with his view of the religious man as the κοσμοπολίτης and his state as the original world (*Opif* 142-44). Any sense of history and eschatology is weakened. See H. Braun, "Das Himmlische Vaterland bei Philo und im Hebräerbrief," in Otto Böcher and Klaus Haacker, eds., *Verborum Veritas* (Wuppertal: Rolf Brockhaus, 1970), pp. 319-27. Jerusalem is the soul of man in whom God moves about ὡς ἐν πόλει (*Som* 2. 248), and one seeks the "true city" within his soul (ibid., 2. 250).

[125]The material is conveniently summarized in Schlier, *Galater*, pp. 157-58; Moore, *Judaism*, 2:341-43; Strathmann, "πόλις," *TDNT*, 6:525, Mussner, *Galater*, pp. 325-27. See 2 Bar 4:3-5, 5:1-4, 32:2-4, 1 Enoch 90:28-29 (". . . a new house greater and loftier than the first . . ."), 4 Ezra 7:26 (". . . the city that is now invisible . . ."), 10:27, 13:36 (Sion shall come . . .").

[126]Moore, *Judaism*, 2:342-43, the new Jerusalem takes
the place of the old and is in many ways old Jerusalem.

[127]Russell, *Method*, pp. 297-300, summarizes the attitude of apocalyptic to the other nations and to Israel. Its
eschatological hopes are on the whole nationalistic. The
righteous equal Israel, the wicked equal the Gentiles. There
is a generous attitude to Gentiles in the Sibylline Oracles 3,
Test Benj, Lev, and Naph; but the attitude is harsh in 2 Baruch,
most of 1 Enoch and especially the Similitudes, the Psalms of
Solomon, Jubilees, the Assumption of Moses, and 4 Ezra.

[128]Klaus Koch, *The Rediscovery of Apocalyptic*, trans.
Margaret Kohl (Naperville: Alec R. Allenson, 1970), p. 30.

[129]See Koch, ibid., pp. 30-31; and Gerhard von Rad,
Wisdom in Israel, trans. (R. Mcl. Wilson) (Nashville: Abing-
don Press, 1972), p. 273, on the way the idea of determinism,
God's control over history, and pessimism concerning the
future, is bound up with the remnant: "Even the concept
Israel begins to disintegrate."

[130]On the apocalyptist as the "wise man," see above,
p. 101, and references; and von Rad, *Wisdom*, p. 277. Participation in God's plan and control of the cosmos now takes
a new form, the gaining of secret wisdom; and it is the "wise"
who now come through the final crisis. See Dan 2:20-22, 12:3,
etc. See the "wise man" and his predestined future glory in
1 Enoch 100:6, 105:1--the "wise" have future security assured.
In 4 Ezra 7:43 Israel (or the remnant), already chosen of God,
in a sense anticipates her eternal destiny: "I will rejoice
over the few that shall be saved, inasmuch as they it is that
make my glory prevail now already. . . ." So God comforts
Ezra with the slogan, "Things present (match) them of the
present, things future them of the future" (8:46; see also
7:15-16 and 1 En 104:1-4), and assures him, "For you is
opened paradise, planted the tree of life," etc. (8:52).

[131]1 Enoch 101:1, "Observe the heaven, ye children of
heaven."

[132]4 Ezra 7:15-16, "Why disquietest thyself that thou
art corruptible? . . . mortal? Why hast thou not considered
what is to come, rather than what is now present?"

[133]There is no question about the intense future
expectations of the apocalyptists. See von Rad, *Wisdom*,
p. 276. As noted above, p. 220, apocalyptic had spatial and
vertical as well as horizontal elements.

[134]A good summary of secondary material is in Mussner,
Galater, pp. 324-27. Hengel, *Judaism*, 1:223, refers to the
idea of heavenly Jerusalem in Qumran, but this writer has not
been able to find it there in the strict sense.

[135]4 QpIsa[a].

[136]1 QM 1:3, 3:11, 12:13-17.

[137]See above references to 1 QS 11:6-9, 1 QH 3:19-24, etc. 1 QH 6:14 concludes, "They are thy courtiers, sharing the high estate of [all the heavenly beings]" (Gaster).

[138]1 QpMic 1:5, commenting on "High places of Jewry, that is, Jerusalem," says, "This . . . refers to those who expound the law correctly, . . . and to all who are willing to join His elect . . . when the latter meet together in the communal council."

[139]This is in keeping too with the strong sense of being the remnant. For instance, in 1 QS 2:25 they are the "ideal society of God" who have separated themselves from apostate Israel. This is not just one feature of their ideology among many, but lies at the very heart of it. See Flusser, "Dead Sea Sect," pp. 215-66.

[140]Though the eschatological gifts of salvation were already in the community, they were only so incompletely, and "this did not exclude a future expectation," Hengel, *Judaism*, 1:223.

[141]See above, pp. 66, 98.

[142]See 1 QSa 2:3-11, "No one who is afflicted with a bodily defect or injured in feet or hands, or who is lame or blind or deaf or dumb, or who has a visible blemish in his body, or who is an old man, tottering and unable to stand firm in the midst of the congregation of the men of renown, for holy angels are (present) in their [congre]gation. . . ." Also in 1 QM 6:4-6, and two other more recently published MSS reported in J. A. Fitzmyer, "A Feature of Qumran Angelology and the Angels of 1 Cor 11:10," *NTS* 4 (1957-58):58 (provisionally designated 4 QD[b] and 4 QM[a]), bodily defects are to be excluded from the presence of angels, and therefore from the congregation of the elect. It is interesting that, in Gal 4:12-20, Paul was once accepted as an angel, but no longer.

[143]For further material on the "remnant" concept in late Judaism, see Gerhard F. Hasel, "Remnant," *IDBS*, 736. He notes the Qumran covenanters' fondness for this self-designation. On the other hand, "In Rabbinic thought the remnant idea recedes, and all Israel has part in the future world."

[144]Schlier, *Galater*, p. 159. For Paul, as for apocalyptic Judaism, heavenly Jerusalem represents the new aeon. The startling thing about his language is that the new aeon is now present. This accords with his stress elsewhere in Galatians on "realised" eschatology. See above, pp. 59-60.

[145]This is not a Platonic dualism, but a salvation-historical dualism resulting from the stress on Christ's death in history. Schlier, ibid., pp. 159-60.

[146]See above, p. 94.

[147]See above, p. 66.

[148]Gnosticism's two Jerusalems, earthly and heavenly,
are opposite aeons standing over against each other in the
typical dualistic pattern of syzygies. So, Schlier, *Galater*,
p. 160; Mussner, *Galater*, p. 327; Pagels, *Paul*, p. 110.
Instances belong mainly to Valentinian or Naasene gnosticism.
The doctrine is part of a cosmic-material dualism which
extends to φύσις and becomes the basis for an attack on
Judaism (Gos Phil 69. 30-35 [*NHL*, 142]) or the "psychic"
Christians of the Great Church (Origen, *Comm Joh* 13:16, 19, 60,
etc.).

[149]Pagels, *Paul*, pp. 9-10. It is for this reason that
the opponents cannot hold a position similar to that of Philo
or Gnosticism, where the two Jerusalems are contrasted: Paul's
antithesis would be no polemic against them. See Mussner,
Galater, p. 327.

[150]στύλος is used in Gal 2:9, 1 Tim 3:15, Rev 3:12,
10:1. The use is clearly apocalyptic in Rev 3:12; and 1 Timothy uses it in connection with the community as God's temple.

[151]Charles K. Barrett, "Paul and the Pillar Apostles,"
in J. N. Sevenster and W. C. van Unnik, eds., *Studia Paulina
in Honorem Johannes de Zwaan* (Haarlem: De Erven F. Bohn,
1953), pp. 1-19; and U. Wilckens, "στύλος," *TDNT*, 7:735.

[152]The church is the temple of God in 1 Cor 3:16 and
Eph 2:21; and the Qumran community is seen in this way in 1 QS
5:5-6, 8:5-6, 9:6, 11:8, 1 QH 1:34, 2:24, etc.

[153]Which is a synonym for God Himself. See 1 QH 1:34,
2:24 etc.

[154]1 QS 8:1. The parallel to Gal 2:9 has been pointed
out by Sherman E. Johnson, "The Dead Sea Manual of Discipline
and the Jerusalem Church of Acts," in Stendahl, *Scrolls*, pp.
133-34; and Gaster, *Scriptures*, p. 39.

[155]See above, pp. 97-98.

[156]More recent works devoted to this phenomenon are
Georgi, *Gegner*; Hadas and Smith, *Heroes*; Tiede, *Charismatic*;
and Fiorenza, ed., *Religious Propaganda*.

[157]Tiede, *Charismatic*, p. 52. The reason for aretalogical propaganda is the focus on the personality of the hero
because of an understanding of the nature of the divine presence and style of religious life. And put more simply by
Hadas and Smith, *Heroes*, p. 9, an aretalogy is "a hagiography
for a cult."

[158]See Hadas and Smith, ibid., p. 17, on the importance
of the Platonic image of Socrates. Tiede, *Charismatic*, pp.
55-99, traces the way two different "Socrates" developed, to
authenticate two different ideas of the θεῖος ἀνήρ: the
miracle-working Socrates appears in Xenophon, etc., while
Diogenes Laertius' Socrates preserves the rationalist image.

Following their models, Lucian of Samosata's Apollonius of
Tyana was a θεῖος ἀνήρ because of his miracles, whereas
Philostratus' Apollonius of Tyana was a θεῖος ἀνήρ because
of his wisdom as a philosopher.

[159]Hengel, *Judaism*, 1:111, notes that the word ἀρετα-
λογία appears for the first time in Jewish literature in
Sirach 36:13. Tiede, *Charismatic*, pp. 101, 237-40, has
examined the different "aretalogical" portrayals of Moses and
Abraham in "apologetic" Jewish literature.

[160]See Hadas and Smith, *Heroes*, p. 88, on the portrayal of Eleazar in 4 Macc in terms of the suffering Socrates;
and Haenchen, *Acts*, p. 517, on Paul in terms of Socrates in
Acts 17:22-31 (see above, p. 46).

[161]Hengel, *Judaism*, 1:136, notes that the "praise of
the fathers" in Sirach "is reminiscent of the glorification
of the heroes in Hellenistic times with its biographical genre
de virus illustribus."

[162]See Hengel, ibid., p. 99, where he notes that
apocalyptic, too, shares this way of viewing history. He
gives references (2:61) to the Genesis Apocryphon, etc.

[163]See Hengel, ibid., 1:136; and on Abraham and Moses
in these presentations, below, pp. 111-12.

[164]Hengel, ibid., pp. 89-90; see below, pp. 111-13.

CHAPTER SEVEN

THE TRADITION OF ABRAHAM AND SEED OF ABRAHAM

[1]Mussner, *Galater*, p. 216; see above, pp. 83-84.

[2]Mussner, ibid., p. 217.

[3]Bligh, *Galatians*, p. 167.

[4]Against Jewett, "Agitators," pp. 200-201, who argues
that the opponents were motivated not by missionary concerns
but by Zealot pressure against Christians in Judea in the
forties and fifties. They hoped that, by circumcising Gentiles, they would remove charges that they were a threat to
the Jewish state and avoid persecution for the cross of Christ.
He thus makes the opponents teach circumcision for expediency.
But Galatians shows that they taught it as an essential for
salvation. See above, pp. 64-65. Jewett's argument might
explain the circumcising activities of Gal 2:1-5, but why a
circumcising mission in Galatia? There are records of circumcising campaigns in Judea (below, p. 144), but not elsewhere. Even if the opponents were placating another party,
circumcision of Gentiles would satisfy that party only if

there were some sort of mission-consciousness. Jewett finds no way of relating the opponents to other missionary but anti-Pauline Christian movements.

[5]Mussner, *Galater*, p. 317.

[6]Bligh, *Galatians*, p. 166. They may have taught that the Mosaic law is the explication of the demand to walk before God and be perfect.

[7]Paul refers to Moses only as the μεσίτης, (3:19). This reluctance to even name him may indicate even more his important place in the debate. See below, p. 116.

[8]Compare Rom 9:4-5, 10:5-13, 7:12. See below, p. 121.

[9]Mussner, *Galater*, p. 221. In these terms Paul is taking up the claims of the opponents, not only for their converts to circumcision, but for themselves. See Georgi, *Gegner*, pp. 51-82, on the use of the title by the Corinthian opponents; and also Barrett, *2 Corinthians*, pp. 293-94.

[10]See Ridderbos, *Paul*, p. 273. Paul gives an eschatological answer to his opponents in 3:16, 28-29. See also Foerster, "κληρονομία," *TDNT*, 3:784. He who belongs to the Messiah is the true σπέρμα 'Αβραάμ.

[11]Mussner, *Galater*, pp. 216, 221, has noticed this difference. See also Stoike, "The Law of Christ," p. 130, and below, p. 118.

[12]On the different salvation-historical schemes in Galatians and Romans, see above, p. 84.

[13]Whereas, in Rom 9:4, "adoption as sons" was a privilege of Israel.

[14]Mussner, *Galater*, pp. 221-22, makes this contrast.

[15]On 'Ιουδαΐζειν, see above, p. 64.

[16]That Paul in Romans may actually use an Abraham-argument close to the one used by the opponents in Galatia, see below, pp. 139-41.

[17]See above, pp. 94, 96.

[18]See above, p. 94.

[19]This is the force of the way Paul always refers to the Galatians collectively. They are all equally in danger of this heresy. See above, p. 28.

[20]On the rarity of the full conversion of Gentiles to Judaism, see below, p. 139.

[21]Gen R. 3a (246); Mekilta *Mishpatim* 18; StrB, 3:195.

[22]Philo, *Virt*; Josephus *Ant* 1. 155-56; also Artapanus, Aristobulus, and especially Eupolemus, in Eusebius, *Praep Evang* 9 and 13. Sources used for this material in Eusebius are M. Seguier de Saint-Brisson, *La Préparation Evangelique d'Eusèbe Pamphile*, 2 vols. (Paris: Gaume Freres, 1846); and Albert-Marie Denis, ed., *Fragmenta Pseudepigraphorum Quae Supersunt Graeca* (Leiden: Brill, 1970). See also Hengel, *Judaism*, 1: 88-95, 2:60-65; and Georgi, *Gegner*, pp. 79-80.

[23]Tanch B לך לך 6 (32a); Jub 18:15-18, 24:11; StrB, 3:539-40.

[24]Gen R. 30:39.

[25]Sifre Deut 47; Moore, *Judaism*, 1:344-45; Sanders, *Paul*, p. 101.

[26]Georgi, *Gegner*, p. 81.

[27]StrB, 3:188-91; Schoeps, *Paul*, p. 215.

[28]1 Macc 2:52: "Was not Abraham found faithful when tested, and it was reckoned to him as righteousness?" See 2 Bar 57:2, 58:1-5; Abraham was justified by works, and so also will Israel be justified, if she obeys the law. See also Jub 18:15, 24:11; StrB, 3:186; Ziesler, *Righteousness*, pp. 99-103; and Mussner, *Galater*, p. 218.

[29]*Abr* 60: "Abraham . . . filled with zeal for piety, the highest and greatest of virtues, was eager to follow God and be obedient to His commands."

[30]Gen 26:5 is also referred to in Qid 4:14. Abraham knew the Torah and kept it perfectly. See StrB, 3:186.

[31]*Abr* 275, referring to Gen 26:5.

[32]Sifra on Lev 19:34: "As the native born is one who takes upon him all the commandments of the law, so the proselyte is one who takes upon him all the commandments of the law. Hence the rule: A proselyte who takes upon him all the commandments of the law with a single exception is not to be admitted." See Moore, *Judaism*, 1:345. The main texts for acceptance of proselytes are *Yebamot* 47a-b, and *Gerim*. Sanders, *Paul*, p. 206, notes that the requirements cannot be precisely recovered but admits that the formal definition of a true proselyte was one who intends to obey all the commandments. See also Bernard Jacob Bamberger, *Proselytism in the Talmudic Period* (New York: KTAV Publishing House, 1968), pp. xxi-xxix.

[33]Sanders, *Paul*, p. 90.

[34]Sir 44:19. Because of the faithfulness of Abraham in testing, his seed was established and would rule from sea to sea, etc. See StrB, 3:187.

[35]Sanders, *Paul*, pp. 96-97.

[36]*Sanh* 10:1; Mekilta *Mishpatim* 10; and Sanders, *Paul*, pp. 147-51.

[37]See StrB, 1:116. Sanders, *Paul*, pp. 183-84, disputes the idea that these merits could be transferred to others, but his argument may be a semantic one.

[38]Mekilta *Mishpatim* 18:20; Sanders, *Paul*, p. 206.

[39]Bik 1:4, on Dt 26:3-4. The proselyte cannot say "our fathers." When he prays alone he must pray, "The God of the fathers of Israel," etc. See also Numbers Rabbah 8. The proselyte cannot claim the merits of the fathers. See StrB 1:119.

[40]Sanders, *Paul*, p. 209. See Bamberger, *Proselytism*, for a positive presentation of Jewish proselytism (he gives four pages of material unfavorable to proselytism, and eight pages of favorable material. But are pages to be counted or weighed?).

[41]Georgi, *Gegner*, p. 63.

[42]Thus Mekilta *Mishpatim* 10: "For the heathen nations there will be no redemption . . . Beloved are the Israelites, for the Holy One, blessed be He, has given the heathen nations of the world as ransom for their souls. . . ." See Sanders, *Paul*, p. 150.

[43]As in 3 Macc 6:3; John 8:33, 39; Targ Ps 22:31; Georgi, *Gegner*, p. 82; and Mussner, *Galater*, p. 217.

[44]Josephus *Apion* 2:282: "The masses have long since shown a keen desire to adopt our religious observances . . . as God permeates the universe, so the law has found its way among all mankind." See also Philo, *Vit Mos* 1:4-21, 209. Judaism appealed as a school of foreign philosophy (Moore, *Judaism*, 1:324); and this form of appeal is to be seen also by the way Tacitus, Suetonius, and Juvenal align Judaism with the mystery-cults. See the summary in Georgi, *Gegner*, pp. 102-5. Goodenough has also described the form in which Judaism was so appealing to the Hellenistic world. See *Symbols*, 12:3. Georgi feels that there may have been an explosive growth in Christianity, making the latter possible. See *Gegner*, pp. 84-86. Jean Juster, *Les Juifs dans l'Empire romain; leur condition juridique economique et sociale*, 2 vols. (New York: Burt Franklin, 1965), 1:209-10, estimates that there may have been four times as many Jews in the Diaspora as in Palestine, with perhaps 6-7 million Jews in the Roman empire. Georgi suggests that this large number must be largely due to conversions. Avigdor Tcherikover, *Hellenistic Civilization and the Jews*, trans. S. Applebaum (Philadelphia: Jewish Publishing Society of America, 1959), pp. 292-93, is more cautious, arguing that proselytes would not have been numbered among Jews anyway. Certainly, complete conversion to Judaism was rare. See below. Tcherikover suggests that there must have been a large number of half-proselytes (God-fearers, Sabbatarians, etc.) who remained officially outside Judaism. This would satisfy Josephus' statement: it does appear that Judaism was very attractive in this semi-official form.

[45]As noted by Drane, *Paul*, p. 82, among others.
Jewett, "Agitators," p. 202, suggests that a particular form
of Judaism may have already appealed to the Galatians before
Paul introduced them to Christianity.

[46]See p. 92 above. Hengel, *Judaism*, 1:70, sees an
apologetic aimed at outsiders only in Philo and Josephus.

[47]See p. 92 above; and Hengel, ibid., 1:88, 91; and
further below on the "Hellenistic" Jewish approach to history.

[48]See p. 92 above, quoting Hengel to the effect that
all Jewish literature of the period could be called "Hellenistic." Tiede, *Charismatic*, p. 107, citing Reitzenstein, points
out that the aretalogy itself, and "divine man" propaganda,
cannot be accounted for from a Greek background alone but
shares in Oriental religious currents. Similarly, Hengel,
ibid., 1:112.

[49]See Hengel, ibid., 1:91. The "apologetic" Abraham
of Josephus and Artapanus also appears in the Genesis Apocryphon from Qumran and, to a degree, in Jubilees. See below.

[50]Hengel, ibid., 1:100, notes that after CE 70 Judaism
broke off these historical accounts and began to concentrate
instead on ahistorical halacha and haggada.

[51]There would no longer be the same impetus to portray
Abraham as the father of all culture and wisdom, etc. The suggestion of this change in the portrayal of Abraham is in Gen R.
44. 10, "You are a prophet and not an astrologer."

[52]See above, referring to Hengel, *Judaism*, 1:100.

[53]That is, the Abraham of Paul's time, even the Abraham of some apocalyptic circles, may now be traced more clearly
by taking into account the literature of the "Hasidic wisdom
tradition."

[54]See above, pp. 105-6.

[55]It has been noticed above that, in apocalyptic
literature, a Gentile mission was encouraged in Tobit 14:6-7,
Test Naph 8:3, Test Asher 7:3, Test Jos 19:11, Test Benj 9:2,
and Sib Or book 3: but this was by no means representative of
apocalyptic attitudes to Gentiles. See above, p. 111, on the
same ambivalence in the material assembled by Bamberger from
Rabbinic sources.

[56]See above, pp. 105-6, on these attempts to combine the
biblical narratives with Babylonian-Greek mythology in order
to confirm the truth of the Old Testament and to present
Judaism as the most ancient and reasonable wisdom.

[57]Hengel, *Judaism*, 1:90.

[58]This tradition appears in Josephus, *Ant* 1. 155-60.
In Philo, too, Abraham is the originator of astrology, which

is part of the essential knowledge of God (*Virt* 212-19). He
rules as a prophet-king in Damascus (ibid., 219), and the
heathen world acknowledges that he is a unique representative
of the divine: "thou art a king from God among us" (*Abr* 261).
In Eupolemus, too, Abraham belongs to the race of supermen,
discovers astrology and art, and teaches the Phoenicians
astrology and wisdom. See Eusebius, *Praep Evang* 9 (summaries
in Hengel, *Judaism*, 1:88-92). In Artapanus, Abraham teaches
Pharethones astrology (*Praep Evang* 9:18); and in Cleodemus
Malchus, Heracles marries a granddaughter of Abraham (see
Hengel, ibid., 1:74).

[59]See Georgi, *Gegner*, p. 64. Hengel, ibid., 1:90
notes this role of Abraham in Eupolemus, Aristobulus, Artapanus, and Josephus. But further, this association of Abraham with astrology made its mark on apocalyptic literature,
making astrology highly prized in Palestinian and Qumran
apocalyptic literature (p. 91). See below.

[60]So, in Jubilees 11:23, Abraham is the inventor of
the plow, and in Artapanus Abraham is placed alongside the
Greek hero Heracles, the bringer of divine order and human
prosperity (Eusebius, *Praep Evang* 9:18).

[61]Tiede notes that the image of wonder-worker is
stressed more in Josephus and Artapanus than in Philo. However, Philo still thinks in terms of the θεῖος ἀνήρ (*Virt*
177), but his natural theology has "taken over" miracle. See
above, pp. 105-6.

[62]Josephus *Ant* 1. 155. In the Genesis Apocryphon,
too, Abraham is the magician and wonder-worker who confounds
the sages of Egypt, and who alone can heal Pharaoh's plague
and exorcise the spirit. See Gaster, *Scriptures*, pp. 366-67.
A similar portrayal of Abraham is in Jubilees.

[63]Georgi, *Gegner*, pp. 147-48.

[64]Artapanus (in Eusebius, *Praep Evang* 9:18) and
Cleodemus Malchus (see Hengel, *Judaism*, 1:74).

[65]Artapanus, in Eusebius, *Praep Evang*, 9. 18-20;
Josephus *Ant* 4. 323-24.

[66]In Josephus, Moses, like Abraham, is the great
inventor; in Philo, the elements obey him as their master
(*Vit Mos* 1. 156). This tradition appears also in apocalyptic
literature. In Bar 59 God reveals to Moses "the measure of
fire, . . . the weight of the winds," etc. So, too, Wis Sol
13.

[67]Philo *Vit Mos* 1. 155-56. In *Virt* 177, Philo makes
Moses a θεῖος ἀνήρ, as does Josephus, *Ant* 3. 181-87.

[68]Josephus *Ant* 3. 180-82.

[69]So, in Philo, *Abr* 60, 275, etc., Abraham still is
the one who obeys all the laws of God.

[70]Sanders, *Paul*, pp. 90, 183-84.

[71]Comparing John 8:38, "We are Abraham's seed, and have never been in slavery . . ." to Matt 3:9, "Do not begin to say, . . . We have Abraham as our father. . . ."

[72]StrB, 1:121.

[73]Sanders, *Paul*, p. 424.

[74]Sanders, ibid., p. 137, also excludes this book from "Rabbinism," because of its perfectionist soteriology.

[75]Gunther, *Opponents*, among others, has suggested a connection between John the Baptist, apocalyptists such as the Qumran community, and Jewish-Christian sects. There are similarities between John and the Qumran group (asceticism, purification by water, prophecy, and eschatological expectations); and Baptist followers moved widely outside Palestine (for instance, the Baptist community at Ephesus). And of course, Jubilees is closely associated with the theology of Qumran. See Charlesworth, *Pseudepigrapha*, p. 143, etc. For Qumran as a reform movement, see, for instance, Fitzmyer, *Ebionites*, p. 222 (on criticism of the laxness of the Jerusalem priesthood in 1 QS and CD, and on Essene avoidance of the sanctuary in Josephus *Ant* 18. 1. 5).

[76]Holladay, *Theios Aner*, p. 235.

[77]Above, pp. 111-12.

[78]Above, pp. 96-97, on the demand that the apostle preach himself as a pneuma-self, etc.

[79]See above, pp. 78-82, on the significance of 3:1-5 as an *interrogatio*, and the function played by the terms ἐνάρχεσθαι and ἐπιτελεῖν.

CHAPTER EIGHT

TRADITIONS OF LAW

[1]See above, pp. 59-61, on 1:4, 4:5, and 6:13-14. δικαιοσύνη in Galatians is not just a forensic declaration, but principally life or salvation. See above, pp. 68, 71, etc., and Sanders, *Paul*, pp. 493-94.

[2]Hence this dispute involves eschatology and, by implication, Christology. See above, pp. 59-61, with authorities cited. Differences over eschatology were a chief cause of division in the early church, and of division between Paul and his opponents too. See Robinson, "Kerygma," pp. 122-23.

[3]See above, pp. 78-82, on ἐνάρχεσθαι and ἐπιτελεῖν; and below, pp. 122-23, on the way 3:1-4 is paralleled by 4:8-11, with its own mystery-expressions.

[4]Schmithals, *Paul*, pp. 30-33, on 3:1-5.

[5]See above, pp. 69-78, on 2:15-21.

[6]Foerster, "κληρονομία," *TDNT*, 3:784, concisely states Paul's four principal arguments against the opponents: Abraham was justified by faith (3:6-9); the promise was given to Abraham before the law was given, so no one can inherit by the law (3:15-18); the two covenants, the Abrahamic and the Mosaic, are antithetical in every way (4:21-31); and he who belongs to the Messiah is the true σπέρμα 'Αβραάμ (3:26-29).

[7]See the whole stress on consistency in the will of God in Paul's argument, and probably in the argument of the opponents, above, pp. 61-62. Also, see above, p. 62, on the salvation-historical nature of Paul's argument: Jesus has not broken the line of salvation-history, but stands in the line of promise that runs from Abraham.

[8]See δυνάμεις, 3:5.

[9]Duncan, *Galatians*, p. 114.

[10]This title was commonly given to Moses in Jewish literature outside the OT: *Ass Mos* 1:14, 3:12; Philo *Vit Mos* 3:19; perhaps Heb 8:6, 9:15, 12:24. See Charles, *Apocrypha and Pseudepigrapha*, 2:415; Lightfoot, *Galatians*, pp. 144-45.

[11]Schweitzer, *Mysticism*, pp. 68-69 suggests that Paul draws on Lev 26:46 and replaces Μωυσῆς with μεσίτης. The LXX of Deut 33:2 has angels present at the giving of the law, as does Acts 7:38, 53: Heb 2:2; Jos *Ant* 15. 136 (τὰ ὁσιώτατα τῶν ἐν τοῖς νόμοις δι' ἀγγέλων παρὰ τοῦ θεοῦ μαθόντων: but some feel that ἄγγελος means prophet here, e.g., W. D. Davies, "A Note on Josephus *Antiquities* 15. 136," *HTR* 47 [1954]:135-40); Jub 1:27-2:1 (where it is particularly "calendrical" laws that the "angel of the Presence" writes for Moses); and Pesiqta *Rabbati* 97a. Philo also has Moses receive the law from the powers rather than from God directly: see Goodenough, *Symbols*, 12:57, on *Som* 1. 139-43. Also the Jerusalem targums on Deut 33:2 add prominence to angels. Paul's logic here is that a mediator does not represent one; so the mediator did not represent God--but the angels. This makes logical the deduction of 4:9-10: obedience rendered to the law is in fact rendered to angels. So also Duncan, *Galatians*, pp. 114-15 (though he cautions that there are at least 300 interpretations of Gal 3:20); see also Lietzmann, on 3:19; Schoeps, *Paul*, p. 183; and Mussner, *Galater*, pp. 247-49, who notes the syllogism here: a mediator is never a mediator for one; God is one; *ergo* the law, which came via a mediator, is not from one (God).

[12]See above, pp. 182-83, on the way this passage breaks up in terms of "mots crochets."

[13]See below, p. 152. This tradition appears in Philo, Rabbinic sources, and Samaritan sources.

[14]Mussner, *Galater*, pp. 248-49, also suggests that this is the dynamic involved in 3:19-20.

[15]Bligh, *Galatians*, p. 277. For Paul, Abraham is the great figure of the Old Testament, and Moses is an interloper. Lightfoot, *Galatians*, has noted the "adventitious character" of the law implied by προστιθέναι (3:19), which parallels ἐπιδιατασσεται, 3:15, and παρερχέσθαι in Rom 5:20.

[16]Anthony Tyrrel Hanson, *Studies in Paul's Technique and Theology* (London: SPCK, 1974), p. 67, points out the particular parallel between 3:11 and 3:12. In the latter verse, referring to the "life" of the law, the stress falls on ὁ ποιήσας αὐτὰ ζήσεται ἐν αὐτοῖς, so that in 3:11 the stress must also fall on ζήσεται.

[17]See Sanders, *Paul*, p. 427, on the different way this verse is used in Romans and Galatians. Also, see above, p. 75.

[18]In Galatians, unlike Romans, nothing intercedes between the original purpose of the law and its historical function. So Drane, "Tradition," pp. 169-70. See Stoike, "Law of Christ," pp. 128-30, on the contrast between Rom 7:10 and Gal 3:21.

[19]Paul also argues here on the basis of the Christ-event. In the death of Christ, law and life are revealed as opposites (3:10-14). Hab 2:4 is used to undergird this assertion. The cross reveals that law brings death; Hab 2:4 says that faith brings life. This argument is then tied into the one concerning Abraham and Moses. The promise comes through Abraham, which Christ fulfilled by making us heirs; the law comes through Moses, which Christ fulfilled by dying.

[20]On the precise meaning of διαθήκη in 3:14, 17, see Burton, *Galatians*, pp. 501-5: Paul may move between "will," "testament," and "covenant" in the OT sense, and the term in 3:17 seems undoubtedly to mean "covenant." However, for the essential argument, the distinction is not important. 4:24 is most naturally understood as "covenant" in the OT sense.

[21]Behm, "διαθήκη," *TDNT*, 2:129. "As a valid will cannot be contested or altered by additions, so the promise of God . . . cannot be invalidated by the law which came later."

[22]Lightfoot, *Galatians*, p. 143, concludes that χάρις, (3:19) probably infers "to create transgressions"; where there is no law, there is no transgression (Rom 4:15), compared to Rom 3:20, 7:7, 13, 5:20. This meaning seems required by Gal 3:21, 22.

[23]Commenting on ἀθετεῖ ἤ ἐπιδιατάσσεται (3:15), Lightfoot, ibid., p. 140, observes that the doctrine of the

Judaisers is presented virtually as the annulling of the
promise and the violating of the covenant.

[24]Paul refers to διαθήκη at Gal 3:15, 17, 4:24, Rom
9:4, Eph 1:27, 2:12, 1 Cor 11:25, and 2 Cor 3:6, 14. The
clearest contrast of covenants outside Galatians is in 2 Cor
3:6, 14, where he refers to the "old" and the "new" covenants.
But here it is the Mosaic and Christ covenants which are contrasted, and the Mosaic covenant is treated slightly differently. Moses is a mystagogue who sees God; it is implied
that the stone-law comes from God; and the chief problem is
with the Israelites, who are not spiritual enough, so that
Moses must be veiled. There is a continuity of δόξα between
the Mosaic and the Christ covenants. The Mosaic covenant is
God's διαθήκη, it has its own δόξα, and it comes from the
same God as the new διαθήκη. Behm, "διαθήκη," TDNT, 2:130.
In Rom 9:4-5 the διαθῆκαι (plural!) are numbered among the
many advantages of Israel in salvation-history and are all
revelations of God and His ἐπαγγελίαι (plural!).

[25]It is also explicable in terms of the opponents'
eschatology, and their attachment of law to cosmology. When
Paul says Christ has brought the new age and release from the
old κόσμος or αἰών, this automatically makes Christ and law
antithetical in the opponents' cosmological terms.

[26]See Conzelmann, Theology, pp. 169-70, on the different handling of salvation-history in Galatians and Romans.
In Galatians the "dark" period of history is only from Moses
to Christ; and, whereas in Rom 5:12-21 the "dark" period is
especially the rule of sin, in Galatians it is especially the
rule of law, the παιδαγωγός, the ἐπίτροποι καὶ οἰκονόμοι, and
the στοιχεῖα τοῦ κόσμου. See above, p. 84.

[27]Law itself is the παιδαγωγός, the tyrant. See
Lightfoot, Galatians, p. 143, who gives four ways in which
the law in its whole character and history is negative.
Elsewhere law is a spiritual, holy, good gift from God (Rom
7:11-14) that has fallen into the wrong hands (Rom 7:11, law
came into a situation in which sin was already "lord"; also
Rom 5:12) and functions negatively not because of its inherent
"nature" but because of its "context," sin, flesh (Rom 8:4).
Charles Harold Dodd, New Testament Studies (New York: Scribner, 1952), pp. 123-24, writes, "Whereas, in Galatians, it
(the law) is the instrument of the angelic powers for the
enslavement of God's people--an enslavement which He per-
mitted until 'the fulness of time' (3:24, 4:4) . . . In
Romans it is in itself holy, spiritual, just, and good, but
because of the weakness of the flesh it was incapable of
effecting its true purpose, to give life (7:12, 14, 8:3)."
Stoike, "Law of Christ," pp. 99-101, contrasts the positive
portrayal of the law in Romans (God's [7:12, 25, 8:7]; fails
because of man [7:14, 8:3-4]; is just, good, and spiritual
[7:13-14]; and gives rise to Abraham's seed, just as faith
does [4:15]) with the negative portrayal in Galatians (given
by angels [3:19]; fails because of its inherent nature [3:3,
4:3, 9]; has a curse [3:13]; is impotent [3:21]; is temporary,
[3:9, 18, 23]; is a cruel taskmaster [3:24]; and Abraham's

seed springs only from faith [3:7, 8-9]).   On the unique presentation of the law and justification by faith in Galatians,
see Sanders, *Paul*, pp. 495-97, quoting a forthcoming book by
Davies, in which the doctrine in Galatians is characterized
as sharply polemical.

[28]Koester, *Trajectories*, pp. 147-48.

[29]See above, pp. 112-13.

[30]John G. Gager, *Moses in Greco-Roman Paganism*,
(Nashville: Abingdon Press, 1972), has collected data on the
positive images of Moses in pagan writings.   His appeal was
particularly as lawgiver, leader of the Exodus, and practi-
tioner of magic.   See pp. 134-61 for primary sources on Moses
as a wonder-worker and the strong appeal of this image to the
Hellenistic world.   Moses' contest with and vanquishing of the
Egyptian in the Exodus also glorified him in pagan eyes.   In
this role he was especially the "leader of superior *theological* wisdom" (p. 132).   Gager notes that these appealing
images of Moses to pagans came predominantly from the apolo-
getics of the Jews themselves--which is borne out by studies
such as that of Tiede (*Charismatic*), who has summarized the
image of Moses in Philo (pp. 101-37), Eupolemos (138-40),
Aristobulus (140-46), Artapanus (146-77), and Josephus (207-
40).

[31]See above, pp. 112-13.

[32]See above, pp. 64-65.

[33]The weight of 1:10, 2:3-4, and 5:11 strongly suggests that Paul is being charged with vacillation over the
question of circumcision, and the grounds are the circumcision of some of his co-workers--perhaps even Titus!   See
Lightfoot, *Galatians*, pp. 62-63, Longenecker, *Paul*, p. 220;
Weiss, *Primitive Christianity*, 1:271-73; Georgi, *Geschichte*,
pp. 14-15.

[34]Stoike, "Law of Christ," p. 201.

[35]Markus Barth, *Ephesians*, The Anchor Bible, 2 vols.
(New York: Doubleday, 1974), 1:287-88, 244-48.   He notes that
"works of law" are mentioned only where imposition of legal
elements on Gentiles is discussed, and the term cannot refer
to a jewish doctrine.   The contexts where the phrase occurs
only with selections of Jewish law are Gal 2:3-4, 12-13
and 4:10.   Stoike, "Law of Christ," pp. 149-52, notes
that the exact phrase occurs six times in Galatians and only
twice more in the rest of Paul's epistles.   This suggests
that it should be defined principally out of Galatians.   Furthermore, five of the six occurrences in Galatians occur in
2:16 and 3:1-5, indicating how the expression is bound up
with the debate concerning the law and justification.

[36]Barth, ibid., pp. 247-48, feels that there are no
significant parallels to this term outside Paul's letters.
However, others see some suggestive parallels in Qumran (the

phrase תורה מצשי is found in 4 Q Flor 1:7, where it is linked
with cultic activity) and apocalyptic literature (similar
expressions occur in 2 Bar 57:2; Test Lev 19:11; and Test
Naph 2:6), where cultic or calendrical law is very much an
issue (see below). See E. Lohmeyer, "Gesetzwerke," in
Probleme Paulinischer Theologie (Stuttgart: Kohlhammer, 1955):
66-67; Bertram, "ἔργον," *TDNT*, 2:645; and Stoike, "Law of
Christ," p. 150.

[37]Bultmann, *Theology*, 1:260: ". . . Paul has specific
occasion to speak of the ritual law . . . in Galatians. . . ."

[38]Against Bligh, *Galatians*, pp. 292-96, who concludes:
". . . the early exegetical tradition (of Justin, Irenaeus,
and the Didascalia Apostolorum) was correct: in v. 19 St Paul
is speaking, not about the whole of the Mosaic law, but only
about the ceremonial laws added after Israel had sinned." In
fact, one of the first to use this distinction was the Gnostic
Ptolemy in his *Letter to Flora*.

[39]See above, p. 13, and Schweitzer's observation
on the difference between Acts 15 and Paul regarding law.
The former attempts to deal with the issue in terms of specific precepts, but Paul deals with it in terms of theological principles.

[40]Bultmann, *Theology*, 1:260: "Paul, . . . did not
define the nature of obedience under the demand of God by contrasting the ethical demands and the cultic-ritual demands and
by criticising the latter from the standpoint of the former. .
. . Thinking Jewishly, he does not evaluate the cultic-ritual
commandments in regard to their content, but considers them
only in regard to the fact that they, like the ethical commandments, are demands. Nevertheless, it is apparent from the
matter-of-fact way in which he names the ethical demands of
the decalogue (Rom 13:8-10, Gal 5:14) as the abiding content
of the law obligatory even for the Christian, that the identity
of meaning in the cultic-ritual and the ethical demands exists
only for the man who has not yet come to faith, and that in
faith itself an unconsciously working principle of criticism
is provided." Barth, *Ephesians*, p. 288, comments: "The sharp
distinction of cultic and moral laws is neither biblical nor
Jewish nor true of the history of religions."

[41]Bultmann, *Theology*, 1:259: "By νόμος . . . Paul
(usually) understands the OT law or the whole OT conceived as
law. . . ." Note 3:22, ἡ γράφη. In 4:21, νόμος equals the
life-ordering norm of the OT. See Mussner, *Galater*, pp.
317-18.

[42]Those laws which stress the difference between Jew
and Gentile, and the superiority of Jews: see above on
'Ιουδαΐζειν. Circumcision made Jews the elite people of God
(StrB, 4:32) and promised a perfection appealing to Hellenists
(Jewett, "Agitators," p. 201).

[43]For instance, Josephus *Apion* 2. 282 on the appeal of
the Jewish calendar to the Gentile world.

[44]In Jub 1:27-2:1, and 1 Enoch 33:3 it is particularly
the laws of calendrical observance that the "angel of the
presence" writes for Moses. See Meinrad Limbeck, *Die Ordnung
des Heils* (Dusseldorf: Patmos-Verlag, 1971), p. 64.

[45]See above, p. 115.

[46]Andrew John Bandstra, *The Law and the Elements of
the World* (Kampen: J. H. Kok, 1964), pp. 48-54. There is an
essential relationship between the reference to the στοιχεῖα
τοῦ κόσμου, and Christ's defeat of the κόσμος. Reicke, "The
Law," p. 265, notes that Paul relates the στοιχεῖα τοῦ κόσμου
to the fallen world. So, in Col 2:20, to die to the κόσμος is
to die to the στοιχεῖα τοῦ κόσμου. The elements have cosmological and theological significance.

[47]As does Bandstra, p. 54.

[48]See Bornkamm, "Colossians," p. 124.

[49]So, in Colossians 2, the στοιχεῖα τοῦ κόσμου
(verses 8, 20) are paralleled to ἀρχαὶ καὶ ἐξουσίαι (verse 15).
See Bornkamm, ibid., pp. 123-24. Even Delling, "στοιχεῖον,"
TDNT, 6:685, admits that in Galatians στοιχεῖον is a strongly
negative term: "The very negative judgment of στοιχεῖα by
Paul is not sufficiently brought out when a reference is seen
to the first principles of human religion."

[50]And in 3:24-25, Israel's experience is only one of
slavery to the παιδαγωγός.

[51]A term characteristic of Jewish polemic against
heathen false gods. See Duncan, *Galatians*, pp. 114-15, and
Conzelmann, *Theology*, p. 233.

[52]See Reicke, "The Law," p. 274. This becomes the
most difficult expression of the passage to account for.

[53]See Duncan, *Galatians*, pp. 134-36; and Delling,
"στοιχεῖον," *TDNT*, 6:684: "Among the στοιχεῖα τοῦ κόσμου in
Galatians 4 is on the one side the torah with its statutes
(4:3-5), and then on the other side the world of false gods
whom the recipients once served, 4:8-11. The expression στοιχεῖα τοῦ κόσμου thus draws attention to something common to
Jewish and pagan religion . . . bondage to the στοιχεῖα."

[54]Noted by Bandstra, *The Law*, p. 124.

[55]Stressed by Bandstra, ibid., pp. 63-67, 100.

[56]See also above on the central place in the whole
argument of periods of history, culminating in the cross
(4:4); Koester, *Trajectories*, pp. 146-47; and Sanders, *Paul*,
pp. 483-84.

[57]Bandstra notes, after an examination of the use of
στοιχεῖον in ancient writers, that it is essentially a "formal"
word. In and of itself it carries no particular content but

has specific meaning in terms of its immediate context (*The Law*, p. 33). Bussmann, *Themen*, pp. 58-59, agrees.

[58]It has already been shown above, pp. 81-82, that 4:8-11 is tied into the whole argument of 3:6-4:11 by "mots crochets"; and that 4:8-11 is essentially a restatement of 3:1-5, the *causa* put into the terms of the Galatians' apostasy from Christianity to the new religion.

[59]Bussmann, *Themen*, pp. 58-74, analyzes the τότε μὲν (4, 8) . . . νῦν δὲ (4:9) sequence as the antithesis of before and after conversion, using the terminology of Hellenistic-Jewish missionary propaganda (not knowing and knowing God). He has not pushed as far as Arthur Darby Nock, *Early Gentile Christianity and its Hellenistic Background* (New York: Harper & Row, 1964), who notes the special significance of "known by God," as in CH 10. 5, "God is not ignorant of man: He knows him thoroughly and would be known of him. For it is only knowledge of God that brings salvation to man."

[60]Mussner, *Galater*, p. 297. See above on the law becoming an issue precisely at the point of calendrical observance.

[61]1 Enoch shows great concern for all the laws of the luminaries of heaven (the sun [ch. 72:1], the moon [ch. 73:1], and others [ch. 74:1]) given in the heavenly revelation of Uriel, which concludes, "And he showed me all the laws for these for every day, and for every season of bearing rule, and for every year, and for its going forth, and for the order prescribed to it every month and every week . . ." (79:2). The language is even closer to Galatians in 82:4, 7-10 (for the lights, months, feasts, years and days did Uriel show me . . .). There is a similar calendrical concern in Jub 2:9, "And God appointed the sun to be a great sign on the earth for days and for sabbaths and for months and for feasts and for years and for sabbaths of years and for jubilees and for all seasons of the year." Also 1:10-14, 6:34-38. Davies, "Scrolls," p. 167, notes, "The phrase which appears in Gal 4:10 recalls exactly 1 QS 1:14" (which reads, "They must not deviate by a single step from carrying out the orders of God at the times appointed for them; they must neither advance the statutory times nor postpone the prescribed season." The precise calculations of the calendar were a leading issue between the sect and Jerusalem Judaism. See below). See also 1 QS 9:26-10:8, 1 QM 14:12-14, 10:15, 14:13-15, 1 QH 1:24. In Jub 1:27-2:1, the heavenly laws written down by the angel are in particular laws of calendrical observance.

[62]Limbeck, *Ordnung*, pp. 65-72. Both man and the elements of nature stand under the same rule of God, and therefore the same law. Knowledge of true cosmic order is essential for salvation (1 En 82:1-4), and there is a mystical connection between the stars, the angels and the righteousness of Israel (1 En 80:1-8, Ps Sol 18:10, Ass Mos 10:9, and 2 Bar 51:10).

[63]See above, pp. 116-19, and also the place of angels in the opponents' self-understanding (Gal 1:8-9).

[64]Reicke, "Law," p. 262.   Paul builds on certain ideas already present, but gives the angels a negative instead of a positive significance.

[65]Ibid., p. 262.

[66]The two passages are connected by Schlier, Reicke, Bornkamm, etc. Schweizer, "Christianity of the Circumcised," pp. 245-60, correctly notes differences: the Jewish character is stronger in Galatians.

[67]See Col 1:19-20, 2:6-15 and the particular presentation of the cross--not a *kenosis* and humiliation as in Phil 2:8-11, but the climax of a life filled with all the fulness of God that triumphs in the conquest of the powers of the cosmos. See Lohse, *Colossians*, p. 3, 99, 114, etc.

[68]Ibid., p. 99.

[69]Ibid., p. 99.

[70]Bornkamm, "Colossians," p. 124.

[71]See how 2:9 (ὅτι ἐν αὐτῷ κατοικεῖ πᾶν τὸ πλήρωμα) is polemical and antithetical, denying the claims the opponents made for the στοιχεῖα, Bornkamm, ibid., p. 124.

[72]Lohse, *Colossians*, p. 99: "στοιχεῖα τοῦ κόσμου" must have played a special role in the teaching of the "philosophers." After adapting so many terms of the opposition to his own purposes (θρησκεία, πλήρωμα, αρχαί καί ἐξουσίαι, ἐθελοθρησκία, etc; Bornkamm, "Colossians," p. 127), the author of Colossians would not be likely to crown his rebuttal with a phrase that had been suddenly introduced into the debate out of the blue.

[73]Bornkamm, ibid., p. 131. It is clear, in Colossians, that the festivals do belong to the heretics. The syncretistic nature of the heresy is evident from its combination of these calendrical observances, which derive from Judaism, with taboos and ascetic requirements which cannot be derived from Jewish law.

[74]Schweizer, "Christianity of the Circumcised," p. 225. It is probably no coincidence that the Stichwort appears only in connection with a legalism which expressed itself among other things in a keeping of feast-days.

[75]See Delling, "στοιχεῖον," *TDNT*, 6:672-83; Schlier, *Galater*, (1962), pp. 191-92, on 4:3; Bandstra, *The Law*, pp. 31-46; Lohse, *Colossians*, pp. 97-98; Stoike, "Law of Christ," pp. 156-68.

[76]Delling, ibid., p. 684.

[77]For the texts, see Delling, "στοιχεῖον," *TDNT*, 6:672-73.

[78]Ibid., p. 673; Charles Harold Dodd, *The Bible and the Greeks* (London: Hodder and Stoughton, 1954), p. 231.

[79]For instance, Apuleius, *Metamorphoses*, 11:5, 1: the one redeemed by Isis is no longer subject to εἱμαρμένη because she is the mother of the στοιχεῖα. See also Hans Dieter Betz, "Schöpfung und Erlösung im hermetischen Fragment 'Kore Kosmou,'" *ZTK* 63 (1966):177-78; and "The Mithras Inscriptions of Santa Prisca and the New Testament," *NT* 10 (1968):64-66. There is a strong suggestion in these sources that they are personal forces.

[80]Philo, *Vit Con* 3; *Conf* 173: "Certain persons, impressed by the nature of each of the worlds, have not only deified them as wholes, but have also deified the most beautiful of their component parts, which they shamefully call gods." Alongside this must be placed the polemic against worship of natural phenomena in Wisdom 13:1-2.

[81]Philo, *Heres* 300-2; *Migr* 178-79.

[82]Herm 4. 13. 3; Tatian *Or Grace* 21. 3; Aristid *Apol* 7. 4; Athen *Suppl* 10. 3; Clem Alex *Prot* 64., *Strom* 1. 5. 6; 52. 24. See Delling, "στοιχεῖον," *TDNT*, 6:677. Lohse, *Colossians*, p. 99, commenting on such references, says, " . . . it cannot be objected that the meaning 'stars,' 'elementary spirits,' or 'spirits of the stars' is not attested in any non-Christian text that can be dated with certainty in pre-Pauline times. . . . It is quite legitimate to make conclusions about earlier traditions on the basis of later witnesses, especially in view of the fact that the combination of angels and heavenly powers is already present in Jewish apocalyptic texts. . . ."

[83]Bultmann, *Primitive Christianity*, p. 154.

[84]Richard Reitzenstein, *Poimandres* (Darmstadt: Wissenschaftliche Buchgesellschaft, 1966), pp. 75-79, notes the roots of religious fatalism and concern for εἱμαρμένη in astrology, in Judaism as well as in Paganism.

[85]Delling, "στοιχεῖον," *TDNT*, 6:679. See the above quote from Philo, *Conf* 173, where the stars and their "component parts" are closely equated. See also *Opif* 27. Wis Sol 13:1-2 also links together the worship of the stars and the elements. In later antiquity, στοιχεῖον comes to mean a star or a constellation: see literature, Delling, p. 681; also Lohse, *Colossians*, p. 97.

[86]Dodd, *The Bible*, p. 138.

[87]Ibid., p. 231. Now, E. Schweizer, "Versöhnung des Alls: Kol, 1:20," in *Jesus Christus in Historie und Theologie*, ed. G. Strecker (Tübingen: J. C. B. Mohr, 1975), pp. 487-501,

concludes that the setting of τὰ στοιχεῖα is the world of
astrological dualism, not Judaism seen as a preparation for
the gospel (against Bandstra).

[88]On dating Poimandres, see Arthur Darby Nock and
A. J. Festugière, *Hermes Trismegistus. Corpus Hermeticum*
(Paris: Societe d'edition "Les Belles Lettres," 1954-60),
pp. xxxvii-xxxviii. The earliest attestation is to sections
31-32 in P. Berol. 9794, dating from the beginning of the
third century. Dodd, *The Bible and the Greeks*, pp. 201-9,
argues that the text was probably established about 250 AD,
though much of the material in it is earlier. He notes kin-
ship to Philo, Wisdom of Solomon, 1 Enoch, and other material
dating from 50 BCE-CE 100; and the developed Gnostic systems
of Valentinus, to be dated 130-140 AD, seem to be later
developments of the gnosis of Poimandres, putting much of
the material of the tractate in the first century.

[89]G. W. MacRae, "Nag Hammadi," *IDBS*, 618. The tractate Eugnostos, which shows no Christian influence, has been
taken over and Christianized in the Sophia of Jesus Christ.
Similarly, the Apocalypse of Adam, showing no Christianisms
but a developed cosmology, must be dated as early as the
first century CE. It may have been given a Christianized form
in the Gospel of the Egyptians. The Letter of Peter which he
sent to Philip also reveals a later Christianizing of an
earlier, pre-Christian Gnostic cosmology. Several have seen
in the Apocryphon of John, which must have existed before
Irenaeus' *Against Heresies* (Robinson, Nag Hammadi, p. 98) a
Gnostic attempt at criticism of the anthropos-myth in Poimandres (Richard Reitzenstein, *Hellenistic Mystery-Religions*,
trans. John E. Steely [Pittsburgh: Pickwick Press, 1978],
p. 62) again suggesting the very early date of the material
in this last tractate.

[90]Dodd, *The Bible*, p. 140.

[91]On the *stoikeia* in Galatians as personal powers,
see Schlier, Duncan, Mussner, Betz, Reicke, Bruce, etc.

[92]On the degree of Gnosticism in Corinth, see Conzelmann, *1 Corinthians*, pp. 14-15; and R. McL. Wilson, "How
Gnostic were the Corinthians?" *NTS* 19 (1972-73):65-74. Both
agree that Schmithals, *Gnosticism in Corinth*, takes an extreme
position.

[93]See the dialogical use of Gnostic terms in 1 Cor
2:6-12, etc. The Pauline tradition can cope well with Gnosticism in Colossians. This suggests that it is unlikely that
the opponents in Galatia were Gnostic.

[94]Conzelmann, *1 Corinthians*, pp. 8-9, 16, etc., and
against Drane, who has misunderstood the pragmatic approach
Paul takes to ethical problems in Corinth, and his refusal to
recognize any fixed norm other than the norm of the cross.

[95]See 1:10-17, 3:4-15, 2:10-15, etc. Also George W.
MacRae, "Anti-Dualistic Polemic in 2 Cor 4:6," *Studia
Evangelica* 4 (1968):420-31.

[96]See Pagels, *Paul*, pp. 5, 162.

[97]As in Jub 1:27-2:1.

[98]Bultmann, *Theology*, 1:268, sees Paul's use of the myth of the giving of the law by angels as an attempt to keep the God of Israel clear of any charges against the law. This indicates how neither the opponents (who must exalt the law as a direct revelation from God) nor Paul (who absolves the OT God of any inferior revelation) could be called "Gnostic" in the second-century sense.

[99]Betz, "Problem," pp. 144-45, notes the un-Gnostic character of the traditions which regard the elements of the universe positively, such as the one in CH 4, which seems to have affinities with Jewish apocalyptic. See also Dodd, *The Bible*, pp. 229, 136.

[100]See above, p. 9.

[101]See Jacques E. Ménard, *L'Evangile selon Philippe* (Paris: Letouzey et Ané, 1967).

[102]Pagels, *Paul*, p. 110.

[103]The Gospel of Philip uses in a Gnostic way Paul's assessment of Israel in Galatians 3 and 4, combining the Gnostic demiurge, the demiurge of Greek myth, and the God of the Jews, in an exegesis of Genesis 3, 55 (*NHL*, 133), 63 (*NHL*, 138). The law becomes the tree of knowledge, given by the demiurge, to bring death to the human race.

[104]Pagels, *Paul*, pp. 5, 162. Paul is neither Gnostic nor anti-Gnostic.

[105]Hengel, *Judaism*, 1:217. Both Palestinian and "Hellenistic" Judaism shared in this movement. See above, pp. 91-92. For instance, Aristobulus and the Wisdom of Solomon share a concept of inspiration, ibid., 1:136. Within this movement one can speak of "gnosis," e.g., in Philo, apocalyptic, and Qumran (ibid., 1:228-32). But this is not strictly "Gnosticism," though the latter shares in this movement.

[106]As in Prov 8, Wis Sol 7, and Ecclus 24 etc. See von Rad, *Wisdom*, pp. 144-46. The revelation of wisdom is the revelation of the order of the universe and of the stars, and even of the course of history. Wilckens, "σοφία," *TDNT*, 7:504.

[107]Sirach 24:1-12. See Wilckens, "σοφία," *TDNT*, 7:503; Moore, *Judaism*, 1:264; and Hengel, *Judaism*, 1:168, who notes that this makes the idea begin in Palestine.

[108]See Ps Sol 17; Sirach 19:20, 21:11, 34:8, 24. Hengel, ibid., 1:157, notes that all the phenomena in the world, and their ordering, are an expression of the "wisdom of God"; and the individual who accepts the call to walk in God's way receives a share in the cosmic wisdom.

[109]Hengel, ibid., 1:155.

[110]The central demand of the apostle-tradition, the demand for ἀποκαλύψεις and self-proclamation as a pneuma-self, grows directly out of this doctrine of revelation and inspiration. See above, pp. 99-100.

[111]*Vit Mos* 1. 158.

[112]*Praem* 2.

[113]*Vit Mos* 1. 158-59, *Virt* 177.

[114]See *Vit Mos* 2. 118-22, 123-26, 133-35; *Cong* 116-21; *Decal* 102-5, etc., on the connection between the commandments and astrology.

[115]*Opif* 3.

[116]*Vit Mos* 1. 162 (Moses is the law personified).

[117]*Praem* 2.

[118]*Vit Mos* 1. 158. See Erwin R. Goodenough, *An Introduction to Philo Judaeus* (New York: Barnes and Noble, 1963), pp. 148-49.

[119]The master of the world is the truest lawgiver, and to follow the law is to live in accordance with the universe (*Vit Mos* 2. 48, 52; *Opif* 3). The enemies of the law are the enemies of nature and the universe (*Vit Mos* 2. 53, 285); the observance of the Sabbath keeps man in harmony with nature (ibid., 211-12); the temple is in fact an exact reflection of the cosmos (ibid., 2. 88, *Cong* 117).

[120]Philo uses the Platonic doctrine of the four elements, (*Opif* 52, 109, *Cher* 127, etc.). They are the material from which the cosmos was compounded. In fact, they are the instruments of God (*Vit Mos* 1. 155-57). Therefore, in the "miracles" of Moses, the elements are obeying the lawgiver, and Moses himself (*Vit Mos* 2. 154, 267). God gave Moses a share in His sovereignty over the elements (ibid., 1. 156). Philo rejects "miracles" in a popular sense, and seeks natural causes for them. See Tiede, *Charismatic*, p. 240. But in another sense, his natural theology has removed the distinction between the ordinary and the miraculous. What appears on the one hand to be a wonder, on the other is quite natural. See Georgi, *Gegner*, pp. 155-56.

[121]Betz, "Problem," pp. 146-47, notes Philo's vacillation regarding the elements. He has the Chaldeans see the true harmony between heavenly and earthly: but also has Moses disagree with their divinising of fate and necessity (*Migr* 178-79). In *Vit Con* 3 he opposes the identification of the στοιχεῖα as Greek deities; but on the other hand he can say that heaven is the dwelling place of the astral deities (*Opif* 27).

[122]See *Abr* 69, 71 on Abraham the astrologer; and *Vit Mos* 2. 118-22, 123-26, 133-35, etc., on Mosaic religion and astrology. He can even refer to the stars as divine beings, ψυχαί . . . ἀκήρατοί τε καὶ θεῖαι (*Gig* 8, *Migr* 263).

[123]*Conf* 173; *Heres* 300-12; *Migr* 178-79.

[124]Goodenough, *Introduction*, pp. 82-83, notes this incongruity in Philo's scheme. He does not deny the existence of lesser gods, but only denies that they should be worshipped (*Decal* 53).

[125]*Vit Con* 3.

[126]For instance, Josephus, *Ant* 13. 172, τὸ δὲ τῶν Εσσηνῶν γένος πάντην τὴν εἱμαρμένην κυρίαν ἀποφαίνεται, καὶ μηδὲν ὃ μὴ κατ' ἐκείνης ψῆφον ἀνυρώποις ἀπαντᾶ. See Richard Reitzenstein, *Poimandres* (Darmstadt: Wissenschaftliche Buchgesellschaft, 1966), p. 75. Hengel, *Judaism*, 1:236, commenting on a parallel report in Josephus *Bell* 2. 128, says, "the symbolic significance of the sun in Essenism could at least be understood by the Jewish observer." Perhaps he could have better said, "misunderstood."

[127]See Goodenough, *Symbols*, 2:168-69, 203 (commenting on Wis Sol 13:1-2, 4 Macc 14:7, 17:5). Jews were wearing magic amulets as early as 2 Macc 12:32-45. In volume 12, p. 164, he comments on the four portraits of Moses at Dura-Europos: in the last, Moses stands under the arch of heaven in which are the sun, the moon, and the seven stars. He summarizes some magical material on pp. 62-63. Note that it is not only Essenes who do homage to εἱμαρμένη, but Pharisees (Hippol 9. 4, Epiphaneus 1. 16. 2) and Sadducees (Josephus *Ant* 13. 172). See Reitzenstein, ibid., pp. 73-79.

[128]So Reicke, "The Law," p. 273, comments that the law-tradition in Philo is close to that of apocalyptic literature.

[129]See Josephus *Ant* 3. 181-87, on the wonders worked by Moses and his defeat of the Egyptian magicians. Moses is here a θεῖος ἀνήρ. This characteristic is even more prominent in Artapanus: see Tiede, *Charismatic*, pp. 146-47.

[130]See above, p. 282, note 66, on Moses' genius for invention.

[131]Josephus *Apion* 2. 279.

[132]Josephus *Ant* 3. 75-78, 88.

[133]Aristobulus presents the same interest in the divine ordering of creation in terms of the Sabbath. To him it reveals the principle of the number seven which orders the cosmos. The entire natural process is shaped after the structure of seven, which permeates and orders the world and is the basis of the human capacity for knowledge and wisdom. *Judaism*, 1:166.

^{134}Josephus *Bell* 5. 213; *Ant* 3. 183, "The tapestries
woven of four materials denote the natural elements (τὴν τῶν
στοιχείων φύσιν)." See above, p. 129. In *Ant* 3. 181-83, the
tabernacle has cosmic significance, and it is made clear that
this meaning was intended by Moses himself. Holladay, *Theios
Aner*, pp. 82-83, suggests that, behind this tabernacle allegory
of Philo and Josephus, lies a common tradition, and a Palestinian tradition at that. He gives Rabbinic parallels to many
details in the allegory. The Most Holy Place symbolizes
heaven, earth, and the sea; the seven-branched candlestick
symbolizes the seven planets, etc. In this allegory, νόμος
for Josephus comes to have cosmic proportions. Man, being
κοσμοπόλιτης, must order his life by cosmic νόμος.

^{135}This does not seem to be an "apologetic" theology
of law, but a law-tradition common to Judaism in both Palestine and the Diaspora, here put to "apologetic" use.

^{136}All of Jubilees is an esoteric revelation to Moses
on Sinai. See also 2 Bar 4:2-7, chap. 59, Ps Philo 11:15-12:1,
19:8-16. See also below, p. 152; and Meeks, "Moses," pp. 356-
64.

^{137}Limbeck, *Ordnung*, pp. 64-70. The stars of heaven
are obedient to the Torah (1 Enoch 33:3); and the law-keeping
of nature is a pattern for the law-keeping of man (1 Enoch
2:2). Thus the goal of revelation is to bring man into conformity to the order of the cosmos (1 Enoch 36:4, 41:17).
This strong sense of relationship between earth and heaven,
law of God, and cosmic order, is because creation is not seen
as spiritless impersonal reality, but as a world in which the
elements are ruled by angels and spirits, the "middle beings"
who interpose between God and man. Fruitfulness and prosperity
are bound up with observance of calendrical, cosmic, and
angelic law, 1 Enoch 80:2-8, 82:4-6. There is also an eschatological relationship between the cosmos and obedience to law.
The end of time is determined by the stars (Sib Or 3:81-90;
2 Enoch 65:7; 1 Enoch 72:1; Jubilees 50:5); and if one is to
"know God," and be prepared for the consummation of the age,
one must also know the cosmological mysteries. In Jub 1:26-
29 the "times" of God are bound up with preparation for the
time "when heaven and earth shall be renewed." See also
1 Enoch 72:1.

^{138}All this movement will be concealed from sinners,
and the result will be disastrous for them (1 Enoch 80-82).
The ordering of the cosmos has meaning for salvation, because
the stars (angels) and the righteousness of Israel are in
mystical relationship (Ps Sol 18:10; Ass Mos 10:8-12; 2 Bar
51:10). See Limbeck, *Ordnung*, pp. 65-69.

^{139}The righteous are given a knowledge of this order,
but the wicked are not, and consequently "evil shall be multi-
plied upon them. . . ." (1 Enoch 80:8).

^{140}There is a direct relationship between the laws of
heaven and the laws of God (1 Enoch 2:2). Knowledge of order

is bound up with the Torah in 2 Bar 48:1-24. After surveying
the terrifying cosmos which is governed by God, Baruch
declares, ". . . the law which is amongst us will aid us, and
the surpassing wisdom which is in us will help us."

[141]In Jub 1:27-2:1, the heavenly laws given Moses by
the angel are laws of calendrical observance. See also
2 Baruch 59, where God reveals to Moses the secrets of cosmic
order; and Wis Sol 13.

[142]In Jub 1-2, 50, the Sabbath and the feast of weeks
had been celebrated in heaven before they were given to Moses
and were thus an expression of the heavenly ordering of time.
In Jub 2:9, 17-19 angels keep the Sabbath along with men; and
in 4:15-20, God's angels descend and teach justice, righteousness, and wisdom--and days, months, and Sabbaths. On the
intense calendrical concern in Jubilees, see Joseph M. Baumgarten, *Studies in Qumran Law* (Leiden: Brill, 1977), pp. 101-
14.

[143]See above, p. 130.

[144]Along with the eschatology of the imminence of the
age to come goes an intensified demand that Israel be obedient
to the law of God. See 4 Ezra 7:20, 45, 72 (the reason the
nations are to be judged is that they had the law and did not
keep it), 7:88-90 (future rewards are for those who keep the
Torah), 9:36, 37 (the law abides for ever), etc. See also
2 Bar 84:2-4, 48:23-24. Limbeck, *Ordnung*, pp. 38-39.

[145]4 Ezra 7:60, 61; 8:1, 3; 9:22, etc. Determinism
and freedom are not thought through philosophically. See von
Rad, *Wisdom*, p. 263.

[146]See above, p. 101. Wise men become prophets, and
prophets become inspired wise men. See Hengel, *Judaism*, 1:206,
228-32.

[147]See Wilckens, "σοφία," *TDNT*, 7:503; von Rad, *Wisdom*,
p. 277; and Vielhauer, *NTA*, 2:597-98, on wisdom features in
apocalyptic (dream-interpretation, figurative utterance,
knowledge of the cosmos, neglect of salvation-history, etc.).
On wisdom and redemption, see 4 Ezra 8:52, and 1 Enoch 92:1,
101:8.

[148]Especially in terms of the myth of hidden wisdom
in 1 Enoch 42 (wisdom found no place on earth etc.), 94:5,
and 98:3. See also 4 Ezra 5:9, 2 Bar 48:33-36, and 3:9-12
(the way of the commandments as the way of wisdom). Wisdom
(Torah) remains God's, and only He can give it (2 Bar 14:9).

[149]In 4 Ezra 4:21 the dwellers on earth can understand
only what is on the earth, and they who are above the heavens
that which is above the heavenly heights. Hence, in 13:53-56,
these things have been revealed to Ezra because "you searched
out My law; thy life hast thou ordered unto wisdom and hast
called understanding thy mother."

[150]Just as wisdom is a hidden mystery (1 Enoch 42:1-3, etc.), the law itself is a mystery. 1 Enoch 49:1-4 and 48:5 speak of the "secrets of righteousness" (calendrical and cosmic order, 1 Enoch 72-82). Wilckens, "σοφία," *TDNT*, 7:499-503, suggests that Jewish wisdom-speculations are related to Hellenistic mystery-speculations, and pass into Gnosticism, where a central place is given to Sophia.

[151]In 1 Enoch 18:1-5, 75:1, the elements of nature are ordered by heavenly spirits, or angels (66:1-8, 69:22-24). See also 12:2, 20:1, 39:12, 40:2, 61:12, 71:7; and Ass Mos 12:9-13. Limbeck, *Ordnung*, pp. 64-66; Reicke, "The Law," p. 147.

[152]Betz, "Problem," p. 127.

[153]So 2 Baruch 48:89, ". . . Thou givest commandment to the flames, and they change into spirits. . . . Thou makest wise the spheres so as to minister to their orders."

[154]See Test Sol 8:2, "We are the elements, the cosmic rulers of darkness (ἡμεῖς ἐσμεν στοιχεῖα κοσμοκράτορες τοῦ σκότους);" and 18:2, "We are the thirty-six elements, the world rulers of the darkness of this age." Charlesworth, *Pseudepigrapha*, pp. 197-99, suggests a date within the first century CE for the original Jewish composition.

[155]See Charlesworth, ibid., p. 199, and the suggestive parallels to the Qumranic temple scroll.

[156]See above, pp. 59-61, 62-63, 115, etc., on the essential place of eschatology in the debate concerning δικαιοσύνη.

[157]Reicke, "The Law," p. 273: "It is quite possible that Paul's opponents in Galatia really embraced doctrines similar to those in the books of Enoch and Jubilees." He suggests that they saw a close association between the angels and the στοιχεῖα.

[158]See above, pp. 105-6.

[159]Barrett, in *2 Corinthians*, and Georgi, in *Gegner*, both see the opponents of 2 Corinthians as being Palestinian Jews, using a combination of Palestinian traditions and Hellenistic propaganda techniques.

[160]Hengel, *Judaism*, 1:228.

[161]See Gaster, *Scriptures*, pp. 8-9; R. Huntjens, "Contrasting Notions of Covenant and Law in the Texts from Qumran," *RQ* 8 (1972-75):380, comments, "The whole object of their intense legalism and searching of the Torah was to be ready for the eschaton." Hengel, *Judaism*, 1:222, refers to the sect as an "eschatologically radicalized . . . movement of sanctification." On the place of apocalyptic traditions and literature in Qumran, see Russell, *Method*, pp. 38-47, noting, on the one hand, fragments of Jubilees, 1 Enoch, the Testament of Levi,

and other apocalyptic literature; and, on the other, the community's own apocalyptic works, such as the commentaries on
Isaiah, Hosea, Micah, and Nahum, the Zadokite Document, the
War Scroll, the Midrash on the Last Days, etc. For the striking affinities of the traditions of Qumran with Jubilees, see
James C. VanderKam, *Textual and Historical Studies in the Book
of Jubilees* (Missoula, MT: Scholars Press, 1977), pp. 258-80.

[162]Gaster, *Scriptures*, p. 4. See the titles chosen
by the sectaries to designate continuity with previous remnants
(1 QH 6:14, 8:6, 10). Priests are "sons of Zadok," etc. (1 QS
5:2, 9:14).

[163]See especially 1 QS and CD. The sectaries accused
the priests of failing to observe laws of ritual purity etc.,
and so entered into a covenant to avoid the temple. See
Fitzmyer, "Ebionites," pp. 222-23.

[164]They apparently allowed prayers, lustrations, etc.,
in the place of sacrifices (ibid., p. 230; Philo *Prob* 1. 75;
CD 6:11-13; Josephus *Ant* 18:1-5; and Flusser, "Dead Sea Sect,"
p. 229).

[165]See above, pp. 102-3, on the designation of the
community as Jerusalem.

[166]Gaster, *Scriptures*, p. 5.

[167]The term was especially important to the sectaries
(CD 6:14, 18-19; 20:11-12).

[168]See particularly 1 Q 22, a paraphrase of Moses'
farewell speech in Deuteronomy. It takes the form of a
covenant-renewal, indicating the sectarians' understanding
of "new covenant."

[169]See above, p. 101, on חכמ in Qumran, and the correlation of פשר and רז. Saving knowledge becomes a divine mystery (Hengel, *Judaism*, 1:222); vision and ecstasy are the confirmation of the "prophetic wise man" (207), and visionary
pseudonymity has retreated (205).

[170]Gaster, *Scriptures*, p. 7. In 1 QS 5:11-12 the
laws are "that which was hidden from Israel but found by the
man who searches." It is interesting to compare 1 QH 5:11,
"thou . . . hast hidden Thy Torah (within me)," and 1 QH 5:25,
"the mystery which thou hast hidden in me." In 1 QS 4:6 also
the law is an esoteric doctrine. See also 1 QS 1:9, 3:24;
1 QM 1:3; CD 13:12. Divine revelation is needed, even if one
is to be able to know the mysteries of the divine revelation
in scripture (1 QH 12:11-13). Hengel, *Judaism*, 1:222.

[171]In the sense of obedience, e.g., CD 3:13-17, "But
with the remnant which held fast to the commandments of God,
He made His covenant with Israel for ever, revealing to them
hidden things . . ."; and in the sense of continual meditation
on the Torah, searching for its hidden meaning. See above,
p. 101, and Hengel, *Judaism*, 1:177.

[172]Gaster, *Scriptures*, p. 7.

[173]Hengel, *Judaism*, 1:178. See also Jerome Murphy O'Connor, "An Essene Missionary Document? CD 2:14-6:1," *RB* 77 (1970):201-29.

[174]Especially 1 QS 10:1-4, 1 QS 1:14, and 1 QH 1:10-20, which concludes, "Or ever spirits immortal took on the form of ho(ly) angels, Thou didst assign them to bear rule over divers domains: over the sun and the moon, to govern their hidden powers; over the stars, to hold them in their courses; over (rain and snow), to make them fulfill their functions . . . Thou hast assigned the tasks of men's spirits duly, moment by moment. . . . By (Thy will all things ex)ist, and without Thee is nothing wrought."

[175]Limbeck *Ordnung*, p. 67.

[176]For example, CD 6:14, 18-19: "They shall be careful to act according to the exact interpretation of the law . . . to observe the Sabbath day according to its exact interpretation and the festivals and the day of fasting according to the (interpretations) of those who have entered the New Covenant. . . ." In 1 QH 4:10-11 the enemies of Israel are guilty of "exchanging the law . . . that they may gaze on their folly concerning their festival days." Huntjens, "Covenant," p. 365, concludes, "The question of the calendar . . . was the single most decisive issue that led to the secession of the sect." This is in particular a solar calendar (CD 3:13-16, 1 QS 1:14, 10:1-9). Compare this to the Essene devotion to the sun in Philo and Josephus (above, p. 130) and the misunderstanding to which these accounts were open). There is an association between the Covenanters' traditions and Jubilees especially in connection with calendrical law. "While the theological parallels . . . strongly suggest that the Qumran covenanters and Jub's author belonged to the same theological tradition, the fact that they adhered to a unique calendar makes the case overwhelming" (VanderKam, *Jubilees*, p. 270). See also Joseph M. Baumgarten, *Studies in Qumran Law* (Leiden: Brill, 1977), pp. 102-14.

[177]Hengel, *Judaism*, 1:235. See how this echoes the concerns of Jubilees and 1 Enoch.

[178]See above, CD 6:14, 18-19. There is a similar concern in Jub 6:36-37.

[179]Huntjens, "Covenant," p. 363. See CD 6:14, 18-19 and 1 QS 1:14-15 ("They must not deviate by a single step from carrying out the orders of God at the times appointed for them . . ."); also 1 QH 1:24-25. In 1 Q22 1:8, 2:8, and 3:3 the Sabbath is identified with the covenant. Huntjens, ibid., p. 308, notes that the amount of legal material in the texts is very small, there being nothing like Mishnaic halakha. The demand for law-obedience is principally in terms of calendrical feasts. In CD 10:14-12:18 there is a reworking of a portion of Leviticus; but more than half of it is on the Sabbath.

[180]CD 3:13-17: "But with the remnant that held fast
to the commandments of God, He made His covenant with Israel
forever, revealing to them the hidden things . . . His holy
sabbaths and His glorious festivals."

[181]Davies, "Scrolls," p. 167, on 1 QS 1:14, quoted
above (p. 123); Herbert Braun, *Qumran und das Neue Testament*,
2 vols. (Tübingen: J. C. B. Mohr, 1966), 1:229-30, sees a
parallel in 1 QM 10:10-14: "Thou art He who decreed the day
of the Sabbath rest and the holy festivals, the turning-points
of the years and (all) the appointed seasons."

[182]Ringgren, *Qumran* pp. 56-57, quoting 1 QH 1:8-15:
"Before they became (holy) angels, (Thou madest them) as ever-
lasting spirits in their dominions, the luminaries for their
mysteries, the stars for the courses. . . ."

[183]See 1 QS 3:20; CD 5:18; and 1 QM 10:10-14, where
אור may mean an astral spirit. Braun, *Qumran*, 1:229-30, sees
this doctrine too as being close to the στοιχεῖα τοῦ κόσμου
of Gal 4:3, 9.

[184]See the references above, p. 94, to the community's
sense of the presence of angels in the congregation. Gaster,
Scriptures, p. 7, comments, "He (the sectarian) breaks the
trammels of his mortality . . . he becomes one with the nonmortal beings of the celestial realm--the "holy ones" who
stand forever in direct converse with God."

[185]In 1 QM 10:10-12, there is a direct connection
between the rule of the cosmos by heavenly spiritual beings,
and the institution of the calendrical festivals. See also
1 QS 1:14-15.

[186]See Gaster, *Scriptures*, pp. 8-9. The sectaries
sought escape from the cycle of the ages and the elements of
the universe, release not just from sin but from mortality.

[187]Especially the astrological fragments from Cave 4,
some of which are reproduced in Hengel, *Judaism*, 1:237-38.
Further references are given in 2:158-59.

[188]Ibid., 1:239. Jub 12:16-18 is in effect a polemic
against astrology.

[189]See especially Ziesler, *Righteousness*, pp. 85-103,
and Sanders, *Paul*, pp. 305-12; and above, p. 70.

[190]God and man are contrasted in 1 QS 1:21-2:4, 10:23,
and 1 QH 1:26, 4:29-31. This sense of the overwhelming righteousness of God is the foundation of the doctrine of righteousness by grace.

[191]1 QH 11:31 (man is cleansed through God's mercy);
and 1 QS 11:14 (God will judge the psalmist through צדקה
[righteousness]).

[192]Here man's righteousness is derived from God's righteousness, and man's way is only perfected by the grace of God. See especially the parallelism in 1 QS 11:13-14:

> As for me,
>> If I stumble, the mercies of God
>>> shall be my eternal salvation;
>> If I stagger because of the sin of my flesh,
>>> my justification (משפט) shall be
>>>> by the righteousness of God (צדקתי אל).

Here משפט is parallel to salvation, righteousness to mercy.

[193]See 1 QH 7:12. Here the distinction is between the righteous and the wicked.

[194]1 QH 12:9, 7:30, 4:31.

[195]1 QS 11:17 (righteousness equals perfection of way); and 1 QH 7:28-31 (righteousness is the opposite of transgression).

[196]Man is righteous by God's mercy; but the only way to remain righteous is to do the commandments of God as specified by the sect's covenant. See Sanders, *Paul*, p. 312.

[197]Once having bound himself to the Torah, the member will observe it even at the price of death. See 1 QS 5:8, CD 15:2, 6, etc.

[198]Sanders, ibid., p. 312. He disagrees with Ziesler regarding his proposed distinction between the use of the verb (forensic) and noun and adjective (ethical) forms of the root צדק. There is no distinction in use.

[199]See Huntjen, above, and also Black, in *Scrolls*, p. 125. There are at least two notions of law and covenant in Qumran, one legalist, one more spiritual.

[200]Similar to the suggestions of Barrett and Georgi regarding the opponents in 2 Corinthians. See above, p. 132.

[201]As must be all borrowings in religion: Moore, *Judaism* 2:394-95: "Borrowings in religion . . . are usually in the nature of appropriation of things in the possession of another which the borrower recognizes . . . as belonging to himself . . . the necessary complements of his own (ideas)."

[202]See above, p. 133, on the lack of halakha in the documents, and the replacement of the Temple law observance with their own rites.

[203]See above, p. 111, quoting Josephus *Apion* 2:282, which refers to the popularity of Jewish law among Pagans in terms of the Sabbath, fasts, and food laws.

[204]For instance, Augustine (*Civ Dei* 6:11), quoting earlier satirists of Jews on Jewish law.

CHAPTER NINE

THE TRADITION OF THE SACRAMENTS

[1]Bultmann, *Theology*, 1:135, who goes on to say, ". . . if the act is consummated according to the prescribed rite, then the supernatural powers go into effect, and the act . . . is itself a supranatural ceremony which works a miracle." See also Schoeps, *Paul*, pp. 111-13; and Schweitzer, *Mysticism*, pp. 174-75.

[2]See Bultmann, ibid., pp. 135-36; Schoeps, ibid., p. 113; and on baptism in Galatia, Mussner, *Galater*, p. 263.

[3]*Encyclopaedia Judaica*, 16 vols. (New York: Macmillan, 1971-72), 5:567-69, s.v. "Circumcision."

[4]Goodenough, *Symbols*, 6:144. The *Encyclopaedia Judaica* admits that failure to carry out circumcision leads to "excision at the hand of heaven from the community." See Meyer, "περιτέμνω," *TDNT*, 6:80-81. Circumcision is a "precondition, sign, and seal of participation in Abraham's covenant," and failure to carry it out leads to a loss of salvation. Hence Goodenough calls it "a visible sign of an invisible grace," adding, "One strongly suspects that before the Christians came to have those sacraments which the Jews sharply rejected, circumcision would have been freely called a sacrament. . . ."

[5]See Conzelmann, *1 Corinthians*, p. 126. The principle is that of κλῆσις: one must remain in the particular place allotted to him in the world. There is a difference here from Galatians, as there is no sign of Judaizing demands. Note also Drane, *Paul*, pp. 5-59, on the difference between Gal 5:6 and 1 Cor 7:19.

[6]Thomas Walter Manson, *Studies in the Gospels and Epistles*, ed. Matthew Black (Manchester: Manchester University Press, 1962), p. 169. Drane, *Paul*, notices the entirely different attitude between Galatians 5 on the one hand, and 1 Cor 8, 10:14-30 and Romans 14 on the other, where Paul pleads the rights of the "weaker" Jewish-Christian brother. In Rom 14:5-6 Paul says, "Observe whatever day you like!" But in Gal 4:10-11 he says, "You observe days . . . I am afraid I have labored over you in vain." Circumcision and calendrical observances apparently occupy an entirely different place in Galatians.

[7]Meyer, "περιτέμνω," *TDNT* 6:72, and below.

[8]As in Philo. See below, p. 144.

[9]See the discussion of the mystery language in 3:3, above, pp. 78-82. Baptism evidently comes under ἐνάρχεσθαι, and circumcision under ἐπιτελεῖν. In Qumran baptism was not an unrepeatable occurrence, but probably a daily routine. See Ringgren, *Qumran*, p. 245. John's baptism was less than

an eschatological rite, being only a baptism of "repentance" (Luke 3:3; see also Acts 19:1-7 and the unacceptability of John's baptism to the Pauline churches: Gunther, *Opponents*, pp. 137-38). Among Gnostics, too, baptism was only one of up to five "sacraments," and only a preliminary one, the climactic rite being the "bridal chamber." See E. Segelberg, "The Coptic-Gnostic Gospel according to Philip and its Sacramental System," *Numen* 7 (1960); and Gunther, ibid., pp. 138-40, on "hemerobaptist" Jewish-Christian sects.

[10]See Col 2:11-15, apparently polemically countering a Christian system of perfection in which circumcision was one of the final rites. See further below, pp. 142-43.

[11]On the difference between Romans and Galatians here, see Werner Foerster, "Auffassung und Ziel des Galaterbriefes," in Walther Eltester, ed., *Apophoreta: Festschrift für Ernst Haenchen zum seinem 70. Geburtstag am 10. Dezember 1964* (Berlin: A. Töpelmann, 1964), p. 139, etc. "Beachtet man das ἄρα (3:7), ὥστε (3:9), ἵνα (3:14), διό (4:31), mit denen jeweils der Zielpunkt der Erörterung erreicht ist, so wird deutlich, Paulus argumentiert gegen ein bestimmte fest umrissens These, die auch im Rom so nicht begegnet, nämlich gegen die These: ihr seid solange nicht wirchklich Kinder Abrahams, wie ihr nicht das Zeichen des Abrahamsbundes, die Beschneidung, auf euch nehmt."

[12]Kuhn, "προσήλυτος," *TDNT*, 6:732-33, notes that of all Italian inscriptions referring to Jews (554), only eight refer to full proselytes, and six of these proselytes are women. See also Munck, *Paul*, p. 129, on the rarity of acceptance of circumcision among Gentiles.

[13]See above, p. 111. Josephus refers instead to the Gentile fondness for Sabbaths, feasts, etc.

[14]Sib Or 2:238, 4:24, 162-64, and especially 8:393. This probably represents the missionary propaganda of Diaspora Judaism. See Meyer, περιτέμνω, *TDNT*, 6:79.

[15]Schoeps, *Paul*, pp. 223-24.

[16]Meyer, "περιτέμνω," *TDNT*, 6:78. Both Herodotus and Hadrian equate it with castration, and for long periods it was prohibited throughout the Empire.

[17]Ibid., p. 79.

[18]Meyer, ibid., p. 78, makes this suggestion.

[19]Koester, *Trajectories*, p. 145.

[20]See above, p. 77: Baptism is not one step among many, but makes effective the finality of Christ's deliverance of the believer from the present evil aeon.

[21]Above, pp. 59-64. In Wrede's words, the doctrine of δικαιοσύνη in Galatians deals with "Christ and redemption from the powers of the present world."

[22]Above, pp. 60-61, and also below, pp. 146-56, on the significance of the phrase ἄρσεν καὶ θῆλυ. John W. Drane, "Tradition, Law, and Ethics in Pauline Theology," NovT 16 (1974):170-71, 178-79, among others, suggests that it may have been an apparently enthusiastic doctrine of baptism such as in Gal 3:27-29 that was partly behind the excesses of 1 Corinthians.

[23]Bornkamm, "Colossians," pp. 123-24, notes that the book explicitly contends with the heresy in 2:4-23, and that, further, the "positive unfolding of the gospel in 1:15-20 is already determined, in terminology and in thought, by antithesis to the heresy, and the structure of the letter as a whole becomes transparent and its peculiarity comprehensible in view of this confrontation." See also Jervell, Imago Dei, pp. 231-32, and Lohse, Colossians, pp. 127-29, reconstructing the Colossian heresy from the "catchwords" taken up especially in Colossians 2.

[24]Bornkamm, Colossians, p. 124, notes the evidently polemical intent of Col 2:9 (ὅτι ἐν αὐτῷ κατοικεῖ πᾶν τὸ πλήρωμα τῆς θεότητος σωματικῶς) and 2:10 (καὶ ἐστὲ ἐν αὐτῷ πεπληρωμένοι). He also concludes, from the polemical use of ἀποθνήσκειν (2:20) and ἀπέκδυειν (2:11) that the philosophy "celebrated a mystery of rebirth" (p. 128).

[25]Lohse, Colossians, p. 102: "'Circumcision' is . . . understood as a sacramental rite by which a person entered the community and gained access to salvation. The reference to the phrase ἀπέκδυσις τοῦ σώματος τῆς σαρκός suggests the practice of the mystery cults."

[26]Lohse, ibid., p. 130, suggests that it can no longer be discerned whether an actual or only a figurative circumcision is referred to. That it is a physical circumcision, see Lohmeyer, Kolosser, pp. 108-9; Dibelius, Kolosser, on 2:11 and excursus on 2:23; Gunther, Opponents, p. 83; and Barth, Ephesians, 1:122, on the parallel between Ephesians and Colossians on circumcision. See Bornkamm, Colossians, p. 127: "Possibly circumcision also belonged to the religious practices of the false teachers, perhaps with the altered meaning of a mystery-like initiation."

[27]See the terminology of Eph 2:11 (τῆς λεγομένης περιτομῆς ἐν σαρκὶ χειροποιήτου), an obvious reference to literal circumcision: Barth, Ephesians, 1:125-26.

[28]Lohse, Colossians, p. 102. The OT uses the term to refer to graven images and idols the pagans made for themselves: LXX Lev 26:1, 30; Isa 2:18, 21:9, etc. See also Gunther, ibid., p. 84. The word is also used in Mark 14:58, Acts 7:48, 17:24, Heb 9:24.

[29]The claims the philosophy makes for circumcision can be gathered from the paraenesis that follows in 3:1-17, built around the idea of "putting off" and "putting on." The letter takes the scheme of the philosophy itself, but twists it in terms of an ethical thrust. See also Jervell, *Imago*, pp. 231-33, and below.

[30]For instance, Lohse, *Colossians*, p. 102, citing Gospel of Thomas 53: "His disciples said to Him, Is circumcision profitable or not? He said to them: If it were profitable, their father would beget them circumcised from their mother. But the true circumcision in spirit has become profitable in every way." The point is that, wherever circumcision is spiritualized, it is (as here in the Gospel of Thomas) in terms of baptism. But the heresy cannot mean "baptism" by "circumcision," because Colossians opposes its "circumcision" with baptism. And if the heresy's circumcision is not a baptism--what is it? Some of the other evidence produced by Schmithals in favor of a literal Gnostic circumcision will be examined below.

[31]See Bornkamm, *Colossians*, p. 124, on the polemical intent of πλήρωμα in 2:9-10. The philosophy regarded the divine fulness as residing in the elements, which, along with angels, were to be worshipped as divine beings. Such a dualism is in the Isis mystery in Apuleius, and Corp Herm 13:11, 13. See also Lohse, *Colossians*, p. 128, n. 115, agreeing with Bornkamm's interpretation of the relation of the elements to the πλήρωμα: "In no way" is it possible to identify the στοιχεῖα τοῦ κόσμου with the archons of Gnosticism.

[32]Foerster, *Apophoreta*, p. 138, commenting on the role of the στοιχεῖα τοῦ κόσμου in Galatians (close to their role in Colossians): "Die Gnosis dient ihnen nicht und verehrt sie nicht (ie persönlich gefassten Engelmachten), sondern verachtet sie."

[33]So, Gunther, *Opponents*, p. 83, who notes the Colossian heretics' three motives for circumcision, judging by the polemical claims made instead for baptism: it was a prophylactic against sins; it was a way of imitating the angels (see on Jub 15 below); and it was for deliverance from evil angels.

[34]For the deduction that a more or less fixed confessional formula stands behind the baptismal passages of Gal 3:28, 1 Cor 12:13, and Col 3:11, see Meeks, "Androgyne," pp. 180-84, Jewett, *Imago*, pp. 231-32, and below, pp. 146-48.

[35]For instance, the different issues with which σῶμα is connected in 1 Cor 6:13-20, 7:4, 34, 9:27, 10:16-17, 11:24-29, 12:12-27, 15:35-44, strongly suggests that the Corinthians gave an important place to speculations concerning the σῶμα.

[36]For instance, 1 Cor 6:11 where Paul bases his imperative on the Corinthians' own sacramentalism. See

Conzelmann, *1 Corinthians*, p. 107, and especially notes 45,
46; the comments of Lohse and Dinkler; and 1 Cor 10:1-13 on
the Israelites' baptism into Moses as a τύπος of the Corinthians' identification with Christ. Paul does not debate the
effectiveness of baptism in introducing the believer into the
aeon of Christ, but debates the nature of the aeon. Baptism
itself is not a saving event, but is that which unites the
baptized with God's pilgrim people, who are not in the angelic
heights but in the desert, tempted and in danger of falling.
Baptism heightens responsibility. Robinson, *Trajectories*,
p. 62; and Käsemann, *Römer*, pp. 151-52.

[37]For instance, Rom 6:1-4 and the "eschatological
reservation" introduced into what was probably a purely sacramental understanding of baptism, similar perhaps to Col 2:11-
13 and Eph 2:5-6. See Bultmann, *Theology*, 1:133, 140; Käsemann, *Römer*, p. 151; Robinson, *Trajectories*, p. 30; and Bornkamm, *Experience*, p. 73. Baptism indeed "imparts to the initiate a share in the fate of the cult deity" (Bultmann), but
the surprise is that it brings a share in Christ's death; and
there is a distinction between the life of the believer and
the resurrection life of Christ.

[38]Schmithals, *Gnosticism in Corinth*, pp. 239-40, suggests that Gal 3:26-28 was probably taken over from the opponents and altered by the insertion of διὰ τῆς πίστεως; Betz,
"Composition," p. 357, also suggests that Paul may have taken
over this confession.

[39]Kuhn, "προσήλυτος," *TDNT*, 6:731-33, and 741. Palestinian Judaism wanted no loose adherents, only circumcised
proselytes.

[40]Meyer, "περιτέμνω," *TDNT*, 6:77. See 1 Macc 1:60-61,
2 Macc 6:10, 4 Macc 4:25.

[41]Ibid., pp. 77-78. See Josephus *Bell* 4:270-82; *Ant*
14:403; and *Ant* 13:395-96 for the period under Alexander Jan-
naeus.

[42]Josephus *Ant* 16:220-25, etc.

[43]Josephus *Ant* 20:34-38 and the interesting roles
played by Hellenistic and Palestinian Jews. Foerster, *Apophoreta*, p. 137, suggests that this incident shows a remarkable
parallel to the situation in Galatia. The Galatian opponents
have an attitude similar to the Palestinian Jew.

[44]*Spec Leg* 1:304-6.

[45]Ibid., 1:1-11.

[46]*Migr Ab* 92

[47]1 QS 5:4-5, 26-28; 1 QpHab 11:13.

[48]For instance, 1 QS 5:5: "Men of truth are to circumcise in the community the foreskin of desire and obduracy."

[49]Meyer, *TDNT*, 6:79.   See the later Tannaitic and
Rabbinic views of circumcision in StrB 4:28-31.

[50]As well as Lohse and others mentioned above, p. 142,
see Jewett, "Intruders," p. 201.   Schmithals, *Paul*, pp. 37-38,
has proposed a literal Gnostic circumcision, using especially
Patristic evidence, and his star witness is Cerinthus.   But
many feel now that this evidence is worthless: see A. F. J.
Klijn and G. J. Reininck, *Patristic Evidence for Jewish-
Christian Sects* (Leiden: Brill, 1973), pp. 6, 8, 12, 19, and
the discussion below, p. 145.

[51]Schmithals, *Paul*, pp. 37-38: "Gnostic circumcision
could never obligate one to keep the law in the Pharisaic
sense. . . .   It never did so in Galatia, as stated above--an
important argument for the correctness of our thesis."   It is
suggested that it is precisely at this point--the removal of
nomism from the argument of Galatians--that Schmithals has
committed his most basic error.

[52]Jubilees 30:1-8; see also 15:26, "And every one
that is born, the flesh of whose foreskin is not circumcised
on the eighth day, belongeth not to the children of the covenant which the Lord made with Abraham, but to the children of
destruction; nor is there, moreover, any sign on him that he
is the Lord's."   This is the tenor of the traditions the work
elaborates on.   A similar emphasis is in Test Lev 6:1-9.

[53]Jub 15:27.

[54]2 Bar 41:4-5.   See Charles' commentary on this text,
Baruch, p. 68.

[55]Though Schmithals doubts that actual circumcision
was in question in Colossians and asserts that this was a
Gnostic circumcision.   However, see above, p. 142, on
circumcision among Gnostics; and Bornkamm on the Jewishness
of the Colossian heresy.   It has also been noted that
Schmithals' evidence for a semi-gnostic circumcision among
Jewish-Christians, especially in connection with Cerinthus,
is worthless, as is his allusion to Jerome's opinion that
Galatians was written against Cerinthus (*Paul*, pp. 36-38).
See the above references to Klijn and Reininck.   Cerinthus is
not said to have taught circumcision before Epiphanius.

[56]Goodenough, *Symbols*, 6:144-46.

[57]Ibid., pp. 195-97.   Charlesworth, *Pseudepigrapha*,
pp. 189-90 disputes Goodenough in calling the Odes "Jewish-
Christian," but notes their "strong Jewishness."   He notes
also a close affinity to the Dead Sea Scrolls (where physical
and spiritual circumcision were held together: see above),
and concludes that they must be dated around 70-125.   Others
agree with Goodenough's interpretation of Ode 11's understanding of circumcision, i.e., Schmithals, *Paul*, p. 38, note 74.

[58]See Philo's portrayal of Judaism as a "mystery"
religion, with higher and lower mysteries, below, p. 151;

and Goodenough, Ibid., 12:18-19, 46-47, Aristobulus, Orpheus-
testaments, and Juvenal, *Satire*, 14:96-106; see also Georgi,
Gegner, p. 135.

[59]Georgi, ibid., pp. 135-36. StrB 4:32 cites sources
in which circumcision makes Jews the elite people of God.
Jewett, "Intruders," p. 209, suggests that the promise of
perfection which Jewish tradition attached to circumcision
made it appealing to Hellenists.

[60]See Wayne A. Meeks, "The Image of the Androgyne:
Some Uses of a Symbol in Earliest Christianity," *History of
Religions* 13 (1974):165-208, who notes the language of
"putting off" and "putting on," the listing of pairs, statements that "all" are "one," etc.; Jervell, *Imago*, pp. 231-32,
who notes allusions to Genesis 1-2, without the texts becoming quotations of scripture. There is instead a reference to
a scripture tradition that is well known; Dennis Ronald
Macdonald, "There is no Male and Female: Galatians 3:26-28
and Gnostic Baptismal Tradition," (Ph.D. dissertation, Harvard
University, 1978), who notes the change of verbs from the
first person to the second person in Galatians 3, and the
change of the method of comparison in Gal 3:28 to accord with
LXX Gen 1:27 (pp. 4-15). He suggests that Colossians is
dependent on Galatians rather than on a common tradition; and
that the formula itself is not in question in 1 Corinthians
12. But see the arguments below on Colossians. He admits
that the tradition behind the formula is certainly evident
in Corinth (pp. 96-99).

[61]Assuming with Travis, "Form Criticism," in Marshall,
Interpretation, pp. 154-55, that various instances of a similar form will provide ways of understanding the function of
the form in any one of those instances.

[62]Meeks, "Image," p. 181.

[63]Ibid. Lohse, *Colossians*, p. 141, notes that ἀπεκδυ-
σάμενοι and ἐνδυσάμενοι emphatically stress the relation to
baptism.

[64]See also above, pp. 142-43, on Col 2:11-13 and the
relation of these verbs to the heretical "philosophy," which
has determined the vocabulary and structure of the whole
letter.

[65]The saying in Col 3:9-11 is not introduced or concluded as a baptism-saying (as it is in Gal 3:28 and 1 Cor
12:13). It is understood to be a baptism-saying, though,
because it picks up the language of "putting off" which is
first used in Col 2:11-13 (Jervell, *Imago*, p. 233: in 3:1-17,
2:20 is directly picked up, which itself has picked up 2:11-13.
The "putting off" and "putting on" clearly refer to baptism,
from a comparison with Rom 6:2 and 2 Cor 5:6). Hence 3:9-11
should not be separated from 2:11-13 (Jervell, *Imago*, p. 233).
But it has already been noticed that 2:11-13 is polemical,
taking up the claims of opponents regarding circumcicion and
reinterpreting them in terms of baptism.

[66]See Jervell, *Imago*, p. 233:   "Der Kolosserbrief als
Ganzes zeigt eine Tendenz, Kultus und Ethik der christlichen
Taufe einem Kultus und einer Ethik der Gnosis entgegenzu-
stellen," and 225:   "Gerade in der Taufe fand die Kolosser-
gemeinde Basis und Autorität für ihren Kampf gegen die Irr-
lehre."

[67]See Jervell, *Imago*, p. 232, on the way the saying
refers to Genesis 1-2 without quoting it.   The reference is
to a tradition, eventually resting on Genesis 1-2, which is
well known in the community.   Again, ibid., p. 235, the passage
evidently takes up assumptions already held about ἀπεκδυσά-
μενοι and ἐνδυσάμενοι and twists them, so that they become the
basis for an imperative.

[68]On the way the question of male and female is
involved in the Corinthian situation, see above on 1 Corinthians 11 and 12, and the various problems relating to sex and
the body in 1 Corinthians (e.g., 5:1-13, 6:12-20, 11:2-16,
14:33-36; and chapter 7 [the monotonous parallels of obligations of men and women, indicating that the roles of "male"
and "female" are at issue]), and the significant omission of
ἄρσεν καὶ θῆλυ in 1 Cor 12:13 when compared with Gal 3:28,
this being Paul's "eschatological reservation" of the Corinthians' own enthusiastic interpretation of the tradition,
appearing in 1 Cor 11:10, 15:35-50, 70:1, etc.   See Meeks,
"Androgyne," pp. 199-201; D. L. Balch, "Backgrounds of
1 Corinthians 7: Sayings of the Lord in Q; Moses as an
Ascetic θεῖος Ἀνήρ in 2 Corinthians 3," *NTS* 18 (1972):356,
364; Macdonald, "Male and Female," pp. 96-99.   See further,
below, pp. 153-54.

[69]The expression in Gal 3:28 is in fact reminiscent
of the language of the mysteries, in which one came to share
in the powers of the mystery-god.   Lohse, *Einheit*, p. 236,
refers to the parallels to the mystery in Apuleius, *Metamorphoses*.   Bultmann, *Theology*, 1:140, and Käsemann, *Römer*,
p. 151, both note that the language and thought is foreign to
the Old Testament; though Paul does not build his baptism-
theology on the mystery-cults, but criticizes them.   However,
in this instance, the language of ἐνδυειν may have first
belonged to the opponents.   See above, pp. 78-82, on the
mystical and even magical terms used here, in which the opponents evidently present their program (ἐνάρχεσθαι, ἐπιτελεῖν,
βασκαίνειν, ἀνόητος).   The mystical language of "putting on"
may reflect, then, the opponents' own sacramental theology,
as it does in Colossians, in the debate with the speculative-
Jewish φιλοσοφία.

[70]See Jervell, *Imago*, pp. 232-33, on the close parallels between Ephesians and Colossians, and the way they deal
with similar issues.   Derwood Smith, "The Two Made One: Some
Observations on Eph 2:14-18," *Ohio Journal of Religious Studies*
1 (1973):34-54, notes the expressions in these verses which
stand close to the above formula, especially ὁ ποιήσας τὰ
ἀμφότερα ἕν, ἵνα τοὺς δύο κτίσῃ ἐν αὐτῷ εἰς ἕνα καινὸν ἄνθρωπον, and ἀποκαταλλάξῃ τοὺς ἀμφοτέρους ἐν ἑνὶ σώματι.   He notes
further that these expressions stand particularly close to

Greek traditions of duality and its resolution, as in Plato
Symposium 189-91, 191d, *Timaeus* 31 b-c, and the later stoics.
Particularly significant are the words ἀμφότερα and δεσμός,
and the inexplicable use of the neuter ἕν in Ephesians 2,
which Plato uses for the overcoming of duality. These Greek
traditions also involved an original androgyne that was afterwards divided (Plato *Symposium* 189e). For Ephesians, he concludes that the context is polemical: the duality of the
letter stands over against a more speculative kind of duality
centering on male and female, which draws also on Genesis 1-2
and Judaism (circumcision etc.) and follows the pattern of
urzeit and endzeit and the return to the Adamic condition.

[71]Macdonald, "Male and Female," p. 120, also notes
the many allusions to Genesis 1-3 in 1 Cor 11:3-16, where the
roles of male and female seem very much to be at issue.

[72]Meeks, "Androgyne," p. 185; Macdonald, "Male and
Female," pp. 4-15.

[73]Meeks, ibid., p. 185; Smith, "Two Made One," p. 43.

[74]Lightfoot, *Galatians*, p. 149, noted that Gal 3:28
has parallels both in the Fathers and in the Gnostics, and
that the form of the parallels suggests that they go back to
a common tradition that is also behind Gal 3:28, resting perhaps on Luke 20:34-36. See Meeks, "Androgyne," pp. 189-93;
Smith, "Two Made One," pp. 39-41, and Macdonald, "Male and
Female," pp. 13-14.

[75]The saying also occurs in Hippol *Ref* 4. 7, Clem
Alex *Strom* 3. 985 (Theodotus), Acts of Peter 38 ("Concerning
this the Lord says in a mystery, 'Unless you make what is on
the right hand as what is on the left and what is on the left
hand as what is on the right and what is above as what is
below and what is behind as what is before, you will not
recognize the kingdom.'" The context is Peter's crucifixion,
when he is told by the Lord, "It is time for you, Peter, to
surrender your body"), Acts of Philip 140, Acts of Thomas 147
(in a prayer of Judas: "The inside I have made the outside,
and the outside [inside]"), Gospel of Truth 32:10-16 ("Thus
it is with him who lacks the one; that is, the entire right
which draws what was deficient and takes it from the left-hand
side and brings it to the right, and thus the number becomes
100"), and Clem Alex *Strom* 6:47-48. See Meeks, "Androgyne,"
pp. 184, 189-90; and Jacques E. Ménard, *L'Evangile selon
Philippe, introduction, texte, traduction, commentaire* (Paris:
Letouzey et Ané, 1957), p. 188.

[76]The text of the Gospel of Philip here requires some
reconstruction. Ménard, *Philippe*, p. 188, follows Schenck,
Isenberg, and most others in the reconstruction that is
basically used here.

[77]Macdonald, "Male and Female," p. 59. So Gos Thom 37
asks, "When will you appear to us?" In 2 Clem the saying is
in answer to the question, When will Christ's kingdom come?

Notes: Chapter Nine

313

[78]"When the two become one" (Gos Egypt); "When you make the two one" (Gos Thom); "When the two shall be one" (2 Clem); "[I came to unite] them in that place" (Gos Phil).

[79]ὑμεῖς εἷς ἐστε (Gal 3:28); εἰς ἓν σῶμα (1 Cor 12:13); πάντα καὶ ἐν πᾶσιν Χριστός (Col 3:10-11); εἷς, μια, ἕν, (Eph 4:5); οἱ ἀμφότεροι ἐν ἑνὶ πνεύματι (Eph 2:14-18).

[80]"When you have trampled on the garment of shame" (Gos Egypt), probably a reference to the freeing of the soul from the body (compare to Philo *Leg All* 2. 55, *Immut* 56; and Meeks, "Androgyne," p. 194). J. Z. Smith, "The Garments of Shame," *History of Religions* 5 (1965):224-20, notes that expressions such as undressing, being naked, and treading on the garments of shame are parallels, used in Christian baptismal contexts.

[81]Though not in the saying itself, the concept is elsewhere in the Gospel of Philip. See the references given above. In these sayings, the reference is not merely to social equality of male and female, but to an eradication of the sexes entirely and to a new order of humanity.

[82]See the references in Gos Thom 84-86 (*NHL*, 127) to Adam, the creation of images in the beginning, etc. Macdonald, "Male and Female," p. 50, points to the references here to a return to the primordial state. In Gos Phil 70. 10-25 (*NHL*, 142) there is the reference to Adam and Eve, the fall, and the entrance of sin into the world. Macdonald, ibid., pp. 23-26, points to the evidence of speculation on Genesis 1-2 in Cassianus' teachings (it is Cassianus who has cited the saying referred to as coming from the Gospel to the Egyptians: see Clem Alex *Strom* 3). Jervell, *Imago*, pp. 122-70, has analyzed the prominent use of Gen 1:27 in Gnosticism; and Pearson, *Pneumatikos*, pp. 51-76, examines the use of Gen 2:7 in Gnostic exegesis, concluding that "Gen 2:7 is a focal point for Gnostic speculation" (p. 51). He gives examples from the Apocryphon of John, the Gospel of Truth, the Apocalypse of Adam, the Hypostasis of the Archons, etc., and shows the close connections here with Rabbinic literature.

[83]The debate between Clement and Cassianus and his followers revolves around interpretations of Matt 22:30 and the attainment of the resurrection state. See Clem Alex *Strom* 3. 6. 47-48; and Macdonald, ibid., p. 26. The saying in the Gospel of Thomas is clearly a baptism-saying.

[84]In both 2 Clem 12:3-4 and Clem Alex *Strom* the saying is understood by Clement as referring to the soul's leaving the body. It then loses its physical form, and changes to unity (*Strom* 3. 93). The Gospel of Philip belittles baptism, applying the unification-saying to the final rite of the bridal chamber. See Meeks, "Androgyne," pp. 191-92. In many Gnostic systems, the elite or τελείοι reached their exalted state in the sacrament of sacred marriage; see Gos Phil 69. 20-30 (*NHL*, 142): "Baptism is the holy building. Redemption is the holy of the holy. The holy of the holies is the bridal chamber . . . the bridal chamber is that which is superior to it

(i.e., baptism)." See also Gos Phil 72. 30-73. 10 (*NHL*, 143-
44); and Hipp Ref 6. 14. 6, 6. 9. 10. Macdonald, "Male and
Female," p. 73, equates baptism and the bridal chamber, which
seems to be correct in some Gnostic systems (e.g., the Tri-
partite Tractate [*NHL*, 54-97]) but not in others (e.g., Gos
Phil referred to above, and On the Anointing [*NHL*, 435], which
is specifically devoted to Gnostic sacraments, and in which
the Bridal Chamber is a postbaptismal unction).

[85]In the New Testament, the formula is already working polemically in respect to baptism. It is interesting
that, in these later sayings, it is the Syrian Gos Thom and
the Valentinian Cassianus who are closest to Paul in Gal 3:28.

[86]In fact, the citation formula in 2 Clement is both
the longest and the most emphatic: ἐπερωτηθεὶς γὰρ αὐτὸς ὁ
κυριος ὑπο τινος, πότε ἥξει αὐτου ἡ βασιλεια, εἰπεν. . . .
Clement, in *Stromata* 3, doesn't object to the saying but only
to Cassianus' interpretation of it. See Macdonald, ibid.,
p. 27. Smith, "Two Made One," pp. 41, 47, seems to be correct
in saying that the tradition itself is not gnostic. Meeks,
"Androgyne," p. 166, says the Gnostic forms show bizarre variations of the original tradition.

[87]Summarized in Macdonald, ibid., p. 60.

[88]See Jervell, *Imago*, p. 232 (see above, p. 147).

[89]Jervell, ibid., the canonical sayings themselves
draw on a widely known tradition.

[90]See the conclusions of Macdonald, "Male and Female,"
p. 142; and Meeks, "Androgyne," p. 166.

[91]Edmund Leach, "Genesis as Myth," in *Myth and Cosmos*,
ed. John Middleton, p. 4. See Smith on Plato (above, p. 148).

[92]F. C. Grant, *Hellenistic Religions, The Age of Syncretism* (New York: Liberal Arts Press, 1953), pp. 28-30; and
Arthur Darby Nock, *Conversion* (London: Oxford University
Press, 1961), p. 217. The shrine dates from C2-C1 BCE, and
the inscription is more significant in that these distinctions
were starkly apparent in "outside" society. The "Three
Reasons for Gratitude" of Thales or Plato were "That I was
born a human being and not a beast, next, a man and not a
woman, thirdly, a Greek and not a Barbarian" (for the text,
etc., see Meeks, "Androgyne," p. 167). This saying was taken
over by Judaism; "Blessed (art Thou), who did not make me a
Gentile; blessed (art Thou), who did not make me a woman;
blessed (art Thou), who did not make me a boor," Tosefta,
Berakot 7. 18.

[93]Meeks, "Androgyne," p. 170.

[94]Delcourt, *Hermaphrodite*, ch. 1. Meeks, ibid., p.
184, cites examples of transvestism in initiation rites in
pagan mysteries. The initiate momentarily transcended the
distinction between male and female.

[95]See Meeks, ibid., p. 171, who refers to Diogenes
Laertius 5. 12, 7. 175. The Epicureans also sought a community in which normal social roles of sexes were abolished
(ibid., pp. 174, 179).

[96]Davies, *Paul*, pp. 53-55. Adam was created from
material from the four corners of the earth, so that in him
there was "neither Jew nor Greek" (Pirke de R. Eliezer, # 11,
pp. 76-77); and he was also bisexual (Gen R. 8. 1; b Erub 18a;
b Ber 61a; StrB, 1:802, and further below).

[97]There was no enduring realization of the aspirations
of the mysteries, θίασοι, etc. See Nock, *Conversion*, passim.
The rites had to be repeated.

[98]So Meeks, "Androgyne," p. 183, notes that "The
structures of the myth and the structures of social relationship" had to "mutually enforce one another." See also Hengel,
Judaism, 1:74.

[99]Meeks, ibid., p. 166. See how Col 3:11 adds, "Barbarian, Scythian," terms which have no relation to the context,
suggesting that the saying at this point is drawing on a basic
formula that was known in an even wider circle.

[100]See Leach, "Genesis as Myth," referred to above; and
Delcourt, *Hermaphrodite*, ch. 1.

[101]Meeks, ibid., p. 185. See Smith, "Two Made One,"
pp. 36-38, referring to Plato's androgyne in *Symposium* 189e,
and *Timaeus* 31 b-c. On these references, see also Dodd, *The
Bible*, p. 165. Gressmann, *Orientalisch Religion*, pp. 86-87,
notes that Zeus was portrayed as bisexual (a godly, exalted
condition) as far back as the fourth century BCE.

[102]See above, pp. 147-48, on the references to Genesis
1-2 in the sayings and their contexts.

[103]Smith, "Two Made One," p. 38, traces the way the
tradition passed into Hellenistic Judaism, probably at a time
before Philo.

[104]See Davies, *Paul*, pp. 53-55; Jeremias, "ἄνθρωπος,"
TDNT, 1:364-66; Jervell, *Imago*, pp. 59-62, Richard A. Baer, Jr.,
Philo's Use of the Categories Male and Female (Leiden: Brill,
1970); Macdonald, "Male and Female," pp. 25-26, 92-95. In
Philo, see *Leg All* 1. 31-33, 53, 88-92; *Plant* 44; *Heres* 57,
164; *Qu Gen* 1. 4, 8, 56; 4. 160; and *Opif* 134, 151-52.

[105]*Opif* 134; *Leg All* 1, 31, 2. 12-13. See Baer, *Male
and Female*, pp. 21-22, 28. Philo here uses a Platonic construction of form (or genera) and then the empirical.

[106]*Op Mun* 151-52. See Baer, ibid., pp. 37-38.

[107]*Quaest in Gen* 1. 53; 4. 78. See Macdonald, ibid.,
pp. 95-96.

[108]The soul (i.e., the "higher" soul) was called the
"inside," and the body the "outside." So, *Leg All* 3. 40-41,
239-40; *Heres* 81-85. See Baer, *Male and Female*, pp. 30-31;
and Macdonald, "Male and Female," pp. 92, 94-96.

[109]See *Leg All* 2. 55, 80; *Som* 1. 43 (ἐκδυειν the body)
Migr Ab 192; *Poster* 137 (ἀποδυειν); *Immut* 56 (casting off,
[ἐπαμφιασασθειν], the garment of flesh [τὸ σάρκον περιβλήμα]).
Philo regards the νοῦς or "higher" soul as male, and the
created world, "body and soul," or αἰσθήσις, in female terms.
In fact, the female is only imperfect male; (*Qu Ex* 1. 7, *Qu
Gen* 1. 25). Soteriology is a matter of "becoming male" (*Qu
Gen* 2. 49) as it is in Gos Phil and other later Gnostic texts.

[110]*Vit Mos* 2. 888.

[111]Moses here is quit of the body altogether, that is,
he has left behind completely the ἄνθρωπος of Genesis 2. His
final state corresponds to the ἄνθρωπος κατ' εἰκονα τοῦ θεοῦ,
ὁ κατ' ἀληθειαν ἄνθρωπος, the rational soul of man in its
isolation and purity. See Baer, ibid., pp. 49-50.

[112]See *Leg All* 3. 71: "When the mind soars aloft and
is being initiated into the mysteries of the Lord, it judges
the body to be evil and hostile." Philo uses many mystery
terms to characterize Judaism. Moses' leading of the repent-
ant into obedience to the law is μυσταγωγεῖν (*Virt* 178); the
technical mystery term ἱεροφάντης is used for God, Moses, the
seventy elders, the high priest, etc. (*Spec* 1. 41, 2. 201, 4.
176, etc.); there are lesser mysteries, τὰ μικρὰ μυστήρια, and
greater mysteries, τὰ μεγάλα μυστήρια (*Abr* 122, *Leg All* 3.
100). Philo shares in a larger tradition in which Moses'
ascension becomes the paradigm of mystical experience: see
Wayne A. Meeks, "Moses as God and King," in Jacob Neusner,
ed., *Religions in Antiquity* (Leiden: Brill, 1968), pp. 354,
369.

[113]*Vit Con* 90.

[114]Ibid., especially 83-87. See also Baer, ibid.,
p. 100. He suggests the ritual was perhaps part of a Pente-
cost celebration.

[115]Macdonald, "Male and Female," p. 117, makes this
suggestion. Marc Philonenko, *Joseph et Asêneth. Introduction, texte critique, traduction et notes* (Leiden: Brill,
1968), pp. 108-9, dates the tractate cautiously late in the
first century BCE or early in the first century CE.

[116]Jos As 14. 12, ἀπόθου τὸν χιτῶνα ὅνπερ ἐνδέδυσαι;
compare with Gen 3:21 (ἐποίησεν κύριος . . . χιτῶνας . . .
καὶ ἐνέδυσεν αὐτούς). See Macdonald, "Male and Female,"
p. 117.

[117]Jos As 15. 4 ("You will be renewed and recreated
and will receive a new life").

[118]Jos As 15. 10 (στολὴν γάμου, τὴν στολὴν τὴν ἀρχαῖαν
τὴν πρώτην).

[119]Jos As 16. 9.

[120]Jos As 15. 1. Philonenko sees this as a reference
to the androgyny of an initiate into the mystery cults and
gnosis, similar to Gos Thom 114. Macdonald, ibid., p. 119,
notes the obvious relevance to the language of 1 Cor 11:10.

[121]Gen 1:27 and 5:2 are translated "Male and female
created He *him*" (Bab Talmud, *Megilla* 9a; Mekilta, *Pisha* 14,
which Lauterback translates, "a male with corresponding female
parts created He him" [1:111-12]). See also Gen R. 8. 1;
b 'Erub. 18a; b Ber. 61a; StrB, 1:802.

[122]Meeks, "Androgyne," p. 186, notes that in Gen R.
8. 1, Adam was created διπρόσωπον, a word used synonymously
with ἀνδρογύνος; and, in the creation of Eve, the two "sides"
or "bodies" were separated. The similarity to the language
and thought of Plato *Symposium* 189b is striking. See also
Lev R. 14. This would seem to explain the reference to making
"what is on the right hand as what is on the left," etc., in
Acts of Peter 38, above. Philo also speaks of Eve as "half
of his (Adam's) body" (*Qu Gen* 1. 25, *Opif* 151).

[123]Gen R. 4. 20. 12; Apoc Mos 20:1-3.

[124]Smith, "Two Made One," pp. 41-42, notes the use in
Gen R. 39. 14 of the verb of Gen 1:26 and 12:5 to refer to the
making of a proselyte. "He who brings a Gentile near is as
though he created him." Notice the similarity to the language
of Joseph and Asenath 15. 4, above.

[125]Smith, ibid., p. 42.

[126]Moses' ascent on Sinai was a focal point for a
cluster of Moses-traditions, as becomes apparent from a comparison of various sources. In Philo *Vit Mos* 1. 155-58,
Moses is declared to have become god and king on Sinai, a
mediator between God and men. His office is founded on his
Sinai-ascent as a mystic vision, using Ex 7:1. This glorification of Moses on Sinai is referred to in terms of a restoration of the lost Adamic image of God in *Qu Ex* 2. 46, Debarim R.
11. 3, Yalkut ha-Makiri on Prob 31:29, Ps 49:21, and 68:13
(reproduced in Meeks, "Moses," p. 364), as well as the Samaritan Memar Marqar 5. 4, 6. 3. Meeks concludes that the primary
function of this tradition is to guarantee an esoteric teaching. Moses' ascension has this function in Jubilees (all of
which is an esoteric, angelic revelation to Moses on Sinai),
4 Ezra, and Talm Yer Peah 2. 4. Moses takes heavenly journeys
and receives cosmological secrets in Ps Philo 11:15-12:1,
19:8-16, and 2 Bar 4:2-7.

[127]Adam's original glory is referred to in Apoc Mosis
20-21; 2 Enoch 30:11; 4 Ezra 3:6-7; 2 Baruch 23:4. The righteous are reclothed in this glory in 4 Ezra 7:95-97; 8:51;
2 Baruch 48:49; 49:3; 54:15, 21: 1 Enoch 39:7-9; 50:1; 58:2;
103:2, etc. See Jervell, *Imago*, p. 46. The expression "glory
of Adam (or man)" appears in the Qumran writings in 1 QS 4:23,
CD 3:20, and 1 QH 17:15.

[128]See Vita Adae 4:2, 12-17, 33; Apoc Mosis 7:20;
Jub 3:15; 2 Enoch 30:11, 14; 1 Enoch 69:11. See also Smith,
"Two Made One," p. 43; and Meeks, "Moses," p. 361.

[129]See 1 Enoch 51:1-4 in the β-recension (Charles,
Enoch, p. 101): 1 Enoch 104:4-6 ("ye shall become companions
of the host of heaven"); and 2 Baruch 51:5-12 ("They shall be
made like unto the angels"). In 2 Bar 51:7, this hope is for
those who are saved by works, and those to whom the law has
been a hope--reminiscent of the "works of law" of Gal 2:16,
etc. There is a similar promise in Jub 1:29, 4:26, and 2 Baruch
32:6.

[130]For instance, Jubilees, which seems to have affinities with the theology of the opponents in certain other
respects (the "apologetic" Abraham, calendrical laws, etc.)
also has ascetic tendencies.

[131]4 Ezra 7:128. See also StrB, 1:891. This belief
was not taken up by the Rabbis (ibid., 1:897). They believed
that married life would continue after the resurrection, as
would eating, drinking, etc.

[132]4 Ezra 7:96-101; and 2 Baruch 51:10 ("equal to the
stars"). Charles, *Pseudepigrapha*, 2:589, comments that, in
this period, stars and angels were closely related. So, in
Galatians, the opponents are concerned to fellowship with
angels and are devotees of the στοιχεῖα τοῦ κόσμου, which must
be associated with astral worship.

[133]See above, the references to Clem Alex *Stromata* 3
and 2 Clem 12.

[134]There are allusions to Genesis 1-3 in Poimandres
in connection with creation and fall, androgyny, and restoration to the primeval condition. See Dodd, *Bible*, pp. 146-65.

[135]See Dodd and MacRae, cited above, p. 289.

[136]See the account of the resolution of the fall, the
putting off of the seven fallen characteristics, and the
return to the condition of the seven governors, who are ἀρσενο-
θῆλυς (## 18-21). It is also a return to the image of God:
the goal of man is ἐν θεῷ γίνονται, θεωθῆναι (# 26). See
Jervell, *Imago*, p. 147.

[137]See the soteriological value of gnosis (# 18).
Liturgy is suggested in ## 9, 14, and 17, pointing to the
ritual and cultic activity of a particular community. # 26,
"This is the good end of those who have had knowledge, to be
deified," suggests a liturgy of investiture, or part of it.
There is a sudden change of person, and repetition of certain
elements.

[138]See above, pp. 149-50.

[139]See the material above, p. 147.

^{140}See Meeks, "Androgyne," pp. 165, 180-81; and Macdonald, "Male and Female," pp. 96-97.

^{141}Meeks, ibid., pp. 191-92. The two opposite and simultaneous errors into which the Corinthians have fallen is most explicable in terms of an Adamic androgyne myth which has left the church in total confusion as to sexual roles in the present age. See Macdonald, pp. 102, 107.

^{142}Jervell, *Imago*, pp. 292-94; Macdonald, ibid., pp. 96-99. Just as, for Philo, the first Adam was a heavenly, incorporeal one and the second was made of the earth and given "coats of skin," so, for the Corinthians, in baptism they have put off the earthly and put on the heavenly man. But Paul reverses the order of the two men; and says that we still bear the image of the earthly and await the heavenly.

^{143}See above, p. 151. In apocalyptic, the resurrection body is an astral body. See Conzelmann, *1 Corinthians*, p. 282.

^{144}See how baptism is involved in the enthusiastic self-understanding of the Corinthians, 1 Cor 1:12-17, 6:11, 10:1-11, 15:29. Robinson, *Trajectories*, pp. 30-46, suggests that the Corinthians were interpreting Jesus-traditions concerning baptism and the resurrection similar to those which found their way into the Gospel of Thomas and the Gospel of Philip.

^{145}See above, p. 143.

^{146}Macdonald, "Male and Female," pp. 96-97.

^{147}See above, pp. 78-82, on the terminology of 3:1-5; and pp. 147-48 on ἐνδυειν in 3:27 and mystery-language.

^{148}See above note. This terminology is used nowhere else in Paul. His typical way of using baptismal formulae is dialectical, that is, he takes over the statements of others and reinterprets them, as in Rom 6:1-9 as compared with Colossians 2-3; 1 Cor 6:11, 10:1-11. So the language Paul uses here also can be expected to be part of the debate.

^{149}See above, pp. 116-19. See how this accords with the widespread Jewish tradition of Moses' Sinai ascent as a divinizing, and restoration of the lost glory of Adam, see above, p. 152.

^{150}Which also rings of Philo's presentation of Judaism as a mystery, enabling the soul to escape the body. See above, p. 151.

^{151}Also to be borne in mind are, firstly, the place of baptism in Paul's whole argument, and the way it runs throughout the letter (see above, p. 74). When Paul speaks of baptism in 3:27-29, he has not left behind his main argument); and, secondly, the significance of the rhetorical

structure of Galatians as a whole (Paul is throughout debating
the Galatians' acceptance of the opponents' theology).

[152]See above, p. 150. Note especially the striking
citation formula in 2 Clem 12:1, and the ready acceptance of
the saying itself in "orthodox" circles (p. 150).

[153]Macdonald, "Male and Female," p. 68, correctly
observes that no noted authorities have ever attributed the
saying originally to Jesus. Lightfoot, *Galatians*, p. 149,
suggested that the saying may have been founded on Luke 20:35.

[154]See above, pp. 152-53.

[155]Other Gnostics also sought union with the angels
through baptism. See Gos Phil 65. 19-26, quoted above, p. 348;
and Excerpta ex Theodoto 21, 22, 36, where males are joined
with the logos, females become male, and the whole church is
changed into angels. The Marcosians, *Adv Haer* 1. 21. 3,
believed they were baptised into union with the "powers."
This suggests a borrowing from apocalyptic Judaism.

[156]David L. Dungan, *The Sayings of Jesus in the
Churches of Paul* (Philadelphia: Fortress Press, 1971), Paul
here quotes dominical sayings very accurately and is vitally
concerned with the ongoing development of the interpretation
of the sayings of Jesus.

[157]Robinson, "Kerygma," pp. 127-31, finds that "only
in Q and 1 Corinthians does the term "'kerygma' occur prior
to the pastorals, and only in Q and 1 Corinthians is Sophia a
Christological title, and only in Q (Matt 22:38-42 = Luke
11:29-32) and 1 Corinthians (1:17-2:7) are the two rare uses
combined with each other and with the rejection of 'signs'
required by this 'evil generation,' (Q), 'the Jews' (1 Corinthians)." He concludes that "1 Corinthians and Q have in
common . . . the issue of Jesus and wisdom . . . the Q material
may in part have had such a Sitz im Leben as the conflict in
Corinth."

[158]Balch, "Backgrounds," pp. 355-56.

[159]Ibid., p. 356.

[160]Ibid., p. 357.

[161]The Q material is treated differently by Matthew
and Luke respectively on this question. One insists that a
man leave his wife for the kingdom (Luke 18:29) and the other
does not (Matt 19:29 = Mark 10:29); etc. See Balch, ibid.,
pp. 353-54. When it comes to the saying about the resurrection, the angelic state, and marriage, one puts the end of
marriage in the present tense (Luke 20:34-35) and the other
puts it in the future (Matt 22:30 = Mark 12:25). The implication is that Luke follows Q, and Matthew follows Mark. So, in
Q, the resurrection-saying was used to forbid marriage--just
as the saying in Corinth was being used to forbid marriage.

[162]See above, pp. 147, 153-54.

[163]See above, pp. 153-54.

[164]This suggested function of the resurrection-saying in Q and 1 Corinthians indicates how this same saying came to be understood later by Gnostics as forbidding marriage, etc. They may actually be following a traditional interpretation of the dominical saying which existed in the earliest Christian circles.

[165]See above, pp. 146-48, 150-53.

[166]There is θρησκεία τῶν ἀγγέλων in Colossians (2:18); in 1 Corinthians the woman is told that she must ἐξουσίαν ἔχειν ἐπὶ τῆς κεφαλῆς διὰ τοὺς ἀγγέλους (11:10), the enthusiasts speak in the tongues τῶν ἀνθρώπων . . . καὶ τῶν ἀγγέλων (13:1), and, in connection with the resurrection, Paul must discuss σώματα ἐπουράνια καὶ σώματα ἐπίγεια (15:40). The treatment of the dominical resurrection-saying in 1 Corinthians follows the ascetic tendencies of Q, 4 Ezra, and apocalyptic Judaism, which are bound up with interest in fellowship with angels; and in Galatians, the opponents' interest in angels intrudes in 1:8, 3:19, 4:14, and traditions of revelation and inspiration, law, and the στοιχεῖα, etc. See above, pp. 152-54.

[167]See above, pp. 150-53, on the different understandings of baptism, resurrection, and androgyny, in Clement, Cassanius, and Gos Phil.

[168]Balch, "Backgrounds," p. 364, and Jervell, *Imago*, pp. 309-12, among others, have suggested that the traditions cherished by the Corinthians may have included Gal 3:28.

[169]See the rhetorical analysis, pp. 46-49; the opponents as efficient missionaries, 59; the significance of such words as βασκαίνειν, 69, and the way restatements of the *causa* run throughout the letter, 68-69.

[170]See pp. 68-69, on 2:19-20, 3:1-5, 3:27-29, 4:6-7, and 5:24.

[171]See particularly above, p. 64; on the way that circumcision stands for attempts at justification by works in 5:4-6.

[172]In place of the efficacy of circumcision (works), he argues for the efficacy of the Galatians' past baptism; in place of the claims made for works of law, he argues for the realities already actualized in baptism.

[173]See above, pp. 59-61, 75-76. Nothing can be added to the lordship of Christ, so nothing can be added to the believer's justification.

[174]See above, p. 64, on the essential place of circumcision in the opponents' soteriology; and above, p. 139, a definition of sacrament.

[175]See above, p. 74, quoting Stählin: in 3:6-22, the lines of salvation-history end in Christ; in 3:27-29, they end in baptism. This suggests the essential place of the pericope in the argument.

[176]See above, pp. 150-52.

[177]See above, pp. 147-48.

[178]See above, pp. 143-44.

[179]This conclusion rests partly on the deductions about the way in which the saying functions polemically in 1 Corinthians and Colossians. See above, pp. 142-43, 146-47.

[180]See above, pp. 149-50. The examination of these extra-Biblical formulae also helps to confirm the traditional form of the saying and the myth behind it.

[181]See above, pp. 150-53.

[182]As well as examples from Plato, Hellenistic mythology, the Stoics, etc., Judaism knows the myth in Philo, Joseph and Asenath, the later rabbis, and, in certain respects, apocalyptic Judaism. In Poimandres there is another apparently pre-Christian form of the myth, showing heavy dependence on Genesis 1-2. See above, pp. 151-53.

[183]See above, pp. 151-53. Mention could also be made of the χρίσμα τῆς ἀφθαρσίας by which Asenath is "made new" and her head is made "as the head of a young man" (Jos and As 15:4).

[184]This is made the more likely in light of the fact that Judaism believed that Abraham was "made new" by the rite of circumcision, even referring to this event in the language of Gen 1:26; see above, p. 152.

[185]On the place of the androgyny-myth in 1 Corinthians and Colossians, see above, pp. 147-48, 153-54.

[186]See above, pp. 78-82, on the language of 3:1-5; also above, pp. 139-40, on the opponents' probable use of Abraham's righteousness by faith, then his circumcision, as the "ordo salutis" for Gentiles.

[187]As the "circumcision" of the Colossian opponents seems to do. See above, pp. 142-43, 147-48.

[188]See above, p. 143.

[189]See how justification is presented in apocalyptic/cosmic terms in the opening and closing of the letter (above, pp. 59-61); and as freedom from the enslaving powers of the present evil aeon (pp. 63-66). The two antithetical spheres of σάρξ and πνεῦμα are used to characterize the two programs of "works" and "faith," and to epitomize the whole debate (pp. 78-81).

[190] See an analysis of some of the mystery-terms (pp. 78 - 82); and the law-tradition as one which lays itself open to the charge of devotion to the στοιχεῖα τοῦ κόσμου (pp. 130-134). This same tradition is interested in fellowship with angels and draws on astral religion (pp. 130-31).

[191] On the unusual presentation of Abraham and circumcision in Galatians, see above, pp. 82-83. (Abraham here is justified by "faith alone"), and p. 139 (in Galatians, circumcision is not one of the ἀδιάφορα); and on the unusual Gentile acceptance of circumcision.

[192] See above, pp. 150-51, on the pagan and Jewish parallels to the saying, also connected with experiments in breaking down sexual roles.

[193] Meeks, "Androgyne," p. 204. Colossians uses the mythical language of reconciliation to speak of human unity within the congregation (3:9), and the same occurs in Eph 2:11-12, where the divisive threat is a "circumcision made with hands." See also Gunther, *Opponents*, p. 84.

[194] See above, p. 151.

[195] See above, pp. 150-53, on the function of cultus in the change of societal roles. Meeks, "Androgyne," p. 204, points out that the same was true in Christian circles. In Ephesians 5 and Colossians 3 Christ's relation to the church is in terms of a mythical or metaphorical concept of marriage between the Redeemer and the community (see also 2 Cor 11:2, Rev 19:6-9, 21:2, 9). If this mythical relationship cannot be established, the new societal relationships demanded by Christianity cannot eventuate.

[196] See above, pp. 102-3, on the opponents' consciousness of being the remnant. The Qumran community, which saw itself in these terms, also claimed that there was a new, utopian relationship between the members of the community. So, 1 QS 4:4, "Abounding love for all who follow the truth." See below, p. 172. The Essenes also experienced some breakdown of the male-female roles. See above, p. 151.

[197] The opponents no doubt agreed that baptism joined the believer to Jesus. The phrase ὅσοι γάρ of 3:27 suggests that the claim is taken for granted. The term ἐνδύειν Χριστόν may also belong to them (or perhaps ἐνδύειν Ἰησοῦν). See above, pp. 147-48. But they denied that Jesus was the σπέρμα Ἀβραάμ.

[198] Paul in 3:28 is probably presenting Jesus not only as σπέρμα Ἀβραάμ but as Adam.

[199] This is the implication of 3:29--if you are Christ's, you are *already* Abraham's seed, heirs, etc. To continue the religious quest now is only to abandon heirship, and to turn to pre-Christian religion. Thus this baptism-saying has the same function as other restatements of the *causa*, e.g., 3:1-5, 4:8-11.

[200]Koester, *Trajectories*, p. 145. There seems to be much in his suggestion that Jesus' role is mythologized, along with that of Abraham and Moses. Jesus is apparently made an equal with them in a succession of heroes in Israel's religion. He becomes the last in a series of acts of God, elevating the old covenant to cosmic dimensions.

[201]Many have noticed the few references to the parousia in Galatians. The stress is instead on the present deliverance from the cosmic forces of the old age.

[202]See above, p. 156.

[203]See above, pp. 96-97, on the apostle-tradition and the demand for ἀποκαλύψεις, etc., which is operating in both Galatia and Corinth; in both contexts also are concern for fellowship with angels, interest in Spirit, miracles, etc.

[204]The wisdom-speculation behind 1 Corinthians is clear. See Wilckens, "σοφία," *TDNT*, 6:519-22; and Conzelmann, *1 Corinthians*, pp. 45-48. This wisdom-speculation shows affinities with apocalyptic literature; and the literature of Qumran, which reveals some striking parallels to the opponents' theology, also belongs in the "Hasidic wisdom tradition." See above, pp. 101, 132-33.

[205]On the differences between 1 Corinthians and 2 Corinthians, see Robinson, cited below; and Georgi, *Gegner*, p. 303, etc. But there are also important similarities between the "opponents" in each instance. Balch, "Backgrounds," pp. 362-64, mentions interest in the exegesis of the OT in both; the use of Moses-traditions in both (1 Corinthians 7 and 2 Corinthians 3), and the affinities with the theology of Q in both (such as depreciation of the passion and the humanity of Jesus, interest in miracles and divine men, etc.).

[206]Robinson, "Kerygma," pp. 114-15; and his *Trajectories*, pp. 62-66.

[207]Ibid., *Trajectories*, p. 65, resting especially on 2 Cor 13:4 ("For He was crucified in weakness, but lives by the power of God"); 2 Cor 4:5 ("we preach not ourselves, but Jesus Christ as Lord, and ourselves as your servants because of Jesus"); and 2 Cor 5:16 (the irrelevance of knowing Christ after the flesh)--all contrasting starkly with the relation of the human Jesus to the kerygma, the task of the church and the lives of believers in 1 Cor 1:18-2:5 etc.

[208]Ibid., "Kerygma," p. 143.

[209]See their search for δόξα (2 Corinthians 3), and their heroic understanding of Moses and Jesus (Georgi, *Gegner*, pp. 286-88); their fascination with ὀπτασίας καὶ ἀποκαλύψεις κυρίου, (2 Cor 12:1); their performance of δυνάμεις καὶ τέρατα as signs of their apostleship (2 Corinthians 12); their concern for πνεῦμα (2 Cor 3:17); etc.

[210]See 2 Cor 3:4-18. Gunther, *Opponents*, p. 86, even
credits them with interest in circumcision, because of the
use of καταδουλοῦν in 2 Cor 11:20, compared with Gal 2:4.

[211]2 Cor 11:2.

CHAPTER TEN

ETHICAL TRADITIONS

[1]See above, pp. 15-17, 26-31. Schmithals, closely
followed by Marxsen, assumes that the whole letter is against
Gnostics; and the nature and content of the ethical section is
a principal part of the argument of both.

[2]See above, pp. 27-31. Lütgert and Ropes propounded
a two-front theory. In the ethical portions of the letter,
libertines are confronted, who must be different opponents
from the legalists. The paraenetic materials must directly
reflect the situation in Galatia, which must be libertine, and
cannot therefore be in view in the earlier part of the letter.
The "implied two-front" theorists also assume that, in the
ethical portions, Paul faces a different opponent. There are
perhaps two groups in the Galatian congregation. Jewett has
most recently propounded a variant of this theory, assuming
again that suggestions of sexual immorality, impurity, and
licentiousness reflect the actual behavior of the Galatians.

[3]See above, pp. 27-30. Jewett has noticed that Galatians deals with the congregations as a homogeneous group
(1:6, 3:1-5, 5:7, etc.). The entire congregation seems as
much in danger of one extreme (if they are extremes) as of
the other, and there are the same concerns in the so-called
anti-legalist and anti-libertine sections, i.e., νόμος, σάρξ,
πνεῦμα, 3:1-5, 5:13-24, 6:1-2, 7-8; ἐλευθερία, 4:21-31, 5:1-
13. But against Jewett it must be said that he has no way of
holding the letter together. By starting with the ethical
portion, and making it entirely contextual, and applying it
to the whole congregation, there is no way of explaining how
the Galatians are tempted with nomism.

[4]See above, p. 74. Furnish, *Theology*, p. 110,
has noted that it is typically, in Paul, the same gospel which
finds expression now in theological statements, now in ethical
exhortations.

[5]See above, pp. 53-54. Theologically, there is always
an intimate relationship between indicative and imperative,
and between the human predicament under law and that same
predicament under the tyrant sin.

[6]Schmithals has shown convincingly that the lists of
virtues, in the ethical section of the letter, are integral
to the argument against circumcision. A quarter of the letter
is against "*sarkic*" conduct, and such stress cannot be detached
from the central concerns of the letter.

[7]See above, p. 53, on 5:1, 5:13, and 5:25.

[8]See above, pp. 81-82.

[9]See above, pp. 78-82, and the form the attempt takes here--a beginning (ἐνάρχεσθαι) and ending (ἐπιτελεῖν) which actually results in a complete fall from the status of πνευματικοί: the Spirit has come εἰκῇ. In 6:1-10, the self-styled πνευματικοί are in mortal danger (πλανᾶν) because their "biting and devouring" (5:13-15, 5:26) is placing them under their own retributive law of sowing and reaping which will annihilate "worldly" sinners. See above, p. 82.

[10]See above, p. 54. For instance, Furnish, *Theology*, pp. 71-72, notes that Paul "supports his own exhortations by relating them to what, on other grounds, his readers are already willing to acknowledge."

[11]See above, pp. 53-54, on the way a *refutatio* sought to destroy an opponent's argument on his own terms. Paul's claim here, in effect, is that the intruders' program has brought about the very situation it was supposed to prevent.

[12]On the suggested significance of Gal 3:28 in the overall argument, see above, pp. 146-57.

[13]On the opponents' claims to be community-apostles, see above, pp. 52, 59.

[14]See above, pp. 159-61.

[15]The rejection of this particular claim of the opponents runs right through the letter, and its central place in the debate is evident from its place in the *conclusio*. See above, pp. 64-65, on 6:12-13.

[16]Martin, *Foundations*, 2:154, who notes the puzzling contrast between freedom in Christ from the claims of Mosaic Torah-religion, and the law of Christ, which allows no moral laxity.

[17]See Stoike, "Law of Christ," pp. 47-49, and other authorities cited there.

[18]The way the passage as a whole is built around this form will be further considered below, pp. 167-71.

[19]Ehrhard Kamlah, *Die Form der katalogischen Paränese im neuen Testament* (Tübingen: J. C. B. Mohr, 1964), pp. 3, 15-27; Conzelmann, *1 Corinthians*, pp. 100-101 (excursus on catalogs of virtues and vices); Siegfried Wibbing, *Die Tugend- und Lasterkataloge im Neuen Testament, und ihre Traditionsgeschichte unter besonderer Berücksichtigung der Qumran-Texte* (Berlin: Töpelmann, 1959), pp. 78-79, who defines the form as "asyndetischer und polysyndetischer Aneinderreihung der einzelnen Glieder"); and Doty, *Letters*, pp. 57-58.

[20]Wibbing, *Tugend- und Lasterkataloge*, p. 78, Conzel-
mann, *1 Corinthians*, p. 101, and others, have complete lists.
Vice catalogs are found at Mark 7:21 and parallels, Matt 15:19,
Rom 1:28-31, 13:13, 1 Cor 5:10, 6:9, 2 Cor 12:20, Gal 5:19-21,
Col 3:5, 1 Tim 1:9, 2 Tim 3:2-5, Tit 3:3, 1 Pet 2:1, 4:13, 15,
Rev 21:8, 22:15. Virtue catalogs are found at 2 Cor 6:6, Eph
4:2, 32, 5:9, Phil 4:8, Col 3:12, 1 Tim 4:12, 6:11, 2 Tim 2:22,
3:10, 1 Pet 3:8, 2 Pet 1:5-7.

[21]Wibbing, *Tugend- und Lasterkataloge*, p. 78, gives
examples from the Stoa, and from late Judaism (Philo, *Rer
Div Her* 168-73, Wis Sol 14:25, 4 Macc, Testaments of Reuben
3:2-8, Levi 14:5-8, Judah 16:1, and Benjamin 6:4, the Assumption of Moses 7, 3 Baruch 4:17, 8:5, 13:4, 1 Enoch 91:6, Jub
21:21, 23:14, Sib Or 2:254-83, 3:36-45, and 1 QS 4); and there
are other examples in Gnosticism (CH 1. 21-23, 13. 7-13; Nag
Hammadi Codex 6, book 4).

[22]Kamlah, *Paränese*, pp. 39-49, traces the form to
Iranian dualism and suggests that the dualistic scheme of the
form rests on a dualistic mythical tradition, not on ethical
monotheism (p. 165). Thus there is an intense dualistic statement involved in the form (see pp. 116-34, on CH 1. 22-23,
where the double catalog is used to assert the two spheres in
which all men live: the vices are those of the natural man
living under the influence of the planets, etc.; the virtues,
which do not at all correspond, express the new sphere into
which the initiate is taken up). The same is true of 1 QS 3-4,
where the state of men is fixed in terms of dualism, and the
virtue- and vice-lists express this intense dualism, being
statements of the other-worldliness of the community (pp. 42-
48).

[23]So Kamlah, *Paränese*, pp. 50ff., defines the form
as one which works out a scheme of sin and righteousness in
two catalogs, irreconcilable opposites, each ending with a
promise of salvation or a threat of destruction.

[24]Kamlah himself suggests that, in the case of the
Christian communities, the life-situation was probably baptism, as is suggested strongly by 1 Cor 6:9 (ibid., p. 3).

[25]Kamlah, *Paränese*, pp. 12-18, has argued from the
dualism of the form that its function is not paraenetic but
indicative and is only the basis for the paraenesis. However, the fact that the life-situation of the form in Christian communities was probably baptism, as Kamlah admits,
suggests a paraenetic function. Doty, *Letters*, p. 58, like
Kamlah, speaks of "descriptive" and "paraenetic" forms but
reverses some of Kamlah's designations, now calling Gal 5:19-
23 paraenetic. It would seem preferable to dispense with
this artificial distinction entirely. Furnish, *Theology*,
pp. 95-110, argues convincingly that neat distinctions between
"theology" and "ethics," "indicative" and "imperative," break
down in Paul's writings. He notes that, in Philemon, the
whole thanksgiving section has a hortatory function, pointing
forward to the imperatives and expressed further on; and that

Paul elsewhere uses indicative statements in order to exhort
(e.g., Gal 4:31). It is possible to speak of the "imperatival
indicative" in Rom 5:1-11, 6:1-14, 7:4, 1 Thess 4:7, and countless other instances.
  Conzelmann, *1 Corinthians*, p. 100, notes that the form
was used principally for apologetic ends, to point out "Pagan
trademarks" and to heighten the separation of the particular
community from "the world." Here again, one could speak of
an "imperatival indicative." It is important to note that,
for this reason, the vice-lists do not speak entirely to the
vices of the community itself, but are to an extent traditional. They are attempts to characterize sin, and the sinful
"world," in terms of ethical catalogs. See Kamlah, *Paränese*,
pp. 116-34; Conzelmann, *1 Corinthians*, pp. 100-101; and Doty,
Letters, p. 57.

  [26]That is, a scheme based on the imagery of two ways,
roads, ways of life, etc., which is paraenetic in function.
The best examples are in Jewish wisdom literature (Ps 1:6,
Prov 4:18, Ps 138-24, Prov 12:28, etc.), CH 1. 22-23, 13. 7-9,
Did 1-6, Barn 18-21, and in the New Testament, Matt 7:13-14,
Rom 13:11-14, Matt 25:31-46, Luke 6:20-26, Gal 5:19-23, and
Col 3:5-17. See Michaelis, "ὁδός," *TDNT*, 5:42-93, and Kamlah,
Paränese, pp. 3, 24-27, 210-14. Hengel, *Judaism*, 1:140, notes
that the form became significant in Jewish wisdom and apoc-
alyptic literature, and that it has Greek parallels (e.g.,
the fable of Heracles at the cross-roads).

  [27]For instance, Kamlah, *Paränese*, pp. 50ff., distinguishes between the "double catalog" and the "two-way
scheme," seeing the latter only in such literature as Did 1-6
and Barn 18-21, where the dualistic scheme of the "double
catalog" becomes a frame for catechetical material, and can
be called a "paraenetic" form.

  [28]Rather than the two-way scheme being a development
of the virtue- and vice-catalogs. Both Michaelis, "ὁδός,"
TDNT, 5:42-93, and Hengel, *Judaism*, 1:140, trace the form
back at least as far as the sophist Prodicus and his fable
of Heracles at the cross-roads (Xenoph *Mem* 2. 1. 21-54).

  [29]Wibbing, *Tugend- und Lasterkataloge*, p. 33, sees a
direct relationship between the virtue- and vice-catalogs of
late Judaism and the scheme of the two ways. He also points
out the basic dualistic structure of this latter scheme, and
its paraenetic function (p. 35), as does Hengel, *Judaism*,
1:40. Wibbing, ibid., pp. 61-64, notes that the two-way
scheme merges with virtue- and vice-catalogs in Test 12,
1 Enoch 91:6ff., and especially 1 QS 4. It is this basic
dualism of both the virtue- and vice-lists and the two-way
scheme, in apocalyptic literature, the New Testament, and
later Christian literature, which distinguishes them from
Stoic lists on the one hand, and Old Testament forms on the
other (Wibbing, ibid., p. 42).

  [30]The proposal that the form is paraenetic in Galatians 5 is confirmed by its use elsewhere in the New Testament.

In Colossians, the dualism of the heretical "philosophy" is
taken over polemically, and so paraenesis is conveyed in the
dualistic form of "old man" and "new man." See Jervell, *Imago*,
pp. 244-48. The way the paraenesis is taken up into the "two-
way" frame, as in Did 1-6 and Barn 18-21, suggests again that
the "two-way" scheme is not a different, later form. Kamlah,
Paränese, pp. 31-34, admits a paraenetic function here. Rom
13:12-14, which also uses dualistic language, is clearly
paraenetic (Kamlah, ibid., pp. 31-34). The single scheme of
Matt 5:3-11 becomes a double scheme in Luke 6:20-26, resulting
in an intensification of both the eschatological element and
the paraenetic force (Davies, *Sermon*, pp. 282-85). Matt
7:13-14 is clearly paraenetic, as is Matt 25:31-46, though
again the eschatological element is sharpened in the extreme
division between the good and the wicked (Kamlah, *Paränese*,
p. 27).

[31]See above, pp. 23-24.

[32]Kamlah, ibid., p. 12; and Dahl, *Paul*, p. 103.

[33]See above, p. 327, note 25, on the traditional
nature of the virtue- and vice-lists; and above, p. 54, on
Paul's use even of the ethics of his opponents.

[34]See Gal 4:5, 2 Cor 5:17, 1 Cor 10:11, and Gal 6:15.
For Paul, the Christian stands at the "end of the ages."
Gunther Bornkamm, *Paul*, trans. D. M. B. Stalker (New York:
Harper and Row, 1971), p. 198, comments: "That which Jewish
and primitive Christian apocalyptic awaited in the future and
described in a great variety of pictures (e.g., Rev 21:5),
Paul, because of God's reconciling the world to Himself in
Christ, proclaimed as an accomplished fact."

[35]Kamlah, *Paränese*, p. 12; and Dahl, *Paul*, p. 102.
Only Christianity speaks in terms of "You have been justified."

[36]Bornkamm, *Experience*, p. 80.

[37]The result is an ethic of "eschatological tension"
between the "already" and the "not yet," not an interim ethic
between the ages, but an ethic of the overlapping of the ages.
See Furnish, *Theology*, pp. 134-35. See also Bornkamm, *Paul*,
p. 204; "The new thing here is not the subject matter, but
rather the context of the admonitions."

[38]Kamlah, *Paränese*, p. 15.

[39]Wibbing, *Tugend- und Lasterkataloge*, p. 40: σάρξ
and πνεῦμα are two "Machtsphären," which are irreconcilable
opposites. Which of the two the Christian stands under
becomes evident from his "Tun," as the following catalog
makes clear.

[40]See Kamlah, *Paränese*, p. 16: Paul typically uses
the aorist to refer to the believer's incorporation into the
death of Christ at baptism. See also above, pp. 64-65. Thus

the aorist here comports with the aorist ἀπέθανον and the
perfect συνεσταύρωμαι in 2:19. Some of those who see baptism
referred to here are Jervell, *Imago*, p. 234, as well as Duncan,
Lagrange, Burton, Oepke, and Schlier. Mussner demurs, because
ἐσταύρωσαν is the active form, whereas Paul usually uses the
passive form for baptism. It would have been difficult to
have expressed the thought of the verse in the passive form.
The active aorist here implies both indicative and imperative.
See Schneider, "σταυρόω," *TDNT*, 7:583. Mussner himself admits
that baptism is at least indirectly in view.

[41]Kamlah, *Paränese*, p. 16.

[42]Ibid., p. 17.

[43]Kamlah, ibid., p. 17, draws attention to the continued polemic against works of law in 5:16, 18, and 23.

[44]Furnish, *Theology*, pp. 128-29, notes Paul's stress
on the arrival of the new age in Galatians 3-4, evident in the
coming of the Spirit, being known of God, the cry of the son
of God, Abba, the possession already of the inheritance, witnessed by the entrance into the age of the Spirit. It is
significant then that 5:24 continues this stress, by proclaiming the defeat of the power of σάρξ, and demanding the walk
in the Spirit.

[45]See above, pp. 75-76.

[46]Bornkamm, *Experience*, p. 84: "The obedience of
believers cannot penetrate further than to what has happened
to us at the beginning. It takes place in the constant
'crawling under baptism' (Luther). In this sense one may
formulate it pointedly: baptism is the dedication of the new
life, and the new life is the appropriation of baptism."

[47]That is, they are the concrete particularity of
"life turned to the future for the first time," the "concrete
ways of Christ in the world." See Furnish, *Theology*, p. 74.

[48]See above, pp. 75-82. It is for this reason that
justification and ethics are two sides of the one reality
"in Christ." Justification is a *life*, the life of the new
age; ethics are the concrete spelling out of that life. See
Furnish, ibid., p. 110.

[49]See above, p. 164.

[50]Wibbing, *Tugend- und Lasterkataloge*, p. 40.

[51]See above, p. 54, quoting various authorities.
Paul's genius shows through in the subtle modification of
vice-lists. See also p. 54 quoting Funk: Paul's customary
method of argument is to adapt traditional ethical material
in a particular way. He suggests three ways to decide the
degree of "contextuality."

[52]The traditional nature of the material is evident
from the assertion that these values are φανερά (5:19). See
Furnish, *Theology*, p. 72. But Wibbing, ibid., pp.
86-108, suggests some contextuality on a statistical basis. Of the
vices, ten occur elsewhere in the vice-lists in Paul's writings (πορνεία, ἀκαθαρσία, ἀσέλγεια, θυμός, ἔρις, φθόνος, μέθη,
κῶμος, ζῆλος, ἐριθεία) and five do not (εἰδωλολατρία, φαρμακεία, ἔχθραι, διχορτασία, αἱρεσις). Of the latter, two are
clearly traditional (εἰδωλολατρία and φαρμακεία typically go
together as in Wisdom of Solomon 12:4, Did 5:1, Barn 20:1),
and ἔχθραι is common in the NT, though not in vice-lists (see
Eph 2:14-16, Luke 23:12). Of the virtues, six occur in other
virtue-lists (ἀγάπη, εἰρήνη, μακροθυμία πραΰτης, ἀγαθωσύνη,
πίστις) and three do not (χαρά, χρηστότης, ἐγκράτεια). Again,
however, they are common virtues outside the lists (see Rom
15:13, 14:17, Col 3:12, etc.).

[53]These vices are normally not the vices of the community, but of the "world." See above, p. 164.

[54]Wibbing, *Tugend- und Lasterkataloge*, pp. 96-97,
notes that ἔρις, ζῆλος, θυμοί, ἐριθεῖαι is a kind of formula,
as these four appear in the same order in 2 Cor 12:20-21.
φθόνοι is repeated again in Gal 5:26.

[55]Wibbing, ibid., pp. 96-97. They are found only in
this vice-catalog in Galatians 5, and are unattested in the
catalogs of the popular preachers.

[56]Wibbing, ibid., p. 106; and Mussner, *Galater*, p. 381.
Paul is not here painting a portrait of the Greek "good man."
Furnish, *Theology*, p. 87.

[57]Furnish, ibid., p. 87.

[58]Remembering that there is typically no attempt to
match vices with corresponding virtues, for the latter belong
to the new age, or to those who have come out of the "world,"
and reflect directly the aspirations of the community. See
for instance CH 1. 22, 23, and 1 QS 4, discussed in Kamlah,
Paränese, pp. 116-35, 165. The refusal to match vices and
virtues appears to be a part of the intense dualism inherent
in the lists. In fact, these are likely to be the opponents'
own community-values, descriptive of the remnant they themselves are claiming to bring into being. See above, p. 163,
on Gal 3:28.

[59]See Furnish, *Theology*, pp. 95-110. For instance,
the thanksgiving section in Philemon is in particular terms,
which then become the basis, at the end of the letter, for
the imperative. Kamlah, *Paränese*, pp. 12-13, notes that the
double catalog is inseparable from the ethical topoi for
which it lays an indicative basis. For instance, the vice
with which the lists begins in 1 Cor 6:9 is πορνεία; and
this is exactly the vice which is taken up in the imperative
passage which follows (6:12-20): φεύγετε τὴν πορνείαν (6:18;
see also 6:13, 15, 16).

[60] Wibbing, *Tugend- und Lasterkataloge*, pp. 110-11, 122-27, stresses the way the call to περιπατεῖν (functioning as does the OT הלך), which is the call to concrete fulfillment of the topoi, grows out of the catalogs, so that the call to περιπατεῖν in Galatians 5-6 is especially the call to ἀγάπη, which stands at the head of the virtues.

[61] That is, 5:1. See above, p. 53.

[62] So, Schlier, *Galater*, p. 166, on 5:15. It is the opponents' theology that is rending the congregation. There is a link between the misuse of freedom and violation of the law of love. The heresy is a nomistic misunderstanding of pneuma-possession, an inauthentic spiritualism. It is the very attempt to be πνευματικοί that leads to ethical breakdown.

[63] Taking up the last of the vices relating to the community, φθόνος (5:21).

[64] Where Paul looks for law-fulfillment in Galatians 5-6, it is not in terms of a rejection of libertine or licentious behavior, but in terms of love of neighbor. Stoike, "Law of Christ," pp. 215-16. It is also significant that there is no different problem dealt with in 5:1-12 and 5:13 (seeing that the former pericope is clearly directed against the circumcision program). At the heart of 5:1-12, legalism is opposed to love, and in 5:13-15, σάρξ-conduct is the opposite of love. The threatening, dualistic, all-encompassing nature of σάρξ must be taken into account in 5:13.

[65] So, Bornkamm, *Paul*, p. 202: "The new life does not go beyond what grace bestows on faith. Accordingly, it is not sufficient to think of the new life . . . as a mere supplementary effect of faith; in itself it is a mode of faith, an appropriation of what God has already assigned. . . . Thus the two come together in equilibrium: to live on the basis of *grace*, but also to *live* on the basis of grace." See also Wibbing, *Tugend- und Lasterkataloge*, p. 122; Schlier, *Galater*, pp. 194-95; and Oepke, *Galater*, Excursus 9.

[66] Picking up the irony of 3:1-5, and 4:8-11. See above, pp. 122-23, etc. This suggests further that the ethical argument continues the argument of chaps. 3 and 4 against the program of righteousness by works. This same irony appears to be in 6:7-10, the eschatological climax that appears suddenly in the midst of the paraenesis, adding new force (Funk, *Language*, pp. 264-70). It is not directed against libertinistic, semi-Gnostic Hellenistic enthusiasm (against Jewett, "Agitators," p. 202, etc.,) but is carrying on the surprising transvaluation of values which appears in the vice-catalog. Failure in the area of love in the community is as deadly as the most "worldly" of conduct. On this point the Galatians have been deceived (μὴ πλανᾶσθε, 6:7), just as Paul says earlier that they have been bewitched (3:1) and are therefore living in deadly danger.

[67]It is significant that, in the ethical section,
Paul's eschatology, far from being radically different from
the eschatology with which he confronts the nomists in 3:1-5
etc. (as it would be expected to be if he were now facing a
very different, libertine opponent), is exactly the same, continuing the "enthusiasm" at the head of the book in 1:4.

[68]Kamlah, *Paränese*, p. 2; and Conzelmann, *1 Corinthians*, p. 102.

[69]Wibbing, *Tugend- und Lasterkataloge*, pp. 79, 81-86;
and also 118-23 where he notes the distance from Stoic models,
and the proximity to Qumran.

[70]Kamlah, ibid., pp. 39-50.

[71]Russell, *Apocalyptic*, pp. 257-58, 278; and Conzelmann, ibid., p. 101.

[72]Kamlah, ibid., pp. 42-50, 165-66; Wibbing, *Tugend-
und Lasterkataloge*, pp. 81-86; and Mussner, *Galater*, p. 392.

[73]Here principally following the analysis of Kamlah,
Paränese, p. 44.

[74]The conception here is strikingly similar to Gal
5:17.

[75]In this introduction there is a strong sense that
the righteous live still in the evil aeon, and need "help"
from the angel of truth.

[76]The Qumran list gives virtues first, then vices,
while Paul has the reverse order.

[77]Here again, the impression is very much that the
righteous live in the present evil age, and the perspective
of hope is a future one.

[78]Once more, the righteous live in the evil age:
"For God has appointed these two things to obtain in equal
measure until the final age." There is here also a statement
very close to Gal 5:17; "Between the two categories He has set
eternal enmity. Deeds of perversity are an abomination to
truth, while all the ways of truth are an abomination to perversity; and there is a constant jealous rivalry between these
two regimes, for they do not march in accord" (Gaster).

[79]Again there is a startling continuity with and contrast to Gal 5:24. Whereas Paul shifts the division of the
ages into the past and can speak already of the "crucifixion
of the flesh," the Qumran catalog here looks *forward* to the
"destroying" of "every spirit of perversity from within his
(i.e., the righteous') flesh." The triumph of the Spirit of
Truth goes "sullying . . . in the ways of wickedness owing to
the domination of perversity" (Gaster).

[80]See above, pp. 152-53, on this hope in Judaism, and its possible connection with Gal 3:28.

[81]Though in 1 QS it is a Spirit/Spirit dualism, and in Galatians it is a Spirit/flesh dualism. See Davies, "Scrolls," pp. 164-65; Brandenburger, *Fleisch*, pp. 142-44; etc.

[82]Davies, ibid., p. 170.

[83]Wibbing, *Tugend- and Lasterkataloge*, pp. 110-11. See 1 QS 4:7, 12 and the two ways as "walks."

[84]In Galatians the tension is between the "already" of the new age and the "not yet"; but in 1 QS the tension is that of the call to law-obedience and life by the Spirit of Truth in an age that is almost totally under the thrall of the spirit of error. See Mussner, *Galater*, p. 395.

[85]See above, pp. 166-67, on the eschatological force of Gal 5:24.

[86]See above, pp. 67-70, on the place of eschatology in the debate over faith and works.

[87]Wibbing, *Tugend- und Lasterkataloge*, pp. 92-93, attempts to find equivalents through the medium of the LXX. He suggests parallels to θυμός (קצור אפים), ζῆλος (קנבת זנות), ἀκαθαρσία (טמאה and other equivalents), πορνεία (ברוב זנות) ἀσέλγεια (possibly synonymous with the previous equivalent), and εἰδωλολατρία (גלולי נדה).

[88]Wibbing, ibid., pp. 104-6. There are possible equivalents for πραΰτης (רוח ענוה), μακροθυμία (אורך אפים), ἀγαθωσύνη (טוב עולמים), χρηστότης (same), πίστις (אמת), and εἰρήνη (רוב שלום). This amounts to two-thirds of Paul's virtues.

[89]See above, p. 167, citing Kamlah, *Paränese*, p. 165.

[90]1 QS 4:4. Mussner, *Galater*, p. 379, sees a further terminological parallel between Gal 5:19-23 and 1 QS in the expression ἔργα τῆς σαρκός, which is close to the מעשי רשע of 1 QS 2:5, and the מעשי רמיה of 1 QS 4:23. Despite the distinction in terminology used for the dualism (Spirit/Spirit in Qumran, Spirit/flesh in Paul), most agree that the dualism itself is strikingly similar.

[91]See above, pp. 150-53, 159-61, etc., on the suggested place of Gal 3:23 in the polemic.

[92]Davies, "Scrolls," p. 170. He and others have seen the parallels between the ethics of 1 QS and Galatians. But the point is, Why should Paul use these ethics? What is their dialogical function in the argument?

[93]See above, pp. 69-78,   on 2:15-21.   The opponents have a kind of "faith" in Jesus as a bringer of "righteousness" in a sense.   See also above p. 20, referring to Georgi.

[94]Davies, *Paul*, p. 138.

[95]Ibid., p. 136.   See also Archibald M. Hunter, *Paul and His Predecessors* (London: SCM Press, 1961).   Although not fully agreeing, Furnish, *Theology*, pp. 53-54, finds convincing parallels between ethical exhortations in the synoptics and those in Paul's letters.   "It is certain . . . that the apostle was familiar with traditions about Jesus' teaching and had possessions of certain elements of that teaching."

[96]See Dungan, *Paul* (Philadelphia: Fortress Press, 1971).   His form-critical comparison of 1 Cor 9:4-8 and 1 Cor 7:1-16 with parallel traditions in the Synoptics indicates that both these passages in 1 Corinthians "are intimately related to that complex of traditions now preserved in the synoptic gospels" (p. 146), even though there is not always evidence of a direct quotation.   The conclusion is that Paul actually used "a considerable number of Jesus' teachings" (p. 149), which are to be recovered, not on the basis of exact quotation, but of indications of the presence of interpretations of traditions of the teachings of Jesus, adapted to particular circumstances.

[97]At the core of the Sermon on the Mount/Plain in Q, in the Two Ways of Did 1:3-5, in Clem 13:2, Polycarp *Phil* 2:2-3, and Barn 18-21.

[98]Robinson, "Kerygma," p. 130.   The description of the opponents in 1 Cor 4:8 suggests the woes of the Sermon on the Plain, using κορεννύναι, πλουτεῖν; and that of himself suggests the blessings, using πεινῶμεν καὶ διψῶμεν . . . λοιδορούμενοι εὐλογοῦμεν, διωκόμενοι ἀνεχόμεθα, verse 12.   Here is no simple quotation of Jesus' sayings, but an adaptation of them to a specific problem, even though the original source remains recognizable.

[99]Dungan, *Sayings*, p. 149, notes that accurate quotation of Jesus' words really belongs to a later period (Tertullian and Irenaeus).   Justin Martyr and Clement cite even more freely, as do Did and Barn (below).   See also James J. C. Cox, "Prolegomena to a Study of the Dominical Logoi as Cited in the Didascalia Apostolorum, Part 2:   Methodological Questions," *AUSS* 15 (1977):11-15, who examines the citation of dominical logoi in the Didascalia, noting that quotations may be with or without citation formulae--and may even have no known parallels.

[100]See especially the catalogs at Matt 7:13-14, 25:31-46, Col 3:5-17, Rom 13:11-14, Luke 6:20-26, Did 1-6, and Barn 18-21.

[101]Kamlah, *Paränese*, sees this happening in Did 1-6, Barn 18-21, and the latin Duae Viae.   It has been noticed above that it is already happening in Col 3:5-17.

[102]Especially Matthew 5-7, Luke 6, and Romans 13-15.

[103]So, Davies, *Paul*, pp. 134-36, has found eight
reminiscences of the words of Jesus in Romans 12-15, the context of the dual catalog of Rom 13:11-14 (Rom 12:14 = Matt
5:44; Rom 12:17 = Matt 5:39-42; Rom 12:21 = Matt 5:38-42;
Rom 13:7 = Mark 12:13-17, Matt 22:15-22, Luke 20:20-26; Rom
13:8-10 = Matt 22:34-40 and parallels; Rom 14:10 = Matt 7:1;
Rom 14:13 = Matt 18:7 and parallels). A significant number
of these come from the Sermon on the Mount/Plain. And he
finds four such reminiscences in the context of the dual
catalog in Colossians (Col 3:5 = Matt 5:29, 30; Col 3:13 =
Matt 6:12; Col 3:12 = Luke 6:38; Col 4:2 = Matt 26:41). And
Luke intentionally puts the Q material of the Sermon on the
Mount/Plain into a dualistic scheme, Luke 6:20-26.

[104]James M. Robinson finds this cluster "at the core
of the Sermon on the Mount/Plain in Q," in the Two Ways of Did
1:3-5, in Clem 13:2, and Polycarp, *Phil* 2:2-3, "Kerygma,"
p. 130.

[105]See how ironical this expression is, in the light
of Paul's radical separation of Christ and law in Galatians
3-4 (above, p. 164).

[106]Charles Harold Dodd, *More New Testament Studies*
(Manchester: Manchester University Press, 1968), p. 141.
See 1 Cor 9:14, ὁ κύριος διέταξεν . . . compared to Matt 10:10;
and 1 Cor 7:10, παραγγέλλω, οὐκ ἐγὼ ἀλλὰ ὁ κύριος, compared
to Matt 5:32 and 19:9. Dungan also sees teachings of Jesus
involved here.

[107]Dodd, *More Studies*, p. 146. See also Davies, *Paul*,
pp. 135-40, and Longenecker, *Paul*, pp. 188-90. Furnish,
Theology, grudgingly concedes that the genitive ἄνομος θεοῦ
of 1 Cor 9:21 is probably a subjective genitive, meaning "without the law of God" (supported by Rom 2:12-13, where ἄνομος
refers to God's law), and that "therefore, Dodd's point that
the antithetical phrase ἔννομος χριστοῦ at least 'implies the
existence' of a law of Christ may be granted." But he denies
that the "law of Christ" is the sayings of Jesus conceived as
law. However, his objection rests on his assumption that the
crux of the ethical passage is 5:25, which seems mistaken.
The crux seems rather to be in 5:24.

[108]It has been shown above, pp. 96-97, that Gal 1:11 etc.
does not mean that there were not traditional elements in the
gospel Paul preached in Galatia. So when Furnish, *Theology*,
and others, use Gal 1:11-12 to argue against the presence of
sayings of Jesus in the Galatian context, there is a misunderstanding of the relation between revelation and tradition.

[109]Stoike, "Law of Christ," pp. 239-46, and others,
reject the possibility on this basis. It is argued that the
only possible explicit saying of Jesus is in 5:14, and this
saying is also well known from the Old Testament and Jewish
ethical teaching. Stoike admits a close connection between
Gal 6:2 and 5:14 (see Burton, p. 329; Mussner, *Galater*,

p. 399), but he cannot explain how 5:14 has come to be called
"the law of Christ." His solution is that the expression
comes from the opponents. But if so, how did they get it,
and what did it mean to them? If it does belong to them, then
Paul has rejected their understanding of law in one sense
(chaps. 3-4) and accepted it in another (5:14, 18, 23, 6:2).
Why can he do this? If the opponents have coined the expression, then what traditions have enabled them to do so (i.e.,
traditions of Messiah and law)? They obviously have an important place for Jesus in their traditions, and great respect
for law-givers. Such important questions are left too much
up in the air. Similar criticisms can be levelled at Furnish,
Theology, pp. 51-65.

[110]See Alfred D. Resch, *Der Paulinismus und die Logia
Jesu* (Leipzig: J. C. Hinrichs'sche Buchhandlung, 1904), pp.
67-72, summarized in Table 2 at the end of the chapter.

[111]See Table 1 at the end of the chapter. On the use
of this form along with sayings of Jesus and their exposition,
see Robinson, *Trajectories*, p. 86.

[112]This raises the question of the βάρη of Gal 6:2,
and the strange juxtaposition with φορτίον in 6:5. It is
probably not important, as Dodd says, to distinguish between
ἀναπληρώσετε and ἀναπληρώσατε. Mussner and others suggest
that 6:2 is repeating 6:1, and that the βάρη are the sins of
fellow-Christians. This is probably right, as the whole
passage seems to grow out of a saying such as Matt 18:15-20.
But Schrenk, "βάρος," *TDNT*, 1:555, seems more correct in saying that this last is only part of the total task of love,
and βάρη here cannot be restricted to any one sphere. The
phrase with which βάρη is connected, ὁ νόμος τοῦ χριστοῦ,
seems to relate directly to 5:14 and Rom 13:10 (ibid.). It
is significant also that in Acts 15:28 and Rev 2:24 βάρος
signifies the burden of the Spirit on the community, the
"yoke" of the law, just as Ab 6:5 speaks of the עֹל תורה.
Thus the idea is probably linked directly with Matt 11:28-30
(ibid., and Dodd)--which, however, uses φορτίον. Paul, then,
may be taking up Matt 11:28-30, and playing with the idea of
the βάρος of the law of Christ which, because it is a "yoke"
(Ab 6:5, "to bear the yoke with one's neighbor"), joins one
to one's neighbor so that he becomes one's own φορτίον.

[113]The expression is that of Cox. See above, p. 173.
So, for example, 1 Clem 13:2, "as ye are kind, so shall kindness be shown you," which suddenly appears in the midst of a
quotation from Matt 5:7, 6:14, 15, and Luke 6:31.

[114]Above all, Gal 5:14 and Matt 22:34-40 and parallels,
especially noting ὅλος ὁ νόμος in Matt 22:40. See Dodd, *More
Studies*, p. 139. There are certain weaknesses in suggesting
that the use in Gal 5:14 of Lev 19:18 goes back to Jewish
ethical traditions. Eduard Schweizer, *The Good News According
to Matthew*, trans. David E. Green (Atlanta: John Knox Press,
1975), pp. 251-52, notes that instances of the combination of
Deut 6:5 and Lev 19:18, as in Matt 22:34-40, are actually

quite rare. Schweizer concludes that it is probably Jesus who
has put the two texts together; and that such an arrangement
as this, making Lev 19:18 of supreme importance, along with
the authority of Jesus, probably lies behind the prominent
use of Lev 19:18 in this sense in early Christian circles,
including Rom 13:8-10 and Gal 5:14. Besides this, a saying
such as the one behind Matt 18:15-20, dealing with church
order, seems to be behind Gal 6:1-5 (Dodd, *More Studies*,
p. 146, and Brice, "Origins," p. 282). As noted above, βάρος
and φορτίον in 6:2, 5 recall Matt 11:28-30.

[115]It is interesting that these implicit parallels
(Gal 6:3 = Matt 5:5, Gal 6:9, 11 = Luke 6:27, Gal 6:6 = Luke
6:40, Gal 6:1 = Matt 6:12, Luke 6:37, Gal 6:1 = Luke 6:37)
come from the Sermon on the Mount/Plain, that is, they are Q
material.

[116]See above, pp. 167-68, for more detail on the
relationship between the catalog and the topoi.

[117]So suggested by Mussner, *Galater*, p. 399, who
stresses the connection between 6:2 and 5:14, as do Dodd,
Bruce, and Schrenk, quoted above. Burton, *Galatians*, p. 329,
feels that it is "probable" that the expression "law of
Christ" refers to a law that Christ had promulgated while on
earth. As is implied above, these more explicit sayings do
not come from Q material. However, Matt 11:28-30 is congruous
with the interest of Q in wise sayings, and with the expectations of the wisdom tradition (Koester, *Trajectories*, p. 183).
Matt 22:34-40 appears to use Markan material (Schweizer,
Matthew, p. 251), though the way Paul uses Lev 19:17 in Galatians and Romans seems to be closest to the way Matthew uses
it (T. W. Manson, *The Sayings of Jesus* [London: SCM Press,
1971], p. 227, notes that "the Markan conclusion [i.e., in
Mark 12:28-34] asserts that no other commandment can take
precedence of these two [i.e., Deut 6:5 and Lev 19:18]. That
is, these two stand in a class by themselves. Matthew's conclusion says something different, that these two commandments
are the fundamental principles upon which all other commandments of Scripture are based." Thus it would seem that the
exaltation of Lev 19:18 to this particular precedence in early
Christian ethics reflects a saying of Jesus [see p. 174
above] which stands behind both Mark 12:28-34 and Matt 22:34-
40. But the way Paul interprets this precedence, that is,
that all law rests on Lev 19:17, parallels the way Matthew
does, rather than the way Mark does). And although this
verse is not in Q (Davies, *Sermon*, p. 373), it does not seem
contrary to Q. Lev 19:18 is taken up in a similar way in
Matt 5:43 and parallels. Matt 18:15-20 is peculiarly Matthean,
but it is interesting that there are striking parallels to it
in 1 QS 5:25-6:1, CD 9:2ff., and CD 14:21. Davies even suggests that Matthew is polemicizing against the sectarians
(ibid., pp. 221-30). This in itself helps the suggestion
that the opponents themselves in a sense own the ethics of
Galatians.

[118]See above, pp. 168-70.

[119]This being the typical way in which Paul works in
his ethical sections. See above, pp. 169-70.

[120]There is already an indirect suggestion of such
an interest in the apparent connection between the traditional
unification-saying and Matt 22:30 and parallels which may be
functioning behind Paul's own use of the tradition in Gal
3:28. See above, pp. 154-57. The opponents certainly have
an interest in Jesus, are gospel-preachers, etc. (see above,
pp. 70 - 71);   but at the same time, they are uncompromising
preachers of law.

[121]As suggested by Stoike, "Christ," pp. 116, etc.,
and Georgi, above, p. 20.

[122]See above, p. 20.

[123]It is interesting that Matthew may polemicize
against just such an interpretation of Christ as lawgiver in
his gospel, where Jesus is a paradox--He is a second Moses,
and yet He is simultaneously a greater than Moses, who does
not overthrow the law of Moses but radicalizes its meaning
as only the Lawgiver Himself can do. A surprising element in
Jesus' teaching is the way law becomes personally attached to
Him. It is His law, the law of the Messiah, and all law
ultimately demands the "imitatio Christi." Davies, *Sermon*,
especially pp. 86-108.

[124]Davies, *Torah*, pp. 85-86, draws his conclusions
from Isa 2:1-5, Mic 4:1-5, Isa 42:1-4, Jer 31:31-34 and the
way these passages were understood in the Targums on Isa 12:13,
Song of Songs 5:10, Song of Songs Rabbah 2:13, Midrash
Qoheleth 2:1 and 12:1, and Yalqut on Isa 26, as Justin, *Dial
Trypho* 11 and Deut R. 8:6.

[125]See CD 6:11, 8:10, though the relationship between
the "Prophet," the "Messiah(s)," and the "Teacher of Righteousness" is a complex one. See Longenecker, *Paul*, pp. 185-86.

[126]As demanded by Schoeps, *Paul*: the abolition of
the law is supposed to be for Paul a "Messianic doctrine"
(p. 171), the result of a "pure aeon-theology" (p. 173); and
the expressions "law of Christ" (Gal 6:2) and "law of faith"
(Rom 3:27), arising out of these traditions, refer to a new
law, after the old law has been abolished. But he has not
considered the possibility that the expression, in Galatians
at least, may belong to the opponents.

[127]See above, pp. 61-62, quoting Davies, Moore,
Jervell, and Sanders. Contrary to Schoeps' assertion, these
traditions stress the continuing validity of Israel's law-
traditions.

[128]That is, Paul may here have taken over not only
a slogan of the opponents, but a source of their ethical tradition. It should be said, too, that it is not possible to
determine the opponents' particular understanding of "Messiah"

in terms of various Jewish traditions and expectations or to
find in their theology a precise distinction between the age
of the Messiah and the new age, etc. The schemes of 2 Baruch
and 4 Ezra are both probably to be dated about AD 100 (for
instance, Arthur J. Ferch, "The Two Aeons and the Messiah in
Pseudo-Philo, 4 Ezra, and 2 Baruch," *AUSS* 15 (1977):143-51;
T. Francis Glasson, "Schweitzer's Influence--Blessing or
Bane?" *JTS* 28 (1977):292-93); and apart from these apocalypses,
there is only variety in Jewish speculation regarding the
division of the ages (Glasson, ibid., pp. 293-302).

[129]Koester, *Trajectories*, p. 135.

[130]Koester, *Trajectories*, pp. 137, 125. So Gnosticism
has preserved traditions of Jesus particularly as a dispenser
of secret wisdom or gnosis. In the Gospel of Thomas, for
example, the sayings naturally lend themselves to individualistic speculations regarding the presence of the divine soul
in the body. The legalistic direction of this tendency is
in the Kerygmata Petrou, and the Gospel of Thomas and Q pay
much attention to legal statements (ibid., pp. 138-39).

[131]See Robinson, "Kerygma," pp. 85-86, 128-29; *Trajectories*, p. 113; Balch, "Backgrounds," pp. 361-62 and
Kümmel, *Introduction*, p. 72.

[132]Koester, *Trajectories*, p. 171.

[133]See above, pp. 153-57.

[134]See above, pp. 160-61.

[135]See above, pp. 65-66.

[136]See above, pp. 166-67. Because Gal 5:24 is a
baptismal statement, it continues Paul's "sacramental" answer
to the opponents begun in 2:19-20. Ethics become eschatological ethics, the other side of the eschatological declaration
of righteousness by faith.

[137]So, Drane, "Tradition," p. 177; and *Paul*, pp. 57-
58.

[138]Bultmann, *Theology*, 1:328. This is his understanding of the "law of Christ." So, too, the earlier Dodd, as
in *The Meaning of Paul for Today* (London: Swarthmore Press,
1920), pp. 146-48. But note how Dodd changed his position to
the one referred to above, p. 369, that is, that Jesus was to
Paul an ethical διδάσκαλος. For Drane, too, the "law of
Christ" is not the teaching of Jesus, but the person of Jesus,
His indwelling life in the believer.

[139]Furnish himself notes "contextuality and concrete
relevance" in Paul's ethic generally; and in Galatians 5-6 in
particular, "Paul describes concretely" how the exhortation
to love is to be fulfilled. The Christian must know the concrete "ways of Christ" in the world. See *Theology*, pp. 72-74.

[140]Furnish, ibid., p. 199, suggests that Gal 5:14, rather than reducing all law to an indefinable requirement to "love," instead requires that the Christian should "obey" the law--now made particularly relevant in terms of love for neighbor.

[141]Funk, *Language*, pp. 264-70, notes the unusual place of the "eschatological climax" in Gal 6:7-10, where it reinforces the law of Christ. The law of retribution has returned in a real sense. See above, p. 164.

[142]Georgi, *Gegner*, pp. 282-89. See, for instance, some of the directions this meditation took, in Corinth, in Q, in later writers such as Polycarp, etc. See Robinson, "Kerygma," pp. 128-31. In the various problem situations the NT writers had to deal with, "it seems to be the trans-mission of traditions about Jesus that is the primary source of the difficulties" (p. 131).

[143]So the frame used in the Gospel of Thomas is a Gnostic anthropological dualism, which makes Jesus the dis-penser of gnostic wisdom. See Koester, *Trajectories*, p. 137.

[144]So the beginning-point of all Paul's theology is Christology. See Käsemann, *Paul*, pp. 73-78, against Bultmann; Bornkamm, *Paul*, p. 136; and Ridderbos, *Paul*, pp. 44-53.

[145]Not only is Mark apparently a criticism of the Christology and eschatology of Q (Davies, *Paul*, p. 142), but Matthew represents a very different meditation again on Jesus (Davies, *Sermon*, pp. 56, 61, 99-104), etc.

[146]See above, pp. 154-57, on Gal 2:15-21. Koester, *Trajectories*, p. 145, notes that it is a "different gospel" which Paul so vigorously attacks, a perversion of the "gospel of Christ" (Gal 1:6-7), which probably means, as it does in 2 Cor 11:4, that it proclaims "another Jesus."

[147]Dodd, *More Studies*, p. 146.

[148]So Mussner, *Galater*, p. 287, writes that the *Nova Lex*, the νόμος τοῦ Χριστοῦ, is not merely the "third use of the law," but the "*usus practicus evangelii*," a totally new order of life.

[149]See above, pp. 97-99.

[150]Bultmann, *Theology*, 1:262.

[151]While man still lives under the old aeon, "Scrip-ture" (here, law) consigns "all things to sin" (3:22), and there is no true fulfillment of law. See Bultmann, *Theology*, 1:263.

[152]Gal 6:15, which, it has been noticed (above, p. 65), was a summary answer to the circumcision program.

[153]That is, realizing that the essential nature of law, any law, is demand. See Bultmann, ibid., pp. 268, 270-71, 330. It is the same in Matthew. There is no law for the Christian but the "law of Christ." Law comes to be personally attached to the Messiah. See Davies, *Sermon*, pp. 94, 106-7. The radical demand of the new age takes up the particularity of the "old time" and goes beyond it. The "better righteousness" becomes finally the demand of the "*imitatio Christi*" (Matt 5:17-20, 21-48, 19:16-22). In the dogmatic sections of his epistles, Paul starkly contrasts works and faith. But his ethics parallel strikingly those of the Messiah in Matthew 5-7. See Davies, *Paul*, pp. 138-46.

[154]Did 3:9 follows as an immediate conclusion from the citation of this text.

[155]This is a commentary on Matt 5:7, 6:14, 7:1, Luke 6:31, not actually a quoted "word of the Lord."

[156]This topos suddenly appears in the midst of the quotation of texts in (2), though there is no such text.

[157]*TDNT*, 1:555 connects with Gal 6:2 by way of the tradition of the βάρος of the law, Acts 15 etc.

[158]Dodd, *More New Testament Studies*, pp. 138-39.

[159]Compare to 1 QS 4:4, "abounding love for all who follow the truth."

[160]Goes on to cite Matt 5:7, 6:14, 15, 7:1, Luke 6:31, 36-38.

[161]Dodd, ibid., p. 146, and Bruce, "Origins," p. 282, note that the main theme of Gal 6:1-5 seems to grow out of Matt 18:15-20.

[162]The topos in Rom combines the thoughts of both Barn and Clem, yet only that of Clem seems to come directly from the *logos* in Luke.

[163]Cited as a parallel in Aland, *Synopsis Quattuor Evangeliorum*, p. 107.

[164]From Resch, *Paulinismus*, pp. 67-72.

CONCLUSIONS

[1]Above, pp. 25-26.

[2]Above, pp. 27-28.   See 1:7, 9; 3:1; 4:17, etc.

[3]Above, pp. 28-29.

[4]Above, p. 28.

[5]Above, pp. 28-31.

[6]Above, pp. 15-17.

[7]Above, pp. 53-54.

[8]Above, p. 28.

[9]Above, pp. 37-39.

[10]Above, pp. 39-45.

[11]Above, pp. 46-49.

[12]Definitions are given, above, pp. 42-45, along with examples and a typical structure, pp. 44-45.

[13]Above, pp. 49-50.

[14]Above, pp. 51-52.

[15]Above, pp. 52-53.

[16]Above, pp. 53-54.

[17]This is suggested by the genre-analysis and methodological considerations. Furthermore, the fact that Paul's paraenetic passages draw on the traditional ethical material makes this the more likely.

[18]Above, pp. 58-59.

[19]Above, pp. 61-67.

[20]Above, p. 67.

[21]Above, p. 63.

[22]Above, pp. 65-66.

[23]Above, pp. 67-70.

[24]Above, pp. 69-78.

[25]Above, pp. 77-82.

[26]Above, pp. 80-81.

[27]Above, pp. 81-83.

[28]Above, pp. 85-87.

[29]Above, pp. 95-96.

[30]Above, pp. 96-102.

[31]Above, pp. 98-99.

[32]Above, pp. 105-6.

[33]Above, pp. 109-11.

[34]Above, pp. 111-13.

[35]Above, p. 113.

[36]Above, p. 113.

[37]Above, pp. 115-16.

[38]Above, pp. 69-71.

[39]Above, pp. 116-19.

[40]Above, pp. 118-20.   On the "Jewishness" of this
program, see pp. 123-24.

[41]Above, pp. 120-26.

[42]Above, pp. 128-38.

[43]Above, pp. 132-39.

[44]Above, pp. 128-35.

[45]Above, pp. 139-41.

[46]Above, pp. 145-46.

[47]Above, pp. 139-42.

[48]Above, pp. 141-42.

[49]Above, pp. 145-46.

[50]Above, pp. 146-51.

[51]Above, pp. 145, 152-53.

[52]Above, pp. 164-68.

[53]Above, pp. 168-70.

[54]Above, pp. 171-72.

[55]Above, pp. 178-81.

[56]This is not to say that the opponents were once
Qumran sectaries. There was variety in the traditions and
doctrines of the Covenanters (see above, p. 135), and a
sharing of traditions by the Covenanters and other circles.
Perhaps the most significant parallels are those between the

opponents and Jubilees (above, pp. 111, 113, 123, 131-32, 145-46,
etc.). The Covenanters were one group in particular who maintained the traditions of Jubilees (above, pp. 131-33), but may
not have been the only one.

[57]On the place of Jesus for the opponents, see above,
pp. 175-77.

[58]He is probably a Messiah in the style of the one in
Test Lev 18, who causes sin to cease, and makes Abraham,
Isaac, and Jacob exult; and the one in Ps Sol 17-18, who
expels unrighteousness, establishes righteousness, gathers
together a holy people, etc.; or perhaps he is a teacher of
the covenant, like the Teacher of Righteousness in the Damascus
Document. See above, p. 62.

[59]See the place of the cross in Paul's polemic with
the intruding theology, above, pp. 65-66.

[60]There is a closeness of the "heresies" in Galatia
and in 2 Corinthians. Both make the same demands of an
apostle, and look for the same proofs of apostleship (pp.
93-95); both are opponents of the cross (see note above, and
2 Cor 13:4); both preach another Jesus (Gal 1:8; 2 Cor 11:4);
both are "nomistic enthusiasts." See above, pp. 160-61.

[61]Robinson, "Kerygma," p. 142. He goes on to quote
Georgi, *Gegner*, p. 289, referring to the situation in Corinth:
"It is not true that Paul developed his Christology in complete ignorance of the contents and tendencies of the developing tradition about Jesus. Rather he knew about them and
hence clearly rejected a motivation that at least at times
clearly asserts itself, namely the objective of using a certain form of presentation to make the life of Jesus an unam-
biguous manifestation of the divine, to cover over the
offense of the cross and the humanness of Jesus in general. . . ."

[62]Reversing Schweitzer, *Paul*, pp. 98-104, where
Christology and soteriology in Paul conform to eschatology.
See above, pp. 65-66, on Christology and eschatology in
Galatians, with references to Käsemann, Ridderbos, and Koester.

[63]As claimed by Jewett. See above, pp. 81-82.

[64]See above, pp. 160-61.

[65]Sanders, *Paul*, pp. 483-85.

[66]See above, pp. 160-61 (quoting Robinson on the
stress on "realized" eschatology in 2 Corinthians, and pointing to the parallel eschatology in Galatians).

[67]See above, pp. 102-5, on the sense of being already
members of Jerusalem above, while the tension between the
present evil age and the coming age is still retained.

[68]See above, pp. 98-99, on the self-understanding of the intruding apostles, and the resultant effects on the Galatian community.

[69]See above, pp. 103-7, especially pp. 103-4, on the opponents' juxtaposition of the earthly and heavenly Jerusalem, and how Paul breaks this juxtaposition.

[70]See above, pp. 160-61.

[71]Lightfoot, *Galatians*, pp. 284-370.

[72]See above, pp. 13, 17, 20-21 (citing Gunther, Stählin, Koester, and Georgi).

[73]Jonas, *Gnostic Religion*, pp. 276-77, notes that "except for a brief period of revolutionary extremism, the practical consequences from Gnostic views were more often in the direction of asceticism than of libertinism." Marcion's antinomianism led to a metaphysical asceticism, ibid., p. 44; and Mani's Gnosticism was also ascetic, ibid., pp. 231-32. In both instances, asceticism results from a rejection of Jewish law. Gnostics are immoral libertines mostly in the reports of the Fathers: Foerster, *Gnosis*, 1:231-36.

[74]See above, pp. 160-61 (citing Robinson on 1 and 2 Corinthians).

[75]See above, p. 20 (citing Stählin).

[76]Hengel, *Judaism*, 1:228 says the "Hasidic apocalyptic wisdom tradition," part of the law-tradition in apocalyptic and especially Qumran literature, which becomes a doctrine of "saving knowledge," could be called "gnostic," though not in the second-century sense. On page 229 he also cites K. G. Kuhn, "Die in Palästina gefundenen Hebräischen Texte und das Neue Testament," *ZTK* 47 (1950):203-4: "A preliminary form of Gnostic thought, planted in the Jewish religion of the law and . . . apocalyptic . . . centuries before the Gnostic texts."

[77]This is where Schmithals is quite wrong, and his theory anachronistic.

[78]See above, pp. 123-24, 142-43, and Koester, *Trajectories*, p. 146.

[79]See above, p. 75 (quoting Bornkamm, *Early Christian Experience*, pp. 79-81, on the finality of baptism, and its function as the basis for imperative). Also above, p. 74, quoting von Soden, "Sakrament und Ethik," on 1 Corinthians 10.

[80]See above, pp. 139-40.

[81]See above, pp. 160-61.

[82]See above, pp. 146-57, on the significance of the function of 3:28 in the argument.

[83]See above, pp. 119-20, on the law-"Tendenz" of the opponents, and on the few parallels to the phrase ἔργων τοῦ νόμου, which suggests a cultic meaning to the term.

[84]See above, pp. 139-41, on 5:2-4, where circumcision epitomizes justification by works of law and stands over against justification by faith.

[85]As propounded by Schweitzer in *Paul*, p. 225. There is no logical way from righteousness by faith to ethics. Ethics arise naturally from dying and rising with Christ. See Furnish, *Theology*, pp. 146-47, 258-59.

[86]See the arguments of method, genre, and structure, referred to above, as well as the analysis of the form and content of the double catalog, and the nature of the asso-ciated topoi.

[87]On the transvaluation of ethics in the vice-catalog, see above, pp. 168-70. All sins take on the same seriousness.

[88]For those who suggest this, see above, pp. 175-77.

[89]See above, p. 176, referring to studies of Jewish expectations of the Messiah and his treatment of law, in Davies, *Torah in the Messianic Age*, and Longenecker, *Paul*.

[90]See above, p. 176, suggesting that there is perhaps a similar debate behind Matthew, where Jesus is pre-sented as a second Moses, and yet a greater than Moses.

[91]See above, p. 164.

[92]See above, pp. 177-78, on the relationship between ethics and justification by faith.

[93]See above, p. 69.

[94]Baptism, usually used to clarify the nature of the new life, is here used to clarify justification. See above, p. 68. The transition from 2:16-21 to 3:1-5 to 3:6 is a transition from justification to life in the Spirit to justi-fication, showing that justification here is life in the Spirit. See also above, pp. 68-69. In Romans we are jus-tified apart from works of law: in Galatians we receive the Spirit apart from works of law.

[95]See above, pp. 74-77, and authorities cited, especially Sanders, *Paul*, pp. 482-84.

[96]Sanders, ibid., pp. 481-82: "It is not Paul's analysis of the nature of sin which determines his view, but his analysis of the way to salvation; not his anthropology, but his Christology and soteriology . . . (noting the par-ticular polemical use of Habakkuk 2 in Galatians 3) *since* salvation is only in Christ, *therefore* all other ways to sal-vation are wrong." See also above, p. 65 (citing Käsemann

and Ridderbos); and Käsemann, *Römer*, p. 129: "so ist die Kreuzestheologie nach unserm Text (Rom 5:8) zugleich der Schlüssel zur paulinischen Gotteslehre, Soteriologie, Anthropologie, und Eschatologie. . . ."

[97]See above, pp. 73-74.

[98]See above, pp. 73-74.

[99]See Mussner, p. 287. Gospel and paraenesis are only different sides of the gospel, because paraenesis belongs to the gospel. The New Testament "*nova lex*" is "*usus practicus evangelii*." For a Protestant viewpoint, see Käsemann, *Römer*. The justified one is also the new creature (p. 128); righteousness by faith is the actuality of eschatological freedom, life in the Spirit (p. 123); and so Paul's ethic is eschatological, just as justification must be (p. 125).

[100]See above, pp. 66, 151-52.

[101]The expression ἀκοῆς πίστεως in 3:2, 5 stands over against "works of law" and is probably best translated "believing what was heard." See Sanders, *Paul*, p. 482.

[102]Ibid., p. 487: "The judicial and participatory statements (in Romans) are not in fact kept in watertight compartments, as we have seen also to be the case in such passages as Phil 3:8-11 and Gal 3:24-29." Sanders disputes Ziesler's distinction between forensic (verbal) and participatory (nominal and adjectival) senses of δικαιοῦν/δίκαιος. But Ziesler himself realizes flexibility in uses of the word-group. In Galatians itself, he notices that the forensic sense is foremost in 2:16 (three occurrences of the verbal form); but with 2:17, Paul begins to fuse the forensic and participatory senses (one verbal form). By 2:21 (a nominal form), after the new language of 2:19-20, δικαιοσύνη has become a new form of existence, the new life of faith, although the forensic sense is still retained: *Righteousness*, pp. 172-73. In 176-77, he tries to make the verb-forms in 3:6-14 forensic, but admits that they cannot be separated from 2:16-21 or the references to the Spirit and baptism in 3:1-5.

[103]Following Sanders, *Paul*, pp. 482-84, and Käsemann, references below. Ziesler, *Righteousness*, p. 180, goes on to say that "the letter's main concern is forensic." He has not seen the full significance of 2:16-21 (and the way it stands at the head of the discussion), or the function of 3:1-5 in the debate. He has relied too heavily on the verbal forms in 3:6-14.

[104]Sanders, *Paul*, p. 491; also Käsemann, "The Righteousness of God in Paul," in *New Testament Questions of Today*, pp. 168-82, and "Justification and Salvation History," *Perspectives on Paul*, pp. 60-78. Bultmann objects ("ΔΙΚΑΙΟΣΥΝΗ ΘΕΟΥ," *JBL* 83 [1964]:12-16). Though he admits that the phrase is a subjective genitive in Rom 3:25, he claims that Paul

reinterprets it in 3:26 so that it becomes a genitive of
origin. However, this would not seem to be the contrast Paul
is making, either in 3:24-26 or in the whole context of
1:18-3:26. The contrast rather seems to be between "then"
and "now" (3:21, 26), and between the two revelations of law
(1:18-3:20) and Christ (3:21-26), stressing that God's righteousness "now" is seen in the justification of the sinner
(3:26). See Klein's mediating conclusion, and further bibliography, in *IDBS*, 750-52.

[105]See Sanders, *Paul*, pp. 486-87, and Käsemann, *Römer*,
pp. 123-26.

[106]Käsemann, ibid., p. 123. The former subdivision
makes justification merely the beginning-point for the moral
life of the redeemed.

[107]Ibid., p. 123.

[108]Sanders, *Paul*, pp. 486-87.

BIBLIOGRAPHY

Primary Sources

Ad C. *Herennium de Ratione Dicendi (Rhetorica Ad Herennium)*. Loeb Classical Library.

The Apostolic Fathers. Translated by Kirsopp Lake. Loeb Classical Library. 2 vols.

Attridge, Harold. *First-Century Cynicism in the Epistles of Heracleitus*. Missoula: Scholars' Press, 1976.

Barrett, Charles Kingsley. *The New Testament Background: Selected Documents*. New York: Harper and Row, 1961.

Box, G. H. *The Apocalypse of Ezra*. London: S.P.C.K., 1917.

Burrows, Millar, ed. *The Dead Sea Scrolls of St. Mark's Monastery*. New Haven: American Schools of Oriental Research, 1950.

Charles, Robert Henry. *The Apocalypse of Baruch*. London: Adam and Charles Black, 1896.

_____, ed. *The Apocrypha and Pseudepigrapha of the Old Testament in English*. Oxford: Clarendon Press, 1913.

_____. *The Assumption of Moses*. London: A. and C. Black, 1897.

_____. *The Book of Enoch*. Oxford: Clarendon Press, 1912.

_____. *The Book of Jubilees*. London: S.P.C.K., 1917.

_____. *The Testaments of the Twelve Patriarchs*. London: S.P.C.K., 1917.

Cicero. Translated by G. L. Hendrickson and H. M. Hubell. Loeb Classical Library. 14 vols.

Denis, Albert-Marie, ed. *Fragmenta Pseudepigraphorum Quae Supersunt Graeca*. Una cum Historicum et Auctorum Judaeorum Hellenistarum Fragmentis. Leiden: Brill, 1970.

DeSaint-Brisson, M. Seguier. *La Préparation Evangèlique d'Eusèbe Pamphile*. 2 vols. Paris: Gaume Frères, 1846.

351

Eusebius of Caesarea. *The Ecclesiastical History.* Trans-
    lated by Kirsopp Lake and J. E. L. Oulton. Loeb
    Classical Library. 2 vols.

Foerster, W., ed. *Gnosis.* 2 vols. Translated by R. McL.
    Wilson. London: Oxford Press, 1972.

Gaster, Theodor H. *The Dead Sea Scriptures.* New York:
    Anchor, 1976.

Hadas, Moses, ed. and trans. *Aristeas to Philocrates.* New
    York: Harper and Row, 1951.

Hennecke, Edgar, and Schneemelcher, Wilhelm. *New Testament
    Apocrypha.* Translated by R. McL. Wilson. 2 vols.
    Philadelphia: Westminster Press, 1963-1965.

James, M. R., trans. *The Biblical Antiquities of Philo.* New
    York: KTAV Publishing House, 1971.

Josephus. Translated by H. St. J. Thackeray, Ralph Marcus,
    Allen Wikgren, and Louis Feldman. Loeb Classical
    Library. 9 vols.

Klijn, A. F. J., and Reininck, G. J. *Patristic Evidence for
    Jewish-Christian Sects.* Leiden: Brill, 1973.

Malherbe, A. J. *The Cynic Epistles.* Missoula: Scholars'
    Press, 1977.

Midrash Mekilta. Translated by Jacob Z. L. Lauterbach.
    Philadelphia: Jewish Publication Society of America,
    1933-35.

The Mishnah. Translated by Herbert Danby. Oxford: Clarendon
    Press, 1933.

Murphy, James Jerome, ed. *Demosthenes' On the Crown.* New
    York: Random House, 1967.

Nock, Arthur Darby, and Festigière, A.-J. *Hermes Trismegistus.*
    Corpus Hermeticum. 4 vols. Paris: Société d'édition
    "Les Belles Lettres," 1954-60.

Philonenko, Marc. *Joseph et Aséneth. Introduction, texte
    critique, traduction, et notes.* Leiden: Brill, 1968.

Plato. Translated by G. G. Bury. Loeb Classical Library.
    7 vols.

Quintillian. *The Institutio Oratorio.* Translated by H. E.
    Butler. Loeb Classical Library. 4 vols.

Roberts, Alexander, and Donaldson, James, eds. *The Ante-
    Nicene Fathers.* 10 vols. New York: Christian
    Literature Company, 1885-1897.

Roberts, W. R., trans. *Demetrius on Style*. London: Cam-
     bridge University Press, 1902.

Robinson, James M., ed. *The Nag Hammadi Library in English*.
     New York: Harper and Row, 1977.

Schechter, Solomon. *Documents of Jewish Sectaries*. New York:
     KTAV Publishing House, 1970.

Scott, Walter. *Hermetica*. 4 vols. London: Dawsons, 1968.

Seneca. *Epistulae Morales*. Translated by Richard M. Gummere.
     Loeb Classical Library. 3 vols.

Strack, H. L., and Billerbeck, P. *Kommentar zum neuen Testa-
     ment aus Talmud und Midrash*. 4 vols. Munich: C. H.
     Beck, 1922-1926.

                          Secondary Sources

Baer, Richard A., Jr. *Philo's Use of the Categories Male and
     Female*. Leiden: Brill, 1970.

Balch, D. L. "Backgrounds of 1 Cor 7: Sayings of the Lord
     in Q; Moses as an Ascetic in 2 Cor 3," *New Testament
     Studies* 18 (1972):351-64.

Bamberger, Bernard Jacob. *Proselytism in the Talmudic Period*.
     New York: KTAV Publishing House, 1968.

Bandstra, Andrew John. *The Law and the Elements of the World*.
     Kampen: J. H. Kok, 1964.

Barnes, Timothy D. "An Apostle on Trial." *Journal of Theo-
     logical Studies* 20 (1969):407-19.

Barrett, Charles Kingsley. *A Commentary on the Second Epistle
     to the Corinthians*. *Harpers' New Testament Commentar-
     ies*. New York: Harper and Row, 1973.

_____. "Pauline Controversies in the Post-Pauline Period."
     New Testament Studies 20 (1973-74):229-45.

_____. "Paul's Opponents in 2 Corinthians." *New Testament
     Studies* 17 (1970-71):233-54.

Barth, Markus. *Ephesians*. *The Anchor Bible*. 2 vols. New
     York: Doubleday and Co., 1974.

Bauer, Bruno. *Kritik der Paulinischen Briefe*. 2 vols.
     Berlin: Hempel, 1852; reprint ed., Aalen: Scientia
     Verlag, 1972.

Bauer, Walter. *Orthodoxy and Heresy in Earlier Christianity*.
    Translated by Philadelphia Seminar on Christian
    Origins. Philadelphia: Fortress Press, 1971.

_____. *A Greek-English Lexicon of the New Testament and
    Other Early Christian Literature*. 4th German edition,
    translated by W. F. Arndt and F. W. Gingrich. Chicago:
    University of Chicago Press, 1954.

Baumgarten, Joseph M. *Studies in Qumran Law*. Leiden: Brill,
    1977.

Baur, Ferdinand Christian. *Paul. The Apostle of Jesus Christ*.
    Translated by E. Zeller. 2 vols. London: Williams
    and Norgate, 1876.

Beardslee, William A. *Literary Criticism of the New Testament*.
    Philadelphia: Fortress Press, 1970.

Becker, Jürgen. *Das Heil Gottes; Heils- und Sündebegriffe in
    den Qumrantexten und in dem Neuen Testament*.
    Göttingen: Vandenhoeck und Ruprecht, 1964.

Becker, Jürgen; Conzelmann, Hans; und Friedrich, Gerhard.
    *Die Briefe an die Galater, Epheser, Philipper,
    Kolosser, Thessaloniker und Philemon*. NTD, 8.
    Göttingen: Vandenhoeck und Ruprecht, 1976.

Betz, Hans Dieter. "Geist, Freiheit, und Gesetz. Die Bot-
    schaft des Paulus an die Gemeinden in Galatien."
    Zeitschrift für Theologie und Kirche 71 (1974):78-93.

_____. "On the Problem of the Religio-Historical Under-
    standing of Apocalypticism." *Journal for Theology
    and the Church* 6 (1969):134-56.

_____. "Schöpfung und Erlösung im hermetischen Fragment
    'Kore Kosmou.'" *Zeitschrift für Theologie und Kirche*
    63 (1966):167-82.

_____. "The Literary Composition and Function of Paul's
    Letter to the Galatians." *New Testament Studies* 21
    (1975):353-79.

_____. "The Mithras Inscriptions of Santa Prisca and the
    New Testament." *Novum Testamentum* 10 (1968):48-67.

Bianchi, Ugo, ed. *Le Origini dello Gnosticismo, Colloquio di
    Messina 13-18 Aprile 1966*. Leiden: Brill, 1967.

Black, Matthew. *The Scrolls and Christian Origins*. New York:
    Scribners, 1961.

Blevins, James L. "The Problem in Galatia." *Review and
    Expositor* 69 (1972):449-58.

Bligh, John. *Galatians*. London: St. Paul's Publications,
    1969.

Böcher, Otto, and Haacker, Klause, eds. *Verborum Veritas*.
    Festschrift für Gustav Stählin zum 70. Geburtstag.
    Wuppertal: Theologischer Verlag Rolf Brockhaus, 1970.

Bornkamm, Günther. *Early Christian Experience*. Translated
    by Paul L. Hammer. New York: Harper and Row, 1969.

_____. "Formen und Gattungen 2. Im NT." In *Die Religion
    in Geschichte und Gegenwart*. Edited by Kurt Galling.
    Tübingen: J. C. B. Mohr, 1958.

_____. "The Heresy of Colossians." In *Conflict at Colossae*.
    Edited by Fred O. Francis, and Wayne A. Meeks.
    Missoula, MT: Scholars Press, 1975.

_____. *Paul*. Translated by D. M. G. Stalker. New York:
    Harper and Row, 1971.

Brandenburger, Egon. *Fleisch und Geist*. Neukirchen-Vluyn:
    Neukirchener Verlag, 1968.

Brandon, S. G. F. "The Crisis of 70 AD." *Heythrop Journal*
    46 (1947-48):212-23.

Braun, Herbert. *Qumran und das Neue Testament*. Tübingen:
    J. C. B. Mohr, 1966.

Bruce, F. F. "Galatian Problems. 3. The 'Other' Gospel."
    Bulletin of the John Rylands Library of Manchester
    53 (1971):253-71.

_____. "Galatian Problems. 5. Galatians and Christian
    Origins." *Bulletin of the John Rylands Library of
    Manchester* 55 (1973):264-84.

Bultmann, Rudolf. *Der Stil der paulinischen Predigt und die
    kynisch-stoisch Diatribe*. Göttingen: Vandenhoeck
    und Ruprecht, 1910.

_____. "ΔΙΚΑΙΟΣΥΝΗ ΘΕΟΥ." *Journal of Biblical Literature*
    83 (1964):12-16.

_____. *Primitive Christianity in its Contemporary Setting*.
    Translated by Reginald Fuller. New York: Thames and
    Hudson, 1956.

_____. *Theology of the New Testament*. 2 vols. Translated
    by Kendrick Grobel. New York: Scribners, 1951.

Burrows, Millar. *The Dead Sea Scrolls*. New York: Viking,
    1955.

Burton, Edward. *An Enquiry into the Heresies of the Apostolic
    Age*. Oxford: Collingwood, 1829.

Burton, Ernest deWitt. *A Critical and Exegetical Commentary
    on the Epistle to the Galatians*. *The International
    Critical Commentary*. Edinburgh: T. and T. Clark,
    1921.

Bussmann, Claus. *Themen der Paulinischen Missionspredigt auf
    dem Hintergrund der spätjüdisch-hellenistischen
    Missionsliteratur.* Bern: Herbert Lang, 1971.

Calvin, John. *The Epistles of Galatians, Ephesians, Philip-
    pians, and Colossians.* Translated by T. H. L. Parker.
    Grand Rapids: Eerdmans, 1973.

Charlesworth, James H. *The Pseudepigrapha and Modern Research.*
    Missoula, MT: Scholars Press, 1976.

Clark, Donald Lemen. *Rhetoric in Greco-Roman Education.* New
    York: Columbia University Press, 1967.

Conzelmann, Hans. *An Outline of the Theology of the New
    Testament.* New York: Harper and Row, 1968.

_____. *1 Corinthians.* Hermeneia Series. Translated by
    James W. Leitch. Philadelphia: Fortress Press, 1975.

Cox, James J. C. "Prolegomena to a Study of the Dominical
    Logoi as Cited in the Didascalia Apostolorum, Part 2:
    Methodological Questions." *Andrews University Seminary
    Studies* 15 (1977):1-15.

Crownfield, Frederick C. "The Singular Problem of the Dual
    Galatians." *Journal of Biblical Literature* 64 (1945):
    491-500.

Dahl, Nils Alstrup. *Studies in Paul.* Minneapolis: Augsburg
    Publishing House, 1977.

Dana, H. E., and Mantey, Julius R. *A Manual Grammar of the
    Greek New Testament.* Toronto: Macmillan, 1927.

Danielou, Jean. *The Theology of Jewish Christianity.* Trans-
    lated by John A. Baker. London: Darton, Longman,
    and Todd, 1964.

Davenport, Gene L. *The Eschatology of the Book of Jubilees.*
    Leiden: Brill, 1971.

Davies, W. D. *Paul and Rabbinic Judaism.* London: S.P.C.K.,
    1977.

_____. "Paul and the Dead Sea Scrolls: Flesh and Spirit."
    In *The Scrolls and the New Testament.* Edited by
    Krister Stendahl. New York: Harper and Row, 1957.

_____. *The Setting of the Sermon on the Mount.* Cambridge:
    Cambridge University Press, 1966.

_____. *Torah in the Messianic Age and/or the Age to Come.*
    Philadelphia: Society of Biblical Literature, 1952.

Deissmann, Gustav Adolf. *Bible Studies.* Translated by
    L. R. M. Strachan. Edinburgh: T. and T. Clark, 1901.

Deissmann, Gustav Adolf. *Light from the Ancient East*. Trans-
    lated by L. R. M. Strachan. London: Hodder and
    Stoughton, 1911.

_____. *St. Paul: A Study in Social and Religious History*.
    Translated by William E. Wilson. London: Hodder and
    Stoughton, 1926.

Dibelius, Martin. *An die Kolosser, Epheser, und Philemon*.
    HNT, 12. Tübingen: J. C. B. Mohr, 1927.

_____. *From Tradition to Gospel*. Translated by Bertram
    Lee Woolf. New York: Scribners, 1965.

_____. *Studies in the Acts of the Apostles*. Translated
    by Mary Ling. New York: Scribners, 1956.

Dinkler, Erich, ed. *Zeit und Geschichte: Danksgabe an Rudolf
    Bultmann zum 80. Geburtstag*. Tübingen: J. C. B. Mohr,
    1964.

Dodd, Charles Harold. *More New Testament Studies*. Manchester:
    Manchester University Press, 1968.

_____. *New Testament Studies*. New York: Scribners, 1952.

_____. *The Bible and the Greeks*. London: Hodder and
    Stoughton, 1954.

_____. *The Meaning of Paul for Today*. London: Swarthmore
    Press, 1920.

Doty, William G. *Contemporary New Testament Interpretation*.
    Englewood Cliffs, NJ: Prentice-Hall, 1972.

_____. *Letters in Primitive Christianity*. Philadelphia:
    Fortress Press, 1973.

Drane, John W. *Paul, Libertine or Legalist?* London: S.P.C.K.,
    1975.

_____. "Tradition, Law and Ethics in Pauline Theology."
    Novum Testamentum 12 (1974):167-78.

Duncan, George S. *The Epistle of Paul to the Galatians*. The
    Moffatt New Testament Commentary. London: Hodder
    and Stoughton, 1934.

Dungan, David L. *The Sayings of Jesus in the Churches of
    Paul*. Philadelphia: Fortress Press, 1971.

Eckert, Jost. *Die Urchristliche Verkündigung im Streit
    zwischen Paulus und seinen Gegnern nach dem Galater-
    brief*. Regensburg: Friedrich Pustet, 1971.

Ellis, E. Earle. "Paul and His Opponents." In *Christianity,
    Judaism, and Other Greco-Roman Cults. Studies for
    Morton Smith at Sixty*. Edited by J. Neusner.

Ferch, Arthur J. "The Two Aeons and the Messiah in Pseudo-
     Philo, 4 Ezra, and 2 Baruch." *Andrews University
     Seminary Studies* 15 (1977):143-51.

Fiorenza, Elizabeth Schussler, ed. *Aspects of Religious
     Propaganda in Judaism and Early Christianity.* South
     Bend: University of Notre Dame Press, 1976.

Fischer, James A. "Pauline Literary Forms and Thought Pat-
     terns." *Catholic Biblical Quarterly* 39 (1977):209-23.

Fitzmyer, Joseph A. "A Feature of Qumran Angelology and the
     Angels of 1 Cor 11:10." *New Testament Studies* 4
     (1957-58):48-58.

_____. "The Qumran Scrolls, the Ebionites, and Their
     Literature." In *The Scrolls and the New Testament.*
     Edited by K. Stendahl. New York: Harper and Row,
     1957.

Flusser, David. "The Dead Sea Sect and Pre-Pauline Chris-
     tianity." In *Scripta Hierosolymitana.* Edited by
     Chaim Rabin and Yigael Yadin. Jerusalem: Magnes
     Press, 1965. 4:215-66.

Foakes Jackson, F. J., and Lake, Kirsopp. *The Beginnings
     of Christianity.* 4 vols. London: Macmillan and
     Co., 1933.

Foerster, Werner. "Auffassung und Ziel des Galaterbriefes."
     In *Apophoreta. Festschrift für Ernst Haenchen zum
     seiner 70. Geburtstag,* pp. 170-79. Edited by Walter
     Eltester. Berlin: A. Töpelmann, 1964.

Funk, Robert. *Language, Hermeneutic, and Word of God.* New
     York: Harper and Row, 1966.

_____. "The Form and Structure of 2 and 3 John." *Journal
     of Biblical Literature* 86 (1967):424-30.

Furnish, Victor Paul. *Theology and Ethics in Paul.* Nashville:
     Abingdon Press, 1968.

Gaffron, H. B. *Studien zum Koptischen Philippusevangelium.*
     Bonn: Rheinische-Friedrich-Wilhelms-Universitat, 1969.

Gager, John G. *Moses in Greco-Roman Paganism.* Nashville:
     Abingdon Press, 1972.

Georgi, Dieter. *Die Gegner des Paulus im 2. Korintherbrief.*
     Neukirchen-Vluyn: Neukirchener Verlag, 1964.

_____. *Die Geschichte der Kollekte des Paulus für Jeru-
     salem.* Hamburg: Herbert Reich, 1965.

Glasson, T. Francis. "Schweitzer's Influence--Blessing or
     Bane?" *Journal of Theological Studies* 38 (1977):
     292-93.

Goodenough, Erwin R. *An Introduction to Philo Judaeus.* New York: Barnes and Noble, 1963.

_____. *Jewish Symbols in the Greco-Roman Period.* 13 vols. New York: Bollinger Foundation, 1965-68.

Grant, Frederick Clifton. *Hellenistic Religions, the Age of Syncretism.* New York: Liberal Arts Press, 1953.

Gunther, John J. *St. Paul's Opponents and Their Background.* Leiden: Brill, 1973.

Guthrie, Donald. *New Testament Introduction.* Downer's Grove: Inter-Varsity Press, 1976.

Hadas, Moses, and Smith, Morton. *Heroes and Gods: Spiritual Biographies in Antiquity.* London: Routledge and Kegan Paul, 1965.

Haenchen, Ernst. *The Acts of the Apostles.* Translated by Bernard Noble, Gerald Shinn, Hugh Anderson, and R. McL. Wilson. Philadelphia: Westminster Press, 1971.

Hammond, Henry. *A Paraphrase and Annotations upon All the Books of the New Testament.* 7th edition. London: Tho. Newborough and Benj. Tooke, 1702.

Hanson, Anthony Tyrrel. *Studies in Paul's Technique and Theology.* London: S.P.C.K., 1974.

Hasel, Gerhard F. "Remnant." In *Interpreters' Dictionary of the Bible: Supplementary Volume.* Nashville: Abingdon Press, 1976.

Hawkins, John Gale. "The Opponents of Paul in Galatia." Ph.D. Dissertation, Yale University, 1971.

Hengel, Martin. *Judaism and Hellenism.* 2 vols. London: S. C. M. Press, 1974.

Hirsch, Ernst G. "Zwei Fragen zu Galater 6." *Zeitschrift für die neutestamentlicher Wissenschaft* 29 (1930): 192-97.

Holladay, Carl R. *THEIOS ANER in Hellenistic-Judaism: A Critique of the Use of This Category in New Testament Christology.* Missoula, MT: Scholars Press, 1977.

Hunter, Archibald Macbride. *Paul and His Predecessors.* Revised ed. London: S. C. M. Press, 1961.

Huntjens, R. "Contrasting Notions of Covenant and Law in the Texts from Qumran." *Revue de Qumran* 8 (1972-75): 36-82.

Jaeger, Werner. *Paideia: The Ideals of Greek Culture.* Translated by Gilbert Highett. 3 vols. Oxford: Basil Blackwell, 1947.

360   Galatians--Dialogical Response

360   Galatians--Dialogical Response

Galatians--Dialogical Response

360   Galatians--Dialogical Response

360 Galatians--Dialogical Response

Galatians--Dialogical Response

360   Galatians--Dialogical Response

360   Galatians--Dialogical Response

360   Galatians--Dialogical Response

Jervell, Jacob. "Die Offenbarte und die Verborgene Tora." *Studia Theologica* 25 (1971):90-108.

_____. *Imago Dei*. Göttingen: Vandenhoeck und Ruprecht, 1960.

Jewett, Robert. "The Agitators and the Galatian Congregations." *New Testament Studies* 17 (1971):196-218.

Jonas, Hans. *The Gnostic Religion*. Boston: Beacon Press, 1958.

Juster, Jean. *Les Juifs dans l'Empire romain; leur condition juridique économique et sociale*. 2 vols. New York: Burt Franklin, 1965.

Kamlah, Ehrhard. *Die Form der katalogischen Paränese im Neuen Testament*. Tübingen: J. C. B. Mohr, 1964.

Käsemann, Ernst. *An die Römer*. Handbuch zum Neuen Testament ua. Tübingen: J. C. B. Mohr, 1974.

_____. *Die Legitimität des Apostels*. Darmstadt: Wissenschaftliche Buchgesellschaft, 1956.

_____. *New Testament Questions of Today*. Translated by W. J. Montague. London: S. C. M. Press, 1969.

_____. *Perspectives on Paul*. Translated by Margaret Kohl. Philadelphia: Fortress Press, 1969.

Kennedy, George. *The Art of Persuasion in Greece*. Princeton: Princeton University Press, 1963.

Kittel, Gerhard, and Friedrich, Gerhard. *Theological Dictionary of the New Testament*. Translated and edited by Geoffrey V. Bromiley. 9 vols. Grand Rapids: Eerdmans, 1964-72.

Koch, Klaus. *The Rediscovery of Apocalyptic*. Translated by Margaret Kohl. Naperville: Alec R. Allenson, 1970.

Koester, Helmut. "Paul and Hellenism." In *The Bible in Modern Scholarship*. Edited by Philip J. Hyatt. Philadelphia: Fortress Press, 1968.

_____. "The Purpose of a Polemic of a Pauline Fragment." *New Testament Studies* 7 (1961-62):317-32.

Kümmel, Werner Georg. *Introduction to the New Testament*. Nashville: Abingdon, 1975.

Lagrange, Marie Joseph. *St. Paul; Epître aux Galates*. Paris: J. Gabalda, 1950.

Leenhardt, Franz J. *L'Epître de Saint Paul aux Romains*. Neuchâtel: Delachaux et Niestlé, 1969.

Liddell, H. G., and Scott, R. *An Intermediate Greek-English
    Lexicon.* Oxford: Clarendon Press, 1975.

Lietzmann, Hans. *An die Galater.* Handbuch zum Neuen Testament
    10. 3rd ed. Tübingen: J. C. B. Mohr, 1932.

Lightfoot, J. *St. Paul's Epistle to the Galatians.* 2nd ed.
    London: Macmillan and Co., 1866.

Limbeck, Meinrad. *Die Ordnung des Heils. Untersuchungen zum
    Gesetzverständnis des Frühjudentums.* Düsseldorf:
    Patmos-Verlag, 1971.

Lohmeyer, Ernst. *Die Briefe an die Philipper, an die Kolosser
    und an Philemon.* Göttingen: Vandenhoeck und Ruprecht,
    1964.

Lohse, Eduard. *Colossians and Philemon.* Hermeneia Series.
    Translated by W. R. Poehlmann and R. J. Karris.
    Philadelphia: Fortress Press, 1971.

_____. *Die Einheit des Neuen Testaments: Exegetische
    Studien zur Theologie des Neuen Testaments.* Göttingen:
    Vandenhoeck und Ruprecht, 1973.

Longenecker, Richard N. *Paul, Apostle of Liberty.* Grand
    Rapids: Baker, 1964.

Lütgert, Wilhelm. *Gesetz und Geist: eine Untersuchung zur
    Vorgeschichte des Galaterbriefes.* Gütersloh: Ber-
    telsmann, 1919.

Luther, Martin. *Lectures on Galatians.* St. Louis: Con-
    cordia, 1963.

Macdonald, Dennis Ronald. "There Is No Male and Female:
    Galatians 3:26-28 and Gnostic Baptismal Tradition."
    Ph.D. Dissertation, Harvard University, 1978.

MacRae, George W. "Nag Hammadi." In *Interpreters' Dictionary
    of the Bible: Supplementary Volume.* Nashville:
    Abingdon Press, 1976.

_____. "The Jewish Background of the Gnostic Sophia Myth."
    Novum Testamentum 12 (1970):97-112.

Malherbe, A. J. "Ancient Epistolary Theorists." *Ohio Journal
    of Religious Studies* vol. 5, no. 2 (Oct., 1977):3-17.

Manson, Thomas Walter. *Studies in the Gospels and Epistles.*
    Manchester: Manchester University Press, 1962.

_____. *The Sayings of Jesus.* London: S. C. M. Press,
    1971.

Marshall, I. Howard, ed. *New Testament Interpretation.*
    Grand Rapids: Eerdmans, 1977.

Martin, Ralph P. *New Testament Foundations: A Guide for Christian Students.* 2 vols. Grand Rapids: Eerdmans, 1978.

Marxsen, Willi. *Introduction to the New Testament.* Translated by G. Buswell. Philadelphia: Fortress Press, 1968.

Meeks, Wayne A. "The Image of the Androgyne: Some Uses of a Symbol in Earliest Christianity." *History of Religions* 13 (1974):165-208.

_____. "Moses as God and King." In *Religions in Antiquity.* Edited by J. Neusner. Leiden: Brill, 1968.

Ménard, Jacques E. *L'Evangile selon Philippe, introduction, texte, traduction, commentaire.* Paris: Letouzey et Ané, 1967.

Michaelis, W. "Judaistische Heidenchristen." *Zeitschrift für die neutestamentliche Wissenschaft* 30 (1931):83-89.

Michel, Otto. *Der Brief an die Römer.* Göttingen: Vandenhoeck und Ruprecht, 1955.

Momigliano, Arnaldo. *The Development of Greek Biography.* Cambridge, Mass: Harvard University Press, 1971.

Moore, George Foot. *Judaism in the First Christian Century of the Christian Era.* 2 vols. New York: Schocken Books, 1971.

Munck, Johannes. *Paul and the Salvation of Mankind.* Translated by Frank Clarke. Atlanta: John Knox Press, 1977.

Mussner, Franz. *Der Galaterbrief.* Herders Theologischer Kommentar zum Neuen Testament: Vol. 11. Freiburg: Herder, 1974.

Nock, Arthur Darby. *Conversion.* London: Oxford University Press, 1961.

_____. *Early Gentile Christianity and Its Hellenistic Background.* New York: Harper and Row, 1964.

Norden, Eduard. *Agnostos Theos.* Stuttgart: B. G. Teubner, 1956.

Oepke, D. Albrecht. *Der Brief des Paulus an die Galater.* Handbuch zum Neuen Testament 9. Leipzig: A. Deichertsche Verlagsbuchhandlung D. Werner Scholl, 1937.

O'Connor, Jerome Murphy. "An Essene Missionary Document? CD 2:14-6:1." *Revue Biblique* 77 (1970):201-29.

O'Neill, J. C. *The Recovery of Paul's Letter to the Galatians.*
London: S.P.C.K., 1972.

Oster, Richard E. "A Historical Commentary on the Missionary
Success Stories in Acts 19:11-40." Ph.D. Dissertation,
Princeton Theological Seminary, 1974.

Pagels, Elaine. *The Gnostic Paul.* Philadelphia: Fortress
Press, 1975.

Pearson, Birger Albert. *The Pneumatikos--Psychikos Terminology
in 1 Corinthians.* Missoula, MT: Scholars Press, 1973.

Rabinowitz, Isaac. "'Pesher/Pittaron:' Its Biblical Meaning
and Its Significance in the Qumran Literature."
Revue de Qumran 8 (1972-75):219-32.

Ramsay, William M. *A Historical Commentary on St. Paul's
Epistle to the Galatians.* London: A. and C.
Black, 1899.

Reicke, B. "The Law and This World According to Paul."
Journal of Biblical Literature 70 (1951):259-76.

Reitzenstein, Richard. *Antike und Christentum.* Darmstadt:
Wissenschaftliche Buchgesellschaft, 1963.

_____. *Hellenistic Mystery-Religions: Their Basic Ideas
and Significance.* Translated by John E. Steely.
Pittsburgh: The Pickwick Press, 1978.

Resch, Alfred D. *Der Paulinismus und die Logia Jesu.* Leipzig: J. C. Hinrichs'sche Buchhandlung, 1904.

Ridderbos, Herman. *Paul. An Outline of His Theology.*
Translated by John Richard de Witt. Grand Rapids:
Eerdmans, 1975.

_____. *The Epistle of Paul to the Churches of Galatia.*
Grand Rapids: Baker, 1953.

Rigaux, Béda. *The Letter of St. Paul.* Translated by Stephen
Yonick. Chicago: Franciscan Herald Press, 1968.

Ringgren, Helmer. *The Faith of Qumran. Theology of the Dead
Sea Scrolls.* Translated by Emilie T. Sander.
Philadelphia: Fortress Press, 1963.

Robinson, James M. "Kerygma and History in the New Testament." In *The Bible in Modern Scholarship.* Edited
by Philip J. Hyatt. Philadelphia: Fortress Press,
1968.

Robinson, James M., and Koester, Helmut. *Trajectories Through
Early Christianity.* Philadelphia: Fortress Press,
1971.

Ropes, James H. *The Singular Problem of the Epistle to the Galatians.* Cambridge, Mass: Harvard University Press, 1929.

Russell, David Syme. *The Method and Message of Jewish Apocalyptic.* London: S. C. M. Press, 1964.

Sampley, J. R. "'Before God, I do not lie,' (Gal 1:20). Paul's Self-Defense in the Light of Roman Legal Praxis." *New Testament Studies* 23 (1971):477-82.

Sanders, E. P. "Patterns of Religion in Paul and Rabbinic Judaism: A Holistic Method of Comparison." *Harvard Theological Review* 66 (1973):455-78.

_____. *Paul and Palestinian Judaism. A Comparison of Patterns of Religion.* Philadelphia: Fortress Press, 1977.

Sanders, J. T. "Paul's Autobiographical Statements in Gal. 1-2." *Journal of Biblical Literature* 85 (1966):335-43.

_____. "The Transition from Opening Epistolary Thanksgiving to Body in the Pauline Corpus." *Journal of Biblical Literature* 81 (1962):352-62.

Sandmel, Samuel. *Philo's Place in Judaism.* Cincinnati: Hebrew Union College Press, 1956.

Schlier, Heinrich. *Der Brief an die Galater. Kritisch-exegetischer Kommentar über das Neue Testament.* 11th ed. Göttingen: Vandenhoeck und Ruprecht, 1951.

Schmithals, Walter. *Gnosticism in Corinth.* Translated by John E. Steely. Nashville: Abingdon Press, 1971.

_____. *Paul and the Gnostics.* Translated by John E. Steely. Nashville: Abingdon Press, 1972.

_____. *The Office of Apostle in the Early Church.* Translated by John E. Steely. Nashville: Abingdon Press, 1969.

Schoeps, Hans Joachim. *Paul. The Theology of the Apostle in the Light of Jewish Religious History.* Philadelphia: Westminster Press, 1961.

Schubert, Paul. *Form and Function of the Pauline Thanksgivings.* Berlin: Alfred Töpelmann, 1939.

_____. "The Place of the Areopagus Speech in the Composition of Acts." In *Transitions in Biblical Scholarship.* Edited by J. Coert Rylarsdaam. Chicago: University of Chicago Press, 1968.

Schweitzer, Albert. *The Mysticism of Paul the Apostle.* Translated by W. Montgomery. London: A. and C. Black, 1912.

Schweizer, Eduard. "Christianity of the Circumcised and
    Judaism of the Uncircumcised." In *Jews, Greeks, and
    Christians: Religious Culture in Late Antiquity*.
    Edited by Robert Hammerton-Kelly and Robin Scroggs.
    Leiden: Brill, 1976.

_____. *The Good News According to Matthew*. Translated
    by David E. Green. Atlanta: John Knox Press, 1975.

_____. "Versöhnung des Alls: Kol, 1:20." In *Jesus
    Christus in Historie und Theologie*. Edited by G.
    Strecker. Tübingen: J. C. B. Mohr, 1975.

Segelberg, E. "The Coptic-Gnostic Gospel According to Philip
    and its Sacramental System." *Numen* 7 (1960):42-56.

Selby, D. J. *Towards an Understanding of St. Paul*. Engle-
    wood Cliffs: Prentice-Hall, 1962.

Sevenster, J. N., and van Unnik, W. C., eds. *Studia Paulina
    in honorem Johannis de Zwaan, Septuagenarii*. Haarlem:
    De Erven F. Bohn, 1953.

Sherwin-White, A. N. *Roman Society and Roman Law in the New
    Testament*. Oxford: Clarendon Press, 1963.

Smith, Derwood, "The Two Made One: Some Observations on Eph
    2:14-18." *Ohio Journal of Religious Studies* 1 (1973):
    34-54.

Smyth, Herbert Weir. *Greek Grammar*. Cambridge, Mass: Har-
    vard University Press, 1974.

Stählin, G. "Galaterbrief." In *Die Religion in Geschichte
    und Gegenwart*. Edited by Kurt Galling. Tübingen:
    J. C. B. Mohr, 1958. 2:1187-90.

Stoike, Donald Allen. "'The Law of Christ:' A Study of
    Paul's Use of the Expression in Galatians 6:2."
    Th.D. Dissertation, School of Theology at Claremont,
    1971.

Tannehill, Robert C. *Dying and Rising with Christ*. Berlin:
    Töpelmann, 1967.

Tcherikover, Avigdor. *Hellenistic Civilization and the Jews*.
    Translated by S. Applebaum. Philadelphia: Jewish
    Publication Society of America, 1959.

Thyen, Hartwig. *Der Stil der jüdisch-hellenistischen Homilie*.
    Göttingen: Vandenhoeck und Ruprecht, 1955.

Tiede, David Lenz. *The Charismatic Figure as Miracle-Worker*.
    Missoula, MT: Society of Biblical Literature, 1972.

Turner, Nigel. *Grammatical Insights into the New Testament*.
    Edinburgh: T. and T. Clark, 1965.

Tyson, J. B. "Paul's Opponents in Galatia." *Novum Testamentum* 10 (1968):241-54.

Van Manen, W. B. "Marcions Brief van Paulus aan de Galatiërs."
Theologisch Tijdschrift 21 (1887):382-404, 451-533.

Van Unnik, W. C. *Tarsus or Jerusalem: The City of Paul's
Youth.* Translated by G. Ogg. London: Epworth Press,
1962.

Veltman, Frederick. "The Defense Speeches of Paul in Acts:
Gattungsforschung and Its Limitations." Th.D. Dissertation, Graduate Theological Union, 1975.

Von Mosheim, Johann Lorenz. *Institutes of Ecclesiastical
History.* 4 vols. London: Longman, Brown, et al.,
1845.

Von Rad, Gerhard. *Wisdom in Israel.* Translated by R. McL.
Wilson. Nashville: Abingdon Press, 1972.

Weiss, Johannes. *The History of Primitive Christianity.*
2 vols. Translated by Frederick C. Grant. New York:
Wilson-Erickson, 1937.

Wendland, Paul. *Die hellenistisch-römisch Kultur in ihren
Beziehungen zu Judentum und Christentum. Die ur-
christlichen Literaturformen.* Tübingen: J. C. B.
Mohr, 1912.

White, John Lee. *The Form and Function of the Body of the
Greek Letter.* Missoula, MT: Society of Biblical
Literature, 1972.

Wibbing, Siegfried. *Die Tugend- und Lasterkataloge im Neuen
Testament, und ihre Traditionsgeschichte unter
besonderer Berücksichtigung der Qumran-Texte.* Berlin:
Töpelmann, 1959.

Wilckens, Ulrich. *Rechtfertigung als Freiheit.* Neukirchen-
Vluyn: Neukirchener Verlag, 1974.

Wilder, Amos N. *Early Christian Rhetoric.* London: S. C. M.
Press, 1964.

Wilson, Robert McL. "Gnostics--in Galatia?" *Studia Evangelica*
4 (1968):358-67.

_____. *The Gnostic Problem.* London: A. R. Mowbray, 1964.

Wrede, William. *Paul.* Translated by Edward Lummins. Lexing-
ton: American Theological Library Association, 1962.

Ziesler, J. A. *The Meaning of Righteousness in Paul.*
Cambridge University Press, 1972.